PARISIORVM

BEUDE

e siècle.

First Edition

Tout Paris Guides are published by The Palancar Company Ltd
The Courtyard, 12 Hill Street, St. Helier, Jersey, C.I.

Printed in France by Imprimerie Union

TOUT PARIS

the

SOURCE GUIDE

to

THE ART OF FRENCH DECORATION

by

PATRICIA TWOHILL LOWN

and

DAVID LOWN

ILLUSTRATED BY FRANÇOISE McAREE

♕ The Editors have selected artisans, dealers and suppliers who are considered the best in their fields. Amongst all these, however, are a select few who are outstanding. The reader will find these indicated by a Crown.

NOTE: The telephone numbers listed in the Guide are generally for the City of Paris. When calling from abroad, it is first necessary to access long distance, then dial the country code (33) for France followed by the city code (1) for Paris. Most cities in France have 8 digit telephone numbers. When making a call anywhere outside Paris or between cities in France, it is necessary to dial (16) followed by the 8 digit number. The first 2 digits are the city code, so when dialing a country town from abroad, one dials (33) for France followed directly by the 8 digits. The city code (1) is only dialed for Paris.

THE ART OF FRENCH DECORATION

The subject of decoration is so vast that no single work can embrace it all. As is true of all the arts, there was no single seminal beginning. The Art of Decoration has evolved, with creative ideas giving birth to new forms and designs, crossing borders with inter-marriage, wars, and man's endless search for new customers for his products and skills.

French Decoration owes a great deal to the work of the artists and artisans of the Orient and the Middle East. According to legend, their secrets were brought back from Jerusalem by the Knights returning from the Crusades. These precious secrets included knowledge of the forces of gravitation, geometrical formulae, techniques in stone cutting, masonry and carpentry, as well as highly developed skills in mosaics, glass, painting, weaving, gilding, etc. Their talents were closely guarded and passed on by word of mouth from generation to generation of artisans.

These remarkable men designed and built the great Cathedrals and Castles of Europe in the midst of the "Dark Ages" while the the population went through long periods of plague, war and paralyzing poverty. The Church, which was all powerful, became the great patron of architecture, decoration and the arts.

Finally, however, it was not the Church, nor the Kings who were responsible for the advances in art and decoration, but the individual artisan, the "Compagnon", with a pack of tools on his back and a staff in his hand travelling from town to town, selling his skill to whomever could afford to pay.

This Guide has made every effort to be independent, objective and clear in its selection of merchants, artists and artisans who can best serve the honorable professions of Architect and Decorator anywhere in the world.

CATEGORY INDEX

ANTIQUE DEALERS

Antiquaires

The City of Paris and surrounding areas house more than five thousand Antique Dealers.

To the delight of most professionals and knowledgeable amateurs, most of the better dealers are concentrated in particular Arrondissements or in organized markets. Without prejudice, we have tried to organize our listing of antique dealers by quality and by neighborhoods or marketplace.

Most notable of these concentrations is the area known as the "Golden Triangle" near the Elysée Palace in the 8th Arrondissement. This triangle is formed by the Rue du Faubourg-Saint-Honoré, the Avenue Matignon and the Rue de Miromesnil. Here can be found a concentration of some of the greatest antique dealers in the world.

Also important is the center known as "Le Louvre des Antiquaires" in the 1st Arrondissement. It is situated conveniently opposite the Louvre Museum, on the Rue de Rivoli and the Rue Saint-Honoré. The Palais Royal is just across the street.

For more treasures it is suggested that you visit an area on the Left Bank called the "Carré Rive Gauche". It is directly across the river from the Louvre Museum, bounded by the Rue du Bac, the Quai Voltaire, the Rue des Saints-Pères and the Rue de l'Université. Several of the best antique and art dealers from the Right Bank also have galleries in the Carré. Don't miss it.

After you've explored all these, you will still have all of Paris at your feet. This Guide lists a selection of antique dealers by Arrondissement. Some are top quality with high prices. Others fall into almost every price range. Finally, at the end of the guide, you will find a listing of the best dealers in the organized "Markets".

Standing all alone amongst the thousands of antique dealers in Paris is the "crème-de-la-crème", the best of the best. As you might expect, Old Masters and "Museum" quality furniture are not inexpensive. We have chosen nine of the top "Antiquaires" and listed them first. We suggest you start with them so your eye can become adjusted to the marvels of the Art of French Decoration.

The very best of the Antique Dealers

♛ DIDIER AARON & CIE

118 rue du Faubourg-Saint-Honoré, 75008 Paris ■ Tel: 47 42 47 34 - Fax: 42 66 24 17 ■ Mon-Sat 10:00-12:30/14:30-18:30 ■ Lise Guenot speaks English ■ Prices high ■ Professional discounts

Very high quality XVIII century French furniture, paintings and art objects. There is also a remarkable collection of Chinese objects. Lise Guenot is very knowledgable.

Note: Didier Aaron has galleries in London and New York.

♛ AVELINE - JEAN-MARIE ROSSI

20 rue du Cirque, 75008 Paris ■ Tel: 42 66 60 29 - Fax: 42 66 45 91 ■ Mon-Sat 9:30-19:00 ■ English spoken ■ Prices high ■ 10% negotiable professional discount

Very high quality XVII, XVIII, XIX century furniture.

♛ GISMONDI

20 rue Royale, 75008 Paris ■ Tel: 42 60 73 89 - Fax: 42 60 98 94 ■ Tues-Fri 10:00-19:00/Sat 10:00-18:00 ■ English spoken ■ Prices high ■ Professional discounts

Excellent quality Italian XVII century furniture and art objects. French XVIII century furniture, art objects and XVII, XVIII and XIX century paintings and old drawings.

♛ JEAN LUPU ANTIQUITES

43 rue du Faubourg-Saint-Honoré, 75008 Paris ■ Tel: 42 65 93 19 - Fax: 42 65 49 16 ■ Mon-Fri 10:00-13:00/14:00-18:30/Sat by appointment ■ English spoken ■ Prices very high ■ 10 to 20% discount to professionals

Top grade XVII, XVIII century furniture, art objects, paintings.

♛ MICHEL MEYER

24 av. Matignon, 75008 Paris ■ Tel: 42 66 62 95 - Fax: 49 24 07 88 ■ Mon-Sat 10:00-13:00/14:00-19:00 ■ Celia and Michel Meyer speak English ■ Prices high ■ Discounts can be negotiated

Superb quality furniture and art objects of the XVIII century.

♛ YVES MIKAELOFF

10 & 14 rue Royale, 75008 Paris ■ Tel: 42 61 64 42 - Fax: 49 27 07 32 ■ Mon-Sat 10:00-19:00 ■ Yves Mikaeloff and Nicolas Joly speak English ■ Prices very high ■ Professional discount

Very high quality XVIII century furniture, old master paintings and drawings, extraordinary carpets and tapestries.

♛ JACQUES PERRIN

98 rue du Faubourg-Saint-Honoré, 75008 Paris ■ Tel: 42 65 01 38 - Fax: 49 24 04 08 ■ Mon-Sat 10:00-13:00/14:00-19:00 ■ Everyone in the gallery speaks English ■ Prices high ■ 10% professional discount

Highest quality XVIII century furniture, art objects, paintings and drawings. Feast your eyes.

✦ MAURICE SEGOURA

20 rue du Faubourg-Saint-Honoré, 75008 Paris ■ Tel: 42 65 11 03 - Fax: 42 65 16 08 ■ Mon-Sat, 9:00-19:00 ■ Maurice, Pierre and Marc Segoura speak English ■ Prices high to very high ■ Professional discounts possible

Superb antiques, French furniture and objects of the XVIII century, old master paintings.

✦ BERNARD BARUCH STEINITZ

75 rue du Faubourg-Saint-Honoré, 75008 Paris ■ Tel: 47 42 31 94 - Fax: 49 24 91 16 ■ 108 rue du Faubourg-Saint-Honoré 75008 Paris ■ Tel: 47 42 38 40 ■ Mon-Sat, 9:00-19:00 ■ English spoken ■ Prices high ■ Professional discounts negotiated

Very high quality French furniture, art objects, architectural elements, paintings of the XVIII and XIX century. Bernard Steinitz is considered a genius in the field.

Note: There is also a Steinitz Gallery on the rue Rossini near the Drouot Auction Rooms. By appointment only. Tel: 48 24 89 34.

Note: Steinitz maintains an extensive restoration workshop in Saint-Ouen in the heart of the Marché aux Puces, where his artisans do superb restoration and finishing of his own inventory.

Le Louvre des Antiquaires

2 place du Palais-Royal, 75001 Paris ■ Tel: 42 97 27 00 - Fax: 42 97 00 14 ■ Administrative Office hours: Mon-Fri 9:00-19:00 ■ Gallery hours: Tues-Sun 11:00-19:00 ■ Catherine Delachaux: Director of Communications

Le Louvre des Antiquaires is comprised of three floors of galleries connected by broad staircases and escalators.

TOUT PARIS editors have arranged the galleries according to category or product so that you might more easily target exactly what you need. Organize your search by subject and then go directly to the merchants who specialize in the treasures you seek. Browsing is also pleasant, educational and rewarding.

ANTIQUE BOXES AND SHOWCASE COLLECTIBLES

DOMINIQUE DELALANDE, 1/2/3 Allée Majorelle ■ Tel: 42 60 19 35

GALERIE SARTO, 9/11 Allée Guimard ■ Tel: 42 61 58 22/29

MONIQUE SENEMAUD, 3 Allée Roentgen ■ Tel: 42 60 19 09

ANTIQUE SILVER

CURIEL-LES BIJOUX DE LOUVRE, 16 Allée Odiot ■ Tel: 42 60 17 67

GALERIE DANIELLE MOREAU, 9 Allée Bellange ■ Tel: 47 03 91 00

GALERIE MAITIA, 17 Allée Desmalter ■ Tel: 47 03 97 84

PIERRE LANDRIEUX, 1/2/4 Allée Cressent ■ Tel: 42 61 56 48

EDOUARD DE SEVIN, 9 Allée Desmalter ■ Tel: 42 61 57 99

SUGER, 6/8 Allée Cressent ■ Tel: 42 61 57 73

ARCHAEOLOGY

GALERIE FRANÇOIS ANTONOVICH, 4 Allée Desmalter ■ Tel: 42 61 57 93

GALERIE PYTHEAS, 4 Allée Molitor ■ Tel: 40 15 93 28

L'ART ET LES HOMMES-GAL. BASSALI, 2 Allée Saunier ■ Tel: 42 60 21 25

JULIETTE NOUJAIM, 1 Allée Roentgen ■ Tel: 42 60 18 92

<hr>
ARMS & MILITARY
<hr>

JOSEPH BRAGHIERI, 1 Allée Jacob ■ Tel: 42 61 58 42

A.C. HAGONDOKOFF, 15 Allée Desmalter ■ Tel: 42 61 58 08
Military antiques and lead soldiers

L'ESPADON, 6 Allée Weisweiller ■ Tel: 42 61 56 44

PATRICE REBOUL, 3/6 Allée Riesener ■ Tel: 42 60 80 80

<hr>
ART OF INDIA AND TIBET
<hr>

SLIM BOUCHOUCHA, 8 Allée Boulle ■ Tel: 42 61 57 25

<hr>
ART NOUVEAU - ART DECO
<hr>

MICHEL CAFLER, 9/11 Allée Carlin ■ Tel: 49 26 01 41
Art Deco furniture and art objects.

DANENBERG, 2 Allée Boulle ■ Tel: 42 61 57 19

FERRE/LEFORT/LESTRINGANT, 37/39 Allée Boulle ■ Tel: 42 61 57 65

GALERIE BRAMY, 22 Allée Boulle ■ Tel: 42 61 57 48

GALERIE FOURNIER, 27 Allée Riesener ■ Tel: 42 61 23 65

GALERIE J. POINT, 9/11 Allée Riesener ■ Tel: 42 61 56 98 - Fax: 49 52 07 21
Art Nouveau/Art Deco glass, furniture, bronze.

GALERIE TOURBILLON, 1 Allée Riesener ■ Tel: 42 61 56 58

GRUNSPAN - PARTOUCHE, 7 Allée Carlin ■ Tel: 42 61 58 39

HUREL, 3 Allée Saunier ■ Tel: 47 03 49 45

W. HUYBRECHTS, 18 Allée Riesener ■ Tel: 49 26 05 81
Pate de Verre, Gallé, Daum, Lalique.

IMPULSION B, 26 Allée Riesener ■ Tel: 42 61 57 09

L'OR VERRE, 12/14 Allée Riesener ■ Tel: 42 60 23 45

LESIEUTRE, 32 Allée Riesener ■ Tel: 42 61 57 13

MAKASSAR-FRANCE, 4/6 Allée Thomire ■ 2 Allée Germain ■ 11/13 Allée Boulle ■ Tel: 42 61 57 79 - Fax: 43 73 78 12
1920 to 1935 furniture, objects, sculpture, paintings, lighting by the great names, Ruhlmann, Chareau, Sue & Mare, Frank, Dunand, Iribe, Leleu.

MEDICIS, 9 Allée Saunier ■ Tel: 42 61 01 92 - Fax: 42 61 01 66

OUAISS ANTIQUITES, 1/3 Allée Guimard ■ Tel: 42 60 22 66

ART OBJECTS & CURIOSITIES

AURELIO BIS, 8 Allée Desmalter ■ Tel: 42 61 57 98

DENIS CORDIER, 41/43 Allée Boulle ■ Tel: 42 61 56 53

DANTEC, 8 Allée Weisweiler ■ Tel: 42 61 56 45

DOMINIQUE DELALANDE, 1/3 Allée Majorelle ■ Tel: 42 60 19 35

DEGRAVE ET FAURE, 30 Allée Riesener ■ Tel: 42 61 57 12

DUBOIS, 4 Allée Boulle ■ Tel: 42 60 19 00

ELIZABETH "M", 1 Allée Bellange ■ Tel: 42 60 18 38

ELSASER, 4 Allée Mackintosh ■ Tel: 42 60 17 99

GALERIE COUR CARREE-G.C.C., 5 Allée Guimard ■ Tel: 42 61 58 19

GALERIE HELENE TRUONG, 2 Allée Roentgen ■ Tel: 42 60 18 95

GALERIE PITTORESQUE, 13 Allée Desmalter ■ Tel: 42 61 58 06

NICOLE KRAMER, 5 Allée Desmalter ■ Tel: 42 61 57 95

LA FILLE DU PIRATE, 1/3 Allée Weisweiler ■ Tel: 42 60 30 30/31

LUCIE SABOUDJIAN, Cour Palais Royal ■ Tel: 42 61 57 85

MARTIN DE BAZINE, 5/7 Allée Weisweiler ■ Tel: 42 61 56 43

OUAISS ANTIQUITES, 20 Allée Riesener ■ Tel: 42 61 56 99

WEEK END, 12 Allée Boulle ■ Tel: 42 61 57 32

BOOKS, OLD AND RARE

PAUL-LOUIS COUAILHAC, 10 Allée Riesener ■ Tel: 42 61 56 91 - Fax: 42 61 10 70
Rare and old books, manuscripts.

LA CARTOTHEQUE, 1 Allée Canabas ■ Tel: 42 61 56 64

BOOKS, CONTEMPORARY ART

LA LIBRAIRIE DES ANTIQUAIRES, 9 Allée Canabas ■ Tel: 42 61 56 79

CANES

LAURENCE JANTZEN, 11 Allée Desmalter ■ Tel: 42 61 58 05 - Fax: 47 09 35 55
XVII to XX century canes.

CARPETS, TAPESTRIES & TEXTILES

AVEDIS, 8 Allée Riesener ■ Tel: 42 61 56 89

L'ART ET LES HOMMES/GALERIE BASSALI, 2 Allée Saunier ■ Tel: 42 60 21 25

CLOCKS

ANTIC-TAC, 1 Allée Boulle ■ Tel: 42 61 57 16

COINS & STAMPS

ALAIN ELEB, 22 Allée Riesener ■ Tel: 42 61 57 04

LA CARTOTHEQUE, 1 Allée Canabas ■ Tel: 42 61 56 64

POSTE D'ANTAN, 23 Allée Boulle ■ Tel: 42 61 57 49

CRYSTAL, OPALINE, GLASS

AURELIO, BIS, 8 Allée Desmalter ■ Tel: 42 61 57 98

BADILLET, 17 Allée Desmalter ■ Tel: 47 03 97 84

DUBOIS, 2 Allée Riesener ■ Tel: 42 60 19 95

GALERIE HELENE TRUONG, 2 Allée Roentgen ■ Tel: 42 60 18 95

PALISSANDRE, 17 Allée Boulle ■ Tel: 42 61 57 38

DOLLS, AUTOMATED TOYS

COLOMBELLE, 14 Allée Boulle ■ Tel: 42 61 57 34

GERARD ETIENBLED, 19 Allée Riesener ■ Tel: 42 60 22 92

FAIENCE, PORCELAIN

AVOA, 6/8 Allée Molitor ■ Tel: 49 27 96 65

M.J. BADIN, 4 Allée Weisweiler ■ Tel: 42 86 86 79

FREDERIQUE BRUYNEEL, 22 Allée Desmalter ■ Tel: 42 61 58 13 - Fax: 42 97 00 14
XVIII & XIX century, porcelain, bronze, mirrors, furniture and art objects

ELSASER, 4 Allée Mackintosh ■ Tel: 42 60 17 99

BERTRAND DE LAVERGNE, 1 Allée Saunier ■ Tel: 42 60 21 63

THEOREME, 18/19 Allée Jacob ■ Tel: 40 15 93 23

DOMINIQUE VIEILLEVILLE, 24 Allée Boulle ■ Tel: 42 61 57 50
XVII to XIX century faience, porcelain, bronze.

PAULE ZELLITCH, 3 Allée Boulle ■ Tel: 42 61 57 20

FANS ANTIQUE

LUCIE SABOUDJIAN, Cour Palais Royal ■ Tel: 42 61 57 85

FIREPLACES, ACCESSORIES

GERARD CONTE, 3b Allée Molitor ■ 13 Allée Jacob ■ Tel: 42 60 18 62/63

PAULE ZELLITCH, 3 Allée Boulle ■ Tel: 42 61 57 20

─────────── **FOLK ART - POPULAR ART** ───────────

LA GALERIE PITTORESQUE, 13 Allée Desmalter ■ Tel: 42 61 58 06
LE COCHELIN, 16 Allée Jacob ■ Tel: 42 61 50 96
L'HERMINETTE, 4/6 Allée Germain ■ Tel: 42 61 57 81

─────────── **FURNITURE - ENGLISH ART OBJECTS** ───────────

BRITISH IMPORT ANTIQUES, 2/4 Allée Topino ■ Tel: 42 60 19 12/13

─────────── **FURNITURE & ART OBJECTS CHARLES X** ───────────

PALISSANDRE, 17 Allée Boulle ■ Tel: 42 61 57 38

─────────── **FURNITURE - ART OBJECTS 1930-1950** ───────────

GALERIE No. 4, 4 Allée Saunier ■ Tel: 42 61 56 55
1940-1950
LES ANTIQUITES DU XX SIECLE, 36 Alllée Riesener ■ Tel: 49 27 03 35
NEO SENSO, 18/20 Allée Boulle ■ Tel: 42 61 57 41

─────────── **FURNITURE & ART OBJECTS, HAUTE ÉPOQUE** ───────────

L'ART ET LES HOMMES/GALERIE BASSALI, 2 Allée Saunier ■ Tel: 42 60 21 25

─────────── **FURNITURE & ART OBJECTS, RENAISSANCE** ───────────

GALERIE FRANÇOIS ANTONOVITCH, 4 Allée Desmalter ■ Tel: 42 61 57 93

─────────── **FURNITURE & ART OBJECTS, XVII, XVIII CENTURIES** ───────────

ALLEE-MACHERET, 4b Allée Desmalter ■ Tel: 42 61 57 94
ANTICHE ARTI DECORATIVE, 26 Allée Boulle ■ Tel: 42 60 53 86
Specialty: Italian
BLEU VERT ANTIQUITES, 21/23/25 Allée Riesener ■ Tel: 42 61 57 02
FREDERIQUE BRUYNEEL, 22 Allée Desmalter ■ Tel: 42 61 58 13
DANTEC, 8 Allée Weisweiler ■ Tel: 42 61 56 45
DEBERNARDI, 1 Allée Thomire ■ Tel: 47 03 45 27
DEPIEDS-PARIENTE, 24 Allée Desmalter ■ Tel: 42 61 18 53
DANIEL DUAULT, 8/10 Allée Saunier ■ Tel: 42 61 56 76
ERMENAULT-MOURET, 2 Allée Jacob ■ Tel: 42 61 58 43
GALERIE FRANÇOIS ANTONOVITCH, 4 Allée Desmalter ■ Tel: 42 61 57 93
GALERIE JACQUES OLLIER, 7 Allée Guimard ■ Tel: 42 61 58 30/31
GALERIE MONTAIGNE, 13/15 Allée Guimard ■ Tel: 40 20 07 13
GALERIE RIVE DROITE, 9 Allée Jacob ■ Tel: 40 15 97 87

GALERIE RIVOLI, 24 Allée Riesener ■ Tel: 42 61 57 05

GALERIE YVES BRUCK, 2 Allée Carlin ■ Tel: 42 60 21 92

GISMONDI GALERIES, 6 Allée Saunier ■ Tel: 42 61 56 71/42 61 66 60

GRUNSPAN-PARTOUCHE, 7 Allée Carlin ■ Tel: 42 61 58 39

HARTER, 1/3 Allée Topino ■ Tel: 40 15 90 46

JEAN REY ET CIE, 3/5 Allée Canabas ■ Tel: 42 61 56 62/63

L'ART ET LES HOMMES/GALERIE BASSALI, 2 Allée Saunier ■ Tel: 42 60 21 25

LES ARCADES DU LOUVRE, 5 Allée Molitor ■ Tel: 47 03 31 62

MARTIN DE BAZINE, 5/7 Allée Weisweiler ■ Tel: 42 61 56 43 - Fax: 42 61 15 27

POSTE D'ANTAN, 23 Allée Boulle ■ Tel: 42 61 57 49

PAULE ZELLITCH, 3 Allée Boulle ■ Tel: 42 61 57 20

──────────── **FURNITURE & ART OBJECTS, XIX CENTURY** ────────────

ALDO BRAGHIERI, 27 Allée Boulle ■ Tel: 42 61 57 54

CROISETTE ANTIQUES, 16 Allée Desmalter ■ Tel: 42 60 20 49

DEBERNARDI, 1 Allée Thomire ■ Tel: 47 03 45 27

DEUTSCH-SALSEDO, 10/12 Allée Desmalter ■ Tel: 42 61 58 02/03
XVIII & XIX century paintings, furniture and art objects.

GALERIE HARTER, 1/3 Allée Topino ■ Tel: 40 15 90 46

ROGER HASSAN, 2 Allée Desmalter ■ Tel: 42 60 21 10

──────────── **GENERALISTS** ────────────

COLETTE AUBINIERE, 30 Allée Boulle ■ Tel: 42 61 57 59

M. J. BADIN, 4 Allée Weisweiler ■ Tel. 42 86 86 79

FREDERIQUE BRUYNEEL, 22 Allée Desmalter ■ Tel: 42 61 58 13

MICHEL CAFLER, 9/11 Allée Carlin ■ Tel: 49 26 01 40

GERARD CONTE, 3b Allée Molitor ■ 13 Allée Jacob ■ Tel: 42 60 18 62/63

CORAIL, 35 Allée Boulle ■ Tel: 42 61 57 64

DAVIA DE FER, 28 Allée Boulle ■ Tel: 42 61 57 55

CATHERINE DESPAS, 3 Allée Cressent ■ Tel: 42 61 56 51

GILBERT DUMAS, 3 Allée Jacob ■ Tel: 42 60 21 55

GALERIE CHARLES SAKR, 6/8 Allée Jacob ■ Tel: 42 61 58 61
Fax: 47 20 38 00
XVIII, XIX and early XX century furniture, paintings and art objects.

GALERIE COLANNE, 5 Allée Topino ■ Tel: 42 60 16 72

GALERIE D'ORSAY, 12b Allée Desmalter ■ Tel: 42 60 23 01

GALERIE JEAN-PIERRE HARTER, 1/3 Allée Topino ■ Tel: 40 15 90 46
Fax: 42 60 49 79
Furniture of the XIX century, 1930-1940, XIX century paintings.

GALERIE LA JOCONDE, 10 Allée Jacob ■ Tel: 42 60 23 52

GALERIE M.D.M., 19 Allée Boulle ■ Tel: 42 86 87 07

GALERIE OLIVIER RENAULT, 34 Allée Riesener ■ Tel:42 61 57 14

GALERIE SABBAN, 31 Allée Boulle ■ Tel: 42 61 57 62

GALERIE SARTO, 9/11 Allée Guimard ■ Tel: 42 61 58 22/29

GALERIE 7, 7 Allée Desmalter ■ Tel: 42 61 57 97

GALERIE THOMIRE - LANTELME, 3 Allée Thomire ■ Tel: 42 61 57 78

INTEMPORAL, 1 Allée Desmalter ■ Tel: 42 60 22 65

GUY KALFON, 15 Allée Jacob ■ Tel: 40 15 08 67

LA TOUR CAMOUFLE, 5/7 Allée Saunier ■ Tel: 42 60 22 32

JACQUES LEVY, 18 Allée Jacob ■ Tel:42 61 58 14

JEAN LOMBARD, 18 Allée Desmalter ■ Tel:42 60 19 83

MONIQUE PHILIPPE-ALAIN CHAUVEL, 10 Allée Boulle ■ Tel: 42 61 57 26

──────────────── ICONS ────────────────

GALERIE MANIC, 20 Allée Desmalter ■ Tel: 42 61 58 12

L'ART ET LES HOMMES/GALERIE BASSALI, 2 Allée Saunier ■ Tel: 42 60 21 25

WEEK END, 12 Allée Boulle ■ Tel: 42 61 57 32

──────────── ILLUMINATIONS - MANUSCRIPTS ────────────

LES ENLUMINURES, 16 Allée Riesener ■ Tel: 42 60 15 58 - Fax: 40 15 00 25
Illuminated manuscripts, drawings & gouaches of the Middle Ages & Renaissance.

──────────────── ISLAMIC ART ────────────────

SLIM BOUCHOUCHA, 8 Allée Boulle ■ Tel: 42 61 57 25

JULIETTE NOUJAIM, 1 Allée Roentgen ■ Tel: 42 60 18 92

──────────────── MARINE & SCIENCE ────────────────

PATRICK ADAM, 11 Allée Bellange ■ Tel: 42 60 17 77

DOMINIQUE DELALANDE, 1/2/3 Allée Majorelle ■ Tel: 42 60 19 35

DIEUTEGARD "LA FILLE DU PIRATE", 1/3 Allée Weisweiler ■ Tel: 42 60 20 30/31

──────────────── MEDICINE, SURGERY ────────────────

NICOLE KRAMER, 5 Allée Desmalter ■ Tel: 42 61 57 95
XVII to XIX century European small art objects - boxes, miniatures, surgical, dental, optical instruments.

ORIENTAL ART AND ANTIQUES

BERTRAND DE LAVERGNE, 1 Allée Saunier ■ Tel: 42 60 21 63 - Fax: 39 55 97 88

XVII & XVIII century Chinese and Japanese porcelain, Compagnie des Indes, tobacco jars.

DUCHANGE - GARMIGNY, 5 Allée Carlin ■ 15/17 Allée Riesener ■ Tel: 42 61 58 38

GALERIE KURITA, 2 Allée Bellange ■ Tel: 42 60 21 06

JAPON ANTIQUE, 7 Allée Riesener ■ Tel: 42 61 56 88

KOUNI, 3 Allée Desmalter ■ 42 60 23 15

PAINTINGS & DRAWINGS BEFORE 1830

DE JONCKHEERE, 9 Allée Boulle ■ Tel: 42 60 20 82

XVI and XVII century Flemish and Dutch paintings.

GALERIE FLORENCE DE VOLDERE, 2 Allée Molitor ■ Tel: 40 15 93 26

GALERIE JACQUES OLLIER, 7 Allée Guimard ■ Tel: 42 61 58 30/31

GALERIE LILIANE ROCHER, 4 Allée Jacob ■ Tel: 40 20 01 34

PAINTINGS & DRAWINGS XIX, XX CENTURIES

ARCADIANE GALERIE, 2 Place Palais-Royal ■ Tel: 42 61 57 75 - Fax: 42 61 57 76

XVIII & XIX century paintings, bronzes, sculptures, furniture. 1900s glass.

PATRICE AUZERAL, 13 Allée Riesener ■ Tel: 42 61 56 93

BERKO GALLERY 7/9 Allée Molitor ■ Tel: 42 60 19 40 - Fax: 42 60 19 41

Late XIX century European paintings and Belgian and French Romantic Schools.

DOMINIQUE BERT, 5/7 Allée Jacob ■ Tel: 42 61 58 50

J. BOUTERSKY, 6 Allée Desmalter ■ Telfax: 42 61 57 96

Paintings, art objects. Paintings of Toshio Bando 1895-1974.

DE JONCKHEERE, 7/9 Allée Boulle ■ Tel: 42 60 20 82

GALERIE JEAN-LOUIS BOSC, 4 Allée Majorelle ■ Tel: 42 60 19 48

GALERIE BOULLE, 21 Allée Boulle ■ Tel: 42 61 57 43

GALERIE BRETONNIERE-BERNAUDIN, 10b Allée Riesener ■ Tel: 42 60 20 91

GALERIE PHILIPPE CEZANNE, 28 Allée Riesener ■ Tel: 42 61 57 11

GALERIE PHILIPPE CEZANNE, 5 Allée Roentgen ■ Tel: 42 60 19 26

GALERIE GIOVANNI, 1/3 Allée Carlin ■ Tel: 42 61 56 73/74

GALERIE LAUMA, 7 Allée Roentgen ■ Tel: 42 60 19 30

GALERIE LAURY-BAILLY, 5 Allée Riesener ■ Tel: 42 61 56 86

GALERIE ROGER MANCHERON, 5 Allée Mackintosh ■ Tel: 42 60 20 26

GALERIE GLADYS SANI, 7 Allée Canabas ■ Tel: 42 61 56 92

GALERIE SARTO, 9 Allée Guimard ■ Tel: 42 61 58 22

GALERIE THOMIRE-R. ROUX, 13b/15 Allée Boulle ■ Tel: 42 61 57 00

GALERIE THOMIRE-LANTELME, 3 Allée Thomire ■ Tel: 42 61 57 78

GALERIE VACHET, 29 Allée Boulle ■ Tel: 42 61 57 56

LEFEVRE-WARME, 16 Allée Boulle ■ Tel: 42 61 57 36

MAGHERA-GALERIE NATAF, 14 Allée Desmalter ■ Tel: 42 60 22 23 - Fax: 42 60 22 29
xix century and modern French and Oriental paintings.

M.F.A. GALERIE ANTINEA, 12/14 Allée Jacob ■ Tel: 42 61 66 78

STE REGARTS (DEVILLE-GUILLAUME), 8/10 Allée Guimard ■ Tel: 42 61 58 24

──────────── **RUSSIAN ART** ────────────

GORKY ANTIQUITES, 6 Allée Odiot ■ Tel: 42 60 22 76

WEEK END, 12 Allée Boulle ■ Tel: 42 61 57 32

──────────── **SACRED ART** ────────────

ALAIN EXCOFFIER, 1/3 Allée Mackintosh ■ Tel: 42 61 44 20

GALERIE COUR CARREE - G.C.C., 5 Allée Guimard ■ Tel: 42 61 58 19

GALERIE MANIC, 20 Allée Desmalter ■ Tel: 42 61 58 12
Icons, statuary, restoration.

──────────── **SCULPTURE** ────────────

GILBERT DUMAS, 3 Allée Jacob ■ Tel: 42 60 21 55

GALERIE PHILIPPE CEZANNE, 28 Allée Riesener ■ Tel: 42 61 57 11

MIGUET FRERES, 2/6 Allée Guimard ■ Tel: 42 61 58 25/26

JACQUES TCHARNY, 33 Allée Boulle ■ Tel: 42 61 75 04

──────────── **TABLE ARTS** ────────────

DANENBERG, 2 Allée Boulle ■ Tel: 42 61 57 19

LA GALERIE PITTORESQUE, 13 Allée Desmalter ■ Tel: 42 61 58 06

SUGER, 6/8 Allée Cressent ■ Tel: 42 61 57 72
European glass, silver and table arts 1840-1940.

──────────── **TOYS** ────────────

LE PETIT GRENIER, 19 Allée Odiot ■ Tel: 42 60 17 69

GERARD ETIENBLED, 19 Allée Riesener ■ Tel: 42 60 22 92

Carré Rive Gauche

The Carré Rive Gauche is a convenient area for the serious buyer of art and antiques. Starting on the Quai Voltaire across from the Louvre, the "Carré" is bounded by the Rue du Bac, the Quai Voltaire, the Rue des Saints-Pères and the Rue de l'Université.

The merchants in this tight little enclave make it one of the greatest art and antique markets in the world. A wide variety of specialties is covered, from old masters to contemporary paintings. You will also find some of the best examples of museum quality antique furniture along with some of the more eclectic disciplines such as old engravings, archaeological artifacts, porcelain, ethnic art, tapestries and carpets. Just about everyone in the area is expert in the decorative arts and ready to share their knowledge and know-how. You'll discover for yourself that most of the dealers are extremely qualified in their field.

Every year, during the month of May, the Carré Rive Gauche holds a "red carpet" open house. The pavements are literally carpeted in red and traffic is barred from late afternoon to evening's end. Most establishments will welcome you with a smile and a glass of champagne.

Try to make it in May. It's the real start of the Paris season for treasure hunting.

Opening hours are generally the same throughout the Carré Rive Gauche: 10:00-13:30/14:30-19:00. For complete information call 42 79 98 37.

The Editors have organized the Carré Rive Gauche on a street by street basis so that you may start at one end and finish up where you started.

MILANO BACSTREET

1 rue du Bac, 75007 Paris ■ Tel: 42 61 24 20 - Fax: 49 27 80 85 ■ Mon 14:30-19:30/Tues-Sat 10:30-19:30 ■ English spoken ■ Prices reasonable ■ 15 to 20% professional discount

Far Eastern furniture, art objects, archaeology, porcelain, bronze, ivory.

GALERIE VERNEUIL

17 rue du Bac, 75007 Paris ■ Tel: 42 61 18 77 - Fax: 42 61 14 99 ■ Mon-Sat 10:00-19:30 ■ Jean-Claude Sieberth speaks English ■ Prices high ■ 10 to 15% professional discount

French ceramics, faience, porcelain.

JOSY ARMENGAUD

19 rue du Bac, 75007 Paris ■ Tel: 47 03 99 07 ■ Mon-Sat 10:30-13:00/14:30-19:00 ■ Josy Armengaud speaks English ■ Price medium, ■ Professional discount

XVIII century French furniture, decorative objects.

FRANÇOIS HAYEM

21 rue du Bac, 75007 Paris ■ Tel: 42 61 25 60 - Fax: 42 61 59 02 ■ Mon-Sat 9:30-19:00 ■ Béatrice de Marcheville speaks English ■ Prices high ■ Professional discount

XVIII century French furniture and art objects.

FLORENCE MARTIN

23 rue du Bac, 75007 Paris ■ Tel: 42 61 52 88 - Fax: 42 61 15 27 ■ Mon 14:30-19:00/Tues-Sat 11:00-19:00 ■ Florence Martin speaks English ■ Prices medium to high ■ Professional discount

XVII, XVIII century French, Italian furniture, art objects.
Small selection of Gothic items.

LEFEBVRE & FILS

24 rue du Bac, 75007 Paris ■ Tel: 42 61 18 40 ■ Mon-Sat 10:00-12:30/14:00-19:00 ■ English spoken ■ Prices very high ■ Professional discount

European ceramics, from the XVI to early XIX centuries.

ALAIN DE LAVALADE

25 rue du Bac, 75007 Paris ■ Tel: 42 61 17 75 - Fax: 40 20 98 94 ■ Mon 14:00-19:00/Tues-Sat 11:30-13:00/14:00-19:00 ■ Alain de Lavalade speaks English ■ Prices medium ■ 10% professional discount

XVII, XVIII and early XIX century French furniture and art objects. Restoration of furniture.

THENADAY

1 quai Voltaire, 75007 Paris ■ Tel: 42 60 77 33
XIX century furniture

JACQUELINE BOCCADOR

1 quai Voltaire, 75007 Paris ■ Tel: 42 60 75 79 - Fax: 42 60 31 27 ■ English spoken ■ Prices medium to high ■ Professional discount
Sculpture and furniture of the Middle Ages and Renaissance.

GALERIE GHISLAINE DAVID

1 quai Voltaire, 75007 Paris ■ Tel: 42 60 73 10 - Fax: 42 96 02 69 ■ Mon-Sat 10:00-13:00/14:00-19:00 ■ Ghislaine David speaks English ■ Prices medium to high ■ 10% professional discount
XVIII century French furniture, sculpture, art objects.
Will research and find special items for professional clients.

☷ GALERIE PERRIN

3 quai Voltaire, 75007 Paris ■ Tel: 42 60 27 20 - Fax: 42 61 32 61 ■ English spoken ■ Prices high ■ Professional discount
Very high quality XVII, XVIII century furniture, fine old drawings, art objects.

L. P. BRESSET & FILS

5 quai Voltaire, 75007 Paris ■ Tel: 42 60 78 13 - Fax: 42 60 59 38 ■ Tues-Sat 10:00-12:30/14:30-19:00 ■ Gilles Bresset speaks English ■ Prices high ■ 10 to 15% discount
Furniture, art objects and sculpture of the XIII to XVII centuries (Middle Ages, Renaissance, Louis XIII).

FREMONTIER ANTIQUITES

5 quai Voltaire, 75007 Paris ■ Tel: 42 61 64 90 - Fax: 42 61 04 96 ■ Mon-Fri 9:00-19:00/Sat 10:00-19:00 ■ English spoken ■ Prices medium to high ■ Professional discount
XVIII, XIX century antiques from all countries.

NICOLIER

7 quai Voltaire, 75007 Paris ■ Tel: 42 60 78 63 ■ Tues-Sat 10:30-12:00/14:30-18:30 ■ Prices medium to high ■ Professional discount
Faience, porcelain of the Far East, IX to XIX centuries.

DIDIER RABES

7 quai Voltaire, 75007 Paris ■ Tel: 42 60 73 13
XVII century furniture and art objects.

GALERIE BELLIER

7 quai Voltaire, 75007 Paris ■ Tel: 42 60 74 72 - Fax: 40 20 93 52 ■ Tues-Sat 10:30-13:00/14:30-19:00 ■ English spoken
XIX, XX century paintings.

RENONCOURT

7 quai Voltaire, 75007 Paris ■ Tel: 42 60 15 63 ■ Mon-Sat 10:00-12:30/14:00-19:00 ■ Prices high ■ 10% professional discount
Late XVIII century to Charles X furniture and art objects.

♚ GALERIE CAMOIN DEMACHY

9 quai Voltaire, 75007 Paris ■ Tel: 42 61 82 06 - Fax: 42 61 24 09 ■ Mon-Sat 10:00-13:00/14:30-19:00 ■ Jocelyne Le Brenn and Alain Demachy speak English ■ Prices high ■ 10% professional discount

Superb display of French and other European XVII, XVIII and XIX century furniture, lighting and objects.
Qualified experts.

GALERIE RATTON-LADRIERE

11 quai Voltaire, 75007 Paris ■ Tel: 42 61 29 79 - Fax: 42 56 00 72 ■ Mon-Sat, 14:30-19:00 ■ English spoken ■ Prices very high ■ 10% professional discount

Statuary and art objects from the Renaissance to the XVIII century, paintings and drawings from the XVI to the XVIII centuries. Specialist in the Haute Epoque (Middle Ages to Renaissance).

GALERIE F. PERREAU-SAUSSINE

11 quai Voltaire, 75007 Paris ■ Tel: 42 61 10 75 - Fax: 42 61 59 49 ■ Tues-Fri 10:30-13:00/14:00-19:00/Mon 15:00-19:00 ■ Rachel Belisha speaks English ■ Prices high ■ Professional discount

Paintings, drawings and sculpture of the great masters of the XIX and XX centuries.
Expert in Théodore Rousseau and XIX and XX century drawings.

♚ GALERIE MICHEL SEGOURA

11 quai Voltaire, 75007 Paris ■ Tel: 42 61 19 23 - Fax: 42 60 01 98 ■ Tues-Sat 10:00-12:30/14:00-18:30 and by appointment ■ English spoken ■ Prices medium to high ■ Professional discount

XVII century Flemish and Dutch paintings and drawings.

ANTONY EMBDEN

15 quai Voltaire, 75007 Paris ■ Tel: 42 61 04 06 - Fax: 42 61 40 89 ■ Mon-Sat 10:30-12:30/14:30-18:30 ■ Antony Embden speaks English

Art objects of the XVI, XVII centuries. Specialist in European sculpture.

GALERIE JEAN-MAX TASSEL

15 quai Voltaire, 75007 Paris ■ Tel: 42 61 02 01
Old master paintings.

♚ GALERIE CHEVALIER

17 quai Voltaire, 75007 Paris ■ Tel: 42 60 72 68 - Fax: 42 86 99 06 ■ Mon 14:00-18:00/Tues-Fri 10:00-13:00/14:00-19:00/Sat 11:00-19:00 ■ English spoken ■ Prices high

Highest quality carpets and tapestries. This is a must if you love great carpets and superb museum quality tapestries. The Chevalier twins are considered the best in the world. Don't be intimidated, everyone in the gallery is charming. They are known world-wide for restoration and cleaning of carpets and tapestries.

GALERIE ALTERO

21 quai Voltaire, 75007 Paris ■ Tel: 42 61 19 90

Art objects and antique glass.

♔ GALERIE DE JONCKHEERE

21 quai Voltaire, 75007 Paris ■ Tel: 42 66 69 49 - Fax: 42 61 23 14 ■ Mon-Sat 10:30-19:00/ Closed Mon 13:00-14:30 ■ English spoken ■ Prices high ■ Professional discount

Old master paintings, drawings.

♔ FRANÇOIS HAYEM

21 quai Voltaire, 75007 Paris ■ Tel: 42 61 01 30 - Fax: 42 61 59 02 ■ Mon-Sat 9:30-19:00 ■ English spoken ■ Prices high ■ 10% professional discount

XVIII century furniture and art objects.

♔ REVILLON D'APREVAL

23 quai Voltaire, 75007 Paris ■ Tel: 42 61 27 36 - Fax: 42 61 43 70 ■ Mon-Sat 10:00-12:30/14:30-19:00 ■ Luc Revillon d'Apreval speaks English ■ Prices medium to high ■ 10% professional discount

Excellent collection of XVII, XVIII, XIX century furniture and art objects.

♔ J. O. LEEGENHOEK

23 quai Voltaire, 75007 Paris ■ Tel: 42 96 36 08

Old master paintings and drawings.

GALERIE CHARLES & ANDRE BAILLY

25 quai Voltaire, 75007 Paris ■ Tel: 42 60 36 47 - Fax: 42 60 54 92 ■ Mon-Sat 10:00-13:00/14:00-19:00 ■ Charles, André and Patricia Bailly speak English ■ Prices medium ■ 5 to 10% professional discount

Old masters, modern and contemporary paintings, drawings, water colors and sculpture. Excellent quality, wide range.

♔ HUGUETTE BERÈS

25 quai Voltaire, 75007 Paris ■ Tel: 42 61 27 91

XIX, XX century paintings.

♔ VAN DER MEESCH

27 quai Voltaire, 75007 Paris ■ Tel: 42 61 23 10 - Fax: 49 27 98 49 ■ Tues-Sat 10:00-12:30/14:00-18:30 ■ English spoken ■ Prices medium to high ■ Professional discount

Faience, porcelain, art objects.

♔ MICHEL OTTIN

33 quai Voltaire, 75007 Paris ■ Tel: 42 61 19 88 - Fax: 42 61 32 41 ■ Mon-Sat 10:00-19:00 ■ Michel and Sandrine Ottin speak English ■ Prices medium to high ■ Professional discount

XVIII century French regional furniture in natural wood.
XVIII century furniture in marquetry, XVIII and XIX century art objects.

RENONCOURT

1-3 rue des Saints-Pères, 75007 Paris ■ Tel: 42 60 75 87 - Fax: 42 60 15 14 ■ Mon-Sat 10:00-12:30/14:00-19:00 ■ Prices high ■ 10% professional discount

Late XVIII century to Charles X furniture and art objects.

MICHEL LALAY

2 rue des Saints-Pères, 75007 Paris ■ Tel: 42 60 71 62 ■ Tues-Sat 10:00-12:30/14:30-19:00 ■ Michel Lalay speaks English ■ Prices medium ■ Professional discount

XVIII, XIX century furniture.

JEAN-FRANÇOIS DE BLANCHETTI

2 rue des Saints-Pères, 75007 Paris ■ Tel: 42 60 22 43 - Fax: 42 96 23 47 ■ Tues-Sat 10:00-13:00/14:00-19:00/Mon 14:00-19:00 ■ Jean-François Blanchetti speaks English ■ Prices medium ■ 10% professional discount
Neo-classical and XIX century furniture, paintings and art objects.

JEAN-PIERRE GROS

6 bis rue des Saints-Pères, 75007 Paris ■ Tel: 42 61 28 15 - Fax: 42 61 44 90 ■ Tues-Sat 10:30-13:00/14:30-19:00/Mon 14:30-19:00 ■ Philippe Claverie speaks English ■ Prices very high ■ 10 to 20% professional discount
XVIII, XIX, early XX century furniture, tapestries, lighting, paintings.

GALERIE BARÈS

7 rue des Saints-Pères, 75007 Paris ■ Tel: 42 60 65 83 - Fax: 49 27 91 63 ■ Mon-Sat 11:00-19:00 ■ Joël Bares speaks English ■ Prices reasonable ■ Professional discount

Paintings, engravings and illustrated books of great XX century artists, Picasso, Chagall, Braque, Miró, Buffet, Poliakoff, Léger.

VERONIQUE GIRARD

7 rue des Saints-Pères, 75006 Paris ■ Tel: 42 60 74 00 - Fax: 47 03 41 54 ■ Tues-Sat 10:30-12:30/14:30-19:00 ■ Véronique Girard speaks English ■ Prices medium ■ 10% professional discount

XVIII, XIX century silver. Repair.

GUY BELLOU

7 bis rue des Saints-Pères, 75007 Paris ■ Tel: 42 60 81 33 ■ Tues-Fri 10:30-12:30/14:30-19:00/Sat 14:30-19:00 ■ Guy Bellou speaks English ■ Prices medium ■ 10 to 30% Professional discount

XVIII century furniture and art objects.

GALERIE DES SAINTS-PÈRES

11 rue des Saints-Pères, 75007 Paris ■ Tel: 42 60 25 94 - Fax: 49 27 95 83 ■ Tues-Sat 13:00-19:00 ■ Anne-Marie Fournier speaks English ■ Prices medium to high ■ Professional discount

Contemporary paintings, drawings and sculpture.
Portraits to order by any one of the gallery's 20 living artists.

GALERIE SAINT-MARTIN

11 rue des Saints-Pères, 75007 Paris ■ Tel: 42 60 83 65 - Fax: 42 60 44 19
■ Mon-Sat 11:00-13:00/14:00-19:00 ■ Charlotte Chapoulart speaks English
■ 15 to 20% professional discount

Furniture of the XVIII and XIX centuries. Paintings of the XVIII, XIX and early XX centuries. Bronzes of the XIX century. Special collection of seals.

GALERIE ROGER DUCHANGE

12 rue des Saints-Pères, 75007 Paris ■ Tel: 42 60 89 55 ■ Mon 14:00-18:30/Tues-Sat 10:00-12:00/14:00-18:30 ■ English spoken

Chinese and Japanese art objects, porcelain, bronze, semi-precious stones, paintings, furniture, ivories.

JEAN WANECQ

12 rue des Saints-Pères, 75007 Paris ■ Tel: 42 60 83 64 - Fax: 42 60 41 48
■ Mon-Sat 10:00-13:00/15:00-18:00 ■ Gertrude Wanecq speaks English ■ 10% professional discount

XVIII, XIX century French furniture, paintings, art objects.

B. FAIVRE-REUILLE

13 rue des Saints-Pères, 75007 Paris ■ Tel: 42 60 28 74

XVIII, XIX century furniture.

DUBRUNOIS

13 rue des Saints-Pères, 75007 Paris ■ Tel: 42 96 90 39

Old drawings.

GALERIE VERNEUIL SAINTS-PÈRES
MORTIER-VALAT

13 rue des Saints-Pères, 75007 Paris ■ Tel: 42 60 28 30 - Fax: 42 60 28 16
■ Tues-Sat, 15:00-19:00 ■ Joëlle Mortier-Valat speaks English ■ Prices high
■ 10 to 15% professional discount

XIX, XX century paintings, sculpture, furniture.

HOPILLIART-LEROUX

14-16 rue des Saints-Pères, 75007 Paris ■ Tel: 42 60 85 55

XVIII century furniture and art objects.

HELENE FOURNIER-GUERIN

25 rue des Saints-Pères, 75007 Paris ■ Telfax: 42 60 21 81 ■ Mon 15:00-19:00/Tues-Sat 11:00-13:00/15:00-19:00 ■ Hélène Fournier-Guerin speaks English ■ Prices medium ■ 10 to 15% professional discount

Chinese porcelain of the XVII, XVIII centuries.
French porcelain of the XVIII century. Faience of the XVII and XVIII centuries.

ATELIER 12

27 rue des Saints-Pères, 75007 Paris ■ Tel: 42 60 81 00

Decorative objects

PARSUA

7 rue de Verneuil, 75007 Paris ■ Tel: 42 86 80 94
Carpets and tapestries.

DES LAMPES

9 rue de Verneuil, 75007 Paris ■ Tel: 40 20 02 58 - Fax: 40 20 08 36 ■ Mon 14:00-19:00/Tues-Sat 11:00-19:00 ■ Antoine Pialoux and Jean Meoule speak English ■ Prices medium ■ Professional discount
Antique lamps.

M.P.A.

9 rue de Verneuil, 75007 Paris ■ Tel: 40 20 08 70 - Fax: 40 20 08 36 ■ Mon 14:00-19:00/Tues-Sat 11:00-19:00 ■ English spoken ■ Prices high ■ Professional discount
XVIII to early XX century furniture and art objects.

NOIR D'IVOIRE

22 rue de Verneuil, 75007 Paris ■ Tel: 42 86 99 11
Decorative objects

BERNARD CAPTIER

25 rue de Verneuil, 75007 Paris ■ Tel: 42 61 00 57 - Fax: 47 49 04 25 ■ Mon 14:30-19:00/Tues-Sat 10:30-19:00 ■ English spoken ■ Prices medium ■ 10 to 15% professional discount
Antique furniture from China and Japan. Old paintings, objects and Japanese screens.

GALERIE B.J.F.

27 rue de Verneuil, 75007 Paris ■ Tel: 42 61 36 46 - Fax: 42 61 22 00 ■ Tues-Sat 14:00-19:00 ■ English spoken ■ Prices medium ■ 10% professional discount
XVIII, XIX century furniture, art objects and paintings.

ANNICK KLAVIER

32 rue de Verneuil, 75007 Paris ■ Tel: 42 61 08 39
Decorative objects.

LE QUELANCAY

40 rue de Verneuil, 75007 Paris ■ Tel: 42 96 39 75
Curiosities, art objects.

THIERRY L'HUILLIER

42 rue de Verneuil, 75007 Paris ■ Tel: 42 60 23 03 ■ Mon-Sat 14:00-19:00 ■ English spoken ■ Prices medium to high ■ Professional discount
XVI to XIX century European ceramics, pewter, porcelain, faience, glass.

PHILIPPE MURAT-DAVID

3 rue de Beaune, 75007 Paris ■ Tel: 42 61 64 53 ■ Mon 14:30-19:00/Tues-Sat 10:30-13:00/14:30-19:00 ■ Philippe Murat-David speaks English ■ Prices medium ■ 10 to 20% professional discount

Furniture and art objects of the XVII, XVIII, XIX centuries.

LORRAINE NORRE

6 rue de Beaune, 75007 Paris ■ Tel: 42 61 68 47

Art Deco, art objects.

M. K.

6 rue de Beaune, Paris 75006 ■ Tel: 42 61 26 86

Art objects.

ALAIN GERARD

7 rue de Beaune, 75007 Paris ■ Tel: 42 61 23 95 - Fax: 40 20 01 92 ■ Mon-Sat 10:00-12:00/14:00-19:00 ■ English spoken ■ Prices medium ■ Professional discount

Art objects, collectibles.

JACQUELINE NICOLAS

7 rue de Beaune, 75007 Paris ■ Tel: 42 61 25 38

Art objects.

LE VIEUX MANOIR (GINTZBERGER)

8 rue de Beaune, 75007 Paris ■ Tel: 42 61 17 50

XVIII century furniture, faience, porcelain.

GALERIE ACTEON

8 rue de Beaune, 75007 Paris ■ Tel: 42 61 23 43 - Fax: 42 61 00 58 ■ Mon-Sat 15:00-19:00 and by appointment ■ Charles de Langlade speaks English ■ Prices medium ■ Professional discount

Architectural paintings, drawings, models of the XVII, XVIII, XIX centuries, architectural furniture, sculpture models. Aviation, automotive, marine, locomotion – everything that moves or flies. Also scientific objects, inventions.

GALERIE DES LYONS

9 rue de Beaune, 75007 Paris ■ Tel: 42 61 16 81 - Fax: 49 48 70 01 ■ Mon-Sat 11:00-12:30/14:30-19:00 ■ English spoken ■ Prices medium ■ 10% professional discount

XIX, XX century paintings.

GALERIE DE BEAUNE (M. RICHER)

10 rue de Beaune, 75007 Paris ■ Tel: 42 86 05 72

Furniture and art objects: Empire, Directoire, Charles X.

MICHEL SONKIN "ART POPULAIRE"

10 rue de Beaune, 75007 Paris ■ Tel: 42 61 27 87 ■ Mon-Fri 14:30-19:00 and by appointment ■ Jeanne Sonkin speaks English ■ Prices medium ■ 15% professional discount

Folk art (Popular art), art objects, objects of curiosity in wrought iron.

MYRNA MYERS

11 rue de Beaune, 75007 Paris ■ Tel: 42 61 11 08 - Fax: 30 82 49 17 ■ Tues-Sat 14:30-18:30 ■ English spoken ■ Prices medium

Far Eastern art, ceramics and textiles.

F. DE NOINVILLE

12 rue de Beaune, 75007 Paris ■ Tel: 49 27 02 99

Glass.

GABRIELLE LAROCHE

12 rue de Beaune, 75007 Paris ■ Tel: 42 97 59 18

Sculpture and furniture of the Middle Ages and Renaissance.

DRAGESCO-CRAMOISAN

13 rue de Beaune, 75007 Paris ■ Tel: 42 61 18 20

Faience, porcelain, glass.

PASCAL IZARN

13 rue de Beaune, 75007 Paris ■ Tel: 42 60 96 69

Art objects, clocks (horlogerie).

ANTIQUITES DE BEAUNE

14 rue de Beaune, 75007 Paris ■ Tel: 42 61 25 42 - Fax: 42 61 24 44 ■ Tues-Sat 11:00-12:30/14:30-19:00/Mon 14:30-19:00 ■ Marguerite and Gérard Horwitz speak English ■ Prices high ■ 5 to 10% professional discount

Furniture in fruit woods, porcelain.

CATHERINE ARIGONI

14 rue de Beaune, 75007 Paris ■ Tel: 42 60 50 99 - Fax: 42 60 24 97 ■ Mon-Tues-Thurs 14:30-19:00/Wed-Fri-Sat 11:00-13:00/14:00-19:00 ■ English spoken ■ Prices high ■ 10 to 15% professional discount

XVIII, XIX, XX century furniture, chandeliers, sconces, lamps, art objects.

GALERIE DELVAILLE

15 rue de Beaune, 75007 Paris ■ Tel: 42 61 23 88 - Fax: 40 15 98 33 ■ Mon 14:30-19:00/Tues-Sat 10:00-12:30/14:30-19:00 ■ English and Spanish spoken ■ Prices medium to high ■ Professional discount

XVIII century French furniture. XVII, XVIII, early XIX century paintings.

PHILIPPE LEROUX

16 rue de Beaune, 75007 Paris ■ Tel: 42 61 18 24 ■ Tues-Sat 14:00-19:00 ■ Prices medium ■ Professional discount

XVII, XVIII, XIX century glass and drawings.

GERARD LEVY
17 rue de Beaune, 75007 Paris ■ Tel: 42 61 26 55 - Fax: 42 96 03 91 ■ Mon-Sat 14:00-18:00 ■ Gérard Lévy speaks English ■ Prices high ■ 10% professional discount

Antiques and art of China. Collection of photographs (1839-1940).

PETROUCHKA
18 rue de Beaune, 75007 Paris ■ Tel: 42 61 66 65

The art of Russia.

F. & D. BIANCARELLI
19 rue de Beaune, 75007 Paris ■ Tel: 42 61 23 05 ■ Mon-Sat 10:30-13:00/14:30-19:30 ■ Mr. Biancarelli speaks English ■ Prices medium

XVI, XVII, XVIII century furniture, paintings, art objects, sculpture.

ALLOU-BORREMANS
21 rue de Beaune, 75007 Paris ■ Tel: 49 27 05 80

Sculpture of the XIX, XX centuries, decorative objects.

LE CABINET DE CURIOSITE
23 rue de Beaune, 75007 Paris ■ Tel: 42 61 09 57

Art objects.

DENIS DERVIEUX
25 rue de Beaune, 75007 Paris ■ Tel: 40 15 99 20 ■ Mon-Sat 14:00-19:00 ■ English spoken ■ Prices medium ■ 10 to 20% professional discount

XVIII century furniture and decorative objects.
Gilded wood (bois doré).

LA ROSE DES VENTS
25 rue de Beaune, 75007 Paris ■ Tel: 42 60 11 17

Marine art and marine art objects.

THENADAY
27 rue de Beaune, 75007 Paris ■ Tel: 42 61 00 84

XIX century furniture.

ANDRE ANTOINE
31 rue de Beaune, 75007 Paris ■ Tel: 42 61 26 06

Sculpture of the XIX, XX centuries.

ANDRE METROT
31 rue de Beaune, 75007 Paris ■ Tel: 42 61 09 06

XVIII century furniture.

────────────────── RUE DE L'UNIVERSITÉ ──────────────────

GALERIE MUGLER-DUGAS
2 rue de l'Université, 75007 Paris ■ Tel: 42 96 36 45

Art objects.

AKKO VAN ACKER
3 rue de l'Université, 75007 Paris ■ Tel: 42 60 22 03
Art objects, curiosities.

ALAIN BERGER
3 rue de l'Université, 75007 Paris ■ Tel: 42 61 55 01
XIX century furniture, art objects.

JOEL LEBAS-MICHEL MORIN
4 rue de l'Université, 75007 Paris ■ Tel 42 86 02 72
Art objects, popular art.

ANNE JAUDEL
5 rue de l'Université, 75007 Paris ■ Tel: 42 60 33 94 ■ Tues-Sat 10:00-13:00/14:00-19:00/Mon 14:00-19:00 ■ Anne Jaudel speaks English ■ Prices medium ■ 10% professional discount
XVIII century French and Italian painted furniture, decorative objects.

CLAUDE VALDI
6 rue de l'Université, 75007 Paris ■ Tel: 47 03 94 90
Decorative objects.

GERARD MONLUC
7 rue de l'Université, 75007 Paris ■ Tel: 42 96 18 19
XVIII century furniture.

GALERIE AGAMEDE
12 rue de l'Université, 75007 Paris ■ Tel: 40 15 93 12
XIX, XX century paintings.

JEANNINE DE BRITO
12 rue de l'Université, 75007 Paris ■ Tel: 42 60 26 27
XVIII century furniture, paintings.

LA CHINE DES T'SING
14 rue de l'Université, 75007 Paris ■ Tel: 42 60 65 93 ■ Mon 14:00-19:00/Tues-Sat 10:00-13:00/14:00-19:00 ■ English spoken ■ Prices reasonable ■ 10% professional discount
Far Eastern art and art objects of the XVII to XIX century.

GALERIE PIERRE M. DUMONTEIL
38 rue de l'Université, 75007 Paris ■ Tel: 42 61 23 38
XIX, XX century paintings, sculpture.

GALERIE MERCIER-DUCHEMIN-CHANOIT
40 rue de l'Université, 75007 Paris ■ Tel: 42 86 00 40 - Fax: 42 86 03 02 ■ Mon-Sat 10:00-12:30/14:00-19:00 ■ English spoken ■ Prices medium ■ 10% professional discount
XIX, XX century paintings, drawings, sculpture.

GALERIE CHEREAU
40 rue de l'Université, 75007 Paris ■ Tel: 42 96 40 58
XIX, XX century paintings, sculpture.

GALERIE LA SIBYLLE

42 rue de l'Université, 75007 Paris ■ Tel: 42 96 16 75 ■ Tues-Sat 14:30-19:30
and by appointment ■ English spoken ■ Prices medium ■ Professional discount
XVIII, XIX early XX century paintings. Landscapes and flowers a specialty.

──────────────── RUE DE LILLE ────────────────

LILLE ANTIQUITES

3 rue de Lille, 75007 Paris ■ Tel: 47 03 33 43 ■ Tues-Sat 14:00-19:00 ■ Prices
high ■ 5 to 10% professional discount
XVIII, XIX century furniture, art objects and paintings.

MAROUN SALLOUM ANTIQUITES

6 rue de Lille, 75007 Paris ■ Tel: 40 15 95 02
XVIII century furniture, art objects.

GALERIE MARIE-ANNE BARON

6 rue de Lille, 75007 Paris ■ Tel: 40 15 97 60 - Fax: 40 29 98 28 ■ Thurs-Fri-
Sat 14:00-19:00 ■ Marie-Anne Baron speaks English ■ Prices medium ■ 15%
professional discount
Antiques from China and Japan. Paintings, screens, lacquer, small furniture,
chests, tables, consoles and art objects.

GALERIE DU RESSORT

12 rue de Lille, 75007 Paris ■ Tel: 49 26 04 89
Contemporary paintings, sculpture.

BASTIEN & ASSOCIES

13 rue de Lille, 75007 Paris ■ Tel: 42 60 76 27 - Fax: 42 66 07 93
XVIII, XIX century furniture.

ROBERT MONTAGUT

15 rue de Lille, 75007 Paris ■ Tel: 42 60 29 25 - Fax: 42 66 07 93 ■ Mon-Sat
8:00-18:00 ■ English spoken ■ Prices medium ■ 5% professional discount
Art objects.

DUO

15 rue de Lille, 75007 Paris ■ Tel: 47 03 92 63 - Fax: 42 61 67 90 ■ Tues-
Fri 14:00-19:00 and by appointment ■ English spoken ■ Prices medium ■ Professional discount
Art Nouveau (1900s) furniture, objects, paintings, lighting, of European
(non-French) origin.
Art Deco (1930s) French furniture, objects, paintings, lighting, and sometimes silver.

GALERIE WEBER & ASSOCIES

15 rue de Lille, 75007 Paris ■ Tel: 42 60 29 25 - Fax: 42 86 84 19 ■ Mon-Fri
13:00-19:00 ■ Bernard-Alexandre Weber speaks English ■ Prices medium
XVIII, XIX century furniture, paintings, art objects.

ASIE ANTIQUE

23 rue de Lille, 75007 Paris ■ Tel: 49 27 04 43 Fax: 48 34 65 91 ■ Tues-Sat 15:00-19:00 ■ Lee Thanapoomikul speaks English ■ Prices medium ■ 10 to 25% professional discount

Sculpture, furniture of China and Japan.

Statuary, bas reliefs, sculptured heads of Khmer, Thailand and Burma.

GABRIELLE LAROCHE

25 rue de Lille, 75007 Paris ■ Tel: 42 60 37 08 - Fax: 49 27 07 31 ■ Mon-Sat 10:00-19:00 ■ Professional discount

Furniture, sculpture, tapestries, objects of the Middle Ages and Renaissance.

GALERIE LAFON POKORNY

25 rue de Lille, 75007 Paris ■ Tel: 40 20 01 79

XIX, XX century paintings, sculpture.

AGNES DEYDIER & CIE

30 rue de Lille, 75007 Paris ■ Tel: 42 61 61 14

Far Eastern art.

MOUGIN

30 rue de Lille, 75007 Paris ■ Tel: 40 20 08 33 - Fax: 40 20 09 22 ■ Tues-Sat 11:30-19:00 ■ Gladys Mougin speaks English ■ Prices high ■ 10% professional discount

Furniture in unique designs by international artists. Limited editions and designs to order. Contemporary furniture in metal.

PHILIPPE VICHOT

37 rue de Lille, 75007 Paris ■ Tel: 40 15 00 81 - Fax: 42 61 07 52 ■ Mon-Sat 10:00-13:00/14:00-19:00 ■ English spoken by Gloria Beaufils de la Torre ■ 10% professional discount

XVIII, XIX century furniture, paintings, art objects (in marble, wrought iron, stone). French carpets.

GALERIE VERONIQUE MASI

38 rue de Lille, 75007 Paris ■ Tel: 42 60 01 30 ■ Tues-Sat 11:00-19:00 ■ Prices medium ■ Professional discount

XVIII century furniture.

JEAN-CLAUDE EDREI

44 rue de Lille, 75007 Paris ■ Tel: 42 61 28 08 ■ Mon-Sat 10:00-19:00 ■ Jean-Claude Edrel speaks English ■ Prices high ■ 10% professional discount

XVII, XVIII century furniture. XVI, XVII, XVIII century tapestries. French and European faience.

GISELE WEINBERGER

48 rue de Lille, 75007 Paris ■ Tel: 42 61 25 09

Sculpture of the Middle Ages, Old Master paintings.

Antique Dealers
by Arrondissement

I

ERIC PHILIPPE
25 Galerie Vero-Dodat, 75001 Paris ■ Tel: 42 33 28 26 - Fax: 42 21 17 93 ■ Tues-Sat 14:00-19:00 ■ English spoken ■ Prices medium ■ Professional discount
European decorative arts of 1900-1950, furniture, lighting, carpets, photography.

III

DEUX ORPHELINES
21 place des Vosges, 75003 Paris ■ Tel: 42 72 63 97 ■ Mon-Sat 11:30-19:00 ■ Prices medium ■ 10% Professional discount
XIX century furniture, objects, lamps, china, antique fabrics and linen.

GUIGUE (Atelier)
11 rue Saint-Gilles, 75003 Paris ■ Tel: 48 04 04 95 ■ Mon-Fri 10:00-18:00/Sat by appointment ■ Prices medium to high ■ 15% professional discount
Painted antique furniture. Custom furniture painted on order. Also gives intensive classes in painting on wood and screens.

ALDO PELLAS
15 rue Payenne, 75003 Paris ■ Tel: 42 78 15 69 ■ Mon & Wed-Sat 10:30-12:30/14:00-18:30/Sun 14:00-18:30 ■ Prices reasonable
XVIII, XIX century mirrors, furniture and paintings.

ANNE PIETRI ET SA FILLE
58 rue Vieille-du-Temple, 75003 Paris ■ Tel: 42 72 70 42 ■ Tues-Sat 12:15-18:45 ■ Frédérique Pietri speaks English ■ Prices medium ■ 10 to 15% Professional discount
Late XIX, early XX century and Art Deco furniture and art objects.

IV

ART DEPOT
3 rue du Pont-Louis-Philippe, 75004 Paris ■ Tel: 47 77 99 02 ■ English spoken ■ Professional discount
Art Deco, aeronautic and industrial designs.

MARTIN BOLTON
48 rue des Archives, 75004 Paris ■ Tel: 42 72 27 19 - Fax: 44 21 38 11 ■ Tues-Thurs-Fri-Sat 11:00-14:00/15:00-19:00 ■ Martin & Mercedes Bolton speak English ■ Prices medium
XIX century English furniture, silver plate, porcelain.

CATH ART

13 rue Ste-Croix-de-la-Bretonnerie, 75004 Paris ■ Tel: 48 04 80 10 - Fax: 48 04 02 08 ■ Mon-Sat 11:30-19:30/Sun 15:00-19:00 ■ Pascal Le Gouet speaks English ■ Prices medium to high ■ 10% professional discount

Humorous pieces: furniture, art objects, lamps, frames, clocks, glass, ceramics in limited editions.

ATELIER MURIEL & JEAN-FRANÇOIS GUIGUE

4 place Edmond-Michelet, 75004 Paris ■ Tel: 42 72 88 74 ■ Mon-Fri 9:00-19:00/Weekends by appointment ■ Prices medium ■ 10 to 20% professional discount

Antique painted furniture, paintings and art objects, decorative panels. Restoration of painted furniture, paintings and art objects.
Classes in decoration on wood.

——————————— V ———————————

INTERIEURS RIVE GAUCHE

37 bd St-Germain,75005 Paris ■ Tel: 46 33 61 40 - Fax: 43 29 95 00 ■ Mon-Sat 10:00-13:00/14:30-19:30 ■ Prices medium ■ 10 to 20% professional discount

Table arts, porcelain, faience, glass, crystal, lamps, miniatures of the XVIII century to 1950.

TORTUE ELECTRIQUE

5 rue Frédéric-Sauton, 75005 Paris ■ Tel: 43 29 37 08 ■ Tues-Sat 14:00-19:00 ■ Georges Monnier speaks English ■ 20% professional discounts

Antique games: chess, cards, magic, circus, mechanical banks.

——————————— VI ———————————

BAROQUES ANTIQUITES

67 rue du Cherche-Midi, 75006 Paris ■ Tel: 45 49 31 14 ■ Tues-Sat 14:30-19:00 ■ Christiane Delrieu speaks English ■ Prices medium ■ Professional discount ■

Period of Napoleon III: furniture, silver, art objects, paintings.

J.M. BEALU & FILS

169 bd Saint-Germain, 75006 Paris ■ Tel: 45 48 46 53 - Fax: 42 84 09 80 ■ Mon 14:00-18:30/Tues-Sat 10:00-12:30/14:00-18:30 ■ Bertrand Bealu speaks English and German ■ Prices high to very high ■ 10% professional discount

XVII, XVIII century furniture and art objects, faience and porcelain.
Experts in porcelain of the XVI, XVII, XVIII centuries.

MADELAINE CASTAING

21 rue Bonaparte, 75006 Paris ■ Tel: 43 54 91 71 ■ Tues-Fri 10:00-13:00/15:00-19:00 ■ English spoken ■ Prices medium to high ■ Professional discount

XIX century French furniture and objects. Restoration, Charles X, Napoléon III. Some English and Russian.

COURTEAUX-ENAULT

41 rue Saint-André-des-Arts, 75006 Paris ■ Tel: 43 26 99 61 ■ Mon-Sat 14:15-19:00 ■ English spoken ■ Prices medium

Superb XVIII century painted panels, screens and sculptured wood. Frames and lamps.

ARIANE DANDOIS

61 rue des Saints-Pères, 75006 Paris ■ Tel: 42 22 14 43 - Fax: 45 48 82 64 ■ Mon-Sat 10:00-12:30/14:00-19:00 ■ English spoken ■ Prices high ■ Professional discount

XIX century European furniture. Chinese, Japanese and Indian art.

DAVID ET SES FILLES

27 rue Bonaparte, 75006 Paris ■ Tel: 43 26 81 40 ■ Tues-Sat 10:30-18:30 ■ Prices medium ■ 10% professional discount

Antique silver, boxes and art objects.

YVES GASTOU

12 rue Bonaparte, 75006 Paris ■ Tel: 46 34 72 17 - Fax: 43 29 62 99 ■ Tues-Sat 11:00-13:00/14:00-19:00 ■ English spoken ■ Prices medium ■ 10% professional discount

Furniture, sculpture, neo-classic painting 1935 to 1950 by Arbus, Poillerat, Du Plantier, Gio Ponti, Adnet, Hermes, Jansem.

GOLOVONOFF GALERIE

13 rue du Vieux-Colombier, 75006 Paris ■ Tel: 42 22 39 06 - Fax: 45 44 88 85 ■ Mon-Fri 11:00-13:00/14:30-19:00 ■ Françoise Golovonoff speaks English ■ Prices medium ■ 10% professional discount

Furniture, decorative objects and chandeliers of the period 1780 to 1850 from Russia, Sweden, Germany, Austria.
Neo-classic and Biedermeyer.

GUDEA GALLERY

22 rue Bonaparte, 75006 Paris ■ Tel: 46 33 78 62 - Fax: 46 33 42 30 ■ Tues-Sat 11:00-12:30/13:30-19:00 ■ Marie-Ange Barbet speaks English ■ Prices medium to high ■ 20% professional discount

Objects of antiquity, archeology: Sumerian,
Egyptian, Greek, Roman.
Expert in the archaeology of the Mediterranean Basin.

L'IMPREVU

21 rue Guénégaud, 75006 Paris ■ Tel: 43 54 65 09 ■ Tues-Sat 14:30-19:00 ■ Jean Rosen speaks English ■ Prices high ■ 10% professional discount

French objects, English majolica, ceramics in the Palissy style, trompe l'œil on faience. All from the second half of the XIX century.

J. PAUL LAGARDE

21 rue des Saints-Pères, 75006 Paris ■ Tel: 42 60 63 81 ■ Mon-Fri 9:30-12:00/14:30-17:30 ■ J. Paul Lagarde speaks English ■ Prices medium ■ 10% professional discount

XVIII, XIX century furniture and art objects.

GALERIE DES LAQUES

74 rue du Cherche-Midi, 75006 Paris ■ Tel: 45 48 88 82 - Fax: 45 44 31 81 ■ Mon-Sat 10:30-12:30/14:00-19:00 and by appointment ■ English spoken ■ Prices high ■ Professional discount

XVII, XVIII, XIX century furniture, objects, gilded wood (bois doré) and Oriental and European lacquered furniture.

GALERIE FELIX MARCILHAC

8 rue Bonaparte, 75006 Paris ■ Tel: 43 26 47 36 - Fax: 46 05 01 58 ■ Mon-Sat 10:00-19:00 ■ English spoken ■ Prices high ■ Professional discount

Art Nouveau, Art Deco furniture, art objects. Symbolist and Orientalist paintings, glass and ceramics of 1900 to 1925.

MME SEBASTIEN MIOCHE

42 rue Bonaparte, 75006 Paris ■ Tel: 43 54 33 37 ■ Tues-Sat 10:30-13:00/14:30-18:30 ■ Tatiana Mioche speaks English ■ Prices medium ■ Professional discount

Louis XIII tables, chairs. Special small yardage of fabrics of high quality – tapestries, silks, damasks and embroideries. Also has upholstering workshop.

LE ONZE

11 rue Jacob, 75006 Paris ■ Tel: 43 29 42 44 ■ Mon-Sat 11:00-13:00/14:00-19:00 ■ Nicolas Sergeeff speaks English ■ Prices modest ■ Professional discount

XVIII and XIX century furniture and art objects.

THIBAULT GALERIE

3 rue Coëtlogon, 75006 Paris ■ Tel: 45 44 75 33 - Fax: 42 22 42 73 ■ Mon 14:00-19:00/Tues-Sat 10:00-19:00 ■ Guillaume Thibault speaks English ■ Prices high ■ 10% professional discount for prompt payment

French furniture and paintings of the XVIII and XIX centuries. Faience, silver, chandeliers and clocks. The Galerie will also handle restoration and repair of furniture and paintings.

GALERIE OLIVIER WATELET

11 rue Bonaparte, 75006 Paris ■ Tel: 43 26 07 87 - Fax: 43 25 99 33 ■ Tues-Sat 10:30-13:00/14:30-19:00 ■ Prices high ■ 10 to 15% discount

Furniture, art objects, paintings of the period 1935-1955: Arbus, Quinet, Poillerat, Berard.

ZERO FIGURE

38 rue de Seine, 75006 Paris ■ Tel: 43 26 85 91 ■ Mon-Sat: afternoons ■ English spoken ■ Prices medium

1900-1930 art objects, Chinese porcelain, Bohemian crystal, Opaline: all in miniature.
Expert in antique miniatures.

ACHKAR CHARRIERE

232 bd Saint-Germain, 75007 Paris ■ Tel: 45 48 93 30 - Fax: 45 49 07 01 ■ Mon-Sat 10:30-19:00 ■ Joseph Achkar speaks English ■ Prices high ■ 10% professional discount

XVII, XVIII century furniture, paintings and art objects.

ANTIQUITES PHILIPPE DELPIERRE

3 rue du Bac, 75007 Paris ■ Tel: 47 03 32 25 - Fax: 49 27 98 28 ■ Tues-Fri 10:00-12:30/14:00-19:00/Sat 11:00-12:30/14:00-19:00 ■ Arnaud Tonder speaks English ■ Prices medium ■ Professional discount

XVIII, XIX century furniture, chandeliers and art objects.

ARCHEOLOGIE

40 rue du Bac, 75007 Paris ■ Tel: 45 48 61 60 - Fax: 45 48 75 25 ■ Mon 14:00-19:00/Tues-Sat 11:00-12:30/14:00-19:00 ■ English spoken ■ Prices high ■ 10% professional discount

Greek terra cotta, Etruscan and Roman bronze, antique marbles, antique jewellery.

ARTS ET BOISERIES

16 rue des Saints-Pères, 75007 Paris ■ Tel: 42 60 23 13 ■ Mon-Sat 14:00-19:00 ■ Guy Leclerc speaks English ■ Prices medium ■ 10% professional discount

French furniture and objets of the XVIII century. Some items of the XV and XVI centuries.

L'AUTRE JOUR

26 av. de la Bourdonnais, 75007 Paris ■ Tel: 47 05 36 60 ■ Mon-Fri 14:30-19:00 ■ Dorothée d'Orgeval speaks English ■ Prices medium

Antiques, curiosities, fabrics.

BASTIEN ET ASSOCIES

13 rue de Lille 75007 Paris ■ Tel: 42 60 76 27 - Fax: 42 66 07 93 ■ Mon-Sat 8:00-18:00 ■ English spoken ■ Prices medium ■ 5% professional discount

XVIII, XIX century French furniture. Restoration.

DU COTE DE CHEZ VIANE

11 rue de Luynes, 75007 Paris ■ Tel: 45 48 57 26 ■ Mon-Sat 11:00-12:45/14:00-19:00 ■ Mme Dyer speaks English ■ Prices medium ■ 10% professional discount

XIX century furniture, art objects, paintings.

AU DIRECTOIRE

12 bd Raspail, 75007 Paris ■ Tel: 42 22 67 09 ■ Mon 14:30-19:00/Tues-Sat 10:30-12:00/14:30-19:00 ■ Thierry Winsall speaks English ■ Prices medium ■ Professional discount

French furniture, art objects: Empire, Directoire, Consulat.

RAYMOND DUBREUIL

25 quai Voltaire, 75007 Paris ■ Tel: 42 61 24 21 ■ Tues-Sat 14:30-19:00 ■
Prices medium ■ 10% professional discount
French furniture of the XVIII century.

MARC FARRAUD-ANTIQUITES

24 rue Surcouf, 75007 Paris ■ Tel: 45 55 51 44 ■ Mon-Sat 11:00-20:00 ■
English spoken ■ Prices medium ■ Professional discounts
French furniture, paintings, decorative objects of the XVIII, XIX centuries.

MARGUERITE FONDEUR

24 rue de Beaune, 75007 Paris ■ Tel: 42 61 25 78 ■ Mon-Sat 14:30-18:00
■ English spoken
Furniture and art objects of the XVIII century.

ANDREE HIGGINS

52-54 rue de l'Université, 75007 Paris ■ Tel: 45 48 75 28 - Fax: 45 48 07 98
■ Tues-Sat 10:00-12:00/13:00-19:00 ■ English spoken ■ Prices medium ■
10% professional discount
Superb collection of XIX century English furniture.
French art objects and lamps.

ILSE B

56 rue de l'Université, 75007 Paris ■ Tel: 45 48 98 96 ■ Mon-Sat 14:00-19:00
■ English spoken ■ Prices medium
Antiques and unusual objects of the XIX century.

BERNARD JULLIEN

26 rue Surcouf, 75007 Paris ■ Tel: 45 51 00 07 ■ Mon-Sat 11:30-19:30 ■
English spoken ■ Prices medium ■ 7 to 10% professional discount
XVIII, XIX century furniture, art objects. Repair of paintings and tapestries.

GALERIE MALTIER-VERCHER

48 rue de Verneuil, 75007 Paris ■ Tel: 47 03 37 46 ■ Mon-Fri 15:00-19:00 ■ Christine Vercher speaks English ■ Prices medium ■ 10% professional discount
Sculptures, paintings, art objects of all periods.
Specialist in the first half of the XX century.

MONIQUE MARTEL

39 rue de Verneuil, 75007 Paris ■ Tel: 42 60 47 97 - Fax: 42 60 47 09 ■ Georges
Franck speaks English ■ Prices reasonable ■ 10% professional discount
Drawings of the XVI to XVIII century. XVIII century furniture.

CLAUDE NICOLET

24 rue de Bourgogne, 75007 Paris ■ Tel: 45 51 30 40 ■ Mon-Fri 9:00-
20:00/Sat 14:00-20:00 ■ English spoken ■ Prices medium ■ 10 to 15% professional discount
French furniture, art objects, chandeliers, clocks of the early XIX century
(1790 to 1830). Especially Parisian furniture in mahogany.

OLIM

92 rue de Grenelle, 75007 Paris ■ Tel: 45 49 45 70 ■ Mon-Sat 11:00-19:00
■ Prices medium to high ■ 15% professional discount
Furniture XVIII, XIX centuries, old and contemporary paintings, art objects,
couturier jewellery, restoration of frames, antique painted furniture.

REFLETS D'EPOQUES

17 bd Raspail, 75007 Paris ■ Tel: 45 48 42 07 ■ Mon-Fri 11:00-19:00 ■
Prices medium ■ 10 to 30% professional discount
XVIII, XIX century furniture, clocks, faience, porcelain and objects of curiosity.

LES RELAIS DU PASSE

11 rue Dupont-des-Loges, 75007 Paris ■ Tel: 47 05 75 70 ■ Tue-Sat 12:00-
19:00 ■ Henriette Saba speaks English ■ 10% professional discount
Specialist in mahogany furniture of the Consulat, Empire and Restoration
periods. Also paintings of the XIX and XX centuries.

CHEZ SWANN

5 rue de Beaune, 75007 Paris ■ Tel: 42 61 27 22 ■ Mon-Sat 14:30-18:30 ■
English spoken
XVIII century furniture and art objects, gilded wood (bois doré) and chairs.

GALERIE THIBAULT DE LA CHATRE

36 rue de Varenne, 75007 Paris ■ Tel: 45 48 82 99 Fax: 45 49 05 84 ■ Mon-
Sat 10:30-13:00/14:30-19:30 ■ English spoken ■ Prices medium ■ 10% pro-
fessional discount
XVIII, XIX century furniture, paintings, decorative objects, chairs.

GALERIE DE VERNEUIL

45 rue de Verneuil, 75007 Paris ■ Tel: 40 15 01 15 ■ Mon-Sat 14:30-19:30
■ English spoken ■ Prices medium ■ 5 to 10% professional discount
XVIII and early XIX century furniture, art objects, silver, paintings and engrav-
ings, faience. Sculptured wood statues of the XII to XVI centuries.

VIA VARENNE

38 rue de Varenne, 75007 Paris ■ Tel: 49 49 06 49 - Fax: 40 49 00 16 ■ Mon-
Sat 14:30-19:30 ■ Christine Mireux speaks English ■ Prices medium ■ 10%
professional discount
Furniture, cabinets of the XVII century, old paintings.

ANNE VINCENT

31 bd Raspail, 75007 Paris ■ Tel: 40 49 02 21 ■ Tues-Sat 11:00-13:00/14:30-
19:00 ■ Anne de l'Harpe speaks English ■ Prices medium ■ Professional discount
Antique furniture and objects of the XIX century to 1950.

―――――――――――――――― **VIII** ――――――――――――――――

L'AIGLE IMPERIAL

3 rue de Miromesnil, 75008 Paris ■ Tel: 42 65 27 33 - Fax: 42 65 90 97 ■
Mon-Sat 10:30-13:00/14:00-19:00 ■ Pierre de Souzy speaks English ■ Prices
high ■ 10% professional discount
Antique historical arms, figurines, military memorabilia.

EUGENE BECKER ANTIQUITES

136 rue du Faubourg-Saint-Honoré, 75008 Paris ■ Tel: 42 89 44 90 - Fax: 42 89 44 91 ■ Mon-Fri 14:00-19:00/Mornings by appointment ■ Eugène Becker speaks English ■ Prices high to very high ■ 15% professional discount
French furniture, sculpture, drawings and art objects of the XVIII century.

PIERRE G. BERNARD

1 rue d'Anjou, 75008 Paris ■ Tel: 42 65 23 83 ■ Mon-Sat 10:30-13:00/13:30-18:30 ■ Marc Higonnet speaks English ■ Prices medium ■ 10% professional discount
Antiques, collectibles

ELIZABETH BUSSON EDITIONS

20 place de la Madeleine, 75008 Paris ■ Tel: 42 65 26 06 - Fax: 47 42 30 06 ■ Mon-Sat 10:00-18:00 ■ Elizabeth Busson speaks English ■ Prices medium ■ 10% professional discount
XVIII century French furniture from Provence, painted furniture, mirrors, pier glasses, faience, Toile de Jouy, chairs, lamps, old screens, decorative country objects.

CARRE D'OR

46 av. George V, 75008 Paris ■ Tel: 40 70 11 00 - Fax: 40 70 96 81
A newly established center for 40 antique dealers, art galleries, silversmiths and jewellers.

COMPAGNIE DE LA CHINE ET DES INDES

39 av. Friedland, 75008 Paris ■ Tel: 42 89 05 45 - Fax: 42 89 11 07 ■ Mon-Sat 9:30-12:00/14:00-18:30 ■ English spoken ■ Prices medium to very high ■ Professional discount
Antiques of the Far East: China, Japan, Tibet, Nepal, India, Khmer, Cambodia. Furniture, art objects, porcelain, sculpture, paintings, Japanese and Chinese screens, bronzes of China, Nepal and Tibet. Pottery Han to Tong. XVIII century Chinese porcelain. 5,000 B.C. to XVIII century.

LA COUR AUX ANTIQUAIRES

54 rue du Faubourg-Saint-Honoré, 75008 Paris ■ Tel: 42 66 38 60 Mme Jaquenoud - Fax: 42 66 96 63 ■ Mon 14:00-18:30/Tues-Sat 10:30-18:30
This attractive courtyard, entered from the rue du Faubourg-Saint-Honoré houses 16 boutiques, which offer a wide range of antiques and art objects, including furniture, lighting, old paintings, sculpture, bronze, faience, porcelain, glass, doll furniture, hunting art and objects, architectural items and jewellery. Well worth a browse.

FABIUS FRERES ANTIQUAIRES

152 bd Haussmann, 75008 Paris ■ Tel: 45 62 39 18 - Fax: 45 62 53 07 ■ Mon-Fri 9:00-12:00/14:30-18:00 ■ English spoken ■ Prices high
XVIII, XIX century furniture, paintings, sculpture.

♛ DE JONCKHEERE

100 rue du Faubourg-Saint-Honoré, 75008 Paris ■ Tel: 42 66 69 49 - Fax: 42 66 13 42 ■ Tues-Sat 11:00-19:00 ■ Georges de Jonckheere and Claude Vittet speak English ■ Prices high
XVI and XVII century Flemish and Dutch paintings.

KRAEMER ET CIE

43 rue de Monceau, 75008 Paris ■ Tel: 45 63 24 46 - Fax: 45 63 54 36 ■
Mon-Sat 9:30-19:30 ■ Mr. Kraemer speaks English

Furniture, chairs, art objects of the XVII and XVIII centuries. Louis XIV, Louis XV, Louis XVI.

👑 KUGEL

279 rue Saint -Honoré, 75008 Paris ■ Tel: 42 60 19 45 - Fax: 42 61 06 72 ■
Mon 14:30-18:30/Tues-Sat 10:00-13:00/14:30-18:30 ■ English spoken ■
Prices high ■ Professional discount

Antiques from the XV to XIX centuries. Silver dominates their marvellous collection.

FRANÇOIS LEAGE

178 rue du Faubourg-Saint-Honoré, 75008 Paris ■ Tel: 45 63 43 46 - Fax:
42 56 46 30 ■ Mon-Fri 9:00-19:00/Sat 10:00-12:45/14:00-18:00 ■
François Leage and Sylvie Ozanne speak English ■ Prices high ■ Professional discounts

French furniture and objects of the XVIII century.

C.T. LOO & CIE

48 rue de Courcelles, 75008 Paris ■ Tel: 45 62 53 15 - Fax: 45 62 07 02 ■
Mon-Sat 10:30-12:30/14:30-18:30 ■ English spoken ■ Prices high ■ Professional discount

High quality furniture, art objects, screens from China, Korea, India and Japan.

LOUIS XV

3 rue du Faubourg-Saint-Honoré, 75008 Paris ■ Tel: 42 66 39 68 - Fax:
42 66 20 52 ■ Mon 14:00-19:00/Tues-Fri 10:00-12:00/14:00-19:00/Sat 14:00-19:00 ■ English spoken ■ Competitive prices ■ 10% professional discount

Furniture, paintings and art objects of the XVII, XVIII centuries.

CLAUDE DE LUPIA

137 rue du Faubourg-Saint-Honoré, 75008 Paris ■ Tel: 43 59 56 56 - Fax:
42 67 90 28 ■ Tues-Sat 10:00-13:00/14:00-18:30 ■ English spoken ■ Prices medium to high ■ 10% Professional discount

Sumptuous low tables, antique mirrors, decorative objects, paintings, pastels.

ANDREE MACE

266 rue du Faubourg-Saint-Honoré, 75008 Paris ■ Tel: 42 27 43 03 - Fax:
44 40 09 63 ■ Mon-Sat 9:00-12:30/14:00-18:30 ■ English spoken ■ Prices medium to very high ■ Professional discount

XVI to XIX century antiquities in stone and marble.
Specialty: fireplaces of the XVIII century.
Large selection of cast iron fireplace backplates.

A. COLIN MAILLARD

11 rue de Miromesnil, 75008 Paris ■ Tel: 42 65 43 62 ■ Pierre-Jacques Chauveau speaks English ■ Prices high ■ 10% to 20% discount to professionals

Antique generalist, antique lighting and lamps. Custom lampshades.

JEAN-PIERRE MANTION

59 rue du Faubourg-Saint-Honoré, 75008 Paris ■ Tel: 47 66 41 37 - Fax: 42 66 96 63 ■ Mon-Sat 15:00-18:30 ■ Jean-Pierre Mantion speaks English ■ Prices medium ■ 10% professional discount

First Empire, French, Russian, Swedish lighting.
Reproductions of period lighting on special order.
Furniture of the XVII century to the end of the XIX century.

GALERIE JEAN-LUC MECHICHE

182 rue du Faubourg-Saint-Honoré, 75008 Paris ■ Tel: 45 63 20 11 - Fax: 42 25 91 34 ■ Tues-Sat 10:00-13:00/14:30-19:00 ■ Claire Laroquette speaks English ■ Prices high ■ Professional discount

XVIII and XIX century French furniture, contemporary paintings, archeological objects from China. Contemporary furniture in limited edition on order.

GALERIE GERARD ORTS

164 rue du Faubourg-Saint-Honoré, 75008 Paris ■ Tel: 42 89 44 48 - Fax: 45 63 46 66 ■ Mon-Sat 10:00-19:00 ■ Laurence Darrigrand speaks English ■ 10% professional discount

Louis XIV and Empire furniture and art objects.

GALERIE PATRICK PERRIN

178 rue du Faubourg-Saint-Honoré, 75008 Paris ■ Tel: 40 76 07 76 - Fax: 40 76 09 37 ■ Mon-Sat 10:00-13:00/14:00-19:00 ■ Patrick Perrin speaks English ■ Prices high

French drawings 1600 to 1920. Louis XVI mahogany furniture.

FABIO ROMANO POZZOLI

157 rue du Faubourg-Saint-Honoré, 75008 Paris ■ Tel: 40 74 08 58 - Fax: 40 74 08 70 ■ Tues-Fri 10:30-13:00/14:00-19:00 ■ English spoken ■ Prices high ■ Professional discount

Furniture and objects from northern Europe and Russia,1780 to 1940.

JEAN RENONCOURT

77 rue du Faubourg Saint-Honoré, 75008 Paris ■ Tel: 44 51 11 60 - Fax:42 66 25 89 ■ Mon-Sat 10:00-19:00 ■ English spoken ■ Prices high ■ 10% professional discount

Furniture and art objects, late XVIII century to Charles X.

MARC REVILLON D'APREVAL

28 rue de Washington, 75008 Paris ■ Tel: 42 61 27 36 - Fax: 42 61 43 70 ■ Mon-Sat 10:00-12:30/14:30-19:00 ■ English spoken ■ Prices medium ■ 10% professional discount

French furniture and objects of the XVII, XVIII, XIX centuries. Expertise and repair.

J.& A. SCHMITZ

13 rue de La Trémoille, 75008 Paris ■ Tel: 47 23 83 08 ■ Mon 14:00-19:00/Tues-Fri 11:00-19:00 ■ Prices medium ■ 10% professional discount

Parisian furniture, art objects of the XVIII, XIX century.

GALERIE JEAN SOUSTIEL

146 bd Haussmann, 75008 Paris ■ Tel: 45 62 27 76 - Fax: 45 63 44 63 ■ Mon-Fri 10:00-12:00/14:00-19:00 ■ English spoken ■ Prices medium to high ■ Professional discount

Islamic art from North Africa, Egypt, Syria, Turkey, Iran, India. Ceramics, miniatures, textiles.

LE SPHINX

104 rue du Faubourg-Saint-Honoré, 75008 Paris ■ Tel: 42 65 90 96 - Fax: 42 65 90 97 ■ Mon-Sat 10:30-13:00/14:00-19:00 ■ Pierre de Souzy speaks English ■ Prices high ■ 10% professional discount

XIX century antiques, paintings, arms. Specialist in "Napoleonic" memorabilia.

VIVALDI ANTIQUITES

39 rue de Rome, 75008 Paris ■ Tel: 43 87 68 39 ■ Mon-Fri 10:00-19:00 ■ Prices medium ■ Professional discount

XVIII, XIX century furniture, paintings, art objects, clocks, lamps.

IX

MIRON ANTIQUITES

5 rue de Provence, 75009 Paris ■ Tel: 47 70 54 17 - Fax: 48 00 08 71 ■ Mon-Sat 9:00-13:00/14:00-19:00 ■ English spoken ■ Prices medium ■ 10 to 15% professional discount

Furniture and art objects, XVIII, XIX centuries.
Expert in neo-classic furniture.

XIV

LUDION

175 av. du Maine, 75014 Paris ■ Tel: 45 39 56 02 ■ Tues-Sat 11:00-12:30/14:30-19:00 ■ Françoise Besson speaks English ■ Prices medium ■ 20% professional discount

Furniture and art objects of the XIX and early XX centuries.

XV

See VILLAGE SUISSE under Markets.

GODARD DESMAREST

1 bis rue de la Cavalerie, 75015 Paris ■ Tel: 45 66 97 45 - Fax: 43 06 03 32 ■ By appointment only ■ Godard Desmarest speaks English ■ Prices medium ■ Professional discounts

Furniture and art objets of the XVIII century.

LE POILU

20 rue Emile-Duclaux, 75015 Paris ■ Tel: 43 06 77 32 ■ Mon-Sat 9:00-12:00/14:00-19:00 ■ Prices medium

Military articles from 1870 to 1950: uniforms, insignia, decorations, wigs, equipment, documents. Catalogues available.

—————————————————————— XVI ——————————————————————

ANTIQUE 16

19 rue de l'Annonciation, 75016 Paris ■ Tel: 42 88 64 73 - Fax: 42 30 94 36 ■ Mon-Sat 10:00-12:30/14:00-19:00 ■ Prices medium ■ Professional discounts

Furniture, objects, paintings, XVIII and XIX centuries.

GALERIE BEAUSEJOUR
R.R. SOUDIT

35 bd Beauséjour, 75016 Paris ■ Tel: 45 27 97 06 by appointment ■ & Hôtel Ritz, place Vendôme, 75001 Paris ■ Tel: 42 60 38 30 ■ Mon-Sat 10:00-19:00 ■ Florence Delcros, Directrice of the Gallery in the Ritz speaks English ■ Prices medium ■ 3 to 10% professional discount

XIX century silver, paintings, bronzes, porcelain.

COMPTOIR DES OBJETS D'ART

13 av. Théophile-Gautier, 75016 Paris ■ Tel: 40 50 60 92 - Fax: 40 50 66 22 ■ Mon-Sat 11:00-19:00/Sun 15:00-19:00 ■ Farid Zamouri speaks English ■ Prices medium ■ 20 to 35% professional discount

Furniture of all the XIX century, especially Empire, old paintings, engravings and drawings, decorative objects, table arts.

BEATRICE DARLAY

5 rue Isabey, 75016 Paris ■ Tel: 46 47 70 20 ■ Mon-Fri 14:30-19:00 ■ Béatrice Darlay speaks English ■ Prices medium ■ 10% professional discount

XIX century French and English furniture, paintings, decorative objects and gifts with a masculine theme; hunting, skiing, sailing, golf, tennis. Engravings, lamps, quilts.

EUGENIE-VICTORIA

1 rue Lekain, 75016 Paris ■ Tel: 45 25 79 10 ■ Tues-Sat 10:30-12:30/15:30-19:00/Sun 10:30-12:30 ■ Marie-France Theullier speaks English ■ Prices medium ■ 10% professional discount

XIX century antiques and decorative objects.

GALERIE JOSEPH KARAM

61 av. Raymond-Poincaré, 75116 Paris ■ Tel: 44 05 09 21 - Fax: 44 05 09 20 ■ Mon-Sat 10:00-19:00 ■ English spoken ■ Prices medium to high ■ Professional discount

Eclectic mix of XVIII, XIX century French, Italian, Spanish furniture, art objects, archeological objects.

ANTIQUITES MICHEL-ANGE

75 rue Michel-Ange, 75016 Paris ■ Tel: 46 51 74 25 ■ Mon-Sat 10:00-12:30/14:30-19:00 ■ Didier Sambourg speaks English ■ Prices medium ■ 30% Professional discount
Furniture, art objects and old books.

GUY MINOT ANTIQUITES

9 rue de la Tour, 75016 Paris ■ Tel: 45 20 71 27 - Fax: 40 50 76 20 ■ Mon-Sat 11:00-19:30 ■ English spoken ■ Prices medium ■ 10 to 20% professional discount
Furniture, late XIX century to 1950, decorative objects, lighting, tableware.

JEAN-PAUL PINSON

8 rue Eugène-Labiche, 75116 Paris ■ Tel: 45 04 95 18 - Fax: 40 72 60 15 By appointment ■ English spoken ■ Prices medium to high ■ 20% professional discount
Furniture, paintings and art objects of the XVII to the XIX centuries. Architectural drawings and Orientalist paintings.

VILLAGE DE PASSY

19 rue de l'Annonciation, 75016 Paris ■ Tel: 42 88 64 73 - Fax: 42 30 94 36 ■ Mon-Sat 10:00-12:30/14:00-19:00 ■ Prices medium ■ Professional discounts
French furniture of the XVIII, XIX centuries, art objects, paintings.

———————————————— XVII ————————————————

PHILIPPE DE BEAUVAIS

112 bd de Courcelles, 75017 Paris ■ Tel: 47 63 20 72 ■ Mon-Sat 10:00-12:30/14:00-19:00 ■ Philippe de Beauvais speaks English ■ Prices medium ■ 10% professional discount
Furniture and art objects of the XVIII and XIX centuries.

BLEU PASSE

24 bis bd de Courcelles, 75017 Paris ■ Tel: 42 67 57 40 ■ Mon-Sat 11:00-19:00 ■ English spoken ■ Prices medium ■ 10 to 20% professional discount
XIX century furniture, curiosities, paintings, silver, porcelain, embroidered linen.

SERGE MALAUSSENA

10 place de la Porte-de-Champerret, 75017 Paris ■ Tel: 43 80 17 29 ■ Tues-Sat 11:00-19:00 ■ Prices medium ■ Professional discount
XVIII, XIX century furniture and decorative objects. Sculpture, clocks, chandeliers, ceramics, glass.

AUX PORTES DU TEMPS

95 rue de Tocqueville, 75017 Paris ■ Telfax: 47 66 31 66 ■ Mon-Sat 10:30-20:30/Sun 14:30-20:00 ■ Anabel Gautier speaks English ■ Prices medium to high ■ 25% professional discount
Paintings, XVII, XVIII centuries. Porcelain, XVII, XVIII, XIX centuries. Furniture, XVIII, XIX centuries.

JEAN RIGAL

12 av. Mac-Mahon, 75017 Paris ■ Tel: 44 09 02 34 ■ Mon-Sat 11:00-19:00 ■ Jean Rigal speaks English ■ Prices high ■ 20% professional discount
Furniture, art objects and paintings of the XIX and XX centuries.

MARIA SANDORFI

90 rue Jouffroy, 75017 Paris ■ Tel: 47 63 97 57 ■ Mon-Fri 11:00-19:00/Sat 15:00-18:00 ■ Maria Sandorfi speaks English ■ Prices medium ■ 10 to 20% professional discount
XIX century decorative objects, small furniture, paintings, porcelain, silver.

TEMPS QUI PASSE

11 rue Pierre-Demours, 75017 Paris ■ Tel: 45 74 09 36 ■ Tues-Sat 11:00-19:00/Sun 11:00-13:00 ■ Chantal Bartent speaks English ■ Prices medium ■ Professional discount
Antique furniture, objects, tableware, clocks, lighting.

─────────────────────── XVIII ───────────────────────

SOPHIE DUPONT

49 rue Ramey, 75018 Paris ■ Tel: 42 54 69 30 ■ Mon-Sat 10:30-19:30 ■ Sophie Dupont speaks English ■ Prices medium ■ Professional discounts
XVIII, XIX century furniture and objects.

─────────────────────── NEUILLY ───────────────────────

L'ALEORS

158 av. Charles-de-Gaulle, 92200 Neuilly-sur-Seine ■ Tel: 47 22 20 68 - Fax: 46 24 10 70 ■ Tues-Sat 10:00-19:00 ■ Catherine Lejon speaks English ■ Prices medium ■ 10% professional discount
Art objects, curiosities, furniture of the XVIII and XIX centuries. Showcase collectibles and bronzes of the XIX century.

Antique Collectibles

─────────────────── ANTIQUE ARMS & MILITARY ───────────────────

L'AIGLE IMPERIAL

3 rue de Miromesnil, 75008 Paris ■ Tel: 42 65 27 33 - Fax: 42 65 90 97 ■ Mon-Sat 10:30-13:00/14:00-19:00 ■ Pierre de Souzy speaks English ■ Prices high ■ 10% professional discount
Antique historical arms, figurines, military memorabilia.

AUX ARMES D'ANTAN

Village Suisse ■ 1 av. Paul-Déroulède, 75015 Paris ■ Tel: 47 83 71 42 - Fax: 47 34 40 99 ■ Thurs-Mon 10:30-13:00/14:30-19:00 ■ English spoken ■ Prices medium to high ■ 5 to 10% professional discount
Antique arms and military souvenirs.
Qualified expert.

JEAN-CLAUDE DEY

8 bis rue Schlumberger, 92430 Marnes-la-Coquette ■ Tel: 47 41 65 31 - Fax: 47 41 17 67 ■ Tues-Fri 14:00-19:30/Sat-Sun 11:00-12:00/14:00-19:00 and by appointment ■ Delphine Dey speaks English ■ 10% professional discount

Antique arms, XII to XX centuries from all countries. Rifles, carbines, pistols, revolvers, cannons, daggers, sabers, swords, armor, uniforms, helmets, equipment. Historical memorabilia and objects, documents, paintings. Orders and decorations. Lead soldiers. Also restoration in their own atelier. Catalogues on request.
Qualified expert.

LE CIMIER

38 rue Ginoux, 75015 Paris ■ Tel: 45 78 94 28 ■ Mon-Sat 10:00-13:00/14:00-19:00 ■ Jacques Vuyet speaks English ■ Prices high

Historic military figurines, documents on military costumes.

AU PLAT D'ETAIN

16 rue Guisarde, 75006 Paris ■ Tel: 43 54 32 06 ■ Tues-Sat 10:30-12:30/13:30-19:00 ■ English spoken ■ Prices medium

Specialty: soldier "Lucotte" for whom they have founded a collector's club. Antique lead soldiers as well as modern fabrication, CBG - Mignot - Lucotte - TRADITION. Painted figurines.

LE POILU

20 rue Emile-Duclaux, 75015 Paris ■ Tel: 43 06 77 32 ■ Mon-Sat 9:00-12:00/14:00-19:00 ■ Prices medium

Military articles from 1870 to 1950: uniforms, insignia, decorations, wigs, equipment, documents. Catalogues available.

POUSSIERES D'EMPIRES

33 rue Brezin, 75014 Paris ■ Tel: 45 42 42 06 ■ Tues-Sat 11:00-19:00 ■ Prices medium

Historical military memorabilia, especially the French colonies and particularly French Indo-China. Regimental insignia, decorations and orders.

AU SOLDAT D'ANTAN

67 quai de la Tournelle, 75005 Paris ■ Tel: 46 33 40 50 - Fax: 44 07 33 45 ■ Mon-Sat 14:00-19:00 ■ Prices medium to very high ■ Professional discount

Lead soldiers, historical souvenirs, orders, antique arms.

───────────── AUTOMOBILES ─────────────

L'ORANGERIE MODERNE

33 rue de l'Orangerie, 78000 Versailles ■ Tel: 39 50 28 74 - Fax: 33 02 15 02 ■ Tues-Sun 14:15-19:30 ■ English spoken ■ Prices high to very high ■ 10% professional discount

Miniature automobiles 1/43 scale. Specialist in Bugatti and Ferrari.

PRIVILEGE

10 rue Demarquay, 75010 Paris ■ Tel: 40 05 12 43 - Fax: 40 35 03 76 ■ Mon-Sun: call ■ Stéphane Marant speaks English ■ Prices high ■ Professional discount

Producer, creator of crowns, tiaras and diadems in gold plated metal and 24 carat gold, crystal and jewels for collectors, museums, special events, beauty contests, weddings, special collection of Fabergé type eggs.

———— DOLLS ————

LA MAISON DE POUPEE

40 rue de Vaugirard, 75006 Paris ■ Tel: 46 33 74 05 ■ Tues-Sat 14:30-19:00 and by appointment ■ Prices medium ■ Professional discount

Beautiful dolls for the collector. Restoration and expertise.

LES POUPEES RETROUVEES

16 rue Brémontier, 75017 Paris ■ Tel: 48 88 98 77 - Fax: 42 27 55 61 ■ Mon-Fri 14:00-19:00 ■ Arielle Ged speaks English ■ Prices reasonable ■ Professional discount

Antique dolls and toys of the XIX and early XX centuries, documents, books, small furniture. Restoration.

———— GAMES ————

AU COLLECTIONNEUR

15 rue Brey, 75017 Paris ■ Tel: 42 27 64 50 ■ Mon-Sat 11:00-14:30/16:00-19:00 ■ English spoken ■ Prices modest

Collectibles of all kinds, stamps, money, bank notes, etc.

GALERIE 13 RUE JACOB

13 rue Jacob, 75006 Paris ■ Tel: 43 26 99 89 ■ Mon-Sat 14:30-19:00 ■ English spoken ■ Prices medium ■ Professional discount

Antique games: Chess, Backgammon, Mah Jong, others. Objects of curiosity.

MAGASIN LEDUC

9 rue Constance, 75018 Paris ■ Tel: 46 06 81 81 ■ Tues-Fri 16:00-19:30/Sat 11:00-13:00/16:00-19:30/Sun 11:00-13:00 ■ English spoken ■ Prices medium ■ 15% professional discount

Games and antique toys.

TORTUE ELECTRIQUE

5 rue Frédéric-Sauton, 75005 Paris ■ Tel: 43 29 37 08 ■ Tues-Sat 14:00-19:00 ■ Georges Monnier speaks English ■ 20% professional discount

Antique games: Chess, cards, magic, circus, mechanical banks.

GALERIE MICHEL CACHOUX

16 rue Guénégaud, 75006 Paris ■ Tel: 43 54 52 15 - Fax: 46 33 48 69 ■ Tues-Sat 11:00-19:30 ■ Nicole Ruff speaks English ■ Prices medium ■ 10 to 20% professional discount

Minerals, fossils, spheres.

MARINE D'AUTREFOIS

80 av. des Ternes, 75017 Paris ■ Tel: 45 74 23 97 - Fax: 45 74 61 70 ■ Tues-Sat 10:00-13:00/14:00-19:00 ■ Gildas de Kerdrel speaks English ■ Prices medium to high

Models of famous sailing yachts. America's cup yachts of the 1930s to the 1980s. Antique models of yachts and steam vessels. Antique navigation instruments. Antique marine equipment and ship fittings. Marine paintings and old marine photographs. Ship builder's models. Models of ships and yachts on order.

BERTRAND THIEBAUT

4 av. de Villiers, 75017 Paris ■ Tel: 42 94 25 71 - Fax: 40 10 13 08 ■ Every day 9:00-18:00 ■ English spoken

Old scientific instruments, marine curiosities, special furniture, very unusual objects.
Specialty: history of sciences.

PHILIPPE WILMART

37 av. de la Grande-Armée, 75116 Paris ■ Tel: 45 00 65 16 - Fax: 46 04 22 41 ■ Mon-Fri 10:00-18:00 ■ English spoken ■ Prices medium to high ■ Professional discount

Marine objects, ship models, books, boat pictures, navigation instruments, XVIII, XIX century French naval arms, curiosities, physical sciences.
Qualified expert

ANDRE BISSONET

6 rue du Pas-de-la-Mule, 75003 Paris ■ Tel: 48 87 20 15 ■ Mon-Sat 14:00-19:00

Antique European musical instruments.

ORPHEE

8 rue du Pont-Louis-Philippe, 75004 Paris ■ Telfax: 42 72 68 42 ■ Mon-Sat 13:30-19:30 ■ English spoken ■ Prices medium ■ 20% professional discount

Antique musical instruments.

FREDERIC MARCHAND

6 rue de Montfaucon, 75006 Paris ■ Tel: 43 54 32 82 - Fax: 44 07 04 82 ■ Tues-Sat 14:00-19:00 ■ English spoken ■ Prices medium ■ Professional discount

Antique toys and other collectibles, including Art Deco and Art Nouveau biscuit, perfume flacons.

AU PETIT MAYET

10 rue Mayet, 75006 Paris ■ Tel: 45 67 68 29 ■ Mon-Sat 14:00-19:00 ■ Philippe Lepage speaks English ■ Prices medium to high

Antique toys, automated toys.

TOILE D'ARAIGNEE

8 rue Mandar, 75002 Paris ■ Tel: 40 28 47 48 ■ Mon-Sat 11:00-19:30 ■ Prices medium ■ 10 to 15% professional discount

Antique toys in tole, old publicity items, plaster, enamel signs, presentation cases, items of curiosity 1950-1960.

————————— MISCELLANEOUS ANTIQUE COLLECTIBLES —————————

NOSTALGIE BROCANTE

21 rue des Carmes, 75005 Paris ■ Tel: 46 34 59 03 ■ Tues-Fri 13:00-19:00 ■ English spoken ■ Prices medium ■ 20% professional discount

Old phonographs, cameras and stereocopes, dolls, celluloids and restoration of these objects.

BEAUTE DIVINE

40 rue Saint-Sulpice, 75006 Paris ■ Tel: 43 26 25 31 ■ Mon 14:00-19:99/Tues-Sat 10:00-13:00/14:00-19:00 ■ English spoken ■ Prices medium high ■ 10% professional discount

Specialty: perfume flacons, art deco objects, small furniture in the spirit of 1900 to 1930. Old bathroom accessories.

Near and Far Eastern Antiques
Antiquités orientales

ANTIQUITES ET ART D'ASIE

4 av. Bugeaud, 75116 Paris ■ Tel: 45 53 77 48 - Fax: 47 55 02 52 ■ Tues-Sat 10:30-19:00 ■ English spoken ■ Prices medium ■ 5 to 20% professional discount

Archeological objects from China: Neolithic, Bronze Age, Han, Tang, Soong, Yuan dynasties. Sculpture and porcelain of China: Ming and Qing dynasties. Sculptures and Buddha from Tibet, Thailand, Burma, India, Cambodia.

ASIE ANTIQUE

23 rue de Lille, 75007 Paris ■ Tel: 49 27 04 43 - Fax: 48 34 65 91 ■ Tues-Sat 15:00-19:00 ■ Lee Thanapoomikul speaks English ■ Prices medium ■ 10 to 25% professional discount

Sculpture, furniture of China and Japan. Statuary, bas-reliefs, sculptured heads of Khmer, Thailand and Burma.

JACQUES BARRERE

36 rue Mazarine, 75006 Paris ■ Tel: 43 26 57 61 - Fax: 46 34 02 83 ■ Tues-Sat 14:00-19:30 ■ English spoken ■ Prices medium ■ Professional discount

Far Eastern antiques and objects.

BEURDELEY ET CIE

200 bd Saint-Germain, 75007 Paris ■ Tel: 45 48 97 86 - Fax: 45 44 99 11 ■ Mon-Sat 10:00-12:30/14:30-19:00 ■ Prices high

Antiques, archeology, sculpture from China, Japan, Southeast Asia.

LA CHINE DES T'SING

14 rue de l'Université, 75007 Paris ■ Tel: 42 60 65 93 ■ Mon: 14:00-19:00/Tues-Sat 10:00-13:00/14:00-19:00 ■ Martine Tournier speaks English ■ Prices reasonable ■ 10% discount

XVII, XVIII, XIX century porcelain and small collectibles of the Far East. Specialty: blue & white porcelain.

COMPAGNIE DE LA CHINE ET DES INDES

39 av. de Friedland, 75008 Paris ■ Tel: 42 89 05 45 - Fax: 42 89 11 07 ■ Mon-Sat 9:30-12:00/14:00-18:30 ■ English spoken ■ Prices high ■ Professional discount

Far Eastern antiques: China, Japan, Tibet, Nepal, India, Khmer, Cambodia. Furniture, art objects, porcelain, sculpture, paintings, Japanese and Chinese screens, bronzes of China, Nepal and Tibet. Pottery: Han to Tong. XVIII century Chinese porcelain. 5,000 B.C. to the XVIII century.

GALERIE DES LAQUES

74 rue du Cherche-Midi, 75006 Paris ■ Tel: 45 48 88 82 - Fax: 45 44 31 81
■ Mon-Sat 10:30-12:30/14:00-19:00 and by appointment ■ English spoken
■ Prices high ■ Professional discount

XVII, XVIII, XIX century furniture, objects, gilded wood (bois doré), Oriental and European laquered furniture.

YVONNE MOREAU-GOBARD

5 rue des Saints-Pères, 75006 Paris ■ Tel: 42 60 88 25 ■ Mon-Sat 10:00-12:30/14:00-19:00 ■ English spoken ■ Prices high ■ 10% professional discount

Asian archeological objects in stone, bronze, wood, especially Southeast Asia.

JEAN-MICHEL GUENEAU

22 rue de Beaune, 75007 Paris ■ Tel: 42 61 49 94 ■ Mon-Fri 10:30-12:30/14:00-19:00 ■ English spoken ■ Prices medium ■ 10% professional discount

Specialist in Islamic Arms. Antiques, objects, paintings from Europe and Middle East.

ROBERT HALL-FRANCE

22 rue Drouot, 75009 Paris ■ Tel: 42 47 12 04 - Fax: 45 23 10 17 ■ Mon-Fri 9:00-18:00 and by appointment ■ English spoken ■ Prices medium

Antique Chinese tobacco jars as well as documention on the subject.

ANNE-MARIE KERVORKIAN

21 quai Malaquais, 75006 Paris ■ Tel: 42 60 72 91 - Fax: 42 61 01 52 ■ Mon-Sat 10:30-12:30/14:30-19:00 ■ English spoken ■ Prices medium

Antiques of the Near and Far East, archeological objects, Islamic Art, Persian and Indian miniatures.

BERNARD LE DAUPHIN

87 av. de Villiers, 75017 Paris ■ Tel: 40 54 80 91 - Fax: 42 27 14 93 ■ By appointment ■ English spoken ■ Prices high ■ Professional discount

Japanese art objects, especially arms and armour.

C. T. LOO

48 rue de Courcelles, 75008 Paris ■ Tel: 45 62 53 15 - Fax: 45 62 07 02 ■ Mon-Sat 10:30-12:30/14:30-18:30 ■ English spoken ■ Prices high ■ Professional discount

High quality oriental furniture, art objects, screens from China, objects from Korea, India and Japan.

PHILIPPE AND CLAUDE MAGLOIRE

13 place des Vosges, 75004 Paris ■ Tel: 42 74 40 67 ■ Tues-Sat 13:00-18:00 ■ English spoken ■ Prices high ■ 20% professional discount

Specialty: archeology and art of the Orient.

BERNARD ROUSSEAU

2 rue de Provence, 75009 Paris ■ Tel: 45 23 52 65 ■ By appointment ■ English spoken ■ Prices medium

Specialty: graphic arts of Japan from the XVI to the XIX century. Estampes, paintings, illustrated books.

GALERIE JEAN SOUSTIEL

146 bd Haussmann, 75008 Paris ■ Tel: 45 62 27 76 - Fax: 45 63 44 63 ■ Mon-Fri 10:00-12:00/14:00-19:00 ■ English spoken ■ Prices medium to high ■ Professional discount

Islamic art from North Africa, Egypt, Syria, Turkey, Iran, India. Ceramics, miniatures, textiles.

TANAKAYA ARTS DU JAPON

4 rue Saint-Sulpice, 75006 Paris ■ Telfax: 43 25 72 91 ■ Tues-Sat 12:00-19:00 ■ Prices medium ■ Professional discount

Japanese original estampes and antiques. Paintings, bronzes, lacquer, porcelain, stoneware.

TOIT DU MONDE

33 rue Berthe, 75018 Paris ■ Tel: 42 23 76 43 - Fax: 42 57 19 07 ■ By appointment ■ English spoken ■ Prices medium ■ Professional discount

Primitive and classical art and objects from the Himalayan countries: Nepal, Bhutan, Sikkim, Tibet, Northern India.

ARCHITECTURAL ELEMENTS

ETUDE FAURE & REY

14-16 rue d'Angeviller, 78120 Rambouillet ■ Tel: 30 59 77 78 - Fax: 30 59 51 13 ■ Dates of public sales are announced ■ Catalogues available by mail, phone or fax

Hundreds of architectural elements, including statues, basins, fountains, pillars and gates of the XVIII and XIX centuries. Arches, columns in stone, marble, wood panelling of the XVIII and XIX centuries. Antique parquet, fireplace mantels, antique doors, interior and exterior styles from Louis XIII to Louis XVI. Chateaux furniture.

ORIGINES

14 Porte d'Épernon/Maulette, 78550 Houdan ■ Tel: 30 88 15 15 - Fax: 30 88 11 80 ■ Tues-Fri 9:00-12:00/14:00-18:00/Sat 10:00-12:00/15:00-18:00/Sun 15:00-17:00 ■ English spoken by Samuel Roger ■ Prices medium to high ■ 20% professional discount

A remarkable collection of architectural items including fireplaces of all styles and periods in stone, marble, wood. Flooring in tile, terra cotta, stone, parquet. Wood panelling, doors, windows, grills, garden ornaments. All architectural elements interior and exterior of all styles and periods.
Specialty: fireplaces in stone, wood or marble.
Also transport services and installations.

SOCIETE PHILIPPE TOURY

81 bd des Elas, 78110 Le Vésinet ■ Tel: 39 52 03 99 - Fax: 39 52 06 22 ■ Mon-Sat 9:00-12:30/14:00-18:30 ■ Philippe Toury speaks English ■ Prices medium to high ■ 10% professional discount

Fireplaces, doors, beams, staircases, windows, wood panelling from demolitions of old structures.
Also copies of certain items in flooring, fireplaces, doors, wood panelling, windows, gates, grills, beams, staircases.

Cork
Liège

---------------- VII ----------------

AU LIEGEUR (J. PONTNEAU)

17 av. de la Motte-Piquet, 75007 Paris ■ Tel: 47 05 53 10 ■ Tues-Fri 9:00-12:30/14:00-19:00 ■ English spoken ■ Prices medium ■ Professional discount

Cork materials for walls, floors, ceilings as well as gift items in cork.

CREADIFOP

100 av. de Choisy, 75013 Paris ■ Tel: 45 70 74 19 - Fax: 45 85 77 39 ■ Mon-Sat 10:00-13:00/14:00-18:00 ■ English spoken ■ Prices medium ■ Professional discount

Fabrication of products in cork.

AU CHENE LIEGE

74 bd du Montparnasse, 75014 Paris ■ Tel: 43 22 02 15 - Fax: 42 79 81 23 ■ Tues-Sat 9:30-12:30/13:45-18:30 ■ Prices medium ■ Professional discount

The cork source in Paris. Cork fabric for wall upholstery and fashion (sold by the yard). Cork tiles for walls, floors and ceilings. Corks for wine, floor mats, table mats.

Parquet

SOLS MAJEURS

12 rue Jacques-Cœur, 75004 Paris ■ Tel: 42 71 74 28 - Fax: 42 71 74 29 ■ Mon-Sat 9:30-18:30 ■ Elizabeth de Bascher speaks English ■ Prices medium ■ Professional discount

Old style parquet. They make it and install it. Burgundy stone floors. Paving in aged marble and stone, slate, terra cotta. Wrought iron.

GEROCLAIR

27 rue Joseph-Python, 75020 Paris ■ Tel: 40 30 21 46 - Fax: 40 30 23 74 ■ Mon-Fri 8:00-12:00/14:00-18:00 ■ Bertrand Geraud and Nadège Beillevaire speak English ■ Prices medium ■ Professional discount

Wood flooring in oak, maple, ash, teak, and other. Laminated pre-finished floors, acrylic impregnated floors, solid hardwood floors, supplies of teak, portable floors.

ROWI SOL FRANCE

32 bd de Ménilmontant 75020 Paris ■ Tel: 47 97 95 06 - Fax: 47 97 98 81 ■ Tues-Sat 9:00-12:00/14:00-18:00 ■ Gérald Karsenty speaks English ■ Prices medium ■ 10 to 25% professional discount

Floating parquet 8 mm thick. Stratified flooring 8 mm thick. Manufacture and installation.

EURO-PARQUET

217 rue Béranger, 92700 Colombes ■ Tel: 47 85 73 97 - Fax: 47 85 66 92 ■ Mon-Fri 9:00-12:00/14:00-18:00 ■ Prices medium ■ Professional discount

Specialist in flooring. All types of parquet, new and renovated. Marble, stone and granite flooring as well as flagstones and tiles.

ROCS

26 rue Paul-Vaillant-Couturier, 92000 Nanterre ■ Tel: 47 29 01 20 - Fax: 47 21 84 30 ■ Mon-Fri 8:30-12:30/14:00-19:00/Sat 10:00-13:00/14:00-18:00 ■ Prices medium ■ Professional discount

Supply and installation of all types of parquet.

TRADELI SOLS

1 rue Mouillon, 92500 Rueil-Malmaison ■ Tel: 47 49 73 50/47 14 08 14 ■ Mon-Fri 9:00-18:00 ■ Prices medium ■ 10 to 20% professional discount

Installation of all types of parquet.

SEE ALSO WOOD CARVERS.

Marble and Stone
Marbre et pierre

——————————————— XI ———————————————

J. POULAIN ET FILS

7-11 bd Ménilmontant, 75011 Paris ■ Tel: 43 79 04 32 - Fax: 43 79 04 32 ■ Mon-Fri 8:30-12:30/13:30-17:30 ■ Prices medium to high ■ Professional discount

Installation and renovation of marble, stone and granite. Vertical and horizontal interior installations. Bathrooms, stairs and all decorative applications. Flagtones.

——————————————— XV ———————————————

BONNEL INTERNATIONAL

3 rue de l'Arrivée, 75015 Paris ■ Tel: 43 35 01 22 - Fax: 40 47 61 10 ■ Mon-Fri 9:00-17:00 ■ Benoît Chevallier and Régis de Vaujuas speak English ■ Prices medium to high ■ Professional discount

Suppliers of limestone, marble and granite for construction, facings and paving. Specialists in restoration of historical monuments. (Qualification #15).

——————————————— XVII ———————————————

JEAN DARTIGUES

20 rue de la Félicité, 75017 Paris ■ Tel: 42 27 52 36 - Fax: 47 64 10 64 ■ Mon-Fri 9:30-12:00/14:30-18:30 ■ Laurent Dartigues speaks English ■ Prices high ■ 15% professional discount

Transformation, restoration, construction and original creations in marble, stone and granite. Mosaics, bathrooms, furniture and decorative objects.

ALFORTVILLE

SERVICE PARISIEN DE PONÇAGE

121 rue Véron, 94149 Alfortville ■ Tel: 43 75 13 14 - Fax: 49 77 04 14 ■ Mon-Fri 8:00-12:00/13:30-19:00 ■ English spoken ■ Prices medium ■ 10% professional discount

Sanding and crystallization of marble, stone and granite. Maintenance and sale of products for maintenance.

CLICHY

LAUVAL

39 bd Jean-Jaurès, 92110 Clichy ■ Tel: 47 31 32 75 - Fax: 47 31 00 46 ■ Mon-Fri 7:30-19:00 ■ Gérard Grasset speaks English ■ Prices medium ■ 10% professional discount

Supply and installation of marble, granite and limestone for bathrooms, stairs, interiors and exteriors.

COURBEVOIE

TECHNIQUE ET MATERIAUX DE BATIMENT

81 rue Victor-Hugo, 92400 Courbevoie ■ Tel: 47 88 71 91 - Fax: 47 68 89 44 ■ Mon-Fri 9:00-19:00 ■ Elias Chammas speaks English ■ Prices medium to high ■ Professional discount

Marble, stone and granite for construction.

MARCO POLO CREATION

21 rue de Belfort, 92400 Courbevoie-Paris La Défense ■ Tel: 47 89 16 25 Fax: 46 67 74 83 ■ Mon-Fri 10:00-13:00/14:30-18:30/Closed Wednesday ■ Sophie Alix speaks English ■ Prices high to very high ■ 15% professional discount

High quality custom installation of marble, horizontal and vertical, natural stone and granite.

VINCENNES

♛ MADR

22 av. Franklin-Roosevelt, 94300 Vincennes ■ Tel: 43 98 03 00 - Fax: 43 08 16 62 ■ Mon-Fri 8:00-12:00/13:00-17:30 ■ Jean-Yves Rouger speaks English ■ Prices medium ■ Professional discount

Specialist in marble. Restoration of marble and sculptures in marble and other stone. Mounting of bronzes on marble bases. Installation of bathrooms. Member of the Grands Ateliers.

VAM

5 rue de Montreuil, 94300 Vincennes ■ Tel: 43 74 83 17 ■ Prices medium

Supply, installation and maintenance of marble and tiling.

MARBRERIE DU BEL AIR
5 av. Carelle, 94290 Villeneuve-le-Roi ■ Tel: 45 97 32 50 - Fax: 45 97 12 19 ■ Mon-Fri 8:00-17:00 ■ Prices medium ■ 25% professional discount

Installation of marble for interiors. Bathrooms, bathtubs and washbasins, stairs, tables. Flooring in marble and granite. Kitchens in granite. Flagstones.

NHT-CGPM
CARRELAGE-GRANIT-PIERRE-MARBRE
9 bis rue de la Gare, 92130 Issy-les-Moulineaux ■ Tel: 46 42 83 45 - Fax: 46 42 45 16 ■ Mon-Fri 7:30-19:30 ■ Luigi Sanna speaks English ■ Prices medium ■ Professional discount

Supply and installation of natural stone, granite and marble. High quality tiles.

OPUS
La Diane, 28290 Saint-Pellerin ■ Tel: 37 98 83 95 - Fax: 37 98 85 77 ■ Mon-Sat 8:00-19:00 ■ Roseline Olphe Galliard speaks English ■ Prices medium ■ 20% professional discount

Sale of marble and granite blocks.

👑 GUILLAUME PERICAS
SOL FAÇADE
10 place du Carouge, 60820 Boran-sur-Oise ■ Tel:44 21 94 91 - Fax: 44 21 97 60 ■ Mon-Fri 8:30-19:00 ■ Prices medium to high ■ Professional discount

High quality stone, marble and granite for construction and renovation. Restoration of old buildings in sandstone and limestone. Renovation of flagstones. Consultation provided to professionals for materials for construction and renovation.

Antigraffiti

P'INK CITY
126 av. Félix-Faure, 75015 Paris ■ Tel: 40 60 77 79 - Fax: 45 54 26 59 ■ Mon-Fri 8:00-18:00 ■ Arlette Boudon speaks English ■ Prices medium

Special treatment and cleaning of building facades. Graffiti protection for all surfaces.

Shutters, Blinds, Awnings
Volets, stores intérieurs et extérieurs

————————————————— **X** —————————————————

HERGE
50 rue des Petites-Ecuries, 75010 Paris ■ Tel: 47 70 44 79 - Fax: 47 70 13 73 ■ Mon-Fri 9:00-18:00/Sat 9:00-14:00 ■ Jeanine Barrasa speaks English ■ Prices medium ■ Professional discount

Fabrication, installation and maintenance of exterior awnings, interior and exterior blinds, security blinds, rolling shutters. Construction and counsel in window decoration: sheers and curtains, wall upholstery, bed covers.

STORES EURODRAP
3 impasse Bon-Secours, 75011 Paris ■ Tel: 43 70 97 60 - Fax: 43 70 26 99
■ Mon-Fri 9:00-18:00/Sat 14:00-18:00 ■ Prices high
Custom made interior blinds, in all fabrics. High quality.

STORES VOLTAIRE
4 rue Gobert, 75011 Paris ■ Tel: 49 60 91 84/43 79 55 89 - Fax: 43 56 16 54
■ Mon-Sat 9:00-18:00 ■ Prices medium ■ 10% professional discount
Fabrication and installation of interior and exterior blinds of all types. Rolling
shutters and security blinds. Installation of electric controls for all types of
blinds and window fastenings.

STORES AUVRAY CATALA
86 av. du Général Michel-Bizot, 75012 Paris ■ Tel: 43 45 22 22 - Fax:
43 45 21 21 ■ Mon-Fri 8:00-17:30 ■ English spoken ■ Prices medium ■ Professional discount
Blinds, patio awnings, parasols and tents.

STORES BELZACQ
23 bd Garibaldi, 75015 Paris ■ Tel: 42 70 43 43 - Fax: 42 70 97 57 ■ Prices
medium ■ 25% professional discount
Interior and exterior blinds, awnings, tents. All custom made.

NVS
8 rue Gustave-Flaubert, 75017 Paris ■ Tel: 46 22 88 27 - Fax: 47 63 09 16
■ Mon-Fri 9:00-18:00 ■ Sylvie Lafitan and Emanuel Guillard speak English
■ Prices low ■ 10 to 35% professional discount
Interior and exterior blinds. Venetians, horizontal and vertical, in wood and
metal, awnings, canopies. All window decoration.

MODO FRANCE
11 rue Forest, 75018 Paris ■ Tel: 42 93 56 93 - Fax: 45 22 57 63 ■ Mon-Fri
9:00-13:00/14:00-19:00 ■ Olivier Frachon speaks English ■ Prices medium
■ 10% professional discount
The most complete selection of wood venetian blinds.

BIER
28 ter rue Belgrand, 75020 Paris ■ Tel: 47 97 98 41/85 51 15 28 for English
contact - Fax: 85 51 17 87 ■ Tues-Sat 9:00-12:00/13:30-18:00 ■ Patrick
Roos speaks English ■ Prices medium ■ 33% professional discount
All interior and exterior blinds, decorative blinds, closures in wood and
wood trellis.

Tile and Flagstone
Carrelage et dallage

─────── III ───────

TERRA COTTA

7 rue du Pont-aux-Choux, 75003 Paris ■ Tel: 40 27 05 93 - Fax: 40 27 97 28 ■ Tues-Sat 10:00-13:00/14:00-18:30 ■ English spoken ■ Prices high ■ 20% professional discount

Terra Cotta tile of Tuscany for interior and exterior, lighting and ceramics.

─────── VII ───────

EMAUX DE BRIARE

7 rue du Bac, 75007 Paris ■ Tel: 42 61 16 41 - Fax: 42 61 53 31 ■ Mon-Sat 10:00-13:00/14:00-18:00 ■ English spoken ■ Prices medium ■ Professional discount

Manufacturer of ceramics. Tiles, lots of tiles, exterior or interior, for floors or walls. In sizes all the way from 1 cm × 1 cm to 10 cm × 10 cm. Stock or custom. 30 cm square slabs ready to install. They will make tile carpets or ceramic frescoes and friezes to your design or theirs. A very good place.

─────── XIII ───────

OMNIUM DE POSE MARBRES TESTA

6 rue Albert-Bayet, 75013 Paris ■ Tel: 45 87 29 47 - Fax: 45 86 27 19 ■ Mon-Fri 8:00-19:00 ■ Prices medium ■ 2 to 10% professional discount

Specialists in marble, stone, granite, tile and flagstone. For construction and renovation. Staircases and Saracen vaults.

─────── PARIS SUBURBS ───────

PIERRE CHALVIGNAC

6 rue de Baillage, 78000 Versailles ■ Tel: 30 42 52 20 ■ Prices medium ■ Professional discount

Antique flagstones and tiling.

SOCIETE VERSAILLAISE DE CARRELAGE

26 rue du Pont-Colbert, 78000 Versailles ■ Tel: 39 02 01 32 - Fax: 39 50 35 46 ■ Mon-Fri 8:00-19:30 ■ Prices medium ■ 10% professional discount

Supply and installation of all types of tiles and marble.

TUILES LAMBERT

37 rue Pieu, 78130 Les Mureaux ■ Tel: 30 90 42 00 - Fax: 30 99 75 95 ■ Mon-Fri 7:30-12:00/13:30-17:30 ■ Gilbert Le Floch and Frederic Afarian speak English

Fabrication of tiles and accessories in terra cotta: flat and curved tiles in numerous sizes.

SEE ARCHITECTURAL ELEMENTS AND PARQUET

Walls and Ceilings
Murs et plafonds

G S HABITAT ISOLATION

350 rue des Pyrénées, 75020 Paris ■ Tel: 46 36 82 46 - Fax: 47 97 17 86 ■ Mon-Fri 9:15-12:30/14:00-18:30 ■ Prices medium to high ■ Up to 20% professional discount

Supply and installation of stretched PVC ceilings.

———————— OUTSIDE PARIS ————————

CRYSTAL

Z.I. Les Paluds ■ 189 rue de la Maire, 13685 Aubagne Cedex ■ Tel: 42 82 05 77 - Fax: 42 82 01 16 ■ Mon-Fri 8:00-19:00 ■ Pascal Lefebvre speaks English ■ Prices medium ■ Professional discount

Manufacturer and owner of the European and American copyright for the aluminium chassis for stretched fabrics, dropped ceilings, wall panels, advertising billboards.

DG PLAFONDS SUSPENDUS

13 rue Saint-Honoré, 78000 Versailles ■ Telfax: 42 37 61 39 ■ Mon-Fri 8:00-13:00/13:30-19:00 ■ Dominique Grouls speaks English ■ Prices medium

Industrial acoustic insulation, sound proofing, dropped ceilings in metal, wallboard and fiber-board. Movable wall panels. Special flooring for computer installations.

MATFOR

89, rue Robespierre, 93100 Montreuil ■ Tel: 48 59 48 88 - Fax: 48 59 48 64 ■ Mon-Fri 8:00-19:00 ■ Pierre Meyer speaks English ■ Prices low to medium ■ Professional discount

Fabrication and installation of office modular units. Dropped ceilings and closets.

ORION INTERNATIONAL

39 bd Victor-Hugo, 92110 Clichy ■ Tel: 47 31 66 95 - Fax: 47 56 99 82 ■ Mon-Fri 9:00-19:00 ■ Frederic Skinfessel speaks English ■ Prices medium to high ■ 10% professional discount

Fabrication and installation of office modular units. Choice of four different types.

SPID

63 rue Victor-Hugo, 94700 Maisons-Alfort ■ Tel: 43 75 16 08 - Fax: 43 96 58 66 ■ Mon-Fri 8:00-18:00 ■ Prices medium

Dropped ceilings, thermal and acoustic insulation. Technical flooring for computer rooms, movable office partitions.

ORIGINES

Traditional spirit...

16th to 19th Century fire places in stone, wood or marble, antique terra cotta tiles, 17th to 20th Century stone or marble paving, Versailles floorboards, original wooden doors and panelling, gates and pillars, garden ornaments, architectural elements, reeditions from our workshops...

Open Tuesday to Friday from 9 to 12 am and 2 to 6 pm.
Saturday from 10 to 12 am and 3 to 6 pm.

14, Porte d'Epernon - Maulette 78550 HOUDAN   FRANCE
Tél.: 33 (1) 30 88 15 15 - Fax : 33 (1) 30 88 11 80

ART AUCTION HOUSES
Salles des ventes

Auction procedures in France are very different from auctions elsewhere. A special group of highly trained auctioneer/experts called "Commissaires-priseurs" control a monopoly on public auctions in France.

HOTEL DES VENTES DROUOT

9 rue Drouot, 75009 Paris ■ Tel: 48 00 20 20 - Fax: 48 00 20 33 ■ Mon-Sat 11:00-18:00 plus five Sundays per year ■ Prices are high, low and as you might expect

Public auctions of everything from old master paintings to vintage wines. They have several locations in Paris and the suburbs. Ask at any Paris newstand for the "Gazette de Drouot". It contains a complete listing of every one of their auctions in addition to a wealth of detail on estimates, prices and provenance. Their main gallery is a beehive of activity. The best time to attend an auction at the Drouot Galleries is when most of the dealers are attending one of their many salons or expositions, or when they are off on holiday.

LE DEPOT-VENTE DE PARIS

81 rue Laguy, 75020 Paris ■ Tel: 43 72 13 91 - Fax: 43 71 45 43 ■ Mon-Sat 9:30-19:30 ■ Prices low ■ 5% professional discount

Over 25,000 square feet of furniture and antique objects.

SALLE DES VENTES

33 rue Général-Colin, 78400 Chatou ■ Tel: 39 52 10 40/39 52 48 06 - Fax: 30 53 55 36 ■ Every day except Tues 9:30-12:30/14:30-18:30 ■ Prices medium

Auctions of furniture, art objects, tapestries, paintings, collectibles, chandeliers, glass.

CHATEAU DE CHEVERNY

Philippe Rouillac ■ Hôtel des Ventes, route de Blois, 41100 Vendôme ■ Tel: 54 80 24 24 - Fax: 54 77 61 10 ■ Prices as bid

An annual auction event in this beautiful Château where furniture, art objects, paintings, tapestries of high quality and architectural elements are sold. Make a week-end of it and stay for an excellent dinner.

SOTHEBY'S FRANCE

3 rue de Miromesnil, 75008 Paris ■ Tel: 42 66 40 60 - Fax: 47 42 22 32 ■ Wed-Fri 9:30-12:30/14:00-18:00 ■ English spoken ■ Fees are high

Sothebys do not function as auctioneers in France, but provide expertise and counsel for buying or selling art, antiques, anything. They do hold auctions in Monaco.

ART GALLERIES
Galeries d'art

Walk around any corner in Paris and there's a good chance you will find an art gallery. The range in quality is as great as the variation in prices. But remember, there are pictures galore, whether they be oil paintings, water colors, lithographs, engravings or whatever. In any case, there are a couple of things you might keep in mind when searching for the perfect work of art to set off a room, an office or a public building.

First and foremost, establish for yourself whether or not you are looking for a work of art with proven investment value or simply a picture or sculpture that functions beautifully in the atmosphere you are creating. If the latter, your choice is almost limitless. Whatever your goal, we suggest you begin your search in one of the four different gallery concentrations in Paris.

For a combination of fine works by young unknown artists, as well as established names, you might try the galleries on the Left Bank, especially the 6th and 7th Arrondissements.

Some of the better known international dealers have their main galleries in the area of the Rue du Faubourg Saint-Honoré, the Avenue Matignon and the Rue de Miromesnil.

The more daring buyer can explore the area of the Bastille, the Marais or one of the organized markets of Paris: "Le Village Suisse" and "Le Marché aux Puces" at the Porte de Clignancourt.

If you are looking for Old Master drawings, paintings or monumental mediaeval sculpture pre-dating 1850, you need to visit the Antique Dealers.

I

GALERIE D'ART CASTIGLIONE

9 rue Castiglione, 75001 Paris ■ Tel: 42 60 87 91 - Fax: 42 60 27 96 ■ Tues-Sat 10:30-18:30 ■ Mr. Gatellier speaks English ■ Professional discount
Modern paintings.

GALERIE REGIS LANGLOYS

169 rue Saint-Honoré, 75001 Paris ■ Tel: 42 60 56 94 - Fax: 42 60 41 03 ■ Tues-Sat 11:00-12:30/13:30-18:30 and by appointment ■ Regis Langloys speaks English ■ Prices medium to high ■ Professional discount
High quality figurative paintings, expressionist and primitive works, estampes.

MARUMO

243 rue Saint-Honoré, 75001 Paris ■ Tel: 42 60 08 66 - Fax: 40 15 96 04 ■ Tues-Sat 9:30-19:00 ■ English spoken ■ Professional discount
Barbizon school, Post Impressionists, Dutch and XIX century schools.

GALERIE MARWAN HOSS

12 rue d'Alger, 75001 Paris ■ Tel: 42 96 37 96 - Fax: 49 27 04 99 ■ English spoken ■ Prices medium ■ Professional discount
Works by established XX century artists: James Brown, Calder, Feininger, Dubuffet, Dufy, Ernst, Giacometti, Léger, Lipchitz, Matisse, Miro, Ben Nicholson, Picasso.

LES MUSARDS
JEAN-CLAUDE D'OZOUVILLE

91 rue Saint-Honoré, 75001 Paris ■ Tel: 42 33 96 33 ■ Mon-Sat 12:00-19:30 ■ Jean-Claude d'Ozouville speaks English ■ Prices medium ■ 20% professional discount
Primitive art, drawings, paintings, art objects.

GALERIE ERIC PHILIPPE

25 Galerie Vero Dodet, 75001 Paris ■ Tel: 42 33 28 26 - Fax: 42 21 17 93 ■ Tues-Sat 14:00-19:00 ■ Eric Philippe speaks English ■ Prices medium ■ Up to 20% professional discount
Photography of 1900 to 1950.

II

GALERIE J. HAHN

10 rue de Louvois, 75002 Paris ■ Tel: 47 03 42 55 - Fax: 47 03 42 34 ■ Mon-Sat 10:00-19:00 ■ Emeric Hahn speaks English ■ Prices high
XVII and XVIII century French and Italian paintings, XIX century French school, sculpture of the XVIII and XIX centuries.

RYAUX

67 rue Sainte-Anne, 75002 Paris ■ Tel: 42 60 37 47 - Fax: 42 60 31 41 ■ Mon-Fri 9:30-13:00/16:00-18:30 ■ Jean-Luc and Selma Ryaux speak English ■ Prices high
Old paintings, drawings and sculptures
Expert: Cour de Cassation.

GALERIE MARC VILLETTE

50 rue Sainte-Anne, 75002 Paris ■ Tel: 40 20 04 43 ■ Mon-Fri 13:00-19:00 and by appointment ■ Marc Villette speaks English ■ Prices medium ■ 10% professional discount

Old French and Italian drawings and estampes, XVI to early XIX centuries. Old Masters and XIX century drawings.

————————————————III————————————————

GALERIE ALIAS

6 rue Coutures-Saint-Gervais, 75003 Paris ■ NEAR THE PICASSO MUSEUM ■ Tel: 48 04 00 14 - Fax: 48 04 01 36 ■ Tues-Sat 10:30-19:00 (Open Mon PM) ■ Claude-Anne Jacob speaks English ■ Prices medium ■ 20% professional discount

Paintings, sculpture, engravings, works on paper, contemporary tapestries. They offer services to architects and designers for monumental works, decorative panels, etc.

AREA

10 rue de Picardie, 75003 Paris ■ Tel: 42 72 68 66 - Fax: 42 72 53 49 ■ Wed-Sat 14:00-19:30/Thu 14:00-21:00/Sun 15:00-19:00 ■ English spoken ■ Prices medium ■ Professional discount

Contemporary art, limited print editions, books.

ASKEO

19 rue Debelleyme, 75003 Paris ■ Tel: 42 77 17 77 - Fax: 42 77 27 77 ■ Mon-Fri 14:00-19:00/Sat 11:00-19:30 ■ Fati speaks English ■ Prices medium ■ 10 to 15% professional discount

Contemporary painting, sculpture, photos.

CATHERINE ET STEPHANE DE BEYRIE

5 rue de Saintonge, 75003 Paris ■ Tel: 42 74 47 27 - Fax: 42 74 47 31 ■ Tues-Sat 10:30-19:00 ■ Catherine and Stéphane de Beyrie speak English ■ Prices medium ■ 5 to 15% professional discount

Contemporary paintings and sculpture

GALERIE BERNARD BOUCHE

123 rue Vieille-du-Temple, 75003 Paris ■ Tel: 42 72 60 03 - Fax: 42 72 60 51 ■ Tues-Sat 14:00-19:00 ■ English spoken ■ Prices high ■ Professional discount

Impressionist and contemporary masters, paintings, sculpture, drawings.

GALERIE FARIDEH CADOT

77 rue des Archives, 75003 Paris ■ Tel: 42 78 08 36 - Fax: 42 78 63 61 ■ Tues-Sat 10:00-19:00 ■ Farideh Cadot speaks English

Contemporary paintings and sculpture.

GALERIE PHILIPPE CASINI

13 rue Chapon, 75003 Paris ■ Tel: 48 04 00 34 - Fax: 48 04 06 08 ■ Tues-Sat 14:30-19:00 ■ English spoken ■ Professional discount

Contemporary sculpture.

GALERIE FREDERIC CASTAING

13 rue Chapon, 75003 Paris ■ Tel: 42 74 69 09 - Fax: 42 74 00 89 ■ Tues-Fri 10:00-12:00/14:30-18:00 ■ Frederic Castaing speaks English ■ Prices high ■ 10% professional discount

Letters, manuscripts, musical scores, historic documents, from François I to François Mitterrand, including Chopin, Marie-Antoinette, Voltaire, Monet, Freud, Victor Hugo, etc. Well worth a visit.
Mr. Castaing is an expert and member of SNCAO and SLAM.

GALERIE RAPH DEBARRN

16 rue de Poitou, 75003 Paris ■ Tel: 42 78 80 84 - Fax: 42 78 81 84 ■ Tues-Sat 14:00-19:00 ■ Murielle Villani speaks English ■ Prices reasonable

Contemporary French and international paintings and some sculpture. Promising young unknowns.

DI ROSA RL/L'ART MODESTE

43 rue de Poitou, 75003 Paris ■ Tel: 40 27 92 82 - Fax: 40 27 02 84 ■ Mon-Sat 10:00-19:00 ■ English spoken ■ Prices reasonable

Contemporary art, specializing in the works of Hervé and Richard Di Rosa, lithographs, seriographs and glass.

GALERIE EMGET ART 97

97 rue Vieille-du-Temple, 75003 Paris ■ Tel: 42 77 51 21 or 42 77 64 70 ■ Mon-Sat 14:30-19:00 ■ Prices medium

Contemporary paintings, water colors, estampes, designs in acrylics.

GALERIE FROMENT PUTMAN

33 rue Charlot, 75003 Paris ■ Tel: 42 76 03 50 - Fax: 42 72 87 50 ■ Tues-Sat 10:30-13:00/14:00-19:00 ■ Cyrille Putman and Almine de Froment speak English ■ Prices medium

Contemporary painting, sculpture, drawings, installations.

PASCAL GABERT

80 rue Quincampoix, 75003 Paris ■ Tel: 48 04 94 84 - Fax: 42 71 48 73 ■ Tues-Sat 11:00-12:30/14:00-19:00 ■ English spoken

Contemporary paintings.

GALERIE PHILIPPE GRAVIER

7 rue Froissart, 75003 Paris ■ Tel: 42 71 55 01 - Fax: 42 71 05 56 ■ Tues-Sat 14:00-19:00 ■ English spoken ■ Prices medium ■ Professional discount

Contemporary painting and sculpture.

GALERIE KARSTEN GREVE

5 rue Debelleyme, 75003 Paris ■ Tel: 42 77 19 37 - Fax: 42 77 05 58 ■ Tues-Sat 10:00-13:00/14:30-19:00 ■ English spoken

Contemporary paintings.

MAISON MANSART (Association culturelle)

5 rue de Payenne, 75003 Paris ■ Tel: 48 87 41 03 ■ Tues-Sun 15:00-19:00 ■ Guy-Alain Thiollier and Suzanne Pauphilet speak English ■ Prices medium

Contemporary paintings, drawings, engravings, sculpture.

GALERIE DIANE MANIERE

11 rue Pastourelle, 75003 Paris ■ Tel: 42 77 04 26 - Fax: 42 72 62 43 ■ Tues-Sat 14:00-19:00 ■ English spoken ■ Professional discount

Contemporary paintings.

GALERIE ERIC DE MONTBEL

55 rue Charlot, 75003 Paris ■ Tel: 42 78 79 16 - Fax: 42 78 79 17 ■ Tues-Sat 11:00-13:00/14:30-19:00 ■ Eric de Montbel speaks English ■ Prices medium

Modern art, abstract and figurative paintings and sculptures of little known artists.

GALERIE NATHALIE OBADIA

8 rue de Normandie, 75003 Paris ■ Tel: 42 74 67 68 - Fax: 42 74 68 66 ■ Tues-Sat 11:00-19:00 ■ Delia Colombani speaks English ■ Prices medium ■ 10 to 20% professional discount

Contemporary French and international paintings, drawings and sculpture.

GALERIE CLAUDINE PAPILLON

59 rue de Turenne, 75003 Paris ■ Tel: 40 29 98 80 - Fax: 40 29 07 19 ■ Tues-Sat 14:00-19:00 ■ English spoken ■ Professional discount

Large collection of contemporary paintings.

GALERIE POLARIS

8 rue Saint-Claude, 75003 Paris (in courtyard) ■ Tel: 42 72 21 27 - Fax: 42 76 06 29 ■ Tues-Fri 14:00-19:00/Sat 11:00-13:00/14:00-19:00 ■ English spoken ■ Prices medium ■ Professional discount

Contemporary paintings, sculpture and photography by young artists. Editions of lithos, serios and art books.

GALERIE SAMIA SAOUMA

16 rue Coutures-Saint-Gervais, 75003 Paris ■ Tel: 42 78 40 44 - Fax: 42 78 64 00 ■ Tues-Sat 13:00-19:00 ■ Kelli Wilde speaks English ■ Prices medium to high ■ Professional discount

Contemporary European and American paintings, drawings, sculpture and photography.

GALERIE VERONIQUE SMAGGHE

24 rue Charlot, 75003 Paris ■ Tel: 42 72 83 40 ■ Wed-Sat 14:00-19:00 ■ Véronique Smagghe speaks English ■ Prices medium ■ 5 to 10% professional discount

XIX and XX century as well as contemporary paintings, sculpture, illustrated books.

GALERIE THORIGNY

13 rue de Thorigny, 75003 Paris ■ Tel: 48 87 60 65 - Fax: 48 87 87 27 ■ Tues-Sat 11:00-13:00/14:00-19:00/Sun by appointment ■ Patricia Heuilliet speaks English ■ Prices medium ■ 10 to 15% professional discount

Contemporary art, Duchamp, Man Ray, Rotella, Bertini and young artists. Exhibitions by theme.

GALERIE TROISIEME ŒIL

98 rue Vieille-du-Temple, 75003 Paris ■ Tel:48 04 30 25 - Fax: 48 04 09 98 ■ Tues 14:00-19:00/Wed-Sat 10:30-12:30/14:00-19:00 ■ Anne-Marie Marquette and Fausto Mata speak English ■ Prices medium

Contemporary paintings, drawings, sculptures and engravings, from 1950s to the present.

GALERIE MARQUET DE VASSELOT

18 rue Charlot, 75003 Paris ■ Tel: 42 76 00 31 - Fax: 42 72 04 21 ■ Wed-Sat 14:00-19:00 and by appointment ■ English spoken ■ Prices medium ■ Professional discount

Painting and sculpture of little known young artists.

GALERIE RENOS XIPPAS

108 rue Vieille-du-Temple, 75003 Paris ■ Tel: 40 27 05 55 - Fax: 40 27 07 16 ■ Tues-Sat 10:00-13:00/14:00-19:00 ■ English spoken

Modern and contemporary paintings and sculpture, catalogues of expositions.

GALERIE ZURCHER

56 rue Chapon, 75003 Paris ■ Tel: 42 72 82 20 - Fax: 42 72 58 07 ■ Tues-Fri 14:00-19:00/Sat 11:00-19:00 ■ English spoken ■ Prices medium to high ■ Professional discount

Contemporary painting and sculpture by young artists.

———————————————— **IV** ————————————————

GALERIE AMYOT

20 rue Saint-Louis-en-l'Ile, 75004 Paris ■ Tel: 43 26 74 30 ■ Also 60 rue Saint-Louis-en-l'Ile, 75004 Paris ■ Tel: 44 07 23 41 - Fax: 44 07 23 48 ■ Tues-Sat 11:00-12:30/14:30-19:30/Sun 11:00-12:30/14:30-19:00 ■ English spoken ■ Prices medium

Figurative paintings, water colors, pastels.

A L'IMAGE DU GRENIER SUR L'EAU

45 rue des Francs-Bourgeois, 75004 Paris ■ Tel: 42 71 02 31 - Fax: 42 78 66 77 ■ Mon-Fri 10:00-19:00/Sat 11:00-13:00/14:00-19:00 ■ Florence Penault and Geraldine Vales speak English ■ Prices medium ■ 10% discount for purchases over 10,000 Francs

Posters, estampes, postcards, books, photos, old original documents of the XIX to XX centuries classified by theme and country of origin. Specialty: Art Nouveau and Art Deco.

GALERIE DES ARCHIVES

39 rue Beaubourg, 75004 Paris ■ Tel: 42 78 05 77 - Fax: 42 78 19 40 ■ Tues-Fri 11:00-13:00/14:00-19:00/Sat 14:00-19:00 ■ English spoken ■ Prices 5,000 to 200,000 Francs

Contemporary paintings, sculpture and videos of living artists.

GALERIE ART EN TETE

7 rue Saint-Merri, 75004 Paris ■ Tel: 48 04 09 60 - Fax: 48 04 89 66 ■ Mon-Sat 11:00-19:00 ■ Nai Ollivier speaks English ■ Prices medium to high

Special custom creations of unique art objects, i.e. vases, screens, sculpture by contemporary artists in limited edition.

ART FORMEL

9 rue Saint-Paul, 75004 Paris ■ Tel: 48 04 93 33 ■ Thurs-Mon 14:00-19:30/Sun 15:30-19:30 ■ English spoken ■ Prices medium

Paintings, bronzes, ceramics and glass of 1890 to 1960.

CROUSEL-ROBELIN-BAMA

40 rue Quincampoix, 75004 Paris ■ Tel: 42 77 38 87 - Fax: 42 77 59 00 ■ Tues-Sat 11:00-13:00/14:00-19:00 ■ Francine Tagliaferro speaks English ■ Prices low, medium, high ■ Occasional professional discount

Contemporary paintings, sculpture, photographs and installations.

GALERIE BARBIER-BELTZ

7 rue Pecquay, 75004 Paris ■ Tel: 40 27 84 14 - Fax: 40 27 81 15 ■ Tues-Sat 14:00-19:00 ■ English spoken ■ Prices high ■ Professional discount

Contemporary paintings, sculpture and photography.

GALERIE BELLINT

28 bis bd de Sébastopol, 75004 Paris ■ Tel: 42 78 01 91 - Fax: 42 76 00 69 ■ Tues-Fri 14:00-19:00/Sat 11:00-13:00/14:00-19:00 ■ Annie-Josi Lemant speaks English ■ Prices medium ■ 10% professional discount

Contemporary abstract paintings, engravings and sculpture.

GALERIE ALAIN BLONDEL

4 rue Aubry-le Boucher, 75004 Paris ■ Tel: 42 78 66 67 - Fax: 42 78 47 90 ■ Tues-Fri 11:00-13:00/14:00-19:00/Sat 14:00-19:00 ■ Also: GALERIE ALAIN BLONDEL 2 ■ 50 rue du Temple, 75004 Paris ■ Tel: 42 71 85 86 - Fax: 48 04 33 97 ■ Tues-Sat 14:00-19:00 ■ Alain Blondel speaks English ■ Prices medium ■ 10% professional discount

Contemporary paintings and sculpture (Realism).
Qualified expert.

GALERIE ISABELLE BONGARD

4 rue de Rivoli, 75004 Paris ■ Tel: 42 78 13 44 - Fax: 42 78 13 90 ■ Tues-Sat 14:00-19:00 ■ Isabelle Bongard speaks English ■ Professional discount

Contemporary paintings, sculpture, photography, mixed media and art books.

GALERIE HENRY BUSSIERE

15 rue des Tournelles, 75004 Paris ■ Tel: 42 72 50 37 ■ Tues-Sat 14:00-19:00 ■ English spoken ■ Prices 5,000 to 100,000 Francs ■ Professional discount

Contemporary sculpture and paintings.

GALERIE DU CENTRE

1 rue Pierre-au-Lard, 75004 Paris ■ Tel: 42 77 37 92 - Fax: 42 77 26 31 ■ Tues-Sat 10:00-13:00/14:00-19:00 ■ English spoken ■ Professional discount

Contemporary paintings of living artists.

GALERIE MARIE-THERESE COCHIN

49 rue Quincampoix, 75004 Paris ■ Tel: 48 04 94 16 - Fax: 48 04 92 83 ■
Tues-Sat 14:00-19:00 ■ Marie-Thérèse Cochin speaks English ■ Prices
medium

Contemporary paintings, sculpture, lithographs.
Specialty: Eastern Europe, former Soviet Union.

GALERIE EUROPA

22 rue des Jardins Saint-Paul, 75004 Paris ■ Tel: 42 77 64 04 ■ Mon-Thurs-
Fri-Sat 14:00-19:00 ■ Prices reasonable

Contemporary paintings, sculpture of young artists.

GALERIE JEAN FOURNIER

44 rue Quincampoix, 75004 Paris ■ Tel: 42 77 32 31 - Fax: 48 87 34 65 ■
Mon-Sat 10:00-13:00/14:00-19:00 ■ Jean Fournier speaks English

Modern and contemporary painters, J. Bishop, S. Bordarier, P. Buraglio,
S. Fauchiere, S. Francis, Hwang Ho Sup, Shirley Jaffe, F. Lucien, Joan
Mitchell, B. Piffaretti.

GALERIE CATHERINE GUERARD

82 rue Saint-Louis-en-l'Ile, 75004 Paris ■ Tel: 46 33 73 11 - Fax: 46 33 73 11
■ Daily except Mon 14:00-19:00 ■ Catherine Guerard speaks English ■
Prices medium ■ Professional discount

Contemporary figurative painting, Hours, Kleinman, Merard, Mazilu,
Goinand, Mesterou, Chapaud.

GALERIE INSTANTS F. DESJOURS

17 quai aux Fleurs, 75004 Paris ■ Tel: 46 33 45 51 - Fax: 44 07 18 02 ■ Mon-
Fri 9:00-13:00/15:00-19:00 ■ Philippe Lapouyade speaks English ■ Prices
medium to high ■ 20% professional discount

Unique and unusual portraits in three dimensions by laser and reproduction of hands and other parts by moulage.Sculpture, old carved wooden figurines and santons.

GALERIE BERNARD JORDAN

54 rue du Temple, 75004 Paris ■ Tel: 42 72 39 84 - Fax: 42 72 48 24 ■ Tues-
Sat 14:30-19:00 ■ English spoken ■ Prices medium to high ■ 10 to 20% professional discount

Contemporary, abstract, young French painters.

LA GALERIE DES INDEPENDANTS

17 place des Vosges, 75004 Paris ■ Tel: 42 77 50 03 - Fax: 42 77 31 36 ■
Every day 14:00-19:00 ■ Sylvie Ferrandon speaks English ■ Prices reasonable ■ 10% professional discount

Contemporary figurative paintings.

GALERIE LAAGE SALOMON

57 rue du Temple, 75004 Paris ■ Tel: 42 78 11 71 - Fax: 42 71 34 49 ■ Tues-
Fri 10:30-12:30/14:30-19:00/Sat 11:00-19:00 ■ Pascal Bouchaille, Gabrielle
Salomon and Elizabeth de Laage speak English ■ Prices medium ■ Pro-
fessional discount

Contemporary sculpture and paintings.

JEAN-CLAUDE LEVET
FINE ART GALLERY

51 rue Saint-Louis-en-l'Ile 75004 Paris ■ Tel: 43 54 36 47 ■ Every day 9:00-19:00 ■ Jean-Claude Levet speaks English ■ Prices medium ■ 10 to 20% professional discount

Late XIX century and early XX century post Impressionist paintings.

GALERIE GABRIELLE MAUBRIE

24 rue Ste-Croix-de-la-Bretonnerie, 75004 Paris ■ Tel: 42 78 03 97 ■ Tues-Sat 14:00-19:00 ■ English spoken ■ Prices medium

Avant-garde and contemporary art.

👑 GALERIE MAEGHT

4 rue Saint-Merri, 75004 Paris ■ Tel: 42 78 43 44 - Fax: 42 78 27 61 ■ Tues-Sat 10:00-13:00/14:00-19:00 ■ English spoken ■ Prices medium to high ■ Professional discount

Contemporary paintings, Miró, Calder, Giacometti, young artists. Also a book shop of art editions in this magnificent XVII century private house in the center of the Marais.

GALERIE NELSON

40 rue Quincampoix, 75004 Paris ■ Tel: 42 72 24 56 - Fax: 42 71 74 58 ■ Tues-Sat 13:00-19:00 ■ Philip Nelson speaks English ■ Prices low to medium

Contemporary art.

GALERIE REGARDS

11 rue des Blancs-Manteaux, 75004 Paris ■ Tel: 42 77 19 61 - Fax: 44 09 91 47 ■ Tues-Sat 14:30-19:00 ■ Martine Devarrieux speaks English ■ Prices medium

Contemporary paintings and sculpture.

GALERIE CLAUDE SAMUEL

18 place des Vosges, 75004 Paris ■ Tel: 42 77 16 77 - Fax: 42 77 88 80 ■ Tues-Sat 14:00-19:00 and by appointment ■ English spoken ■ Professional discount

Contemporary painting, sculpture and photography by young artists.

GALERIE SAINT MERRI ART INUIT

9 rue Saint-Merri, 75004 Paris ■ Tel: 42 77 39 12 - Fax: 40 71 02 20 ■ Tues-Thurs 14:00-19:00/Fri-Sat 11:00-19:00 ■ Prices medium to high

Specialist in Eskimo Art. Sculpture, engravings, books and documentation.

GALERIE LE SOUS-SOL

12 rue du Petit-Musc, 75004 Paris ■ Tel: 42 72 46 72 - Fax: 42 71 90 59 ■ Tues-Sat 14:30-20:00 ■ Eric Bailoni and Stephane Crasnianski speak English ■ Prices low to medium ■ Discounts depend on purchase

Contemporary paintings, sculpture, photos, videos.

GALERIE DU TEMPLE

31 rue du Temple, 75004 Paris ■ Tel: 48 87 15 72 ■ Tues-Sat 14:30-19:30 ■ Maud Tykaert and Catherine Vago speak English ■ Prices reasonable

Contemporary paintings by young artists.

GALERIE VIDAL-SAINT PHALLE

10 rue du Trésor, 75004 Paris ■ Tel: 42 76 06 05 - Fax: 42 76 05 33 ■ Tues-Sat 11:00-13:00/14:00-19:00 ■ Bernard Vidal speaks English ■ Prices 3,000 to 120,000 Francs ■ Professional discount

A very exciting and energetic new gallery showing the works of well known international artists as well as young and upcoming French artists. Amenoff, Lemos, Mackendree, Pizzi Canella, Nicolaiev, Hartmann, Villa, Corlay, Van den Broek, Neumann.

GALERIE VIEILLE DU TEMPLE

23 rue Vieille-du-Temple, 75004 Paris ■ Tel: 40 29 97 52 - Fax: 42 71 39 75 ■ Tues-Sat 14:30-19:30 and by appointment ■ Marie-Hélène de la Forest Divonne speaks English ■ Prices reasonable

Contemporary paintings, sculpture and photography.
Permanent exhibits of Abidine and George Ball.

———————————————————— V ————————————————————

ART ET COMMUNICATION

6 rue de Lanneau, 75005 Paris ■ Tel: 43 26 13 55 ■ Mon-Fri 14:00-19:00 or by appointment ■ Lise Cormery speaks English

Contemporary paintings, sculpture, engravings, art objects, table arts.

GALERIE CHRISTINE COUDERC

6 rue de la Bûcherie, 75005 Paris ■ Telfax: 43 29 44 41 ■ Tues-Sat 14:00-19:00 ■ Christine Couderc speaks English ■ Prices medium ■ 20% professional discount

Paintings, both old and contemporary, art objects.

GALERIE PIERRE-MICHEL DUGAST

70 rue Gay-Lussac, 75005 Paris ■ Tel: 43 29 63 64 - Fax: 43 29 65 20 ■ Tues-Sat 11:00-12:30/15:30-19:00 ■ Prices medium ■ 10 to 20% professional discount

Paintings, sculpture and drawings by contemporary and little known young artists.

GALERIE JEAN-JACQUES DUTKO

13 rue Bonaparte, 75005 Paris ■ Tel: 43 25 96 13 - Fax: 43 29 21 91 ■ Tues-Sat 10:30-12:30/14:30-19:00/Mon 14:30-19:00 ■ Marie-France Vellieux speaks English ■ Prices medium

Art Deco and Primitive Art. Also contemporary paintings and sculpture.

GALERIE EMPREINTES

16 rue des Carmes, 75005 Paris ■ Tel: 46 33 00 90 ■ Tues-Sat 15:00-19:00 ■ Ghyslaine Bargiarelli speaks English ■ Prices medium ■ 10% professional discount

Contemporary figurative paintings and sculpture.

IMAGERIE

9 rue Dante, 75005 Paris ■ Tel: 43 25 18 66 - Fax: 43 25 18 08 ■ Tues-Sat 10:30-13:00/14:00-19:00/Mon 14:00-19:00 ■ Anne Martiniere speaks English ■ Prices medium ■ 10% professional discount

Original posters, drawings, estampes XVIII century to 1950.
Library of 5,000 ektachromes.

GALERIE MICHEL

17 quai Saint-Michel, 75005 Paris ■ Tel: 43 54 77 75 ■ Mon-Sat 9:00-19:00 ■ Everyone in the gallery speaks English

Estampes and original drawings from the XVI to XX centuries.

GALERIE SAPHIR RIVE GAUCHE

84 bd Saint-Germain, 75005 Paris ■ Tel: 43 26 54 22 - Fax: 43 80 23 49 ■ Sun-Thurs 14:00-19:00 ■ Francine and Elie Szapiro speak English ■ Prices medium ■ 5 to 10% professional discount

Paintings, drawings and lithographs of the XIX and XX centuries. Old and new books and ancient Jewish art.

STUDIO DE L'IMAGE

14 rue des Carmes, 75005 Paris ■ Tel: 43 54 88 73 - Fax: 43 29 85 04 ■ Tues-Sat 15:00-20:00 ■ Philippe Grand speaks English ■ Prices medium

Paintings, photographs, books, and designs specially related to the theatre or film world.

VI

GALERIE DE L'ACADEMIE-MARCEL FLAVIAN

6 rue de Seine, 75006 Paris ■ Telfax: 43 54 80 26 ■ Tues-Sat 10:00-12:00/15:00-18:00 ■ English spoken

XIX and early XX century French paintings and sculpture.

GALERIE AITTOUARES

35 rue de Seine, 75006 Paris ■ Tel: 40 51 87 46 - Fax: 42 47 03 90 ■ Tues-Sat 10:00-13:00/14:00-19:00 ■ Ghislaine Drouault speaks English ■ Prices medium ■ 10% professional discount

Impressionist and abstract paintings, sculpture.

GALERIE AKKA-VALMAY

22 rue de Seine, 75006 Paris ■ Tel: 43 54 66 75 - Fax: 43 25 01 32 ■ Tues-Sat 11:30-13:00/14:30-19:30 ■ Laurent Deschamps speaks English

Contemporary painters, (figurative and abstract), French, Polish, Spanish. Some sculpture.

GALERIE ALEXANDRE-ATELIER SAINT-ALBAN

73 rue de Seine, 75006 Paris ■ Tel: 43 26 53 22 - Fax: 43 28 80 29 ■ Mon 14:00-19:00/Tues-Sat 11:00-19:00 ■ Marite Borel speaks English ■ Prices medium

Figurative, Impressionist, Post Impressionist paintings, landscapes, water colors, sculpture.

GALERIE ANTIPODES

3 rue des Beaux-Arts, 75006 Paris ■ Telfax: 43 29 45 68 ■ Jean-Luc and Jacqueline André speak English ■ Prices medium ■ 20% professional discount

Primitive art of South Asia and Asiatic archaeological objects.

GALERIE ARNOUX

27 rue Guénégaud, 75006 Paris ■ Tel: 46 33 04 66 - Fax: 46 33 25 40 ■ Tues-Sat 11:00-13:00/14:00-19:00 ■ Muriel Rousset speaks English ■ Prices high ■ Professional discount

Modern and contemporary art. Abstract art of the period 1910 to 1960. Artists known and little known.

GALERIE BARBIZON

71 rue des Saints-Pères, 75006 Paris ■ Tel: 42 22 18 12 - Fax: 42 22 69 74 ■ Tues-Sat 11:00-13:00/14:30-19:00/Mon 14:30-19:00 ■ Renée Tiger and Sylviane Chevallier speak English ■ Prices medium ■ 10 to 20% professional discount

XIX century and Barbizon School paintings, modern and classic paintings. Contemporary paintings and art objects, i.e. screens, etc.

♔ GALERIE CLAUDE BERNARD

7-9 rue des Beaux-Arts, 75006 Paris ■ Tel: 43 26 97 07 - Fax: 46 33 04 25 ■ Tues-Sat 9:30-12:30/14:30-18:30 ■ English spoken ■ Professional discount

Old and contemporary paintings, sculpture.

GALERIE BERTHET-AITTOUARES

29 rue de Seine, 75006 Paris ■ Tel: 43 26 53 08 - Fax: 43 26 95 66 ■ Tues-Sat 11:00-13:00/14:30-19:00 ■ Claire Leadley speaks English ■ Prices medium ■ 10% professional discount

Contemporary and modern art, particularly paintings and works on paper.

GALERIE FABIEN BOULAKIA

10 rue Bonaparte, 75006 Paris ■ Tel: 43 26 56 79 - Fax: 43 25 91 92 ■ Tues-Sat 10:00-13:00/14:30-19:00 ■ English spoken ■ Prices medium ■ Professional discount

Modern and contemporary paintings.

GALERIE BOURDON

79 bd Raspail 75006 Paris ■ Tel: 43 48 01 39 ■ Tues 14:00-19:00/Wed-Thurs 8:00-12:00/14:00-19:00/Fri 8:00-12:00 ■ Possible professional discount

Modern paintings on consignment.

GALERIE BREHERET

9 quai Malaquais, 75006 Paris ■ Tel: 42 60 74 74 - Fax: 40 68 92 41 ■ Mon-Sat 10:30-19:00 ■ Michel Ducros and Gérard Poser speak English ■ Prices medium

Contemporary works, engravings, lithographs, water colors, oils in small format.

GALERIE JEANNE BUCHER

13 rue de Seine, 75006 Paris ■ Tel: 43 26 22 32 - Fax: 43 29 47 04 ■ Tues-Fri 9:00-13:00/14:00-18:00/Sat 9:30-12:30/14:30-18:30 ■ English spoken ■ Professional discount

Modern and contemporary art.

GALERIE CALLU MERITE

17 rue des Beaux-Arts, 75006 Paris ■ Tel: 46 33 04 18 - Fax: 40 51 82 21 ■ Tues-Fri 13:00-19:00/Sat 10:00-19:00 ■ Prices medium ■ Professional discount

Contemporary paintings and sculpture often of historical themes, Chaissac, Peyrissac, Lacasse, Bryen, Springer.
Young artists (Art "Actuel"). Specialty: European abstract art of the 1950s.

GALERIE DE CASTELNOU

20 rue de l'Abbé Grégoire, 75006 Paris ■ Telfax: 42 22 08 39 ■ Tues-Sat 11:00-19:00 and by appointment ■ Prices medium ■ 20% professional discount

Paintings, water colors, drawings, sculpture, engravings, books, photo art, architecture, French contemporary - essentially figurative.

GALERIE COLETTE CREUZEVAULT

58 rue Mazarine, 75006 Paris ■ Tel: 43 26 67 85 - Fax: 43 25 25 70 ■ Tues-Sat 14:30-18:30 ■ Colette Creuzevault speaks English ■ Prices medium ■ 10 to 15% professional discount

Sculpture of the great masters, also high quality paintings. Germaine Richier, César, Niki de Saint Phalle, exclusive representation of the young sculptor Sophido. Paintings by Matta, Lam, Kijno, Fassianos.

GALERIE DEA

30 rue Bonaparte, 75006 Paris ■ Tel: 46 34 69 00 - Fax: 44 07 26 76 ■ Mon-Sat 10:00-19:00 (often closed 13:00-14:00) ■ English spoken ■ Prices medium ■ 15 to 20% professional discount

Contemporary paintings, furniture and articles of decoration. Beautiful and unusual works in glass and metal. Will take custom orders.

GALERIE DAMBIER-MASSET

5 rue des Beaux-Arts, 75006 Paris ■ Tel: 46 33 02 52 - Fax: 43 26 07 05 ■ Tues-Sat 10:00-13:00/14:30-19:00 ■ Prices medium

Contemporary paintings.

♛ GALERIE DI MEO

9 rue des Beaux-Arts, 75006 Paris ■ Tel:43 54 10 98 - Fax: 43 54 88 65 ■ Tues-Sat 10:00-13:00/14:30-19:00 ■ English spoken ■ Professional discount

Modern and contemporary paintings, mostly young living artists.

GALERIE DOCUMENTS

53 rue de Seine, 75006 Paris ■ Tel: 43 54 50 68 - Fax: 43 29 10 25 ■ Tues-Sat 10:30-12:30/14:30-19:00 ■ Mireille Romand speaks English ■ Prices medium ■ 10% professional discount

Antique original posters 1870 to 1950, estampes.

GALERIE RAYMOND DREYFUS

3 rue des Beaux-Arts, 75006 Paris ■ Tel: 43 26 09 20 - Fax: 43 29 67 81 ■ Tues-Sat 10:30-12:30/14:30-18:30 ■ Raymond Dreyfus speaks English ■ Prices medium

Modern and contemporary paintings, lithographs, contemporary sculpture.

GALERIE DUPERRIER

14 rue des Beaux-Arts, 75006 Paris ■ Tel: 43 54 38 64 ■ Tues-Sat 10:00-12:30/14:30-19:00 ■ English spoken ■ Prices medium ■ 10% professional discount

Primitive art from Africa, Oceania, Indonesia, North America.

GALERIE LUCIEN DURAND

19 rue Mazarine, 75006 Paris ■ Telfax: 43 26 25 35 ■ Tues-Sat 11:00-13:00/14:30-19:00 ■ English spoken ■ Prices reasonable to medium 10,000 to 50,000 FF ■ Professional discount

Contemporary paintings, young artists.

GALERIE DE L'EMPEREUR

61 rue Bonaparte, 75006 Paris ■ Tel: 43 26 87 10 - Fax: 46 33 57 67 ■ English spoken

Realistic and "poetic" paintings, Brianchon, C. Caillard, Leguelt, N. Limouse.

GALERIE ERVAL

16 rue de Seine, 75006 Paris ■ Tel: 43 54 73 49 - Fax: 43 25 68 72 ■ Tues-Sat 11:00-13:00/14:30-19:00 ■ English spoken ■ Prices medium ■ Professional discount

Contemporary art, mostly paintings.

GALERIE FLAK

8 rue des Beaux-Arts, 75006 Paris ■ Tel: 46 33 77 77 - Fax: 46 33 27 57 ■ Mon-Sat 11:00-13:00/14:30-19:30 ■ Edith Flak speaks English ■ Prices medium to high ■ Professional discount

Modern and contemporary paintings, sculpture, drawings, estampes, rare books.

GALERIE CHRISTIANE FLAMENT

113 rue du Cherche-Midi, 75006 Paris ■ Tel: 42 22 13 09 ■ Tues-Sat 11:00-19:00 ■ Christiane Flament speaks English ■ Prices medium ■ 10% professional discount

Contemporary estampes, engravings, water colors, original lithographs, drawings.

GALERIE DU FLEUVE

6 rue de Seine, 75006 Paris ■ Tel: 43 26 08 96 - Fax: 43 28 28 91 ■ Tues-Fri 11:00-13:00/14:30-19:00/Sat 11:00-19:00 ■ English spoken ■ Prices medium ■ Professional discount

Modern and contemporary painting and sculpture.

GALERIE FRAMOND

3 rue des Saints-Pères, 75006 Paris ■ Tel: 42 60 74 78 - Fax: 49 27 01 63 ■ Mon-Sat 10:00-12:30/14:00-19:00 ■ English spoken ■ Prices medium ■ 15 to 25% professional discount

Modern and contemporary paintings, engravings, lithographs.

GALERIE LILIANE FRANÇOIS
15 rue de Seine, 75006 Paris ■ Tel: 43 26 94 32 ■ Tues-Sat 10:30-12:30/14:00-19:00 ■ Liliane François speaks English ■ Prices medium ■ 20% professional discount

Contemporary drawings, paintings, lithographs, sculpture.

GALERIE MARIE-JANE GAROCHE
33 rue de Seine, 75006 Paris ■ Tel: 43 26 89 62 - Fax: 46 33 69 44 ■ Mon 14:30-19:00/Tues-Sat 10:30-12:30/14:30-19:00 ■ Jean-Jacques Rigalleau speaks English ■ Prices medium ■ Professional discount

Contemporary and Post Impressionist paintings.

GALERIE ARLETTE GIMARAY
13 rue de Seine, 75006 Paris ■ 12 rue Mazarine, 75006 Paris ■ Tel: 46 34 71 80 - Fax: 46 33 06 22 ■ Tues-Sat 10:30-13:00/14:00-19:00 ■ Prices low

Contemporary paintings, estampes, sculpture.

GALERIE GRILLON
44 rue de Seine, 75006 Paris ■ Tel: 46 33 03 44 - Fax: 46 33 93 81 ■ Mon 14:00-19:00/Tues-Sat 10:30-12:30/14:00-19:00 ■ Lida and Guy Apelbaum speak English ■ Prices low to medium ■ Professional discount

XIX, XX century original estampes, lithographs, engravings from Daumier to Picasso. Also suppliers of wall decoration for hotels, offices and public buildings.

GALERIE GUENEGAUD
25 rue Guénégaud, 75006 Paris ■ Tel: 46 34 77 61 - Fax: 46 34 77 62 ■ Tues-Sat 10:30-13:00/14:00-19:00 ■ English spoken

Contemporary paintings (especially 1950s).

GALERIE MARIE DE HOLMSKY
80 rue Bonaparte, 75006 Paris ■ Tel: 43 29 08 90 - Fax: 45 00 59 97 ■ Tues-Sat 15:00-19:00 ■ Prices medium ■ 10% professional discount

XIX and XX century paintings, sculptures and art objects. Specialty 1930s.

GALERIE LA HUNE BRENNER
14 rue de l'Abbaye, 75006 Paris ■ Tel: 43 25 54 06 - Fax: 40 46 84 81 ■ Tues-Fri 10:00-13:00/14:00-19:00/Sat 10:00-19:00 ■ Annie Maillet speaks English ■ Prices medium ■ Professional discount

Contemporary lithographs, engravings, pastels, water colors, art books.

J. G. M. GALERIE
8 bis rue Jacques-Callot, 75006 Paris ■ Tel: 43 26 12 05 - Fax: 46 33 44 83 ■ Mon by appointment/Tues-Fri 10:00-19:00/Sat 11:00-19:00 ■ English spoken ■ Prices varied ■ Professional discount

Contemporary sculpture.

GALERIE JONAS
12 rue de Seine, 75006 Paris ■ Tel: 43 26 50 28 - Fax: 43 29 65 66 ■ Tues-Sat 9:30-12:30/14:30-18:30 ■ English spoken ■ Prices high ■ Professional discount

Paintings of the XIX century, Romantic and Barbizon Schools. Expert in XIX century paintings.

GALERIE KRIEF

10 rue Mazarine, 75006 Paris ■ Tel: 43 29 32 37 - Fax: 43 26 99 81 ■ Tues-Fri 10:30-13:00/14:00-19:00/Sat 10:30-19:00 ■ English spoken ■ Prices low to high ■ Professional discount

Modern and contemporary paintings and sculpture.

GALERIE JULIETTE LAURENT

25 rue Dauphine, 75006 Paris ■ Tel: 43 29 10 31 - Fax: 43 29 08 14 ■ Mon-Sat 11:30-18:30 ■ Juliette Laurent speaks English ■ Prices low to medium ■ Professional discount

Modern paintings, water colors, drawings, sculptures, art objects, curiosities, antiquities.

GALERIE ARNAUD LEFEBVRE

30 rue Mazarine, 75006 Paris ■ Tel: 43 26 50 67 - Fax: 44 07 05 19 ■ Mon-Sat 14:00-19:00 ■ English spoken

Contemporary paintings and sculpture.

GALERIE LEFOR-OPENO

29 rue Mazarine, 75006 Paris ■ Telfax: 46 33 87 24 ■ Tues-Sat 11:00-13:00/14:00-19:00 ■ Claude Jamon speaks English ■ Prices medium ■ 20 to 30% professional discount

Contemporary painting and sculpture.

GALERIE CLAUDE LEMAND

16 rue Littré, 75006 Paris ■ Tel: 45 49 26 95 - Fax: 45 48 45 12 ■ Tues-Sat 14:00-19:00 ■ Claude Lemand speaks English ■ Prices medium ■ 10 to 25% professional discount

Exclusive representation of contemporary international painters and sculptors. Unique pieces in bronze, estampes, illustrated books, works on paper.

GALERIE LOFT

3 rue des Beaux-Arts, 75006 Paris ■ Tel: 46 33 18 90 - Fax: 43 54 56 14 ■ Tues-Sat 10:00-13:00/14:30-19:00 ■ English spoken ■ Prices 2,000 to 50,000 FF ■ Professional discount

Young artists - figurative, narrative paintings.

GALERIE J. & H. LUHL

19 quai Malaquais, 75006 Paris ■ Tel: 42 60 76 97 ■ Tues-Sat 14:00-19:00 ■ English, German, Spanish spoken ■ Prices medium to high ■ Professional discount

Japanese estampes, paintings and books.

GALERIE MEYER

17 rue des Beaux-Arts, 75006 Paris ■ Tel: 43 54 85 74 - Fax: 43 54 11 12 ■ Mon-Sat 10:30-13:00/14:30-19:00 ■ English spoken ■ Prices medium to high ■ Professional discount

Art of Oceania.

GALERIE FRANÇOISE MITAINE

60 rue Mazarine, 75006 Paris ■ Tel: 40 51 70 60 - Fax: 40 51 70 33 ■ Tues-Sat 14:00-19:00 ■ English spoken ■ Prices low to medium ■ Professional discount

Contemporary paintings, engravings, lithographs and sculpture.

GALERIE MONTENAY

31 rue Mazarine, 75006 Paris ■ Tel: 43 54 85 30 - Fax: 43 29 42 21 ■ Tues-Sat 11:00-13:00/14:30-19:00 ■ Frédéric Giroux and Anne Mabin speak English ■ Prices medium to high

Contemporary art.

GALERIE MOSTINI

18 rue de Seine, 75006 Paris ■ Tel: 43 25 32 18 - Fax: 43 54 93 55 ■ Tues-Sat 11:00-13:00/14:00-19:00 ■ Elizabeth Mostini speaks English ■ Prices low to medium ■ 10% professional discount

Contemporary painting and sculpture, art objects, ceramics, lighting.

CLAUDE DE MUZAC

1 rue de l'Abbaye, 75006 Paris ■ Tel: 43 54 09 55 - Fax: 43 25 32 92 ■ Mon-Sat 10:00-18:30 ■ Claude de Muzac speaks English ■ Prices high ■ 10% professional discount

Unique presentation of art objects, frames, archeological objects, paintings, fans, framing and mounting on plexi, metal in various finishes, marble. Art objects mounted as lamps.

GALERIE 1900-2000

8 rue Bonaparte, 75006 Paris ■ Tel: 43 25 84 20 - Fax: 46 34 74 52 ■ Mon 14:00-19:00/Tues-Sat 10:00-12:30/14:00-19:00 ■ English spoken ■ Prices reasonable ■ 5 to 10% professional discount

Modern and contemporary paintings. Specialty: Surrealism and Dada.

GALERIE PIXI ET CIE

95 rue de Seine, 75006 Paris ■ Tel: 43 25 10 12 ■ Tues-Sat 10:30-13:00/14:30-19:00 ■ Prices medium ■ 10% professional discount

Paintings, sculpture, drawings of young artists.

GALERIE LA POCHADE

11 rue Guénégaud, 75006 Paris ■ Tel: 43 54 89 03 - Fax: 43 29 75 11 ■ Tues-Sat 11:00-13:00/14:00-19:00 ■ Alain Digard and Philippe Fravelles speak English ■ Prices low to high ■ 10 to 30% professional discount depending on quantity

Modern and contemporary works on paper and paintings of known and little known young artists. Specialists in works 1945 to 1980: Calder, Bertini, Gleizes, Fautrier.

PRIVARTE

6 rue des Beaux-Arts, 75006 Paris ■ Tel: 46 33 74 11 - Fax: 46 33 07 34 ■ Mon-Sat 10:00-13:00/14:00-18:30 ■ Lionel and Sandrine Pissarro speak English ■ Prices medium to high ■ Professional discounts

XIX, XX century paintings, drawings, sculpture and art objects. Impressionist and modern paintings.

GALERIE PROTEE

38 rue de Seine, 75006 Paris ■ Tel: 43 25 21 95 - Fax: 40 46 04 02 ■ Tues-Sat 10:00-12:30/14:00-19:00 ■ Laurence Izern speaks English ■ Prices medium to high ■ 5 to 10% professional discount

Contemporary painting and sculpture, internationally known painters: abstract, lyric and classic. Also young discoveries.

PAUL PROUTE

74 rue de Seine, 75006 Paris ■ Tel: 43 26 89 80 - Fax: 43 25 83 41 ■ Tues-Sat 9:00-12:00/14:00-19:00 ■ English spoken ■ Prices medium to high ■ Professional discount

Original drawings and estampes of the XVI to the XX centuries. Documentary and decorative estampes.

GALERIE SYLVIE RESCHE

53 rue de Seine, 75006 Paris ■ Tel: 43 26 93 48 - Fax: 43 26 90 04 ■ Tues-Sat 10:30-13:00/14:00-19:00 and by appointment ■ English spoken ■ Prices medium to high ■ 10% professional discount

XIX, XX century paintings and water colors.

GALERIE SAMAGRA - PARIS - MUNICH

52 rue Jacob, 75006 Paris ■ Tel: 42 86 86 19 - Fax: 44 74 03 31 ■ Mon 14:00-19:00/Tues-Sat 10:30-12:30/14:00-19:00 ■ English spoken ■ Prices medium to high ■ 5 to 25% professional discount

Contemporary abstract and expressionist paintings, sculpture. Humour and derision. Rental of paintings. Creation of artistic environments.

GALERIE SAMARCANDE

13 rue des Saints-Pères, 75006 Paris ■ Tel: 42 60 83 17 - Fax: 42 61 41 64 ■ Mon-Sat 10:00-12:30/13:30-19:00 ■ English spoken ■ Prices medium ■ 10% professional discount

Archeology: principally Greece and Rome, Egypt, Sumeria, Asia, Middle East, European Middle Ages and Renaissance. Paintings.

GALERIE SEGUIER

10 rue Séguier, 75006 Paris ■ Tel: 43 25 73 23 - Fax: 40 51 73 09 ■ Tues-Sat 15:00-19:00 ■ Prices reasonable ■ 20% professional discount

Contemporary art.

GALERIE NATALIE SEROUSSI

34 rue de Seine, 75006 Paris ■ Tel: 46 34 05 84 - Fax: 46 33 03 37 ■ Mon-Sat 10:00-13:00/14:00-19:00 ■ English spoken

Mostly modern and contemporary paintings.

GALERIE SERRES

15 rue Bonaparte, 75006 Paris ■ Tel: 43 25 78 27 - Fax: 46 33 55 32 ■ Tues-Sat 10:30-19:00 ■ Jean-Philippe Mariaud de Serres speaks English ■ Prices high ■ 10% professional discount

Archeological objects: Mesopotamian, Egyptian, Greek, Roman and Celtic. Qualified expert.

DARTHEA SPEYER
6 rue Jacques-Callot, 75006 Paris ■ Tel: 43 54 78 41 - Fax: 43 29 62 39 ■
Tues-Fri 14:00-19:00/Sat 11:00-19:00 ■ English spoken

Contemporary paintings and sculpture.

GALERIE THIERRY SPIRA
19 rue Guénégaud, 75006 Paris ■ Tel: 46 33 18 19 - Fax: 46 33 20 21 ■ Mon-Sat 14:00-18:00

Paintings and sculpture from 1950 to the present.

GALERIE STADLER
51 rue de Seine, 75006 Paris ■ Tel: 43 26 91 10 - Fax: 46 34 23 97 ■ Tues-Sat 10:00-12:30/14:00-19:00 ■ English spoken ■ Prices medium ■ Professional discount

Contemporary paintings.

GALERIE PATRICE TRIGANO
4 bis rue des Beaux-Arts, 75006 Paris ■ Tel: 46 34 15 01 - Fax: 46 34 64 02 ■ Tues-Sat 10:00-13:00/14:30-18:30 ■ English spoken ■ Prices medium ■ Professional discount

Sculpture and paintings since 1940. Abstract art and realism.

GALERIE VALLOIS
41 rue de Seine, 75006 Paris ■ Tel: 43 29 50 84 - Fax: 43 29 90 73 ■ Tues-Sat 10:00-13:00/14:00-19:00 ■ Michèle Bohbot speaks English ■ Prices medium ■ 10% professional discount

XX century sculpture.
Expert in Rodin.

GALERIE VENDOME-V.R.G.
23 rue Jacob, 75006 Paris ■ Tel: 43 26 29 17 - Fax: 43 29 69 02 ■ Tues-Sat 11:30-13:00/14:30-19:30 ■ English spoken ■ Prices medium ■ Professional discount

Contemporary paintings, sculpture and glass objects by living artists.

GALERIE ALINE VIDAL
70 rue Bonaparte, 75006 Paris ■ Tel: 43 26 08 68 - Fax 43 29 62 10 ■ Tues-Fri 13:00-18:00/Sat 14:00-19:00 ■ Aline Vidal speaks English ■ Prices medium

Contemporary art.

GALERIE LUCIE WEILL-SELIGMANN
ZALBER & DE NOBLET
6 rue Bonaparte, 75006 Paris ■ Tel: 43 54 71 95 - Fax: 40 51 82 88 ■ Tues-Sat 11:00-13:00/14:30-19:00 ■ Charles Zalber and Gonzague de Noblet speak English ■ Prices medium. The rugs cost in the range of 40,000 FF

Drawings by modern and contemporary masters. Works on paper by artists of the XIX and XX centuries. Rugs of the Marie Cuttoli collection by Picasso, Arp, Miro, Klee, Léger, Laurens, Calder.

GALERIE HÉLÈNE APPEL

75 rue Saint-Dominique, 75007 Paris ■ Tel: 45 51 28 17 ■ Tues-Fri 11:00-18:00 ■ Helene Appel speaks English ■ Prices medium ■ Professional discount

Original figurative paintings of living artists.

ART 50

50 rue de Verneuil, 75007 Paris ■ Tel: 40 15 99 50 ■ Tues-Fri 14:00-19:00/Sat 11:00-13:00/14:30-19:00 ■ Claudine Legrand speaks English ■ Prices medium ■ Professional discount

Contemporary painting and sculpture.

L'ART EN MOUVEMENT

17 rue Duvivier, 75007 Paris ■ Tel: 45 55 03 16 - Fax: 47 05 74 07 ■ Mon-Fri variable hours by appointment ■ Antoine Villeneau speaks English ■ Prices medium ■ 15% professional discount

Paintings, lithographs, sculpture. Tapestries, all periods. Art services to corporations and associations.

♛ GALERIE BELLIER

7 quai Voltaire, 75007 Paris ■ Tel: 42 60 74 72 - Fax: 40 20 93 52 ■ Tues-Sat 11:00-13:00/14:30-19:00 ■ Mr. Bellier speaks English ■ Prices high

Late XIX and XX century paintings.

♛ GALERIE HUGUETTE BERÈS

25 quai Voltaire, 75007 Paris ■ Tel: 42 61 27 91 - Fax: 49 27 95 88 ■ Mon-Sat 10:00-13:00/14:00-19:00 ■ Huguette Berès and Anisabelle Berès speak English

Japanese estampes. French paintings, drawings, estampes of the XIX and XX centuries, especially Post Impressionist and Nabis.

♛ GALERIE ANTOINE VAN DE BEUQUE

15 place Vauban, 75007 Paris ■ Tel: 44 18 30 04 - Fax: 44 18 30 05 ■ Mon-Fri 10:00-18:00 by appointment only

Principally a broker of high and very high priced masters of the XIX and XX centuries. Offers expertise and will travel.

GALERIE DENIS BLOCH

52 rue de l'Université, 75007 Paris ■ Tel: 42 22 25 26 - Fax: 45 48 73 73 ■ By appointment only ■ Denis Bloch speaks English ■ Prices reasonable ■ Professional discount

Lithographs and engravings by XX century masters.

GALERIE SYLVIE BRULEY

27 rue de l'Université, 75007 Paris ■ Tel: 40 15 00 63 ■ Tues-Sat 14:30-19:00 ■ Sylvie Bruley speaks English ■ Prices low ■ 15% professional discount

Contemporary paintings and sculpture.

♛ GALERIE CAMOIN

9 quai Voltaire, 75007 Paris ■ Tel: 42 61 82 06 - Fax: 42 61 24 09 ■ Mon-Sat 10:00-13:00/14:30-19:00 ■ English spoken ■ Prices high to very high ■ Professional discount

Old master paintings.

AU CHAT DORMANT

31 rue de Bourgogne, 75007 Paris ■ Tel: 45 50 38 06 ■ Tues-Sat 11:30-19:00 ■ Prices medium ■ 5 to 10% professional discount

Old and contemporary animal art, especially the cat. Paintings, bronzes and porcelain. Sculptures in wood, marionettes, screens, ink wells.

GALERIE CHISSEAUX RIVE GAUCHE

33 av. de la Bourdonnais, 75007 Paris ■ Tel: 45 55 49 17 ■ Tues-Sat 13:30-19:00/Sun 15:00-18:00 ■ English spoken ■ Prices medium ■ 10% professional discount

Contemporary paintings, water colors, period pastels.

LE CYGNE VERT

41 rue de Verneuil, 75007 Paris ■ Tel: 40 20 08 41 ■ Mon-Sat 11:00-19:00 ■ Julien Dufay speaks English ■ Prices medium ■ 20% professional discount

XIX, XX century sculpture and paintings.

GALERIE LINA DAVIDOV

210 bd Saint-Germain, 75007 Paris ■ Tel: 45 48 99 87 - Fax: 42 23 36 70 ■ Tues-Sat 11:30-12:30/14:00-19:00 ■ Lina Davidov speaks English ■ Prices medium ■ 10% professional discount

Contemporary Spanish artists.

ANNICK DRIGUEZ

39 rue de Verneuil, 75007 Paris ■ Tel: 42 86 00 42 ■ Tues-Sat 15:00-19:00 ■ Annick Driguez speaks some English ■ Prices medium ■ Professional discount

XIX, XX century and contemporary sculpture and drawings by sculptors. A tendancy toward the classic "figurative".

GALERIE DUPUTEL

20 rue de Beaune, 75007 Paris ■ Telfax: 42 97 47 92 ■ Mon-Fri 11:00-19:00 ■ David Duputel speaks English ■ Prices medium ■ Professional discount

XIX and XX century paintings, Barbizon School. Sculpture of the XIX century.

GALERIE EFTE

7 rue du Bourgogne, 75007 Paris ■ Tel: 45 51 45 89 - Fax: 45 56 09 01 ■ Mon-Sat 10:00-19:00 ■ English spoken ■ Prices medium ■ Professional discount

Contemporary paintings and sculpture.

EPOCA

60 rue de Verneuil, 75007 Paris ■ Tel: 45 48 48 66 - Fax: 45 44 85 82 ■ Mon-Fri 11:00-19:00/Sat 14:30-19:00 ■ English spoken ■ Prices medium to high ■ Professional discount

A remarkable collection: Indian art, paintings, sculpture, modern art, unusual objects and furniture. " creation of atmospheres". Sale and rental.

GALERIE ESCALE A PARIS-CHRISTIAN DESBOIS EDITIONS

14 av. de la Bourdonnais, 75007 Paris ■ Tel: 45 55 85 53 - Fax: 45 56 06 16 ■ Tues-Sat 15:00-19:00 ■ Christian Desbois speaks English ■ Prices medium ■ Professional discount

Estampes, seriographs, lithographs, paintings, water colors, pastels by artists of the cartoon genre.
Specialist in "Bande Dessinée" (cartoons).

GALERIE DANIEL GERVIS

14 rue de Grenelle, 75007 Paris ■ Tel: 45 44 41 90 - Fax: 45 49 18 98 ■ By appointment ■ English spoken ■ Prices medium ■ Professional discount

Modern and contemporary paintings, sculpture, lithographs, engravings in limited editions.

GALERIE MICHEL GILLET

54 av. de la Bourdonnais, 75007 Paris ■ Tel: 47 53 72 73 - Fax: 45 56 90 03 ■ Mon-Fri 10:00-19:00/Sat 14:00-19:00 ■ Michel Gillet speaks English ■ Prices reasonable ■ 10% professional discount

Contemporary figurative painting and sculpture.

GALERIE DE HESDIN

46 rue du Bac, 75007 Paris ■ Tel: 45 48 13 29 - Fax: 45 48 19 28 ■ Tues-Fri 10:30-13:00/14:00-19:00/Sat 13:00-19:00 ■ English spoken ■ Prices reasonable ■ 10% professional discount

Contemporary paintings, drawings, pastels by young artists, known and unknown.

KIN LIOU

81 rue du Bac, 75007 Paris ■ Tel: 45 48 80 85 - Fax: 42 84 32 78 ■ Tues-Sat 10:30-19:00/Mon 14:00-19:00 ■ English spoken ■ Prices medium

Paintings, unique art objects, bronze candlesticks, chandeliers in tole, XIII to XIX centuries. Small format furniture.

GALERIE SAMY KINGE

54 rue de Verneuil, 75007 Paris ■ Tel: 42 61 19 07 - Fax: 42 61 53 94 ■ Tues-Sat 14:30-19:00 ■ Samy Kinge speaks English ■ Prices medium ■ 15% professional discount

Modern post 1945 paintings, young contemporary artists. Surrealist and New Realist paintings.

♔ GALERIE LEEGENHOEK

23 quai Voltaire, 75007 Paris ■ Tel: 42 96 36 08 ■ Tues-Sat 14:30-18:30 ■ English spoken ■ Prices high

Old master paintings.

ANDRE LEMAIRE

43 rue de Verneuil, 75007 Paris ■ Tel: 42 61 12 55 ■ Tues-Sat 15:00-19:00 ■ Catherine Hamelin speaks English ■ Prices reasonable ■ Professional discount

XIX century paintings and sculpture, Official Academy art.

GALERIE MALTIER-VERCHER

48 rue de Verneuil, 75007 Paris ■ Tel: 47 03 37 46 ■ Tues-Fri 15:00-19:00 or by appointment ■ Christine Vercher speaks English ■ Prices medium ■ 10% professional discount

Paintings, sculpture, art objects of all periods, particularly the first half of the XX century.

♛ GALERIE MAEGHT

42 rue du Bac, 75007 Paris ■ Tel: 45 48 45 15 - Fax: 42 22 22 83 ■ Tues-Sat 10:00-13:00/14:00-19:00 ■ English spoken ■ Prices medium to high ■ Professional discount

Lithographs and engravings of Miró, Calder, Giacometti, Matisse and young artists. Art editions.

GALERIE MERCIER-DUCHEMIN-CHANOIT

40 rue de l'Université, 75007 Paris ■ Tel: 42 86 00 40 - Fax: 42 86 03 02 ■ Mon-Sat 10:00-12:30/14:00-19:00 ■ English spoken ■ Prices medium ■ 10% professional discount

Antique and modern paintings, drawings and sculpture.

GALERIE MONEGIER DU SORBIER

14 rue de Beaune, 75007 Paris ■ Tel: 42 61 69 00 - Fax: 42 61 32 28 ■ Mon-Sat 10:30-12:30/15:00-19:00 ■ English spoken ■ Prices medium ■ 10% professional discount

Paintings of the second half of the XIX century to the early XX century, especially from Provence.

GALERIE ANDRE-FRANÇOIS PETIT

196 bd Saint-Germain, 75007 Paris ■ Tel: 45 44 64 83 - Fax: 45 44 32 04 ■ Tues-Sat 10:30-12:00/14:30-18:30 ■ English spoken ■ Professional discount

Surrealistic and historical art.

DENISE RENE

196 bd Saint-Germain, 75007 Paris ■ Tel: 42 22 77 57 - Fax: 45 44 89 18 ■ Tues-Sat 10:00-13:00/14:00-19:00 ■ English spoken ■ Prices medium to high ■ Professional discount

Abstract art and art constructions.

GIANNA SISTU

29 rue de l'Université, 75007 Paris ■ Tel: 42 22 41 63 - Fax: 45 44 93 85 ■ Mon-Sat 10:00-19:00 ■ English spoken

Post impressionist, modern and contemporary art.

--------------------- VIII ---------------------

GALERIE ARIEL

140 bd Haussmann, 75008 Paris ■ Tel: 45 62 13 09 - Fax: 42 25 98 46 ■ Tues-Fri 10:00-12:30/14:30-18:30 ■ English spoken ■ Prices medium ■ Professional discount

Paintings of the Paris School, new figurative and abstract paintings, Cobra movement. Sculpture by Reinhoud and Subira-Puig.

ART ACTUEL

6 rue de Lisbonne, 75008 Paris ■ Tel: 45 22 01 66 - Fax: 42 93 76 01 ■ Mon-Thurs 9:00-13:00/14:00-18:00/Fri 9:00-13:00/14:00-17:00 ■ Hélène Patrick speaks English ■ Prices medium ■ Professional discount
Rental and sale of the works of contemporary artists, estampes, sculpture.

ARTCURIAL

9 av. Matignon, 75008 Paris ■ Tel: 42 99 16 16 - Fax: 43 59 29 81 ■ Tues-Sat 10:15-19:15 ■ English spoken ■ Prices high
Excellent quality modern and contemporary paintings and sculpture by living artists. Books.

ART FRANCE

36 av. Matignon, 75008 Paris ■ Tel: 43 59 17 89 - Fax: 45 63 84 83 ■ Mon-Sat 10:30-18:30 ■ Carole Senille and Claude Verrier speak English ■ 10 to 15% professional discount
Modern paintings, pastels, drawings, tapestries, sculpture, lithographs. Qualified expert with the Court of Appeals and the French Customs.

ARTS VIVANTS-GALERIE LANCRY

33 rue de Miromesnil, 75008 Paris ■ Tel: 42 66 16 48 - Fax: 42 66 16 30 ■ Mon-Fri 10:00-19:00 ■ Abraham Lancry speaks English ■ Prices medium ■ 25% professional discount on purchases over 20,000 FF
Figurative paintings by living painters. Sculptures and lithographs.

GALERIE ATELIER MATIGNON-LEANDRE QUESNEL

33 ter av. Matignon, 75008 Paris ■ Tel: 42 66 63 87 - Fax: 49 24 07 90 ■ Mon-Fri 15:00-18:00 and by appointment ■ English spoken ■ Prices high ■ Professional discount
Modern paintings. Specialist in Jean Dufy.

GALERIE JACQUES BAILLY

38 av. Matignon, 75008 Paris ■ Tel: 43 59 09 18 - Fax: 45 63 56 71 ■ Mon-Sat 10:00-12:30/14:30-18:30 ■ English spoken ■ Professional discount
Art of the second half of the xx century.

GALERIE BARLIER

36 rue de Penthièvre, 75008 Paris ■ Tel: 49 53 00 05 - Fax: 45 63 47 37 ■ Mon-Sat 10:30-13:00/14:30-19:00 ■ English spoken ■ Prices medium to high ■ Professional discount
Figurative art from the 1950s to the present.

GALERIE D'ART DE LA PLACE BEAUVEAU

94 rue du Faubourg-Saint-Honoré, 75008 Paris ■ Tel: 42 65 66 98 - Fax: 49 24 93 82 ■ Mon 14:00-19:00/Tues-Sat 10:30-19:00 ■ Régine Minet speaks English ■ Prices medium to high ■ 10% professional discount
Contemporary figurative paintings and sculpture.

♛ GALERIE HENRI BENEZIT

20 rue de Miromesnil, 75008 Paris ■ Tel: 42 65 54 56 ■ Mon-Sat 10:30-12:30/14:30-19:00 ■ Jean-Pierre Benezit speaks English ■ Prices medium to high ■ Professional discount

XIX, XX century paintings, drawings and sculpture.
Author of the "Dictionary E. Benezit".

GALERIE MARCEL BERNHEIM

18 av. Matignon, 75008 Paris ■ Tel: 42 65 22 23 - Fax: 42 65 27 16 ■ Mon-Fri 10:00-12:30/14:00-18:30 ■ English spoken ■ Prices high

Top quality Impressionist and Paris School paintings.

♛ GALERIE BERNHEIM-JEUNE

83 rue du Faubourg-Saint-Honoré, 75008 Paris ■ Tel: 42 66 65 03 ■ Tues-Sat 10:30-12:30/14:30-18:30 ■ English spoken ■ Prices high ■ Professional discount

Beautiful gallery with works of the Impressionists and present day artists. Painting and sculpture.

GALERIE PIERRE BIRTSCHANSKY

156 bd Haussmann, 75008 Paris ■ Tel: 45 62 88 86 - Fax: 42 89 41 97 ■ Mon-Fri 10:00-12:00/14:00-18:30/Sat by appointment ■ English spoken ■ Prices medium

Old Master paintings, contemporary artists.

GALERIE BOULAKIA

30 rue de Miromesnil, 75008 Paris ■ Tel: 47 42 55 51 ■ English spoken ■ Prices low to high ■ Professional discount

Modern and contemporary painting and sculpture.

GALERIE MICHELLE BOULET

14 rue La Boétie, 75008 Paris ■ Tel: 49 24 00 63 - Fax: 49 24 01 00 ■ Mon-Sat 11:00-19:00 ■ Michelle Boulet and Hulya Moray speak English ■ Prices medium to high ■ 15 to 35% professional discount

Paintings, drawings, lithographs, contemporary figurative sculpture, "trompe l'œil" paintings, still life and fantasy paintings.

GALERIE BRAME & LORENCEAU

68 bd Malesherbes, 75008 Paris ■ Tel: 45 22 16 89 - Fax: 45 22 01 67 ■ Mon-Fri 9:00-12:30/14:30-19:00 ■ English spoken ■ Prices high ■ Professional discount

Paintings, water colors, drawings, sculpture 1820 to 1920.

CAILLEUX

136 rue du Faubourg-Saint-Honoré, 75008 Paris ■ Tel: 43 59 25 24 - Fax: 42 25 95 11 ■ Mon-Fri 9:00-12:30/14:00-18:00 ■ English spoken ■ Prices medium to high ■ 10% professional discount

High quality XVIII century French paintings and drawings.

GALERIE CAPLAIN-MATIGNON

29 av. Matignon, 75008 Paris ■ Tel: 42 65 04 63 ■ Tues-Sat 10:30-13:00/14:30-19:00 ■ English spoken ■ Prices medium

Hyper-realistic contemporary paintings.

GALERIE LOUIS CARRE

10 av. de Messine, 75008 Paris ■ Tel: 45 62 57 07 - Fax: 42 25 63 89 ■ Mon-Fri 10:00-12:30/ 13:30-18:30 ■ English spoken ■ Prices high

Contemporary abstract painting and sculpture, drawings, water colors.

GALERIE JEANNE CASTEL

3 rue du Cirque, 75008 Paris ■ Tel: 43 59 71 24/42 25 55 63 - Fax: 43 59 52 31 ■ Mon-Fri 10:00-13:00/14:00-19:00 ■ Livia Raffin speaks English ■ Prices medium to high

Modern and contemporary paintings and sculpture.

GALERIE COLLE-GOBEAU

23 rue Jean-Mermoz, 75008 Paris ■ Tel: 42 89 49 64 ■ Mon-Fri 11:30-13:00/14:30-19:00 ■ English spoken ■ Prices low to medium ■ 10% professional discount

Modern and contemporary figurative painting, some XIX century paintings.

▦ GALERIE COLNAGHI

112 rue du Faubourg-Saint-Honoré, 75008 Paris ■ Tel: 42 66 14 51 - Fax: 42 66 23 95 ■ Mon-Fri 10:00-13:00/14:30-18:30 ■ English spoken ■ Prices high

Old Master paintings and drawings of the XIV to XIX centuries.

GALERIE JEAN COULON

32 av. Matignon, 75008 Paris ■ Tel: 42 66 30 80 - Fax: 42 66 96 16 ■ Mon-Fri 10:30-12:30/14:30-18:30 ■ English spoken ■ Prices high

Paintings of the Paris School.

LA CYMAISE

174 rue du Faubourg-Saint-Honoré, 75008 Paris ■ Tel: 42 89 50 20 ■ Mon-Fri 9:30-12:30/14:30-18:30 ■ Amaury de Louvencourt speaks English ■ Prices high ■ 10% professional discount

Sport paintings of the XIX and XX centuries.
Hunting, shooting, racing, polo, coaching.

GALERIE DELORME

21 rue de Miromesnil, 75008 Paris ■ Telfax: 42 66 25 20 ■ Mon-Fri 10:00-18:00 ■ Michel Delorme speaks English ■ Prices reasonable ■ Professional discount

Modern paintings.
Specializes in paintings of Provence and Spain.

GALERIE ELYSEE MATIGNON

28 av. Matignon, 75008 Paris ■ Tel: 47 42 16 88 - Fax: 47 42 20 10 ■ Mon-Sat 10:00-13:00/14:00-18:30 ■ Michel Giraud speaks English ■ Prices medium to high

Modern and contemporary paintings, sculpture, lithographs.

CHRISTIAN MEISSIREL FINE ART

91 bd Malesherbes, 75008 Paris ■ Tel: 42 25 98 85 - Fax: 42 25 98 87 ■ Mon-Fri 14:00-19:00/Mornings by appointment ■ English spoken ■ Prices medium ■ Professional discount

XIX century paintings. Specialty: Orientalist.

GALERIE ELYSEE MIROMESNIL

18 rue de Miromesnil, 75008 Paris ■ Tel: 47 42 50 80 ■ Mon-Fri 10:00-12:00/15:00-18:30/Sat 15:00-18:00 ■ Prices medium ■ Professional discount
Modern paintings and art objects.

GALERIE MATHIAS FELS

138 bd Haussmann, 75008 Paris ■ Tel: 45 62 21 34 ■ Tues-Fri 10:30-12:30/14:30-18:00/Sat 10:30-12:30 ■ Mathias Fels speaks English ■ Professional discount
Paintings of the "New Realists", figurative paintings, narrative and avant-garde paintings.

WALLY FINDLAY GALLERY

2 av. Matignon, 75008 Paris ■ Tel: 42 25 70 74 - Fax: 42 56 40 45 ■ Tues-Fri 10:00-13:00/14:00-19:00 ■ English spoken ■ Prices high ■ Professional discount
Contemporary paintings.

GALERIE FRANCE ET LA LITHOGRAPHIE

31 av. Matignon, 75008 Paris ■ Tel 42 66 34 42 - Fax: 42 66 93 59 ■ Mon 14:30-18:30/Tues-Sat 10:30-12:30/14:30-18:30 ■ English spoken ■ Prices medium ■ 15% professional discount
Lithographs and engravings of artists of the Paris School.
Works of painters who have worked in France between 1950 and the present. Young artists' drawings, paintings, water colors and lithographs.

GALERIE FRANCET

31 av. Matignon, 75008 Paris ■ Tel: 42 66 34 42 - Fax: 42 66 93 59 ■ Mon 14:30-19:30/Tues-Sat 10:30-12:30/14:30-18:30 ■ English spoken ■ Prices medium to high ■ Professional discount
Modern and contemporary estampes and contemporary paintings.

GALERIE ERIC GALFARD

2 rue de Messine, 75008 Paris ■ Tel: 45 62 45 60 ■ Tues-Sat 14:00-19:00 ■ English spoken ■ Prices low to medium ■ 10 to 30% professional discount
Contemporary paintings, engravings and sculpture.

GALERIE MAURICE GARNIER

6 av. Matignon, 75008 Paris ■ Tel: 42 25 61 65 - Fax: 45 61 12 33 ■ Tues-Fri 10:00-13:00/14:30-19:00/Sat until 18:00 ■ Philippe David speaks English ■ Prices medium ■ Professional discount
Works by Bernard Buffet exclusively.

GALERIE GUIGNE

89 rue du Faubourg-Saint-Honoré 75008 Paris ■ Tel: 42 66 66 88 - Fax: 49 24 99 96 ■ English spoken ■ Prices medium to high ■ Professional discount
Contemporary figurative painting and sculpture.

GALERIE FANNY GUILLON LAFFAILLE

4 av. de Messine, 75008 Paris ■ Tel: 45 63 52 00 - Fax: 45 61 92 91 ■ Mon-Fri 10:00-12:30/14:30-18:00/Sat by appointment ■ Bernard Guillon speaks English ■ Prices medium ■ 10% professional discount
Modern paintings. Specialist in Raoul Dufy.

♕ HABOLDT AND CO.

137 rue du Faubourg-Saint-Honoré, 75008 Paris ■ Tel: 42 89 84 63 - Fax: 42 89 58 81 ■ Mon-Fri 10:00-18:00/Sat 11:00-17:00■ Thaddee Prate speaks English ■ Prices high

High quality Old Master paintings and drawings.

GALERIE HERAUD

24 av. Matignon, 75008 Paris ■ Tel: 42 66 31 62 - Fax: 42 66 31 62 ■ Mon-Sat 10:00-19:00 ■ Prices responsible ■ Professional discount

Impressionist, Post Impressionist and modern paintings.

♕ GALERIE HOPKINS THOMAS

2 rue de Miromesnil, 75008 Paris ■ Tel: 42 65 51 05 - Fax: 42 66 90 28 ■ Mon-Fri 9:30-13:00/14:30-18:30 ■ Prices high

Impressionist and modern paintings.

♕ DIDIER IMBERT FINE ART

19 av. Matignon, 75008 Paris ■ Tel: 45 62 10 40 - Fax: 42 25 86 03 ■ Mon-Fri 10:00-13:00/14:30-19:00 ■ Gail Brenner speaks English ■ Prices high

Paintings, drawings and sculpture by masters of the XIX and XX centuries. Representative of the estate of Henry Moore. Representative of the Colombian Artist Fernando Botero. Department of antique fans.

GALERIE JEAN-PIERRE JOUBERT

18 av. Matignon, 75008 Paris ■ Tel: 42 65 00 79 - Fax: 47 42 63 87 ■ Tues-Sat 10:30-12:30/14:30-18:30 ■ English spoken ■ Prices medium ■ 10% professional discount

Paintings of the Paris School. Cubist, "reality/poetic" paintings. Sculpture by Volti.

GALERIE LAMBERT ROULON

62 rue La Boétie, 75008 Paris ■ Tel: 45 63 51 52 - Fax: 42 89 59 24 ■ Mon-Sat 10:00-19:00 ■ English spoken ■ Prices medium ■ Professional discount

Contemporary paintings.

GALERIE ROBIN LEADOUZE

2 av. Matignon, 75008 Paris ■ Tel: 42 89 26 83 - Fax: 42 89 27 03 ■ Mon-Sat 10:00-13:00/14:30-19:00 ■ Serge-Yamin Chocron speaks English ■ Prices high ■ Professional discount

Contemporary figurative paintings and sculpture.

GALERIE LOUISE LEIRIS

47 rue Monceau, 75008 Paris ■ Tel: 45 63 28 85 - Fax: 45 63 76 13 ■ Tues-Sat 10:00-12:00/14:30-18:00 ■ English spoken ■ Prices medium to high

Great names in modern art.

GALERIE LELONG

13-14 rue de Téhéran ■ Tel: 45 63 13 19 - Fax: 42 89 34 33 ■ Tues-Fri 10:30-18:00/Sat 14:00-18:30 ■ English spoken ■ Prices low to very high ■ Professional discount

Modern and contemporary paintings and sculpture.

GALERIE DANIEL MALINGUE

26 av. Matignon, 75008 Paris ■ Tel: 42 66 60 33 - Fax: 42 66 03 80 ■ Mon 14:30-18:30/Tues-Sat 10:30-12:30/14:30-18:30 ■ English spoken ■ Prices high ■ Professional discount

Impressionist and modern masters.

GALERIE MARBEAU

4 rue de Miromesnil, 75008 Paris ■ Telfax: 42 66 22 86 ■ Tues-Fri 10:00-13:00/14:30-19:00/Sat 13:00-19:00 ■ English spoken ■ Prices high ■ Professional discount

Great names in modern and contemporary painting and sculpture with a leaning towards the abstract.

GALERIE BRUNO MARTIN-CAILLE

34 rue du Faubourg-Saint-Honoré, 75008 Paris ■ Tel: 42 65 27 50 - Fax: 40 17 04 40 ■ Mon-Fri 10:00-12:00/14:00-18:00 ■ English spoken ■ Prices high ■ Professional discount

Specializes in the great name painters of the XIX and XX centuries.

GALERIE MARTIN-CAILLE MATIGNON

75 rue du Faubourg-Saint-Honoré, 75008 Paris ■ Tel: 42 66 60 71 - Fax: 47 42 55 48 ■ Mon-Fri 9:30-19:00/Sat 10:30-13:00/15:00-19:00 ■ English, Spanish and German spoken ■ Prices medium to high. Pastels start at $2,500 and oils between $8,000 and $40,000. ■ Professional discount

Contemporary Impressionism by Max Agostini.

GALERIE MARTIN-ISHIHARA

62 rue La Boétie, 75008 Paris ■ Tel: 45 61 04 01 - Fax: 42 56 19 95 ■ Mon-Fri 10:00-12:30/15:00-18:30 ■ English spoken

Modern paintings.

GALERIE MATIGNON SAINT-HONORÉ

34 av. Matignon, 75008 Paris ■ Tel: 43 59 38 88 - Fax: 45 61 20 39 ■ Mon-Fri 10:00-19:00/Sat 13:00-19:00 ■ English spoken ■ Prices medium to high ■ Professional discount

Paintings of the Paris School, Vlaminck, Utrillo, etc., XX century painters, Buffet, Kisling.

GALERIE VERONIQUE MAXE

33 av. Matignon, 75008 Paris ■ Tel: 47 42 02 52 - Fax: 42 66 28 34 ■ Mon-Fri 14:30-18:30 ■ Véronique Maxe and Albert Benamou speak English ■ Prices medium to high ■ 3 to 10% professional discount

XIX and XX century sculpture and painting.
Experts in XIX century sculpture: Rodin, Camille Claudel, Dalon, Carpeaux, Brigotti, etc.

GALERIE MATIGNON

18 av. Matignon, 75008 Paris ■ Tel: 42 66 60 32 - Fax: 42 66 48 74 ■ Mon-Fri 10:00-13:00/14:30-18:30/Open Sat for exhibitions ■ English spoken ■ Prices high ■ Professional discount

Impressionist and Post Impressionist painters, Picasso, Chagall, Buffet, Jansem. Sculpture of Bourdelle.

GALERIE MERMOZ

6 rue du Cirque, 75008 Paris ■ Tel: 42 25 42 49 - Fax: 40 75 03 90 ■ English spoken ■ Prices medium to high

Pre-Columbian specialists, North and South America.

👑 GALERIE YVES MIKAELOFF

10 & 14 rue Royale, 75008 Paris ■ Tel: 42 61 64 42 - Fax: 49 27 07 32 ■ Mon-Sat 10:00-19:00 ■ Yves Mikaeloff and Nicolas Joly speak English ■ Prices high ■ Professional discount

High quality Old Master paintings and drawings. Antique furniture, carpets and tapestries.

GALERIE ENRICO NAVARRA

75 rue du Faubourg-Saint-Honoré, 75008 Paris ■ Tel: 47 42 65 66 - Fax: 42 66 21 36 ■ Mon-Fri 10:30-19:00 ■ English spoken ■ Prices high

Specialty: Marc Chagall, Jean-Michel Bastia and others.

GALERIE NICHIDO

61 rue du Faubourg-Saint-Honoré, 75008 Paris ■ Tel: 42 66 62 86 - Fax: 42 66 91 97 ■ Mon-Sat 10:00-12:30/13:30-18:00 ■ English spoken ■ Prices low to medium ■ Professional discount

Contemporary Japanese, French and American paintings, water colors, lithographs. Sometimes sculpture.

LES OREADES

52 rue de Moscou, 75008 Paris ■ Tel: 43 87 59 20 - Fax: 43 87 99 20 ■ Mon-Sat 11:00-19:00 and by appointment ■ Edmond Rosenfeld speaks English ■ Prices medium ■ Professional discount

Russian and French paintings of the XIX and XX centuries.
Specialty: Russian paintings, water colors and drawings. Organizes expositions of paintings with Russian provenance.

GALERIE PETRIDES

63 rue du Faubourg-Saint-Honoré, 75008 Paris ■ Tel: 42 66 42 32 ■ Mon-Fri 9:30-12:00/14:00-17:45 ■ English and German spoken ■ Prices medium to high

The grand XX century painters, especially Utrillo and Valadon, Vlaminck, Fujita, Laurencin, Dufy, Kisling, Buffet, Van Dongen, Renoir, Picasso, Hamburg, Lorjou, Rouault, Léger, etc. Sculpture: Michel Tardy, Corzou.

GALERIE DE LA PRESIDENCE

90 rue du Faubourg-Saint-Honoré, 75008 Paris ■ Tel: 42 65 49 60 - Fax: 49 24 94 27 ■ Mon-Sat 10:00-13:00/14:30-19:00 ■ English spoken ■ Prices of the market ■ Professional discount

Late XIX and early XX century Post Impressionist painters.

RENOU & POYET

164 rue du Faubourg Saint-Honoré, 75008 Paris ■ Tel: 43 59 35 95 - Fax: 42 56 24 29 ■ Mon-Fri 9:30-12:30/14:30-18:30 ■ Maurice Covo speaks English ■ Prices high ■ 10 to 15% professional discount

Impressionist and modern masters of painting.
Qualified expert in French and Spanish Schools.

GALERIE ETIENNE SASSI

14 av. Matignon, 75008 Paris ■ Tel: 42 25 64 77 - Fax: 42 25 22 71 ■ Mon-Fri 10:00-13:00/14:30-18:30 ■ English spoken ■ Prices medium ■ Professional discount

Impressionist, Post Impressionist paintings, sculpture and ceramics.

GALERIE JOHN SAYEGH

178 rue du Faubourg-Saint-Honoré, 75008 Paris ■ Tel: 42 25 76 21 - Fax: 45 62 02 99 ■ Mon 14:30-19:00/Tues-Sat 10:30-19:00 ■ John Sayegh speaks English ■ Prices very high

Impressionist and modern paintings and sculpture. Picasso, Laurencin, Zempicka, Modigliani, Kisling, Rodin, Maillol.

GALERIE SORDELLO

25 rue de Penthièvre, 75008 Paris ■ Tel: 42 25 41 62 - Fax: 40 75 01 59 ■ Mon-Sat 10:00-19:00 ■ Meg and Marc Sordello speak English ■ Prices medium to high ■ 10% professional discount

Contemporary art glass. Major French and international masters of art in glass.

TAMENAGA

18 av. Matignon, 75008 Paris ■ Tel: 42 66 68 94 - Fax: 47 42 99 14 ■ Mon-Sat 10:00-19:00 ■ English spoken ■ Prices very high ■ Professional discount

Impressionist masters and modern painters. Currently featuring Aizpiri, Bardone, Cottavoz, Fusaro, Guiramond, Haijima, Weisbuch.

UNIVERS DU BRONZE

29 rue de Penthièvre, 75008 Paris ■ Tel: 42 56 50 30 ■ Mon-Sat 10:30-12:30/14:00-19:00 ■ English spoken ■ Prices medium ■ 20% professional discount

XIX and XX century sculpture in bronze: Barye, Mene, Frémiet, Pradier, Renoir. Exclusivity with Busato-Hogomatt.

──────────── IX ────────────

GALERIE AITTOUARES

10 rue de la Grange-Batelière, 75009 Paris ■ Near the Drouot Auction House and Musée Grévin ■ Tel: 45 23 41 13 - Fax: 42 47 03 90 ■ Mon-Fri 10:00-13:00/14:00-18:00 ■ Prices medium ■ Professional discount

Quality Impressionist paintings and drawings. Abstract, Cubist and Surrealist art of the early XX century.
Sculpture in bronze by César, Rodin, Daumier. Water colors and works on paper. Drawings of Rodin and Carpeaux.

NORBERT BOUTET

9 rue de la Grange-Batelière, 75009 Paris ■ Tel: 44 79 03 71 - Fax: 48 00 00 76 ■ Mon-Fri 10:00-13:00/14:00-18:30 ■ English spoken ■ Prices medium ■ Professional discount

Paintings by XVIII and XIX century masters, primitive art, objects of curiosity.

GALERIE AKIE ARICHHI

26 rue Keller, 75011 Paris ■ Tel: 40 21 64 37 - Fax: 42 74 26 60 ■ Tues-Sat 13:00-19:00 ■ Akie Arichhi speaks English ■ Prices reasonable

Contemporary paintings, sculpture, lithographs, engravings.

GALERIE ART CONTEMPORAIN J. & J. DONGUY

57 rue de la Roquette, 75011 Paris ■ Tel: 47 00 10 94 - Fax: 40 21 83 84 ■ Tues-Sat 13:00-19:00 ■ Jacques Donguy and Anne Mortley speak English ■ Prices medium to high ■ Professional discount

Contemporary art, painting, objects, visual poetry, space for artistic activity, expositions, exhibitions of new visual technologies.

ARTCODIS

5 rue de Charonne, 75011 Paris ■ Tel: 47 00 80 43 - Fax: 47:00 60 18 ■ Mon-Sat by appointment only ■ Hubert Cuille speaks English ■ Prices medium ■ 10 to 20% professional discount

Engravings, lithographs, seriographs, of well known contemporary French and international artists in limited editions.

GALERIE CLAIRE BURRUS

16 rue de Lappe, 75011 Paris ■ Tel: 43 55 36 90 - Fax: 47 00 26 03 ■ Tues-Fri 14:00-19:00/Sat 11:00-19:00 ■ English spoken ■ Prices medium ■ Professional discount

Contemporary painting, sculpture, installations, video.

GALERIE LILIANE AND MICHEL DURAND-DESSERT

28 rue de Lappe, 75011 Paris ■ Tel: 48 06 92 23 - Fax: 48 06 92 24 ■ Tues-Fri 11:00-13:00/15:00-19:00/Sat 11:00-19:00 ■ Mr. Robin speaks English

Large collection of modern and contemporary painters.

GALERIE LA FERRONNERIE

40 rue de la Folie-Méricourt, 75011 Paris ■ Tel: 48 06 50 84 ■ Tues-Thurs 14:00-20:00/Wed/Fri/Sat 13:30-19:00 ■ Brigitte Negrier speaks English ■ Prices medium

Contemporary young artists, paintings, engravings, seriographs, sculptures.

GALERIE ALAIN GUTHARC

47 rue de Lappe, 75011 Paris ■ Tel: 47 00 32 10 - Fax: 40 21 72 74 ■ Tues-Fri 14:00-19:00/Sat 11:00-19:00 ■ Alain Gutharc speaks English ■ Prices medium

Contemporary paintings, sculpture, installations and photography.

GALERIE JOUSSE SEGUIN

34 rue de Charonne, 75011 Paris ■ Tel: 47 00 32 35 - Fax: 40 21 82 95 ■ Mon 15:00-19:00/Tues-Sat 11:00-13:30/14:30-19:00 ■ Laurence Bergerot speaks English ■ Prices medium ■ 10% professional discount

Contemporary art. Art Appliqué of the 1950s. Furniture by Jean Prouvé, Charlotte Perriand, Jean Royère.

K ART

45 rue Amelot, 75011 Paris ■ Tel: 40 21 09 32 ■ Mon-Sat 11:00-19:00 ■
Simone Kervern speaks English ■ Prices medium ■ Professional discount
Contemporary abstract paintings and sculpture.

GALERIE LAVIGNES BASTILLE

27 rue de Charonne, 75011 Paris ■ Tel: 47 00 88 18 - Fax: 43 55 91 32 ■
Tues-Sat 11:00-19:00 ■ Jean-Pierre Lavignes speaks English ■ Prices medium ■ Professional discount
Contemporary paintings, drawings and sculpture.

GALERIE OZ

15 rue Keller, 75011 Paris ■ Tel: 47 00 66 23 - Fax: 47 00 44 63 ■ Tues-Sun
15:00-19:30 ■ Jean-Luc Richard speaks English ■ Prices medium
Contemporary art. Contemporary baroque art. Post cards.

GALERIE PRAZ-DELAVALLADE

10 rue Saint-Sabin, 75011 Paris ■ Tel: 43 38 52 60 - Fax:43 38 45 02 ■ Tues-Sat 14:00-19:00 ■ English spoken ■ Prices medium ■ Professional discount
Contemporary painting and sculpture by young living artists, installations.

GALERIE DE TUGNY LAMARRE

5 rue de Charonne, 75011 Paris ■ Tel: 48 05 84 16 - Fax: 40 21 82 95 ■ Tues-Sat 14:00-19:00 ■ Florence de Tugny speaks English ■ Prices medium ■ 10%
professional discount
Contemporary painting, sculpture, photography.
Contemporary furniture by artists.

───────────────── **XII** ─────────────────

GALERIE METEO

4 rue Saint-Nicolas, 75012 Paris ■ Tel: 43 42 20 20 - Fax: 43 42 30 20 ■ Tues-Sat 14:30-19:30 ■ Prices reasonable ■ 20% professional discount
Contemporary art.

───────────────── **XIII** ─────────────────

SERGE BENOIT

Cité Fleurie, Atelier # 25 ■ 65 bd Arago, 75013 Paris ■ Tel: 43 31 80 74 ■
Tues-Sat 10:00-12:00/14:00-18:00 ■ Prices medium ■ 20% professional discount
The atelier sells only the paintings and sculpture of Serge Benoit, the artist
and owner.

───────────────── **XIV** ─────────────────

ART 14

3 rue Edouard-Jacques, 75014 Paris ■ Tel: 43 27 52 85 ■ Tues-Sat 14:00-19:00 ■ Farouk Bey Boumezrag speaks English ■ Prices medium
Contemporary painters, engravers and sculptors. Artisans of art.

GALATEE GALLERY

132-136 bd du Montparnasse, 75014 Paris ■ Tel: 43 20 22 35 or 30 36 73 68 ■ Tues-Sat 14:30-18:00 ■ Fernando and Yvette Gualtieri speak English ■ Prices high

This studio/gallery sells the work of Fernando Gualtieri exclusively. Gualtieri is an artist who paints realistic, poetic paintings. He also does trompe l'œil on order.

ORIGAMI

138 bd du Montparnasse, 75014 Paris ■ Tel: 43 20 49 14 - Fax: 43 35 41 14 ■ Mon-Fri 9:00-19:00 by appointment only ■ Françoise Echard speaks English ■ Prices medium ■ 10 to 20% professional discount

Contemporary paintings, tapestries and Origami sculptures.

GALERIE ROBERT MARTIN

234 bd Raspail, 75014 Paris ■ Tel: 45 61 04 41 - Fax: 42 56 19 95 ■ Mon-Sat 10:00-12:30/15:00-18:30 ■ Sandra Jonquières speaks English

Modern paintings.

───────────────── **XV** ─────────────────

LA GALERIE D'ART

102 rue Cambronne, 75015 Paris ■ Tel: 42 73 19 99 ■ Tues-Sat 10:30-13:00/14:30-19:30 ■ Danielle Feinstein speaks English ■ Prices medium ■ 10% professional discount

Contemporary classic paintings, landscape, still life, flowers, water colors, pastels. Also frames and framing.

GALERIE GUY LECOMTE

49 av. de la Motte-Picquet, 75015 Paris ■ Tel: 47 34 73 02 - Fax: 47 34 16 65 ■ Tues-Sat 10:30-13:00/15:30-19:00 ■ Guy Lecomte speaks English ■ Prices medium ■ 10% professional discount

Contemporary "Figurative" paintings and art objects.

MARIE-THERESE PEYRALADE

54 bis av. de la Motte-Picquet, 75015 Paris ■ Tel: 47 34 69 94 ■ Thurs-Mon 14:00-19:00 ■ English spoken ■ Prices medium ■ 20% professional discount

XIX and early XX century paintings.

I. S. THOMAS GALERIE

46 av. de Suffren, 75015 Paris ■ Tel: 45 67 13 46 - Fax: 45 67 33 16 ■ Tues-Sat 15:00-19:00 and by appointment ■ Ives Thomas speaks English ■ Prices reasonable ■ 10% professional discount

Contemporary French, Spanish, American and Japanese artists.

───────────────── **XVI** ─────────────────

ART D'ASIE

4 av. Bugeaud, 75116 Paris ■ Tel: 45 53 77 48 - Fax: 47 55 02 52 ■ Tues-Sat 10:30-19:00 ■ Some English spoken ■ Prices medium ■ Professional discount

Sculpture from China, Japan, India, Thailand, Southeast Asia.

GALERIE CAPAZZA

100 av. Président-Kennedy, 75016 Paris ■ Tel: 42 24 50 30 ■ By appointment only ■ Gérard and Sophie Capazza speak English ■ Prices medium to high ■ 10% professional discount

Contemporary painting, sculpture and art objects.
NOTE: They also have a Gallery in Sologne. It's worth a visit if you are passing by.

GILLES DIDIER

38 rue Boileau, 75016 Paris ■ Tel: 40 71 04 41 - Fax: 47 43 09 68 ■ Every day by appointment ■ English spoken ■ Prices low to very high ■ Professional discount

Expert and dealer in antique and contemporary posters. Specialist in Cassandre, Lautrec and Cheret.

GALERIE NORBERT HANSE

38 av. Victor-Hugo, 75016 Paris ■ Tel: 45 01 88 40 ■ Mon-Sat 10:30-12:30/15:00-19:00 ■ English spoken ■ Prices medium ■ Professional discount

Contemporary figurative paintings and sculpture, 1950s to the present.

GALERIE JALLES & CIE

14 av. Pierre-1er-de-Serbie, 75016 Paris ■ Tel: 47 20 80 21 ■ Every day by appointment ■ English spoken ■ Prices medium to high: 5,000 to 200,000 francs ■ Professional discount

Paintings of African and Oriental subjects by occidental artists. Water colors and drawings. Africanist and Orientalist art.

--- XVII ---

GALERIE SERGE GARNIER

12 bd de Courcelles, 75017 Paris ■ Tel: 47 63 06 46 ■ Mon-Fri 13:00-19:00/Sat AM by appointment ■ English spoken ■ Prices medium ■ Professional discount

Contemporary and modern paintings.

GALERIE LAHUMIERE

88 bd de Courcelles, 75017 Paris ■ Tel: 47 63 03 95 - Fax: 40 53 00 78 ■ Tues-Fri 9:30-13:00/14:00-18:30/Sat 11:00-18:00 ■ Anne Lahumiere speaks English ■ Prices medium ■ 10 to 30% professional discount

Modern and contemporary paintings, sculpture, estampes.

GALERIE NUNKI

12 rue de Tocqueville, 75017 Paris ■ Tel: 42 27 60 84 ■ Mon-Sat 11:00-19:30 ■ Claude Cussac speaks English ■ Prices medium ■ 25% professional discount

Contemporary paintings. Specialist in visionary art and paintings of fantasy: Bosch, Durer, Dali, Fini, Di Maccio, Panzetta.

GALERIE SAPHIR RIVE DROITE

69 av. de Villiers, 75017 Paris ■ Tel: 44 40 26 84 - Fax: 43 80 23 49 ■ Sun-Thurs 14:00-19:00 ■ English spoken ■ Prices medium ■ Professional discount

XIX and XX century paintings, drawings, lithographs, beautiful old books, old Jewish art.

GALERIE VARINE GINCOURT

110 bd de Courcelles, 75017 Paris ■ Tel: 42 27 20 16 ■ Tues-Sat 11:00-19:00/Mon 14:30-19:00 ■ English spoken ■ Prices medium ■ 5 to 10% professional discount

xx century figurative paintings, engravings, drawings, lithographs, water colors, sculpture.

—————————————— XVIII ——————————————

GALERIE DU CHEVALIER ET DES COLLECTIONNEURS

42 rue Chevalier-de-la-Barre, 75018 Paris ■ Tel: 42 64 84 93 - Fax: 42 57 40 73 ■ Mon-Sun 10:30-18:30 ■ English spoken ■ Prices reasonable ■ 20 to 30% professional discount

Classic and modern paintings.

GALERIE D'ART CHRISTINE DIEGONI

47 ter rue d'Orsel, 75018 Paris ■ Tel: 42 64 69 48 ■ Tues-Sat 14:00-19:00 and by appointment ■ Prices medium to high ■ Professional discount

Decorative arts of the xx century, ceramics, furniture, art objects, 1930s to 1970.

ESSENTIEL

Art d'aujourd'hui ■ 9 rue Ravignan, 75018 Paris ■ Tel: 42 57 37 40 ■ Tues-Sat 11:00-19:00 ■ Isabelle Clayette speaks English ■ Prices medium

Contemporary artists: water colors, ceramic, wood, glass, leather, marble, terra cotta.

ANDRE ROUSSARD

13 rue du Mont-Cenis, 75018 Paris ■ Tel: 46 06 30 46 - Fax: 42 52 38 00 ■ Mon-Sun 11:00-20:00 ■ English spoken ■ Prices reasonable to high ■ 10 to 30% professional discount

xx century paintings, original and exclusive lithographs, estampes, books, catalogues and posters. Specialty: painters who worked in Montmartre. Restoration and framing.

TRANSPARENCE

42 rue Caulaincourt, 75018 Paris ■ Telfax: 42 23 74 45 ■ Tues-Sat 10:30-12:30/14:30-19:30 ■ Marie Savary speaks English ■ 20% professional discount

xix, xx century paintings.

—————————————— XIX ——————————————

GALERIE LEONARDO

62 rue de Hautpoul, 75019 Paris ■ Tel: 42 40 13 11 ■ Mon-Sat 11:00-19:00/Closed Wed ■ English spoken ■ Prices medium 5,000 to 30,000 francs ■ Professional discount

Sculpture in exclusivity: Brazilian - Moreira, American - Kurhajec. Paintings by Milet, Bajalska, Guanse.

ART FACTS

145 rue Pelleport, 75020 Paris ■ Tel: 43 58 62 04 - Fax: 43 58 62 83 ■ By appointment ■ English spoken ■ 10 to 20% professional discount
Post war and contemporary prints, works on paper and illustrated books.

GALERIE ART ET PRESTIGE

9 cours de Vincennes, 75020 Paris ■ 80 Galeries Nation (Level 1) ■ Tel: 40 09 03 62 ■ Tues-Sat 11:00-19:00 ■ English spoken ■ Prices medium to high ■ Professional discount
Contemporary painting and sculpture.

Special categories of art

———————————————— AFRICAN ART ————————————————

NAST A PARIS

10 rue d'Alger, 75001 Paris ■ Tel: 47 03 34 74 - Fax: 42 61 23 87 ■ Tues-Sat 14:00-18:30 ■ Jean-Claude Reveillaud speaks English ■ Prices high ■ 15% professional discount
Black African art: modern and contemporary paintings and sculpture. Specialty: art of Zaïre.

GALERIE SCHAUER

153 rue Saint-Martin, 75003 Paris ■ Tel: 48 87 81 71 ■ Wed-Sat 11:00-13:00/14:00-19:00 ■ English spoken ■ Professional discount
African and Arab painting and sculpture. (Installations).

YVES DEVELON

11 rue Charles-V, 75004 Paris ■ Tel: 42 78 00 55 - Fax: 48 04 01 08 ■ By appointment only ■ English spoken ■ Prices very high ■ 15% professional discount
Antique African art.

GALERIE HELENE ET PHILIPPE LELOUP

9 quai Malaquais, 75006 Paris ■ Tel: 42 60 75 91 - Fax: 42 61 45 94 ■ Tues-Sat 10:30-12:30/14:00-19:00 ■ English spoken ■ Prices high
Unique art objects of black Africa, Oceania, Indonesia. Pre-Columbian art.

BABACAR BADIANE

14 rue Claude-Tillier, 75012 Paris ■ Tel: 40 24 03 42 ■ Mon 14:00-18:00/Tues-Sun 10:00-18:00 ■ Babacar Badiane speaks English ■ Prices medium ■ 10% professional discount
Paintings, art objects, drums and musical instruments, sculpture, contemporary and traditional, of Black Africa.

GALERIE URUBAMBA

4 rue de la Bûcherie, 75005 Paris ■ Tel: 43 54 08 24 - Fax: 43 29 91 80 ■ Tues-Sat 14:00-19:30 ■ Roberta Rivin speaks English ■ Prices medium

Art objects relating to or created by Indians of the Americas. Books in English and French on the theme of American Indians.

AUTOMOBILE ART

GALERIE ACTEON

8 rue de Beaune, 75007 Paris ■ Tel: 42 61 23 43 - Fax: 42 61 00 58 ■ Mon-Sat 15:00-19:00 or by appointment ■ English spoken ■ Professional discount

Automobile art, aviation, architectural, locomotion, everything that moves or flies, in drawings, paintings or models.

GALERIE VITESSE

48 rue de Berri, 75008 Paris ■ Tel: 42 25 48 13 - Fax: 48 25 06 04 ■ Mon-Sat 12:30-19:00 ■ Isabelle Nicolosi speaks English ■ Prices medium ■ 5% professional discount

Paintings, sculpture, lithographs on the themes of automobiles and aviation. Rentals for advertising and film productions.

CHRISTIAN AZAIS

48 rue Jean-Longuet, 92220 Bagneux ■ Tel: 47 74 89 58 - Fax: 40 90 97 09 ■ Mon-Sat 10:00-20:00 ■ English spoken ■ 20% professional discount

Paintings and art objects on the theme of automobiles. Antique arms, antique cars.

CINEMA ART

INTEMPORAL

22 rue Saint-Martin, 75004 Paris ■ Tel: 42 72 55 41 - Fax: 42 72 29 25 ■ Tues-Sat 11:30-19:00 ■ Stanislas Choko speaks English ■ 10% professional discount

Film posters and collectibles related to the film world before 1970.

LES FEUX DE LA LAMPE
LIBRAIRIE DU CINÉMA

2 rue de Luynes, 75007 Paris ■ Tel: 45 48 80 97 ■ Tues-Sat 11:00-13:00/14:30-19:00 ■ English spoken ■ Prices medium

Film posters, old and new books, photos, old movie magazines. Everything that concerns the world of cinema.

MARINE AND OCEAN ART

ARTS ET MARINE

8 rue de Miromesnil, 75008 Paris ■ Tel: 42 65 27 85 - Fax: 42 65 30 51 ■ Tues-Frj 11:00-19:00/Sat 14:00-18:00 ■ English spoken ■ Prices medium

XVIII and XIX century marine paintings, estampes, models, arms, instruments, books on marine themes.

GALERIE MEYER

17 rue des Beaux-Arts, 75006 Paris ■ Tel: 43 54 85 74 - Fax: 43 54 11 12 ■
Mon-Sat 10:30-13:00/14:30-19:00 ■ English spoken ■ Professional discount
Primitive art of Oceania: Australia, Melanesia, Micronesia, Polynesia.

———————————— **PHOTO ART** ————————————

GALERIE AGATHE GAILLARD

3 rue du Pont-Louis-Philippe, 75004 Paris ■ Tel: 42 77 38 24 - Fax:
42 77 78 36 ■ Tues-Sat 13:00-19:00 ■ Agathe Gaillard speaks English
Photo art after 1945.

GALERIE ZABRISKIE

37 rue Quincampoix, 75004 Paris ■ Tel: 42 72 35 47 - Fax: 40 27 99 66 ■
Tues-Sat 14:00-19:00 ■ Editha Carpenter speaks English
Photo gallery which also sells contemporary painting and sculpture.

GALERIE CONTREJOUR

96 rue Daguerre, 75014 Paris ■ Tel: 43 21 41 88 - Fax: 43 20 49 45 ■ Tues-
Fri 13:00-19:00/Sat 14:00-20:00 ■ Christel Broussous speaks English ■
Prices medium ■ Professional discount
Photo art and photo collectibles. Books, photo magazines, post-cards, cal-
endars on photography. High quality photo lab for amateur and professional
photographers. Reproductions on metal using old techniques.

———————————— **SPORTS ART** ————————————

ART VIE

69 rue des Entrepreneurs, 75015 Paris ■ Tel: 45 79 60 60 ■ Mon-Sat 9:00-
20:00 ■ Prices medium ■ 10 to 20% professional discount
Paintings, drawings, water colors, estampes, and art objects related to
sports.

LA CYMAISE

174 rue du Faubourg-Saint-Honoré, 75008 Paris ■ Tel: 42 89 50 20 ■ Mon-
Fri 9:30-12:30/14:30-18:30 ■ Amaury de Louvencourt speaks English ■
Prices high ■ 10% professional discount
Sport paintings of the XIX and XX centuries.
Hunting, shooting, racing, polo, coaching.

ST. DALFOUR

IMPORTED FROM FRANCE

All Natural Conserves
Pure Fruit　No Sugar Added

Here is a major culinary achievement. Gifts of nature elevated by French chefs into all natural conserves. At the same time both delectable and nutritious. St. Dalfour Conserves are made in the heart of the French countryside by a old recipe from the Loire Valley. They are pure fruit. No sugar is added. Only the natural sweetness of concentrated grape juice is used. This natural sweetness produces a taste which is much fresher and delicious than the heavy taste of sugar.

ART NOUVEAU/ART DECO

BAIN ROSE

11 rue d'Assas, 75006 Paris ■ Tel: 42 22 55 85 - Fax: 42 22 35 94 ■ Tues-Sat 10:30-13:00/14:00-18:30 ■ English spoken ■ Prices high ■ 10 to 15% professional discount

Bathrooms of 1900 to 1930. Antique and reproduction basins, furniture, faience for the bath in Art Nouveau/Art Deco styles.

GALERIE DUO

15 rue de Lille, 75007, Paris ■ Tel: 47 03 92 63 - Fax: 42 61 67 90 ■ Tues-Fri 14:00-19:00 and by appointment ■ English spoken ■ Prices medium ■ 10% professional discount

Excellent collection of Art Nouveau and Art Deco: furniture, lighting and objects. No glass.

GALERIE LANDROT

5 rue Jacques-Callot, 75006 Paris ■ Tel: 43 26 71 13 ■ Mon-Sat 14:30-19:00 ■ Gérard and Dominique Landrot speak English ■ 10 to 15% professional discount

Art Deco ceramics of Chagall, Matisse, Maillol. Early xx century sculpture and paintings.

GALERIE FELIX MARCILHAC

8 rue Bonaparte, 75006 Paris ■ Tel: 43 26 47 36 - Fax: 46 05 01 58 ■ Mon-Sat 10:00-19:00 ■ English spoken ■ Prices high ■ Professional discount

Art Nouveau, Art Deco furniture, objects. Symbolist and Orientalist paintings, glass and ceramics of 1900 to 1925.

1900 MONCEAU ANTIQUITES

62 bd Malesherbes, 75008 Paris ■ Tel: 43 87 92 80 ■ Mon-Fri 10:00-18:30 ■ English spoken ■ Prices medium ■ Professional discount

Art Deco furniture and objects. Larger choice in their shop in the Marché aux Puces, (Biron stand 44, Allée 1).

NOIR EBENE

5 rue Brea, 75006 Paris ■ Tel: 46 34 72 93 ■ Mon 15:00-19:00/Tues-Sat 11:00-13:00/15:00-19:00 ■ English spoken ■ Prices medium ■ 10% professional discount

Art Deco furniture (1930-1940) bars, chairs, desks, glass, enamels, lamps, objects.

LE ROI FOU

182 rue du Faubourg-Saint-Honoré, 75008 Paris ■ Tel: 45 63 82 59 - Fax: 45 63 40 57 ■ Tues-Sat 10:30-18:30 ■ English spoken ■ Prices medium to high ■ 10% professional discount

Superb choice of Art Deco and Art Nouveau furniture, lamps, chandeliers, sconces, bronzes.

STUDIO SAINT-SULPICE

3 rue Saint-Sulpice, 75006 Paris ■ Tel: 40 51 06 33 ■ Mon-Sat 13:00-19:00 and by appointment ■ English spoken ■ Prices medium ■ Professional discount

Art Deco furniture, mirrors, lamps, objects.

GALERIE VALLOIS

41 rue de Seine, 75006 Paris ■ Tel: 43 29 50 55 - Fax: 43 29 90 73 ■ Mon 14:00-19:00/Tues-Sat 10:00-13:00/14:00-19:00 ■ English spoken ■ Prices high ■ Professional discount

A fine collection of Art Deco furniture and objects: Ruhlmann, Dunand, Printz, Rateau, Chareau, Sue & Mare, Iribe, Eileen Gray, Franck.

GALERIE JACQUES DE VOS

34 rue de Seine, 75006 Paris ■ Tel: 43 26 29 26 ■ 7 rue Bonaparte ■ Tel: 43 29 88 94 - Fax: 40 46 95 45 ■ Mon-Sat 10:30-13:00/14:00-19:00 ■ English spoken ■ Prices high ■ 10% professional discount

The two galleries specialize in Art Deco furniture and art objects of 1920-1940. Furniture of Ruhlmann, Frank, Chareau, Printz. Sculptures of Lambert-Rucki and Csaky.

IMPRIMERIE UNION

ART PRINTERS
Imprimeries d'art

BUSSIERE

21 rue de Châtillon, 75014 Paris■Tel: 45 41 52 60 - Fax: 40 44 69 22■Mon-Fri 7:00-22:00■English spoken■Prices medium■5 to 10% professional discount

Very high quality full printing services for museums, galleries, corporations, individuals. Photo composition and photogravure. Catalogues and art books.

IMPRIMERIE UNION

84 av. de la République, 94700 Maisons-Alfort ■ Tel: 43 78 52 52 - Fax: 43 53 19 20■Mon-Fri 9:00-18:00■English spoken■Prices medium■Professional discount

High quality, printing of books, art books, catalogues, brochures, posters. Excellent service. Their customers include the top galleries, the National Museums, cultural institutions and corporations. They specialize in bichromie (2 color process) and produce superb reproductions of art and high definition black & white photography as well as full color.

Photograph by Pierre Gaudin

ART REPRODUCTIONS
Reproductions d'art

ERMITAGE

32 bis rue de la Voûte, 75012 Paris ■ Tel: 43 45 39 43 - Fax: 43 43 97 74 ■ Mon-Fri 9:00-18:00 ■ Pascal Lamoglia speaks English ■ Prices low ■ Professional discount

Copies of master painters by hand using the same techniques as originally executed works. Gilded wood frames.

MUSEUM COLLECTION

14 rue de Castiglione, 75001 Paris ■ Tel: 42 97 43 11 - Fax: 46 94 11 10 ■ Mon-Fri 10:30-18:00 ■ James Espie, Director and Marie-Alix Desgrees du Lou speak English ■ Prices reasonable ■ 10 to 20% professional discount

Copies of the great masters. True traditional copies painted by hand in oils on canvas. Special commissions accepted for institutions, clubs, universities, restaurants, hotels.

GALERIE TROUBETSKOY

1 av. Messine, 75008 Paris ■ Tel: 45 62 66 02 - Fax: 42 25 99 39 ■ Mon-Fri 9:30-13:00/14:00-19:30/Sat 10:30-18:30 ■ English spoken ■ Prices depend on dimensions. ■ Small: 1,500 Francs, Large 10,000 francs ■ Professional discount

Painted replicas on canvas, 17th century to the present. 18,000 different subjects. Stock of 100 subjects. Sizes up to 2.50 m. On order, any paintings from any museum in the world.

GALERIE VAN M

39 rue Notre-Dame-de-Lorette, 75009 Paris ■ Tel: 49 70 07 77 ■ Mon-Sat 11:00-19:30 ■ Gabriel Salloum speaks English ■ Prices medium ■ 15 to 20% professional discount

Copies of paintings of the great masters in the techniques and styles of the originals. Old Masters, Impressionists, Moderns.

───────────── **OUTSIDE PARIS** ─────────────

FRESSI

48 av. Egle, 78600 Maisons-Laffitte ■ Tel: 39 62 14 24 - Fax: 34 93 07 74 ■ By appointment ■ Prices reasonable ■ 20% professional discount

Specialist in hand painted replicas of the great masters such as Leonardo Da Vinci, Modigliani, the Impressionists, etc. Executed on order by highly qualified artists. Special commissions accepted for paintings of any subjects for restaurants, clubs, hotels, offices, etc.

ARTISANS

From the time of the first Crusades, France has been the world's leader in fine craftsmanship. In France the word "Artisan" is an essential and proud part of the nation's patrimony in spite of the brutal onslaughts of the industrial and electronic revolutions. Today, French artisans continue to produce decorating and architectural products that have become the true standards of excellence throughout the world. The French system of apprenticeship is still a vital part of the nation's economic and cultural fabric. Any canny designer or creative architect can still find men and women whose skills and knowledge produce the best and most beautiful decorating products the world can offer.

The reader will note that many of the Artisans listed as "Contract Craftsmen" in our guide are "Compagnons du Devoir". Literally translated, the title indicates that the Artisan has sworn to fulfill his duty to the trade he practises. In order to be admitted to the "Compagnons", an apprenticeship of three years and one day must be served by travelling to the various regions of France and learning the different applications of his trade. When he has completed his training, he is then required to produce a "Chef-d'Œuvre" (masterpiece). This is then submitted for evaluation to a jury of "Compagnons". If the work is found worthy, he is admitted as a "Compagnon du Devoir".

♛ Bronze Founders
Fondeurs et bronziers d'art

Founders cast bronze, a mixture of copper and tin, using either the lost wax or sand casting process. Their work usually requires the collaboration of three crafts, the "Turner", the "Chiseller" and the "Fitter". Until recently, they constituted three diffent trades, but today often work together in the same workshop.

BLANCHET LANDOWSKI

57 av. Gambetta, 93170 Bagnolet ■ Tel: 43 61 16 41 - Fax: 48 97 17 37 ■ Mon-Fri 8:00-12:00/13:00-17:30/Fri closing 16:30 ■ English spoken ■ Director: Didier Landowski

Specialties: Art foundry statuary, (lost wax process and sand casting). Work experience: Dome of the Invalides, Prefecture of Bobigny, Doors of the French Ministry of Finance.

SOCIETE BRONZALUMAX-FONDERIE THINOT

91 rue de la République, 92230 Châtillon-sous-Bagneux ■ Tel: 42 53 42 65 ■ Mon-Fri 9:00-18:00 ■ Director: Pierre Thinot

Specialties: Statuary, medals, (lost wax, sand casting). Objects in solid silver. Work experience: The sculptors: Maillol, Richier, the Giacomettis, Belmondo and others.

FONDERIE CLEMENTI

29 rue du Lieutenant-Batany, 92190 Meudon ■ Tel: 45 34 56 32 - Fax: 45 34 73 35 ■ Mon-Fri 7:30-12:30/13:30-17:00 ■ Director: G. Clementi

Specialties: Statuary, in the lost wax process, on order from the artist. Work experience: Miro (Galerie Maeght), Artcurial, Musée Bourdelle.

FONDATION DE COUBERTIN

Domaine de Coubertin, Ateliers St Jacques, 78470 St-Rémy-les-Chevreuses ■ Tel: 30 85 69 62 - Fax: 30 85 69 99 ■ Mon-Thurs 8:00-12:30/13:30-18:00/Fri 8:00-12:30 ■ English spoken ■ Director General: Mr. Bonneau

Specialties: Foundry, metal work, carpentry. Work experience: The balconies of Versailles, the Archangel of Mont-Saint-Michel, The Equestrian Statue in lead on the Esplanade of the Louvre. Contracts in the U.S., Japan, Austria and the Middle East.

MEILLEUR

32 rue des Amandiers, 75020 Paris ■ Tel: 43 66 45 13 - Fax: 43 66 45 43 ■ Mon-Fri 8:30-18:00 ■ Catherine Meilleur speaks English ■ Director: Daniel Meilleur

Specialties: Wrought iron work, art bronze, all bronze and iron work for architecture and decoration. Work experience: Bibliothèque Nationale in Paris, Palais de Fontainebleu, Palais de Compiègne, Conseil d''Etat and the Palais Royal (lanterns).

ENTREPRISE TOULOUSE

10 rue Beautreillis, 75004 Paris ■ Tel: 48 87 82 85 ■ Mon-Fri 8:00-12:00/14:00-18:00 ■ Contact: Jean-Claude Toulouse

Specialties: Chiselling of bronze, all metal work, restoration of precious art objects.

Work experience: Paul Getty Museum, Musée du Louvre, Château de Versailles, the treasures of many of Europe's cathedrals.

☛ Cabinet makers, marquetry workers, chair makers
Ébénistes marqueteurs, menuisiers en sièges

The cabinet makers, marquetry workers and chair makers of France not only restore fine furniture, but can reproduce works in period style on order. They are unmatched anywhere else in the world.

MICHEL CHEVILLARD

33 rue Ganneron, 75018 Paris ■ Tel: 43 87 77 83 - Fax: 42 93 45 30 ■ Mon-Fri 7:30-18:00 ■ Director: Michel Chevillard

Specialty: Restoration of XVIII century mahogany furniture. (Vernis au tampon).

Work experience: For the great Antique dealers of France, especially those who participate in the "Biennale des Antiquaires".

JEAN-LOUIS CHODORGE

16 place Saint-Pierre, 55000 Bar-le-Duc ■ Tel: 29 45 07 99 - Fax: 29 77 16 72 ■ Mon-Fri 8:00-17:00 ■ Director: Jean-Louis Chodorge

Specialty: Restoration of antique marquetry.
Diploma of the Ecole Boulle.
Brochure upon request.

MICHEL GERMOND

78 quai de l'Hôtel-de-Ville, 75004 Paris ■ Tel: 42 78 04 78 - Fax: 42 78 22 74 ■ Mon-Fri 8:00-12:00/13:30-18:00 ■ English spoken ■ Director: Michel Germond

Specialties: Restoration of furniture, chairs, marquetry.
Will repair small pieces of furniture on site.
Work experience: Furniture of the Bibliothèque Nationale, Furniture of the Queen's Chamber at Versailles, Château de Compiègne.

SERGE PRONIEWSKI

33 bis route des Châteaux, 33460 Labarde ■ Tel: 56 88 90 46 - Fax: 56 88 36 29 ■ Mon-Sat 9:00-19:00 ■ English spoken ■ Director: Serge Proniewski

Specialty: Restoration of antique furniture, marquetry Boulle of the XVII and XVIII centuries.

Work experience: Works at the Ecole Boulle, Counsel to the Atelier of the Musée du Louvre.

S.E.R.O.D. (SOCIETE D'EXPERTISE ET DE RESTAURATION D'OBJETS D'ART)

42 rue de Varenne, 75007 Paris ■ Tel: 45 44 65 50 - Fax: 45 49 05 38 ■ Mon-Fri 9:00-19:00/Sat 9:00-18:00 ■ English spoken ■ Director: Henri Desgrippes

Specialty: Restoration of furniture of the XVII and XVIII centuries.
Work experience: Partridge House in England. Many years experience abroad.

PATRICK VASTEL

143 rue du Général-Leclerc, 50110 Tourlaville (Cherbourg) ■ Tel: 33 22 46 07 - Fax: 33 22 96 26 ■ Mon-Fri 9:00-12:30/13:30-18:30 ■ Patrick Vastel speaks English

Specialty: Restoration of XVII and XVIII century marquetry.
Work experience: The great dining room of the City Hall of Cherbourg. Clients come to this establishment from all over the world.
Ecole Boulle.

♔ Gilders
Doreurs

Gilders finish or restore indoor and outdoor decoration.

There are three methods of gilding:
– Gold leaf gilding in which thin layers of gold are laid on wood, plaster or sculpted metal. This involves a series of 22 delicate operations;
– Gold or silver plating by means of electroplating;
– Mercury gilding, an alchemical formula which dates back to classical times. While it is the most beautiful, the process is rare, costly and dangerous to use.

ATELIERS ROBERT GOHARD ET BEAUMONT

90-92 rue des Entrepreneurs, 75015 Paris ■ Tel: 45 78 89 68 - Fax: 45 79 78 09 ■ English spoken ■ Contact: Messrs Robert or Fabrice Gohard

Specialty: Restoration, gold leafing on wood, plaster or metal.
Work experience: The Balustrades of the Queen's Chamber at Versailles, the Grills of the Place Stanislas in Nancy, the Dome of the Invalides, the Flame of the Statue of Liberty in New York.

MAISON MAHIEU

15 impasse des Primevères, 75011 Paris ■ Tel: 43 55 88 25 - Fax: 48 06 92 99 ■ Mon-Fri 8:00-12:00/13:00-17:00 ■ English spoken ■ President: Claude Kern ■ Director General: Edith Maurette

Specialty: Gold and silver plating on metal, bronze patinas. One of the last establishments permitted to practise mercury gilding.
Work experience: Metropolitan Opera in New York, Paul Getty Museum in Malibu, decorative hardware for the great apartments of Fontainebleu, the Trianon of Versailles, Château de Champs (Compiègne).

♛ Ornamental Iron Workers
Ferronniers, métalliers, serruriers d'art

The iron worker forges iron into decorative elements for use either indoors (banisters, fireplace accessories, lighting fixtures, furniture) or outdoors (portals, gates, balconies, handrails, garden furniture). Wrought iron work is often adorned with acanthus leaves and flowers. These effects are achieved by highly skilled artisans known as "Chasers" or "Embossers" who cold-hammer the metal.

In contra-distinction, the metal worker is a carpenter in metal. He specializes in roof frames and window and door casings. The two usually work together.

ATELIERS BATAILLARD

7 impasse Marie-Blanche 75018 Paris ■ Tel: 42 23 04 33 - Fax: 42 54 96 80 ■ Mon-Fri 9:00-13:00/14:00-18:00 ■ English spoken ■ Director: J.-P. Guigo-Bataillard

Specialty: Stair railings, balconies, gates, grills, lighting, furniture. Restoration of all metals: wrought iron, stainless steel, bronze, aluminum.

Work experience: Gates for the Presidential Palaces in Yamoussoukro (Ivory Coast) and Yaounde (Cameroun), the Baghdad Airport and the University of Riyadh. Design and installation of wrought iron staircases for private clients in the U.S.A.

FONDATION DE COUBERTIN

Domaine de Coubertin, Ateliers St Jacques, 78470 St-Rémy-les-Chevreuses ■ Tel:30 85 69 62 - Fax:30 85 69 99 ■ Mon-Thurs 8:00-12:30/13:30-18:00/Fri 8:00-12:30 ■ English spoken ■ Director General: Mr. Bonneau

Specialty: Foundry, metal work, carpentry.

Work experience: The balconies of the Château de Versailles, the Archangel of Mont-St-Michel, the Equestrian statue on the Esplanade of the Louvre.

Contracts completed in the U.S.A., Austria, Japan and the Middle East.

MEILLEUR

32 rue des Amandiers, 75020 Paris ■ Tel: 43 66 45 13 - Fax: 43 66 45 43 ■ Mon-Fri 8:30-18:00 ■ Catherine Meilleur speaks English ■ Director: Daniel Meilleur

Specialty: Decorative iron work, decorative bronze, lighting, decorative hardware. All iron and bronze for decoration and architecture.

Work experience: La Bibliothèque Nationale (Paris), Palais Royal (Paris), Palais de Fontainebleau, Palais de Compiègne, the Conseil d'Etat. Numerous major contracts in the United States and elsewhere.

ATELIER METAFER

287 av. du Président-Wilson, 93210 La Plaine-Saint-Denis ∎ Tel: 48 20 49 06
- Fax: 48 20 05 87 ∎ Mon-Fri 7:30-12:00/13:00-16:30 ∎ Director: Marc Nouaille

Specialty: Restoration, iron work, sculpture, metal work. Custom work in all metals: wrought iron, stainless steel, bronze, aluminium.

Work experience: The Presidential palaces in the Ivory Coast and Cameroun, the Royal Guard and Private Hospital in Riyadh, Saudi Arabia. The Marriot Hotel in Atanta, GA.

Sculpture casting: One of 100 meters in height for a hotel in Singapore, the Dolphins of Hong Kong Harbour, the Lalanne Dinosaurs in Santa Monica, CA.

LES METALLIERS CHAMPENOIS

11 rue de l'Etis, 51500 Bezannes ∎ Tel: 26 36 21 33 - Fax: 26 36 22 15 ∎
Mon-Fri 8:00-12:00/14:00-18:00 ∎ English spoken ∎ Director: Jean Bourly

Specialty: Metal work and iron work.

Work experience: The Statue of Liberty in New York, the friezes on the balcony of the King's Chamber at Versailles, the Gates of the Place Stanislas in Nancy.

♛ Carpet, tapestry, embroidery and textile restorers

Restaurateurs en tapis, tapisseries, broderies et textiles anciens

Carpets, tapestries, embroideries and textiles require special care and maintenance. Light and dust as well as normal wear and tear cause deterioration. But remember, a skilled restorer can often work miracles.

The Artisan-specialist needed will depend on the type of restoration. The work can vary from a relatively simple but skilled operation like cleaning a Savonnerie carpet to the restoration of an important historical ensemble. Nine people worked on the Queen's chamber in Versailles for eleven years.

When a tapestry requires re-weaving, a small number of firms still possess the appropriate Jacquard handlooms and can carry out the most delicate restorations from original documents.

SOCIETE BOBIN

27 rue de la Vanne, 92120 Montrouge ■ Tel: 46 57 64 00 - Fax: 46 57 00 42
■ Mon-Fri 8:00-18:30/Sat 8:30-12:30 ■ English spoken ■ Director: J.-L.
Mourier

Specialty: Cleaning and restoration of carpets, tapestries and antique textiles.
Work experience: Musée du Louvre, Château de Versailles, Château de Fontainebleau.
The company has ateliers in Nice and Gennevillers.

MAISON BROCARD

1 rue Jacques-Cœur, 75004 Paris ■ Tel: 42 72 16 38 - Fax: 42 72 04 77 ■
Mon-Fri 9:00-12:00/14:00-17:00 ■ Marie Brocard speaks English

Specialty: Restoration of tapestries, hangings, and old embroideries.
Work experience: The Queen's Chamber in the Château de Versailles, the gold thread embroideries in the Chamber of Louis XIV, the bed hangings in the Chamber of Josephine at Malmaison.
Restoration work done only in the Atelier and estimates provided from micro-photos.

MAISON CHEVALIER

64 bd de la Mission-Marchand, 92400 Courbevoie ■ Tel: 47 88 41 41 - Fax:
43 34 08 99 ■ Mon-Fri 8:30-18:00 ■ English spoken ■ Directors: Dominique
and Pierre Chevalier ■ Contact: Véronique Chevalier

Specialty: Restoration and cleaning of carpets and tapestries. Creators of a machine which allows cleaning without manipulation.
Work experience: Restoration and cleaning of tapestries for the Musée du Louvre (Gobelins XVII century). The Beauvais chairs in the Château de Versailles. Le Musée de Cluny.
The company has ateliers in Bauge, Toulouse, Brignolles, Lyon.

E.C.A.T. (ETUDE ET CONSERVATION DES ANCIENS TEXTILES)

50 bis rue de Paris, 92190 Meudon ■ Tel: 46 26 36 38 - Fax: 46 23 17 70 ■
Mon-Fri 8:00-18:00 ■ English spoken ■ Director: Isabelle Bedat

Specialty: Restoration of antique fabrics for museums and historic monuments.
Work experience: Musée de Cluny, Château d'Ecouen, Musée des Arts de la Mode, Tapisserie de Bayeux, Musée du Louvre, Institut du Monde Arabe, Musée d'Orsay.
Isabelle Bedat is the successor to Margarita Classen-Smith.

ATELIER DE RESTAURATION PIERRECY

118 av. Pablo-Picasso, 92000 Nanterre ■ Tel: 47 74 61 54 ■ Mon-Fri 8:30-
12:00/13:00-17:00 ■ Contact: G. Pierrecy

Specialty: Restoration of antique tapestries, carpets and tapestries of Aubusson and Beauvais.
Work experience: Restoration of the Vendanges (XVII century), Brussels. Royal Manufacture d'Aubusson. Numerous dealers in antique tapestries in the USA.

♔ Restorers of clocks and bells
Restaurateurs d'horloges et carillons

ENTREPRISE MAMIAS

28-30 av. Jean-Jaurès, 93220 Gagny ■ Tel: 43 02 43 88 - Fax: 43 02 94 42 ■ Mon-Fri 8:00-12:00/13:30-17:30 ■ English spoken ■ Director: Etienne Biard

Specialty: Restoration of clocks, carillons and bells.

Work experience: The bells of Notre-Dame de Paris, the Cathedral at Chartres, the Basilica of the Sacré-Cœur in Montmartre, the Carillon in Washington, D.C.

♔ Stained glass window makers
Vitraillistes

ATELIER AVICE

17 rue de Tascher, 72000 Le Mans ■ Tel:43 81 18 60 - Fax: 43 82 15 58 ■ Mon-Fri 8:00-12:00/13:30-18:00/Fri closing 17:00 ■ English spoken ■ Director: Didier Alliou

Specialty: Restoration and creation of stained glass windows in all styles.

Work experience: Restoration of the stained glass windows in the Cathedrals of Chartres, Le Mans, Laval, the Panthéon in Paris and many other churches. Worked with France Vitrail International on the Basilica of Yamassoukro (Ivory Coast).

ATELIERS DUCHEMIN

14 av. Georges-Lafenestre, 75014 Paris ■ Tel: 45 42 84 17 - Fax: 45 42 01 56 ■ Mon-Fri 9:00-12:00/14:00-17:30/ Fri closing 17:00 ■ Director: Dominique Rousvoal-Duchemin

Specialty: Restoration of stained glass windows of the XIX century and of 1900 to 1930. Important documentation and stock of Tiffany glass and printed glass.

Work experience: Chapel of Bang Pa In (Thailand), reconstitution of the stained glass in the Synagogue on the Rue Copernic in Paris. The Chapel of Ste Anne in Paris.

And many other churches.

FRANCE VITRAIL INTERNATIONAL

95 av. de la Liberté, 92000 Nanterre ■ Tel: 47 29 82 73 - Fax: 47 29 13 40 ■ Mon-Fri 8:15-12:15/13:30-17:30/Fri closing 16:30 ■ English spoken ■ Director: Eric Bonte

Specialty: Creation and restoration of all styles of stained glass.

Work experience: 7,500 square meters of stained glass windows for the Basilica of Yamoussoukro, Ivory Coast.

Hotel George V (Paris), Hotel Plaza Athénée (Paris). Thirty churches and cathedrals.

LES ATELIERS GAUDIN

6 rue de la Grande-Chaumière, 75006 Paris ■ Tel: 43 26 65 62 - Fax: 43 54 96 55 ■ Mon-Thurs 7:30-17:15/Fri 7:30-11:30 ■ Director: Sylvie Gaudin

Specialty: Restoration and creation of stained glass windows of all styles. Work experience: Sainte-Chapelle de Paris, St-Etienne-du-Mont, St-Sulpice, Cathédrale de Chartres.

JACQUES LOIRE

16 rue d'Ouarville, 28300 Lèves ■ Tel: 37 21 20 71 - Fax: 37 36 22 33 ■ Mon-Fri 8:00-12:00/13:30-17:30 ■ English spoken ■ Director: Jacques Loire

Specialty: Restoration and creation of stained glass windows in all styles. Work experience: Cathédrale de Chartres, Eglise St-Eustache (Paris), Bon Samaritain. Restorations in Egypt, Ivory Coast, Persian Gulf States, United States.

BRUNO DE PIREY

La Thuasnerie-Allouis, 18500 Mehun-sur-Yèvre ■ Tel: 48 57 13 82 - Fax: 48 57 38 37 ■ Mon-Fri 8:00-12:00/14:00-18:00 ■ English spoken ■ Director: Bruno de Pirey

Specialty: Restoration and creation of stained glass windows of all styles. Work experience: Chapelle du Val-de-Grâce, Paris. Cathédrale St-Etienne, Hotel des Echevins, Bourges.

VITRAUX D'ART WEINLING

823 route de Gray, 21850 St-Apollinaire ■ Tel:80 71 60 39 - Fax: 80 72 23 41 ■ Mon-Fri 8:00-12:00/14:00-18:00 ■ English spoken ■ Director: Jean Weinling

Specialty: Restoration and creation of stained glass windows in any style. Work experience: Eglise de Rouvres en Plaines (Recreation of xiv century window). Fontaines-en-Duesmois (Côte-d'Or).
Restoration of the window "l'Arbre de Jesse", Chapelle des Œuvres (Dijon) and many others.

♛ Wood Carvers
Sculpteurs sur bois

FANCELLI

31 rue Marcel-Bourdarias, 94140 Alfortville ■ Tel: 43 75 47 87- Fax: 43 75 24 72 ■ Mon-Fri 7:30-12:00/13:30-17:30/Fri closing 17:00 ■ Jean-Pierre and Michel Fancelli speak English

Specialty: Wood carving, wood panelling, historic restoration. Work experience: The Queen's Chamber at Versailles, the Apartments of the Château de Fontainebleau, the ceilings of the Château de Chambord, the Château de Rambouillet. The Metropolitan Museum of New York.

ATELIER PAUL MERINDOL

12 bis route de Lyon, 84005 Avignon ■ Tel: 90 82 11 14 - Fax: 90 85 59 77 ■ Mon-Fri 7:00-12:00/13:30-17:00 ■ English spoken ■ Director: Paul Merindol

Specialty: Wood and stone carving.
Work experience: Statue of the Town of Lille, Place de la Concorde in Paris, Dome of the Invalides, portal of the Church of St-Trophime at Arles.

LES ATELIERS PERRAULT FRERES

30 rue Sébastien-Cady, 49290 St-Laurent-de-la-Plaine ∎ Tel: 41 22 37 22 - Fax: 41 22 37 37 ∎ Mon-Fri 7:00-17:00

Specialty: Traditional master carpentry, slate roofing, classic carpentry: doors, windows, staircases, parquets, wood carving.

Work experience: The Louvre, private houses on the Place des Vosges, Ile St-Louis, Chinon, Abbaye de Fontevrault, Cathédrale de Nantes.

♛ Flagstone
Dallage

MONTGOLFIER

Daumeray 49640 ∎ Tel: 41 32 56 99 - Fax: 41 32 59 32 ∎ Mon-Fri 9:00-12:00/13:30-18:00 ∎ Contact: Joël Baudoin

Specialty: Renovation of flagstone following the original documented designs. Fabrication of flagstone, glazed terra-cotta. Installation.

Work experience: Château de Chabanet (XV century) at Pont-Chrétien, Auberge de la Mare au Diable (XV century Dovecote) near Melun, Auberge de la Vignette Haute (XVI century Bergerie) near Colioure.

👑 Contract Craftsmen of Excellence

Listed here are certain firms whose special skills and experience on major projects make them suitable for the decorator or architect who might be working on important homes, landmark buildings and large public projects.

ART ET TECHNIQUE DU BOIS

31 rue Marcel-Thil, 51100 Reims ■ Tel: 26 47 22 74 - Fax: 26 84 90 01 ■ Mon-Fri 7:00-12:15/14:45-18:00 ■ Contact: Jacques Marcille

Specialty: Restoration of historic monuments. Staircases.
Master carpentry and carpentry (framing, panelling, wainscoting, parquet).
Work experience: The Bell Tower of the Eglise St Jacques in Reims, the ducal square in Charleville-Mézières, the Church of Outines.
Compagnon du Devoir.

AUBERT LABANSAT

Route de Coutances, 50190 Périers ■ Tel: 33 46 71 71 - Fax: 33 46 26 20 ■ President: Andre Aubert

Specialty: Historic conservation, carpentry, master carpentry, cabinet making, half-timbering, old style parquets.
Work Experience: 20 churches, 3 abbeys, 3 cathedrals: Rouen, Le Havre and Sées, dozens of châteaux and private homes.

S.A.C. (SOCIETE AUTUNOISE DE CONSTRUCTION)

12 bd Frédéric-Latouche, 71400 Autun ■ Tel: 85 52 30 07 - Fax: 85 52 67 20 ■ Mon-Fri 7:00-19:00 ■ President: Bernard Billier

Specialty: Masonry, stone masonry, master carpentry, roofing.
Work experience: The old Abbaye de Cluny, Eglise de St-Marcel-les-Chalons, Cathédrale d'Autun, Hôtel-Dieu, Beaune, Opéra de Lyon, Eglise de Meursault.

LE BATIMENT ASSOCIE

Zone Industrielle, 51140 Muizon ■ Tel: 26 02 90 02 - Fax: 26 02 94 09 ■ Mon-Fri 7:30-12:00/13:30-18:00/ Fri 17:00 ■ Contact: Pierre Possème

Specialty: Masonry, stone masonry, master carpentry (bell towers).
Work experience: Marne Provincial Capitol building, Caisse d'Epargne, Reims, vaulted wine cellars, a dozen Churches in the Marne.
Compagnon du Devoir.

LE BATIMENT REGIONAL

Z.I. Savipol, 10300 Sainte-Savine ■ Tel: 25 79 00 24 - Fax: 25 79 56 81 ■ Mon-Fri 8:00-12:00/14:00-18:00 ■ Director: Mr. Dominique Naert ■ English spoken

Specialty: Masonry, stone masonry, stone carving, roofing, restoration of facades, heating.
Work Experience: Château de la Mornaire (Montfort-l'Amaury), Château de la Motte-Tilly (Nogent-sur-Seine), Préfecture de Région Champagne-Ardenne (Troyes).
Affiliated with Stone Craft of Los Angeles.

ENTREPRISE BATTAIS

39 quai du Clos-des-Roses, 60200 Compiègne ■ Tel: 44 20 12 49 - Fax:
44 86 34 91 ■ Mon-Fri 8:00-12:00/13:30-17:30 ■ Contact: François Polidor

Specialty: Roofing: tiles, slate or metal. Roof ornaments.
Work experience: The Dome of the Invalides, Paris, the Arrow of the Abbaye
du Mont-St-Michel, Cathédrale d'Amiens.

ENTREPRISE BLANCHON

29 rue de Turcoing, Z.I. Romanet, 87000 Limoges ■ Tel: 55 30 16 70 - Fax:
55 30 46 38 ■ Mon-Fri 8:00-12:00/13:30-18:30 ■ Contact: Bernard Godivier
■ English spoken

Specialty: Masonry, stone masonry, carpentry, roofing, staff.
Work experience: Eglise de St-Michel-des-Lions (Limoges), Château de
Sedières in Corrèze. Empress Place Building (National Museum of Singapore).

BONNIN STAFF

Zone Activité des Granges, 42600 Montbrison ■ Tel: 77 96 01 80 - Fax:
77 58 65 83 ■ Mon-Fri 8:30-12:00/13:30-17:30 ■ Contact: Gilbert Bonnin

Specialty: Staff, plaster and Italian stucco.
Work experience: Hôtel de Ville (Monbrison, Loire), Théâtre Municipal
(Roanne), Musée de la Poupée (Charbonnières).
Compagnon du Devoir.

BOURGEOIS ENTREPRISE

3 av. Roger-Salengro, 69120 Vaulx-en-Velin ■ Tel: 72 37 50 54 - Fax:
72 37 53 73 ■ Mon-Fri 8:00-12:00/13:30-17:30 ■ Director: Guy Bourgeois

Specialty: Master carpentry, roofing, zinc covering, roof ornaments.
Work experience: The Belfry of Amiens, Eglise de Villeneuve-l'Archevêque
(Côte-d'Or), Hôtel de Ville (Lyon).

SOCIETE NOUVELLE CHANZY-PARDOUX

B.P.105, 57004 Metz Cedex 1 ■ Tel: 87 62 26 22 - Fax: 87 65 39 48 ■ Mon-
Fri 8:00-12:00/13:30-17:30 ■ Contact: Jean-Luc Hartert ■ English spoken

Specialty: Masonry, stone masonry, master carpentry, roofing.
Work experience: Restoration of the Cathedral at Strasbourg (35 years of
work), Château de Lunéville (Meurthe-et-Moselle), the Regional Counsel of
Metz, the Façades of the Arsenal of Metz.

LES CHARPENTIERS D'AUJOURD'HUI

16 rue Jules-Ferry, Z.I. Le Pontet, 69360 St-Symphorien-d'Ozon ■ Tel:
78 02 13 33 Fax: 78 02 95 24 ■ Mon-Fri 7:00-18:00/Sat 8:00-12:00 ■
Contact: Mr. Desprat

Specialty: traditional master carpentry, reinforcement of structures.
Work experience: Château de la Croix-Laval (Lyon region), National
Conservatory of Music in Lyon.
Compagnon du Devoir.

LES CHARPENTIERS DE BOURGOGNE

4 rue Lavoisier, 21600 Longvic ■ Tel: 80 66 77 38 - Fax: 80 31 82 01 ■
Contact: Jacques Gainet

Specialty: Master carpentry, roofing, staircases.
Work experience: Eglise de St-Seine-l'Abbaye, Palais des Ducs at Dijon.
Compagnon du Devoir.

LES CHARPENTIERS COUVREURS DU PERIGORD

19 rue des Pêcheurs, 24000 Périgueux ■ Tel: 53 09 40 57 - Fax: 53 54 09 33
■ Mon-Fri 8:00-22:00 ■ Contact: Mr. Houdousse ■ English spoken

Specialty: Master carpentery, classic slate roofing.
Work experience: Eglise de la Mazière-Basse (Corrèze), Château de Beau-regard-de-Terrasson (Dordogne), Eglise d'Ordiap (Pyrénées), Cathedral de Sarlat (Dordogne), Château de Lanquais (Dordogne).

AUX CHARPENTIERS DE FRANCE

Av. de la Plesse, Chemin Départemental 59, 91140 Villebon-sur-Yvette ■ Tel: 69 34 32 60 - Fax: 69 34 70 39 ■ Mon-Fri 7:00-12:00/13:30-16:30 ■ Contact: Michel Delaunay

Specialty: Master carpentry in traditional and modern styles.
Work experience: The Campaniles of the Musée d'Orsay, the Salle des Fêtes of the Elysées Palace in Paris, maintenance of the Paris Opera House.
Compagnon du Devoir.

ENTREPRISE DEGAINE

129 rue de Lancette, 75012 Paris ■ Tel: 44 67 87 10 - Fax: 43 07 08 75 ■ Mon-Fri 8:30-12:00/13:00-18:00 ■ Contact: John-Hubert Plassat ■ English spoken

Specialty: Masonry, reinforced and pre-stressed concrete, stone masonry.
Work experience: Mont-Saint-Michel, Palais de Fontainebleau, Musée d'Orsay, numerous private homes in the Marais, Eglise du Raincy (Seine-St-Denis), Palais des Ducs de Bourgogne (Dijon).

ENTREPRISE DELESTRE

24 allée Francois-1er, 41000 Blois ■ Tel: 54 43 95 63 - Fax: 54 42 39 16 ■ Contact: Mr. Dominique Delestre

Specialty: Master carpentry, roofing, plumbing, zinc covering, roof orna-ments.
Work experience: Restoration of the Châteaux of Blois, Chambord, Valençay, Chaumont-sur-Loire, Cathedrals of Blois and Tours.

DEVILLARD FRERES

01750 St-Laurent-sur-Saône ■ Tel: 85 38 08 99 - Fax: 85 38 89 51 ■ Mon-Sat 8:00-12:00/14:00-19:00 ■ Director: Jean Devillard ■ English spoken

Specialty: Stone masonry, stone carving, fireplaces, staircases on Saracen vaulting.
Work experience: Conseil Général and Préfecture du Rhône (XVIIIc), Palais de Justice de Tournus (XVIIIc), Hôtel de Ville in Mâcon (XVIIc), Cathédrale St-Vincent de Mâcon, Arrow of the Eglise de Lamur (Isère), Bell tower of the Eglise de Marcigny (Saône-et-Loire).

E.R.P.A. (ENTREPRISE DE RESTAURATION DE PATRIMOINE ANCIEN)

22 rue des Vaux-Renard, 89100 Sens ■ Tel: 44 20 12 49 - Fax: 44 86 34 91
■ Mon-Fri 8:00-12:00/13:30-17:30 ■ Director: François Polidor

Specialty: Stone masonry and restoration of old masonry.
Work experience: Cathédrale de Sens, Préfecture de Sens (the old Abbaye St-Germain), Vézelay.

E.T.P.M. (ENTREPRISE DE TAILLE DE PIERRE ET DE MAÇONNERIE)

39 Clos-des-Roses, 60200 Compiègne ■ Tel: 44 86 28 95 - Fax: 44 86 88 58 ■ Mon-Fri 8:00-12:00/13:30-17:30 ■ Director: François Polidor

Specialty: Stone masonry, restoration of old masonry.

Work experience: Palais de Compiègne, Hôtel de la Marine (Place de la Concorde, Paris), Château de Blerencourt in the Aisne (Musée de l'Amitié franco-américaine).

Note: Mr. Polidor groups three companies, EPTM, ERPA, Entreprise Battais.

ENTREPRISE FOURQUET

Le Péage, Pérouges, 01800 Mescimieux ■ Tel: 74 61 03 22 - Fax: 74 34 70 23 ■ Mon-Sat 8:00-12:00/13:30-18:00 ■ Contact: J.-L. Fourquet

Specialty: Roofing, zinc covering, metallic roofing.

Work experience: Abbaye d'Ambronay, Bell Tower of Argentière, lead roofing of the Château d'Eau, Montpellier.

Compagnon du Devoir.

ENTREPRISE GENTIL

Zone Artisanale Fixin, 21220 Gevrey-Chambertin ■ Tel: 80 52 64 70 - Fax: 80 52 96 25 ■ Mon-Sat 8:00-12:30/14:00-20:00 ■ Maurice Gentil speaks English

Specialty: Roofing in flat tiles (specialist of Burgundy tiles).

Work experience: Château de Gevrey-Chambertin, the Cloisters of the Bernardines, Dijon.

Compagnon du Devoir.

ENTREPRISE GOURDON

38 rue de Cernay, 51100 Reims ■ Tel: 26 88 63 91 - Fax: 24 40 47 18 ■ Mon-Fri 7:30-12:00/13:30-17:45/Fri closing 15:00 ■ Contact: Laurent Gourdon

Specialty: Roofing in slate, copper, lead, zinc or flat tiles.

Work experience: Police building, New York City with the Metalliers Champenois, the Dome of Brooklyn Borough Hall, Château de Fléville (Nancy), Abbaye de Mouzon (Sedan).

Compagnon du Devoir.

ENTREPRISE INDELEC

61 chemin des Postes, 59500 Douai ■ Tel: 27 97 28 28 - Fax: 27 87 61 46 ■ Mon-Fri 8:00-12:00/14:00-18:00 ■ Mr. Pullink speaks English

Specialty: Roof ornaments in hand worked copper, weather vanes, lightning rods.

Work experience: Cathédrale d'Amiens, Cathédrale de Lille, Châteaux of Chambord, Cheverny, Blois, Valençay. Supplier of lightning rods for the USA.

ENTREPRISE GEORGE LANFRY

22 route de Dieppe, 76250 Déville-lès-Rouen ■ Tel: 35 74 39 00 - Fax 35 74 43 34 ■ Mon-Fri 8:00-12:15/13:00-18:00 ■ President: Jean-Marc Lanfry

Specialty: Masonry, stone masonry, master carpentry.

Work experience: Cathedral of Notre-Dame and the Palais de Justice, Rouen, Eglise St-Maclou, Eglise St-Ouen, Abbatiale St-Georges-de-Bocherville.

ENTREPRISE LANCTUIT

Restoration: 12 rue du Point-du-Jour, 27027 Vernon ■ Tel: 32 64 52 52 - Fax: 32 51 81 44 ■ Mon-Fri 8:00-12:00/13:30-18:00 ■ Contact: Patrick Debuck (Historic monuments department)

New construction: 19 route de Rouen, 27950 St-Marcel ■ Tel: 32 21 67 19 - Fax: 32 21 67 21 ■ English spoken

Specialty: Masonry, stone masonry, stone carving, master carpentry, roofing, heating, plumbing. All trades required for the restoration of historic monuments.
Work experience: Cour de Cassation, Ile de la Cité, Paris, Château de Gaillon, Abbaye du Bec-Hellouin (Normandy).

ENTREPRISE M. LEFEVRE

27 rue des Mathurins, 75008 Paris ■ Tel: 42 65 37 84 - Fax: 49 24 04 12 ■ Mon-Fri 9:00-18:00 ■ President: Marc-Henry Menard ■ English spoken

Specialty: Masonry, stone masonry, roofing, master carpentry, carpentry.
Work experience: Château de Chambord, Château de Vincennes, Cathédrale de Rouen, Cathédrale de Bourges, Cathédrale du Mans.

🏛 ENTREPRISE LONGEPE

82 rue Pierre-Semard, 92320 Châtillon ■ Tel: 42 53 39 48 - Fax: 47 35 64 09 ■ Mon-Fri 7:30-19:00 ■ Contact: Ephrem Longépé

Specialty: Staircases, handrails, railings, master carpentry.
Work experience: Private homes in the Marais, Paris, Les Halles de Mirecourt, La Cité Internationale des Arts, Paris.
Compagnon du Devoir.

ENTREPRISE MAHE

13 bd Henri-Arnauld, 49000 Angers ■ Tel: 41 87 60 52 - Fax: 41 87 60 14 ■ Mon-Fri 8:00-12:00/13:30-18:00 ■ Director: Henri Pele

Specialty: Slate roofing and zinc covering.
Work experience: Renovation of slate rooves: in XVIII century structure in Maryland and the Anglican Church in Centreville, Mairie de Salanches, Château in Pornic, Catholic University of Angers.

ATELIERS MAINPONTE

62 rue La Fayette, 77610 Fontenay-Trésigny ■ Tel: 64 42 61 50 - Fax: 64 42 61 58 ■ Mon-Fri 9:00-12:00/13:00-18:00 ■ Contact: Roger Bonnefoy ■ English spoken

Specialty: Stone carving of ornaments: gargoyles, statues, ornamental basins, capitals.
Work experience: Numerous historic monuments. The Louvre, most of the great cathedrals and principal châteaux in the Loire Valley.

AUX METIERS DU BATIMENT-T.P.M.R.

Route Nationale 23, 49480 St-Sylvain-d'Anjou ■ Tel: 41 21 27 00 - Fax: 41 21 27 01 ■ Mon-Fri 8:00-12:00/13:00-18:00 ■ Contact: André Cost

Specialty: All types of master carpentry, classic carpentry, staircases, slate roofing, stone masonry.
Work experience: The National Riding Academy of Saumur, the facing of the Pont de Tours, the Abbaye de Fontevrault.

ENTREPRISE MORICEAU

6 rue Jean-Pierre-Florion, 33160 St-Médard-en-Jalles ■ Tel: 56 28 66 69 - Fax: 56 28 92 81 ■ Mon-Fri 7:30-18:00 ■ Contact: Norbert Moriceau ■ English spoken

Specialty: Roofing, zinc covering.
Work experience: Bell Tower of St-Médard, Church of the Sacré-Cœur in Bordeaux, Château Beychevelle (Médoc).
Compagnon du Devoir.

ENTREPRISE PAVY

Z.I. Nord, 35 rue Thomas-Edison, 72650 La Chapelle-St-Aubin ■ Tel: 43 24 68 24 - Fax: 43 23 00 27 ■ Mon Fri 8:00-12:30/13:30-19:00 ■ Director: Michel Pavy

Specialty: Masonry, stone masonry.
Work experience: Eglise du Vieux-Saint-Sauveur, Caen, Gallo-Roman Ramparts, Le Mans, Palais de Justice, Laval.

LES ATELIERS DE PERRAULT FRERES

30 rue Sébastien-Cady, 49290 St-Laurent-de-la-Plaine ■ Tel: 41 22 37 22 - Fax: 41 22 37 37 ■ Mon-Fri 7:00-17:00 ■ President: Bernard Billier

Specialty: Master carpentry in the traditional style. Slate roofing, classic carpentry: doors, windows, staircases, parquets. Wood carving.
Work experience: The Louvre Museum, private homes on the Place des Vosges, and the Ile-St-Louis, Château de Chinon, Abbaye de Fontevrault, Cathedral of Nantes.

ATELIER DE LA PIERRE

30250 Junas ■ Tel: 66 80 33 82 - Fax: 66 77 70 25 ■ Mon-Fri 8:00-17:00 ■ Contact: J. Mercier

Specialty: All stone masonry, hard or soft stone. Stone from the Luberon and Burgundy. Staircases on Saracen vaulting, bas-reliefs, engraving, stone carving.
Work experience: Restoration of the building Conseil General, Nîmes, Bell Tower of Caveirac, Hôtel de Caderousse.
Compagnon du Devoir.

ETABLISSEMENT PIERRE LARROCHE

21 rue Ausone, 33000 Bordeaux ■ Tel: 56 44 76 81 - Fax: 56 48 04 16 ■ Mon-Fri 8:00-12:30/14:00-18:00 ■ Contact: Pierre Larroche

Specialty: Stone masonry, cleaning, renovation of old buildings.
Work experience: Château Larivet du Haut-Brion (Léognan), Eglise Notre-Dame de la Merci (Haillan), Château de la Mission (Pessac).

ENTREPRISE PLEE

Les Grands-Champs, Chanceaux-sur-Choisille, 37001 Tours ■ Tel: 47 41 00 75 - Fax: 47 51 20 63 ■ Mon-Fri 8:00-12:00/13:30-18:00 ■ Contact: Mr. Dominique Plee ■ English spoken

Specialty: Treatment and reinforcement of structures with armatures.
Work experience: Château de Blois, Château d'Azay-le-Rideau, Galerie Vivienne, Paris.

ENTREPRISE PRADEAU-MORIN

41 bd Soult, 75012 Paris ■ Tel: 43 43 32 54 - Fax: 43 40 37 47 ■ Mon-Fri 8:30-12:30/13:00-17:30 ■ Contact: Charles Marceau ■ English spoken

Specialty: Masonry, stone masonry.
Work experience: Renovation of the Louvre Museum (Paris), the National Assembly (Peristyle), Cathédrale de Beauvais, Les Invalides and the Musée d'Orsay (Paris).

AUX QUATRE COURONNES

B.P. 9, Charentilly, 37390 La Touche ■ Telfax: 47 56 79 70 ■ Mon-Fri 8:00-18:00 ■ Contact: Mr. Campistron

Specialty: Restoration of stone constructions.
Work experience: Châteaux de Villandry and Tours, Domaine de Fontenailles. Compagnon du Devoir.

ENTREPRISE QUELIN

95-97 av. Victor-Hugo, 92563 Rueil-Malmaison ■ Tel: 47 10 08 00 - Fax: 47 51 22 22 ■ Mon-Fri 8:00-19:00 ■ Contact: Hervé Quelin

Specialty: Masonry, stone masonry, staircases, balustrades, rose windows.
Work experience: The Arc de Triomphe de l'Etoile, Notre-Dame de Paris, Basilica of Chartres, Cathédrale St-André (Bordeaux), Musée Chateaubriand (Châtenay-Malabry), La Maison Picassiette (Chartres).

RENAUD PLATRE

Route de Bellevue, 16710 Saint-Yriex ■ Tel: 45 95 55 15 - Fax: 45 92 60 10 ■ Mon-Fri 8:00-12:00/14:00-18:30 ■ Director: Guy Renaudeaux

Specialty: Plaster, staff, stucco.
Work Experience: Casino de Dax, Château de Monchaude (Charente), Musée Labanche (Brive-en-Corrèze).
Compagnon du Devoir.

ENTREPRISE SCHERBERICH

162 rue du Ladhof, 68000 Colmar ■ Tel: 89 23 12 23 - Fax: 89 23 41 29 ■ Mon-Fri 8:00-18:00 ■ Contact: René Scherberich

Specialty: Masonry, stone masonry, stone sculpting. Material used: only sandstone of the Vosges and Rouffach.
Work experience: Collégiale St-Martin (Colmar), Collégiale St-Thiebaut, Château du Haut-Koenigsbourg (Bas-Rhin).

ENTREPRISE SORT ET CHASLES

1 bd Seattle, 44300 Nantes ■ Tel: 40 49 03 85 - Fax: 40 52 12 93 ■ Mon-Fri 8:00-12:00/14:00-18:00 ■ Contact: Guy Renaudeau

Specialty: Plaster, staff, Italian stucco.
Work experience: Casino of Gibraltar, Restoration of the ceilings of the Musée d'Orsay, Pyramid of the Louvre, the ship "Le Souverain des Mers" (St-Nazaire). Compagnon du Devoir.

THOMANN HANRY

56 rue Molitor, 75016 Paris ■ Tel: 46 51 23 26- Fax: 47 43 11 03 ■ Mon-Fri 8:30-18:00 ■ Bernard Thomann speaks English

Specialty: Cleaning of facades by a special copyright process called "gommage". This technique is without sand, water, dust, abrasives, chemicals or scaffolding.

"THE GRANDS ATELIERS DE FRANCE"

JEAN ALOT
Gold Leafing on Wood

RÉMY BRAZET
Classic Upholstery

MARIE BROCARD
Restoration of Embroideries, Furnishing Fabrics & Tapestries

MICHEL GERMOND
Restoration of XVIIth, XVIIIth, XIXth Century Furniture

DANIEL MEILLEUR
Lighting and Decorative Hardware in Bronze

ANNE HOGUET
Creation and Restoration of Fans

JEAN-YVES ROUGER
Marble Craftsman

FRANCE BONNIMOND-DUMONT
Restoration of Paintings

GEORGES KRIVOSHEY
Fabric Printing, Decoration & Haute Couture

PHILIPPE MARTIAL
Creation, Chasing and Gilding of Leather Objects

JEAN QUENTIER
Fine Painting, Faux Finishes, Trompe l'Œil

SIMON ETIENNE
Fine Furniture Restoration

ANNE BLAIN
Engraving on Wood and Metal Marquetry

PIERRE-FRANÇOIS BATTISTI
Trompe l'Œil, XVIIIth Century Painted Walls Panels

LES GRANDS ATELIERS DE FRANCE,
8 pl. de la Madeleine
75008 Paris. Tel : 42 96 12 75. Fax : 40 15 98 32.

♔ The Great Ateliers of France
Les Grands Ateliers de France

This select group of Artisans represents some of the very best that France has to offer. Dedicated to the highest standards of craftsmanship and a strict moral code, they provide a last bastion of defense against the destruction of the artisan system. They are self policing in that each member, representing the various specialties, must be re-evaluated every year and then re-elected into the group of "LES GRANDS ATELIERS".

If the quality of their work falls below the high standards required by the group, or if they have lapsed into questionable dealing, then they will be dropped.

ATELIER JEAN ALOT

101 rue de Patay, 75013 Paris ■ Tel: 45 82 80 32 - Fax: 44 24 51 90 ■ Mon-Fri 8:00-18:00/Sat 8:00-12:00 ■ Prices medium ■ Professional discount

Gilder on wood. All types of gilding on wood. Wood sculpture. Restoration of all objects and furniture in gilded wood (bois doré). Specialist in French furniture of the XVII and XVIII centuries. Framing.
Qualified expert.

PIERRE-FRANÇOIS BATTISTI

6 rue Louis-Nicolas-Clérambault, 75020 Paris ■ Tel: 48 20 31 83 - Telfax: 43 58 77 07 ■ By appointment ■ Pierre-François Battisti speaks English ■ Prices high ■ Professional discount

Creation of decorative panels in all styles of all epochs, particularly XVIII century through Art Deco to contemporary. Decorative painting for boiseries, faux finishes, patinas. Trompe l'œil. Member of the Grands Ateliers.

ANNE BLAIN

105 Grand-Rue, 91160 Longjumeau ■ Tel: 64 48 23 66 - Fax: 69 09 03 08 ■ By appointment ■ Anne Blain speaks English ■ Prices medium

Engraving on marquetry furniture and silver. Engraving of crests and monograms, personal "ex-libris" seals. Enamelling on gold and silver and decorations.

FRANCE BONNIMOND-DUMONT

16 rue Saint-Charles, 75015 Paris ■ Tel: 43 33 01 79 - Fax: 47 89 86 67 ■ By appointment ■ Anne Bonnimond-Dumont speaks English ■ Professional discount

Restoration of paintings and painted murals of all periods.
A scientific analysis can be prepared after examination, upon request.

JACQUES BRAZET

22 rue des Belles-Feuilles, 75016 Paris ■ Tel:47 27 20 89 - Fax: 47 55 68 90 ■ Mon-Fri 8:30-18:00 ■ Rémy Brazet speaks English ■ Prices high ■ 15 to 20% professional discount

Traditional upholstery of walls and antique chairs. Fabrication of draperies, slip covers, bedspreads and sheers. Supplier to the National Museums.

MAISON BROCARD

1 rue Jacques-Cœur, 75004 Paris ■ Tel: 42 72 16 38 - Fax: 42 72 04 77 ■ Mon-Fri 9:00-12:00/14:00-17:00 ■ Marie Brocard speaks English

Restoration, historic reconstitution and copies of embroideries and antique tapestries.

MAISON ETIENNE

55 rue Popincourt, 75011 Paris ■ Tel: 47 00 77 81 - Fax: 48 05 14 25 ■ Mon-Fri 8:00-12:00/13:30-18:00 ■ Simon Etienne speaks English

Restoration of antique furniture and art objects.

MICHEL GERMOND

78 quai de l'Hôtel-de-Ville, 75004 Paris ■ Tel: 42 78 04 78 - Fax: 42 78 22 74 ■ By appointment ■ Prices high

Restoration of XVII, XVIII and XIX century furniture in marquetry and chairs. Expert counsel in the purchase of items of collection.
Expert before the Court of Appeals, Paris.

ANNE HOGUET

2 bd de Strasbourg, 75010 Paris ■ Tel: 42 08 19 89 ■ Mon-Fri 8:00-12:00/14:00-18:30

Fabrication and restoration of fans.

ATELIER GEORGES KRIVOSHEY

46 rue Albert-Thomas, 75010 Paris ■ Tel: 40 40 04 35 - Fax: 42 45 88 30 ■ Mon-Fri 10:00-13:00/14:00-19:00 ■ Isabelle Versini speaks English

Decoration of textiles for decoration and haute couture.
Impressions on velvet. Creation of original designs on fabric, reproduction and execution.

MADR

22 av. Franklin-Roosevelt, 94300 Vincennes ■ Tel: 43 98 03 00 - Fax: 48 08 16 62 ■ Mon-Fri 8:00-12:00/13:00-17:30 ■ Jean-Yves Rouger speaks English ■ Prices medium ■ Professional discount

Marble workshop. Restoration of marble and sculptures in marble and other stone. Pedestals for bronzes. Custom bathrooms.

ATELIER PHILIPPE MARTIAL

8 rue du Général-Guilhem, 75011 Paris ■ Tel: 47 00 71 72 - Fax: 43 55 41 56 ■ Mon-Fri 8:30-13:00/14:00-17:30 ■ Prices medium ■ Professional discount

Superb leather work. Creation of diverse objects in wood covered in leather, with or without chasing and gilding. Jewellery cases, boxes in all shapes and sizes, liqueur cases, small cabinets, desk sets, frames, brief-cases, decorative objects. Classic book binding. Restoration of leather. Work for Hermes and other great Houses. Member of Les Grands Ateliers.

MEILLEUR

32 rue des Amandiers, 75020 Paris ■ Tel: 43 66 45 13 - Fax: 43 66 45 43 ■
Mon-Fri 8:30-19:00 by appointment ■ Catherine Meilleur speaks English ■
Prices high to very high ■ Professional discount

Custom work in bronze, brass and iron for interior and exterior decoration.
Lighting: chandeliers, sconces, lanterns, lamps and adjustable reading lamps.
Decorative door and window hardware, special faucets.
Wrought iron balconies, stair railings, lighting.
Restoration of the above for National Museums and private clients.

ATELIER QUENTIER

15 rue Henri-Monnier, 75009 Paris ■ Tel: 48 78 64 35 - Fax: 48 78 22 79 ■
Mon-Fri 8:00-19:00 ■ Prices high ■ Professional discount
Fine painting, faux finishes, trompe l'œil. Restoration of painted or lac-
quered furniture and objects.

Antique Furniture Restoration
Cabinet Makers
Ébénistes

———————————— IV ————————————

⌂ MICHEL GERMOND

78 quai de l'Hôtel-de-Ville, 75004 Paris ■ Tel: 42 78 04 78 - Fax: 42 78 22 74
■ By appointment ■ Michel Collet speaks English ■ Prices high

Restoration of furniture and chairs of the XVII, XVIII, XIX centuries. Specialist in marquetry.
Expert advice on the confirmation of authenticity and the valuation of high
quality antique furniture.
Member of Les Grands Ateliers. Expert to the Cour d'Appel. World renowned expert.

———————————— VII ————————————

ATELIER CALEX BRUGIER

74 rue de Sèvres, 75007 Paris ■ Tel: 47 34 83 27 - Fax: 40 56 91 40 ■ Mon-
Fri 8:00-17:30 ■ Nicole Judet-Brugier speaks English ■ Prices high to very
high ■ 10 to 15% professional discount

Restoration of lacquer: Chinese, Japanese, Art Deco.
Painted furniture. Stock of lacquered panels and screens of the XVII and
XVIII centuries.

JEAN-PAUL JOUAN

10 rue Perronet, 75007 Paris ■ Tel: 45 48 64 20 ■ Tues-Sat 9:00-12:00/14:00-
19:00 ■ Barbara Jouan speaks English ■ Prices medium ■ Professional discount
Restoration of antique furniture and art objects. Especially XVIII century.

———————————— VIII ————————————

REINOLD FILS

233 rue du Faubourg-Saint-Honoré, 75008 Paris ■ Telfax: 47 63 47 19 ■ Mon-
Fri 8:00-12:00/13:00-18:00/Sat 13:00-18:00 ■ English spoken ■ Prices medi-
um to high ■ Professional discount
Restoration of XVIII century European marquetry furniture and chairs.

XI

♛ MAISON ETIENNE

55 rue Popincourt, 75011 Paris ■ Tel: 47 00 77 81 - Fax: 48 05 14 25 ■ Mon-Fri 8:00-12:00/13:30-18:00 by appointment ■ Simon Etienne speaks English ■ Prices medium to high

Restoration of French furniture and objects of the XVII and XVIII centuries. Member of Les Grands Ateliers.

INTARSIO

94 av. Philippe-Auguste, 750011 Paris ■ Tel: 43 48 50 37 ■ Mon-Sat 9:00-18:00 by appointment ■ Claude-Sara Tomor and Sbero Beritognolo speak English ■ Prices medium ■ Professional discount

Restoration of XVII and XVIII century furniture, especially Boulle marquetry. Specialists in making wall panels and tables of Scagliola.

XII

DIDIER MAULET

74 rue de Charenton, 75012 Paris ■ Tel: 43 44 44 08 ■ Mon-Fri 9:00-19:00 ■ English spoken ■ Prices medium ■ Professional discount

Restoration of XVIII century marquetry furniture.

FABRY

4 rue Gramme, 75015 Paris ■ Tel: 42 50 94 64 ■ Mon-Fri 8:30-12:00/13:00-17:30 ■ Jean-François Fabry speaks English ■ Prices high

Restoration of XVIII and XIX century furniture and chairs.

♛ ROLAND INGERT

32 rue Mathurin-Régnier, 75015 Paris ■ Tel: 47 83 57 49 ■ Mon-Fri 8:00-12:00/14:00-18:00 ■ Prices high

Restoration of lacquer furniture and art objects: Chinese and Japanese, 1925 lacquer.
Restoration for museums and châteaux.

DIDIER GILLERY

2 rue Gervex, 75017 Paris ■ Tel: 43 80 98 17 ■ Mon-Fri 9:00-19:00/Sat 12:00-18:00 ■ Prices medium to high

Restoration of XVII, XVIII and XIX century furniture, chairs and objects.

GEORGES LECLERQ

8 rue Ruhmkorff, 75017 Paris ■ Tel: 40 55 06 23 ■ Mon-Fri 9:00-12:00/14:00-18:00 ■ Laurent Leclercq speaks English ■ Prices medium

Restoration of antique furniture. Specialist in Boulle marquetry. Re-caning of chairs and upholstery. Works for the Mobilier National and Historic Monuments.

JEAN-PIERRE BRUNO

6 rue André-Messager, 75018 Paris ■ Tel: 42 23 24 40 - Fax: 42 23 23 90 ■ Mon-Fri 7:30-17:00 ■ Prices high

Restoration of antique furniture. Specialist in the restoration of chairs, consoles and bois doré (gilded wood).

ATELIERS BENE

10 ter rue Bisson, 75020 Paris ■ Tel: 47 97 05 36 ■ Mon-Fri 8:00-18:00 ■ Prices high

Restoration of antique furniture, marquetry, chairs.

JACQUES POISSON

17 Cité Aubry, 75020 Paris ■ Tel: 43 71 73 09 - Fax: 40 24 26 20 ■ Mon-Fri 8:30-18:00 ■ English spoken ■ Prices high ■ 10% professional discount

Restoration of Boulle marquetry.
Qualified expert.

S. PRONIEWSKI

32 bis route des Châteaux, 33460 Labarde ■ Tel: 56 88 90 46 - Fax: 56 88 36 29 ■ Mon-Sat 9:00-19:00 ■ English spoken ■ Prices high

Restoration of antique furniture, especially marquetry, art objects and tortoise shell.

👑 PATRICK VASTEL

143 rue du Général-Leclerc, 50110 Tourlaville, Cherbourg ■ Tel: (16) 33 22 46 07 - Fax: (16) 33 22 96 26 ■ Mon-Fri 9:00-12:00/13.30-18:30/Sat by appointment ■ Patrick Vastel speaks English ■ Prices medium ■ Professional discount

Restoration of XVII and XVIII century furniture.Expert to the Cour d'Appel.

Caning - Repair and Restoration
Cannage

CANNAGE ET PAILLAGE

58 rue de Charonne, 75011 Paris ■ Tel: 48 05 29 40 ■ Mon-Fri 8:00-12:00/13:30-17:30 ■ Prices medium

All types of repairs for cane furniture.

GEORGES LECLERQ

8 rue Ruhmkorff, 75017 Paris ■ Tel: 40 55 06 23 ■ Mon-Fri 9:00-12:00/14:00-18:00 ■ Laurent Leclercq speaks English ■ Prices medium

Re-caning and upholstery of chairs. Restoration of antique furniture.

Clock Repair and Restoration
Horlogerie

— III —

ART DU TEMPS
1 Cité Dupetit-Thouars, 75003 Paris ■ Tel: 48 04 87 27 ■ Mon-Fri 9:00-12:00/14:00-18:00/Sat by appointment ■ Alesandre Matula speaks English ■ Prices low ■ 30% professional discount
Repair and restoration of antique watches, pendulum clocks and carillons. Manufacturer of parts for antique movements.

CENTRE TECHNIQUE REPARATION HORLOGERE
150 rue du Temple, 75003 Paris ■ Tel: 42 72 03 33 - Fax: 42 72 01 90 ■ Mon-Fri 9:00-17:00 ■ English spoken ■ Prices high ■ 20% professional discount
Repair of antique watches and restoration of pendulum clocks. Repair of chronometers of the Ministry of the Army.

MICHEL ROBILLARD
7 bd des Filles-du-Calvaire, 75003 Paris ■ Tel: 48 87 52 38 ■ Tues-Sat 9:30-12:15/14:15-18:45 ■ Prices medium
Specialist in the repair of antique pendulum clocks. Sale and repair of clocks and watches.

— V —

DANIEL GENDRON
281 rue Saint-Jacques, 75005 Paris ■ Tel: 46 33 35 01 ■ Tues-Fri 15:00-19:00/Sat 10:00-13:00 ■ Daniel Gendron speaks English ■ Prices very high
Restoration of antique pendulum clocks and antique watches. Master Artisan.

GENDROT
12 bd Saint-Germain, 75005 Paris ■ Tel: 43 54 18 84 ■ Tues-Fri 14:30-19:00 ■ Prices medium to high ■ Professional discount
Restoration of antique pendulum clocks from the XVI to the end of the XIX centuries.

— VI —

NOEL SENAC
22 rue d'Assas, 75006 Paris ■ Tel: 45 48 40 91 ■ By appointment ■ Prices medium
Repair of antique watches and pendulum clocks.

— IX —

GUY KOBRINE
14 rue Cadet, 75009 Paris ■ Tel: 45 23 18 84 ■ Mon-Fri 9:00-13:30/15:00-18:45 ■ Some English spoken ■ Prices medium
Qualified expert in the repair and restoration of the famous name wrist watches and XIX century pocket watches.

XIII

PHILIPPE BAILLE
68 bd Blanqui, 75013 Paris ■ Tel: 43 36 09 42 ■ Tues-Sat 10:30-12:30/14:00-19:00 ■ English Spoken ■ Prices high
Restoration of antique and modern clocks, watches and music boxes.

♕ JACQUES REVERDY
46 av. des Gobelins, 75013 Paris ■ Tel: 47 07 77 33 ■ Mon-Fri by appointment ■ Prices medium
Restoration of pendulum clocks, watches, barometers, music boxes and all antique clock mechanisms. Will make missing parts.
Recent work: Beauvais Cathedral. Restoration of the 1857 clock made of 90,000 working parts, the world's most complex clock.
Currently restoring the 1424 Atronomical Clock of Bourges Cathedral. Master Artisan. "Meilleur Ouvrier de France 1982".

XIV

LUCIEN COULON
44 rue des Plantes, 75014 Paris ■ Tel: 45 42 95 53 ■ Tues-Sat 10:00-13:00/15:30-19:30 ■ Isabelle Coulon speaks English ■ Prices medium
Forty years experience in the repair of antique and modern pendulum clocks and watches. All types of movements.

GEORGES CROCI
56 rue de la Sablière, 75014 Paris ■ Tel: 45 43 47 71 ■ Tues-Fri 9:00-12:00/13:30-17:00 ■ Prices medium
Repair of all antique and modern watches, pendulum clocks and carillons.

LE TEMPS RETROUVE HORLOGERIE ANCIENNE
123 rue de Rome, 75017 Paris ■ Tel: 42 27 76 28 ■ Tues-Fri 11:00-19:00/Sat 10:00-14:00 ■ Prices medium ■ 15% professional discount
Restoration and repair of all antique clock and watch movements.

BERNARD PIN
7 rue Pierre-Bonnard, 75020 Paris ■ Tel: 43 56 82 34 - Fax: 43 67 86 92 ■ Mon-Sat by appointment ■ Bernard Pin speaks English ■ Prices high to very high ■ Professional discount
Restoration of antique clocks and watches, music boxes, singing birds and musical pendulum clocks.

DANIEL MORNAS
"ATELIER P. MONNETTE"
8 rue des Chantiers, 78000 Versailles ■ Tel: 39 50 50 33 ■ Tues-Sat 10:00-18:00 ■ Prices medium
Restoration of antique pendulum clocks.

Fans - Antique, Custom and Restoration
Éventails anciens sur mesure et restauration

♛ ATELIER HOGUET

2 bd de Strasbourg, 75010 Paris ■ Tel: 42 08 19 89 ■ Mon-Fri 9:00-12:00/14:00-18:30 ■ Prices high

Restoration and custom fabrication of fans in all designs, since 1872.
The Musée de L'Eventail is open to the public on Tuesdays between 14:00 and 17:00. The collection is extraordinary and displays fans from the XVII century to the present.

MARIE MAXIME

34 bd des Batignolles, 75017 Paris ■ Tel: 45 22 44 52 ■ Mon-Fri 12:00-19:00 ■ Jeanne Dermanoukian speaks English ■ Prices high ■ 20% professional discount

Specialist in antique fans. Showcase collectibles.

Gilders on Wood
Doreurs sur bois

———————————————— VII ————————————————

JOHNY BORG
CADRES LAPOLI

45 rue Vaneau, 75007 Paris ■ Tel:42 22 57 96 - Fax: 42 84 07 51 ■ Tues-Sat 14:30-18:30 ■ Prices medium to high ■ Professional discount

Restoration of gilded wood (bois doré) furniture and objects. Custom frames in French, Italian and Dutch styles.

———————————————— XI ————————————————

ATELIER DE LA FEUILLE D'OR

3 rue Titon, 75011 Paris ■ Tel: 43 56 16 32 ■ Mon-Fri 8:30-18:00/Sat by appointment ■ Marie Le Masson speaks English ■ Prices medium ■ 10% professional discount

Restoration of all objects in gilded or painted wood.
Restoration of painted antique furniture. Custom framing.

———————————————— XIII ————————————————

♛ ATELIERS JEAN ALOT

101 rue de Patay, 75013 Paris ■ Tel: 45 82 80 32 - Fax: 44 24 51 90 ■ Mon-Fri 8:00-18:00/Sat 8:00-12:00 ■ Prices medium ■ Professional discount

Gilding on wood, wood sculpture, restoration of all objects and furniture in gilded wood. Specialist in French furniture of the XVII and XVIII centuries. Custom framing.
Master Artisan. Member of Les Grands Ateliers. Expert to the Tribunals.

THELLIER

64 rue de Longchamp, 75116 Paris ■ Tel: 47 04 32 83 - Fax: 47 27 66 02 ■ Tues-Sat 10:00-12:30/14:30-19:00 ■ Philippe-Louis Mexler speaks English ■ Prices medium ■ Professional discount

Gilding and restoration of wood furniture and objects. Restoration of lacquer and patinas. Custom framing

ATELIER DU BOIS DORE

82 av. des Ternes, 75017 Paris ■ Tel: 45 74 67 58 - Fax: 44 74 72 49 ■ Mon-Sat 9:00-12:30/14:00-19:00 ■ English spoken ■ Prices medium to high ■ Professional discount

Restoration of gilded wood furniture, objects and frames.
Antique reproductions of gilded wood furniture in limited editions.

JEAN-PAUL MARCHAIS

61 rue Guy-Moquet, 75017 Paris ■ Tel: 46 27 53 02 ■ Mon-Fri 10:00-13:30/15:00-17:30/Sat 11:00-14:00 ■ Laurent Marchais speaks English ■ Prices medium ■ 10% professional discount

Restoration of all gilded wood and plaster with fine gold leafing.
Supplier to the Mobilier National.

JEAN-PIERRE BRUNO

6 rue André-Messager, 75018 Paris ■ Tel: 42 23 24 40 - Fax: 42 23 23 90 ■ Mon-Fri 7:30-17:00 ■ Prices high

Restoration of all bois doré (gilded wood) chairs, consoles and objects.

ATELIERS JACQUES GOUJON

5 Villa Guelma, 75018 Paris ■ Tel: 42 64 95 83 - Fax: 42 23 95 50 ■ Mon-Fri 9:00-19:00 ■ Jacques Goujon speaks English ■ Prices medium ■ 10% professional discount

Restoration of antique gilded wood. Custom reproductions.
All types of gold leafing. Restoration of antique lacquer.
Wood sculpture and restoration of sculptured wood furniture.

FREDERIC COCAULT

5 rue Ernest-Lefèvre, 75020 Paris ■ Tel: 40 31 54 23 ■ Tues-Sat 10:00-19:00 ■ English spoken ■ Prices medium to high ■ Professional discount

Conservation of polychrome on wood. Gilding and finishes on wood. Specialty: medieval statues in polychrome (wood) and icons.

YOURI DMITRENKO

26 rue des Montibœufs, 75020 Paris ■ Tel: 40 30 40 83 ■ Mon-Fri 9:00-18:30/Sat by appointment ■ Youri Dmitrenko speaks English ■ Prices medium

Restoration of gilded wood furniture, chairs, frames, mirrors, boiseries (wood paneling). Workshop specializes in the restoration of XVIII century French and German furniture and art objects.

NEUILLY

ROBERT DUVIVIER

30 rue de Sablonville, 92200 Neuilly-sur-Seine ■ Tel: 47 22 25 90 - Fax: 46 43 01 49 ■ Tues-Sat 9:00-12:00/14:00-19:00 ■ Prices medium ■ 10% professional discount

Restoration of all types of gilded wood. Custom framing.
Master Artisan.

OUTSIDE PARIS

ATELIER DE DORURE
ANTOINE PALOMARES

1635 rue Louis-Blériot, 78530 Buc ■ Tel: 39 56 01 24 ■ Mon-Fri 9:00-19:00/Sat 9:00-12:00 ■ Prices medium

Restoration of art objects with fine gold leafing on wood and metal.
Master Artisan.

LUCIEN MARIOTTI

35 rue Petit-Leroy, 94550 Chevilly-Larue ■ Tel: 46 86 45 07 - Fax: 46 86 19 23 ■ Mon-Fri 8:30-12:00/13:30-18:30 ■ Prices medium ■ 10% professional discount

Gilding on wood. Restoration of antique gilded wood of the XVII and XVIII centuries. Supplier to the Mobilier National, the National Museums and Palaces. Qualified by the Historic Monuments.
Master Artisan. Qualified expert.

Glass Artists
Artistes sur verre

III

♛ P. DESSERME

17 rue du Pont-aux-Choux, 75003 Paris ■ Tel: 42 72 02 66 - Fax: 42 72 50 91 ■ Mon-Fri 8:00-12:00/13:30-17:30 ■ Some English spoken ■ Prices medium to high

Reputed to be the best glass blower in Paris. Glasses, mirrors, furniture, lanterns, glass covers for clocks and much more. Custom work.

GALERIE DONYA QUIGUER

1 rue Sainte-Croix-Bretonnerie, 75004 Paris ■ Tel: 48 04 72 55 ■ Tues-Sat 13:00-19:00 ■ Donya Quiguer speaks English ■ Prices medium ■ 10% professional discount

Unique pieces of contemporary glass sculpture.

GALERIE LE SUD/LES MAITRES VERRIERS

23 rue des Archives, 75004 Paris ■ Tel: 42 78 42 37 ■ Tues-Sat 10:30-19:00 ■ Sébastien Aschero speaks English ■ Prices medium to high ■ 10% professional discount

Blown glass by the Masters (Maîtres Verriers). Novaro, Pierini, Guillot, Fievet, Deutler, Marion, Monod, Guittet, Durand-Gasselin, Schamschula, Luzoro, Lepage, Baquere, Deniel, Pertshire and others. Decorative objects in Murano glass.

VIRGINIA MO

4 place de l'Odéon, 75006 Paris ■ Tel: 40 51 78 63 ■ Mon 14:00-19:00/Tues-Sat 11:00-19:00 ■ Virginia Mo speaks English ■ Prices medium to high

Art glass. A group of 15 artists who create unique objects in glass and crystal, especially in colour. Some objects are produced in limited editions. All contemporary.

VERRE ET ROUGE

19 rue de Miromesnil, 75008 Paris ■ Telfax: 42 65 75 65 ■ Mon-Fri 10:00-19:00/Sat during December ■ Christiane Follias speaks English ■ Prices medium ■ 10 to 20% professional discount

Personalized engraving on blown glass. Large choice.

BERNARD PICTET

47 rue Oberkampf, 75011 Paris ■ Tel: 48 06 19 25 - Fax: 43 55 31 45 ■ Mon-Fri 9:00-13:00/14:00-18:00 ■ Bernard Pictet speaks English ■ Prices very high ■ Professional discount

Fine quality engraving and decoration on glass.

JEAN VILLETTE

16 passage de la Folie-Régnault, 75011 Paris ■ Tel: 43 73 85 44 ■ Mon-Fri 9:00-17:00 ■ English spoken ■ Prices medium

Restoration and creation of stained glass windows. Expert to the Cour d'Appel, Paris.

JBP BOUTIQUES

21 rue de la Terrasse, 75017 Paris ■ Tel: 47 66 71 71 ■ Tues-Sat 9:00-12:00/14:00-18:00 ■ Prices very high ■ Professional discount

Engraver on glass and crystal. Original dated and signed works. From an individual champagne bottle to display cabinets and glass buildings.

———————————————— XX ————————————————

MME FABIENNE PICAUD

35 rue du Retrait, 75020 Paris (Bldg in courtyard) ■ Tel: 47 97 10 78 ■ Every day by appointment ■ English spoken ■ Prices medium to high

Fabienne Picaud is the glass artist. Unique art objects in blown glass. Sculpture, goblets, vases, perfume flacons, lighting.

———————————— OUTSIDE PARIS ————————————

JEAN-PIERRE BAQUERE

5 rue Bouin, 92700 Colombes ■ Tel: 47 86 09 49 - Fax: 47 85 83 47 ■ Mon-Sat 9:30-17:00 and by appointment ■ Jean-Pierre Baquere and Isabelle Emmerique speak English ■ Prices low ■ 3 to 7% professional discount

Blown glass creations decorated in gold leaf, platinum and palladium. Series of 50 made in a year. Hand made perfume bottles. Restoration of glass.

GUILLAUME SAALBURG

70 rue Jean-Bleuzen, 92170 Vanves ■ Tel: 46 38 76 76 - Fax: 46 38 74 00 ■ Mon-Fri 8:00-18:00 ■ English spoken ■ Prices high

Architectural and structural applications of glass. Engraving and decoration.

Decorative Iron Work
Ferronnerie d'art

▦ ATELIERS BATAILLARD

7 impasse Marie-Blanche, 75018 Paris ■ Tel: 42 23 04 33 - Fax: 42 54 96 80 ■ Mon-Fri 9:00-13:00/14:00-18:30/Sat by appointment ■ Jean-Philippe Daviaud speaks English ■ Prices high ■ 10 to 20% professional discount

Beautiful custom creations in wrought iron: staircases, furniture, chandeliers, lamps, door hardware, sconces, grills, gates, fences, grill work for stair railings. Traditional and contemporary styles.

MEILLEUR

32 rue des Amandiers, 75020 Paris ■ Tel: 43 66 45 13 - Fax: 43 66 45 43 ■ Mon-Fri 8:30-19:00 by appointment ■ English spoken ■ Prices high to very high ■ Professional discount

Custom wrought iron work. Railings, balconies, tables, lighting. Top quality.

PATRICK MILLOT

31 rue Jouye-Rouve, 75020 Paris ■ Tel: 43 58 60 47 - Fax: 43 58 18 89 ■ Mon-Fri 8:00-12:00/13:00-17:00 by appointment ■ Prices high ■ Professional discount

Decorative wrought iron work. All custom. Specialty: curved stair railings. Balconies, furniture, lighting. Custom work in brass, such as display cases for shops, brass framework for fireplaces.

REALISATIONS METALLIQUES DECORS

12 rue Saint-Sabin, 75011 Paris ■ Tel: 47 00 90 78 ■ Mon-Fri 8:00-12:00/13:30-17:30 ■ Prices medium ■ 10% professional discount

Custom creation of all elements in metal, steel, aluminium, brass for furniture, staircases, fireplace facades.

Lacquerers
Laqueurs

———————————— VII ————————————

ATELIER CALEX BRUGIER

74 rue de Sèvres, 75007 Paris ■ Tel: 47 34 83 27 - Fax: 40 56 91 40 ■ Mon-Fri 8:00-17:30 ■ Nicole Judet-Brugier speaks English ■ Prices medium to high ■ Professional discount

Specialists in the restoration of lacquer and painted furniture. Will custom make from old or contemporary designs. Beautiful collection of antique lacquered panels and screens.

———————————— XII ————————————

CATHERINE MARGHIERI

10 impasse Druinot, 75012 Paris ■ Tel: 43 44 93 99 ■ Mon-Fri 9:00-12:00/14:00-18:00 ■ English spoken ■ Prices medium ■ Professional discount

Specialist in lacquer. Restoration and creation of objects and furniture in lacquer. Small tables and consoles, vases and boxes in eggshell.

———————————— XV ————————————

👑 ROLAND INGERT

32 rue Mathurin-Régnier, 75015 Paris ■ Tel: 47 83 57 49 ■ Mon-Fri 8:00-12:00/14:00-18:00 ■ Prices high

Restoration of lacquer furniture and art objects: Chinese and Japanese, 1925 lacquer.
Restoration for museums and châteaux.

———————————— XVI ————————————

GUY HUGUES

21 rue de l'Annonciation, 75016 Paris ■ Tel: 42 24 49 20 ■ Mon-Fri 9:00-12:00/14:00-18:00 ■ Prices high ■ Professional discount

Restoration of Chinese lacquer, old and new. Custom made lacquer furniture. Low tables and cabinets.

ALM DECOR
Formerly ATELIERS SAIN & TAMBUTE & BERNARD ROGER
Meilleur Ouvrier de France ■ 10 rue André-Joineau, 93310 Le Pré-Saint-Gervais ■ Tel: 48 91 98 64 - Fax: 48 91 02 71 ■ Mon-Fri 8:30-12:30/13:30-17:30 ■ Prices medium

Decorative lacquer. Restoration of furniture and objects.Creation of decorative finishes on panels, screens, furniture and objects.

LES LAQUES CLAUDE
CLAUDE CORNEVIN
22 rue du Gué, 92500 Rueil-Malmaison ■ Tel: 47 51 14 88/47 51 91 62 ■ Tues-Sat 10:00-12:00/15:00-19:00 ■ Pierre Cornevin speaks English ■ Prices medium

Restoration of XVIII and XIX century furniture and objects in Chinese lacquer. Creation of low tables, objects, screens, fans and other.

SERGE TIRARD
"La Ferme Gallais" ■ 26 av. des Platanes, 78860 Saint-Nom La-Bretèche ■ Tel: 34 62 10 14 - Fax: 30 56 73 93 ■ Mon-Fri 9:00:12:00/14:00-18:00 ■ Some English spoken ■ Prices medium ■ Professional discount
Fine restoration of European and Oriental lacquer furniture and objects.

Leather - Creation and Restoration
Objets en cuir - Création et restauration

———————————— VI ————————————

ANDRE MINOS
6 rue Gît-le-Cœur, 75006 Paris ■ Tel: 43 54 61 78 ■ Mon-Sat 9:30-13:00/Afternoons by appointment ■ Prices medium
Restoration of leather objects, old books. Book binding.

ATELIER MAZARINE
42 rue Mazarine, 75006 Paris ■ Tel: 43 25 18 52 ■ Mon-Fri 9:00-13:00/14:00-19:00 and by appointment ■ Annick Schneider and Carole Laporte speak English ■ Prices medium ■ 10% professional discount
Custom made leather articles: photo albums, calendars, address books, cases, boxes. Book binding in leather and toile. Restoration of leather.

———————————— XI ————————————

LEWIS ET FILS DOREURS
18 rue du Moulin-Joly, 75011 Paris ■ Tel: 43 57 45 28 - Fax: 47 00 42 33 ■ Mon-Fri 8:30-12:30/13:30-17:30 ■ Marie Santillana speaks English ■ Prices medium
Leather desk sets and accessories in limited éditions. Custom leather work, chasing and gilding.

♛ ATELIER PHILIPPE MARTIAL

8 rue du Général-Guilhem, 75011 Paris ■ Tel: 47 00 71 72 - Fax: 43 55 41 56
■ Mon-Fri 8:30-13:00/14:00-17:30 ■ Prices medium ■ Professional discount

Superb leather work. Creation of diverse objects in wood covered in leather, with or without chasing and gilding. Jewellery cases, boxes in all shapes and sizes, liqueur cases, small cabinets, desk sets, frames, brief-cases, decorative objects. Classic book binding. Restoration of leather. Work for Hermes and other great Houses.

—————————— XVII ——————————

LEMERLE FRERES

62 rue Legendre, 75017 Paris ■ Tel: 46 22 28 56 - Fax: 48 88 01 83 ■ Mon-Fri 7:30-12:00/13:30-18:30 ■ Xavier Lemerle speaks English ■ Prices high ■ Professional discount

Restoration of old leathers of Cordova, leather chairs, desks and all decorative leather. Traditional restoration, hand dyeing of leathers and gold leafing.

Mosaics
Mosaïque

—————————— VII ——————————

DIANA DI COLLOREDO
TESSELLES

Atelier - Ecole de Mosaïque ■ 12 rue Chomel, 75007 Paris ■ Tel: 42 22 41 98 - Fax: 45 44 11 85 ■ Mon-Sat 10:00-18:30 ■ Laurent Ribis speaks English

Execution of all types of mosaics: tables, floors, objects, friezes. Courses in the techniques of Roman mosaics.

MOSAIK

46 rue de l'Université, 75007 Paris ■ Tel: 47 03 44 06 - Fax: 47 30 90 30 ■ Tues-Sat 10:30-19:00 ■ Prices medium ■ Professional discount

All types of custom work in mosaics. Objects in pate de verre, enamelled glass, stoneware.

—————————— XIV ——————————

CESARE BIZI

A807 - 8 rue du Commandant-René-Mouchotte, 75014 Paris ■ Tel: 43 21 28 81 ■ By appointment ■ Prices high ■ Professional discount

Mosaic artist. Creation and installation. Restoration of antique mosaics.

ECLATS DU SUD

5 rue Courat, 75020 Paris ■ Tel: 40 24 22 56 - Fax: 40 24 13 53 ■ By appointment ■ Prices medium to high ■ 20% professional discount

Furniture in mosaics: tables, chairs, screens, mirrors, lamps. Decorative mosaics for kitchens and bathrooms. Custom wall panels for the exterior.

—————————————— OUTSIDE PARIS ——————————————

DELPHINE MESSMER

Bât A, 23 av. Pasteur, 92170 Vanves ■ Tel 45 29 14 63 - Fax 48 39 38 10 ■ Mon-Fri 10:00-20:00 ■ Delphine Messmer speaks English ■ Prices medium

Mosaic art. Custom designs of all types for walls, floors, furniture and objects. Trompe l'œil.

Decorative painting and Trompe l'œil
Peinture décorative et trompe-l'œil

—————————————— IX ——————————————

♔ ATELIER QUENTIER

15 rue Henry-Monnier, 75009 Paris ■ Tel: 48 78 64 35 - Fax: 48 78 22 79 ■ Mon-Fri 8:00-19:00 ■ Prices high ■ Professional discount

Decorative painting and lacquering. Restoration of painted and lacquered furniture and objects. All styles of decorative painting. Member of the Grands Ateliers.

UN OBJET NOMME DESIR

19 rue Victor-Massé, 75009 Paris ■ Tel: 48 78 16 90 - Fax: 44 53 08 16 ■ Mon-Fri 9:30-18:30 by appointment ■ Jean-Sébastien Raud and Kamar Farnane speak English ■ Prices medium ■ 10 to 20% discount

Creation and production of decorative objects, lighting and neo-baroque mirrors in scagliola and other faux finishes.

—————————————— XIV ——————————————

CERAMIQUE DELABRUYERE SANGALLI

15 rue Bardinet, 75014 Paris ■ Tel: 45 45 36 66 ■ Mon-Fri by appointment ■ Lisyane Sangalli speaks English ■ Prices medium ■ Professional discount

Decorative painting on tiles. Bathrooms, kitchens, entrance halls, restaurants, shops, terraces, table tops. Lamps and porcelain vases. Will also work to clients' designs.

MERIGUET-CARRERE

84 rue de l'Abbaye-Groult, 75015 Paris ■ Tel: 48 28 48 81 - Fax: 45 32 57 84 ■ Mon-Fri 8:00-12:00/14:00-18:00 ■ English spoken ■ Prices high

Decorative painting, trompe l'œil, gilding and faux finishes. Restoration of painted objects.Top quality.

⚜ PIERRE-FRANÇOIS BATTISTI

6 rue Louis-Nicolas-Clérambault, 75020 Paris ■ Tel: 48 20 31 83 - Telfax: 43 58 77 07 ■ By appointment ■ Pierre-François Battisti speaks English ■ Prices high ■ Professional discount

Creation of decorative panels in all styles of all epochs, particularly XVIII century through Art Deco to contemporary. Decorative painting for boiseries, faux finishes, patinas. Trompe l'œil. Member of the Grands Ateliers.

JEAN-MICHEL TERRIER

133 rue de Bagnolet, 75020 Paris ■ Tel: 43 67 93 32 - Fax: 40 21 88 37 ■ Mon-Fri 9:30-12:30/14:00-18:30 by appointment ■ English spoken ■ Prices medium to high ■ Professional discount

Restoration of screens. Excellent quality.

MR. JEAN MARY ALJANCIC

41 rue Chasles, 78120 Rambouillet ■ Tel: 34 83 23 74 ■ Mon-Fri 9:30-12:30/14:30-19:30 ■ Prices medium ■ Professional discount

Faux finishes and antique patinas.

MME FABIENNE MARTINEL

43 av. Général-de-Gaulle, 94000 Saint-Mandé ■ Tel: 49 57 01 36 ■ Mon-Fri 8:30-12:00/14:00-18:00 ■ Prices medium ■ Professional discount

Faux finishes, gilding, patinas and stencils.High quality.

VALLIERE

16, rue Georges-Clemenceau, 92170 Vanves ■ Tel: 46 38 38 38 - Fax: 46 38 33 56 ■ Mon-Fri 8:00-12:00/13:30-19:00 ■ Carole Mahe speaks English ■ Prices medium ■ 5 to 10% professional discount

Decorative painting, ceiling clouds and trompe l'œil for residential and commercial clients. Restoration of facades.

Restoration of Paintings
Restauration de tableaux

---------------------------------- I ----------------------------------

ATELIER GENOVESIO

2 rue de Valois, 75001 Paris ■ Tel: 42 61 35 85 - Fax: 42 96 12 33 ■ Mon-Fri 9:00-12:00/13:00-18:00 and by appointment ■ English spoken ■ Prices high

Restoration of paintings and murals. Reproductions. Work for Museums, Historic Monuments, Municipalities, dealers and individual clients.

---------------------------------- III ----------------------------------

THERESE PRUNET - NICOLE TOURNAY

42 rue Meslay, 75003 Paris ■ Tel: 42 77 80 30 ■ By appointment only ■ Therese Prunet speaks English ■ Prices high

Restoration of paintings for the National Museums of France and the Louvre. Thérèse Prunet restores paintings and murals. Nicole Tournay restores paintings.

---------------------------------- VI ----------------------------------

BERNARD DEPRETZ

30 rue Jacob, 75006 Paris ■ Tel: 43 26 60 14 - Fax: 42 56 03 85 ■ Mon-Fri 10:00-12:00/14:00-19:00 ■ Prices medium ■ 20% professional discount

Restoration of old and contemporary paintings.
Re-mounting, transposition, lightening of varnish.

ATELIER PHILLIPPE LAURENT

2 rue du Regard, 75006 Paris ■ Tel: 42 22 98 72 ■ Tues-Sat 9:00-12:00/14:00-18:30

Restoration of paintings from the XV to the XIX century. Work experience, the Château of Versailles.

---------------------------------- VII ----------------------------------

MME MONIQUE DUCHATEAU

4 rue Casimir-Périer, 75007 Paris ■ Tel: 45 55 08 40/60 96 00 93 - Fax: 45 51 56 99 ■ By appointment ■ Prices medium

Restoration of works on paper: drawings, water colors, gouaches, pastels, Japanese estampes, parchment.

---------------------------------- IX ----------------------------------

MME BRIGITTE MALAVOY

21 rue Drouot, 75009 Paris ■ Tel: 42 46 15 25 ■ Mon-Fri by appointment ■ English spoken ■ Prices high ■ Up to 40% professional discount

Restoration of paintings on wood, canvas or copper from the XVI to the XX century. Works for the French Museums.

X

MME CATHERINE LEGRAND

35 rue de la Grange-aux-Belles, 75010 Paris ■ Tel: 42 45 00 98/49 63 28 48 ■ Tues-Sat 14:00-20:00 ■ Catherine Legrand speaks English ■ Prices medium ■ Up to 15% professional discount

Restoration of old paintings and wood sculpture from the IX century to 1950. Expert in paintings of the XVI to XX centuries. Diploma of the Ecole du Louvre.

ATELIER DU TEMPS PASSE

173 rue du Faubourg-Saint-Antoine, 75011 Paris ■ Tel: 43 46 86 27 ■ Mon-Fri 10:00-18:00/Sat by appointment ■ English spoken ■ Prices medium ■ 10 to 20% professional discount

Restoration of paintings, especially easel paintings, all art objects in polychrome and frames.

Work experience includes National Museums and French Embassies all over Europe.

MME SYLVIE BELLUCCI

61 av. de la République, 75011 Paris ■ Tel: 40 21 04 47 ■ By appointment ■ Prices medium to high ■ Professional discount

Conservation and restoration of easel paintings. Re-mounting, backing, impregnation, spot restoration, cleaning, lightening of varnish. Works for Museums, galleries and collectors.

JEAN-JACQUES COQUERY

45 rue Amelot, 75011 Paris ■ Tel: 43 57 52 72 ■ Mon-Fri 10:00-13:00/14:00-18:30 ■ English spoken ■ Prices high

Restoration of easel paintings on canvas from the XVI century to the present. Oils and acrylics.

MME NATHALIE PINCAS

11 rue Schœlcher, 75014 Paris ■ Tel: 43 27 52 27 - Fax: 43 21 70 90 ■ By appointment ■ English spoken ■ Prices medium

Restoration of old and modern paintings.

ATELIER WROBEL

63 rue Daguerre, 75014 Paris ■ Tel: 43 22 23 93 - Fax: 43 20 32 45 ■ By appointment ■ English spoken ■ Prices medium

Restoration of old, modern and contemporary paintings. Expert with the International Council of Museums.

◢ FRANCE BONNIMOND-DUMONT

16 rue Saint-Charles, 75015 Paris ■ Tel: 45 79 29 93/43 33 01 79 - Fax: 47 89 86 67 ■ By appointment ■ 20% professional discount

Restoration of paintings and murals of all periods. Works scientifically with a complete photographic and technical dossier. Expert and member of the Grands Ateliers.

CLAIRE BROCHU

47 rue Ampère, 75017 Paris ■ Tel: 46 22 74 52 ■ Mon-Fri 9:00-12:30/14:30-18:00

Restoration of paintings. Excellent credentials. Over twenty years experience in painting restoration.

ATELIER ANNE ALABASTRI

4 rue Hermann-Lachapelle, 75018 Paris ■ Tel: 42 55 55 60 ■ Mon 9:00-12:00/Tues-Fri 9:30-12:30/14:00-19:00/Sat 10:00-13:00/14:00-16:00 ■ English spoken ■ Prices medium ■ 5% professional discount

Restoration of paintings. Re-mounting using traditional and modern methods, treatment, cleaning, retouching, chemical analyses and examination by ultra-violet, infra-red and X-ray.

MME MICHELLE BOUCARD

75 rue d'Avron, 75020 Paris ■ Tel: 43 56 04 66 ■ Mon-Sat 9:00-18:00 ■ Prices medium ■ 10% professional discount

Restoration of paintings. Cleaning and re-mounting. Cleaning of engravings.

L'ATELIER DU TEMPS

10 rue Bailly, 92200 Neuilly-sur-Seine ■ Tel: 47 45 04 81 ■ Thurs-Sat 10:00-18:00 and by appointment ■ Jean-Claude Blaquière speaks English ■ Prices high

Restoration of XVII and XVIII century paintings. Oils on canvas, panels, murals (frescoes). Advice on conservation and restoration. Maintenance of collections. Treatment and cleaning of old panels, re-fixing, re-mounting, retouching and lightening of varnish.

L'ATELIER
ANNA PONIATOWSKI

Place Mansart, 78610 Marly-le-Roi (Vieux Marly) ■ Tel: 39 58 57 95 ■ Mon-Sat 10:00-19:00 by appointment ■ Prices medium

Restoration of paintings of all periods.

ATELIER DE RESTAURATION DE TABLEAUX
Mme Lucinière de Cornulier ■ 47 av. de Verdun, 78290 Croissy-sur-Seine
■ Tel: 39 76 95 50 - Fax: 30 53 59 30 ■ English spoken ■ Prices medium
Restoration of old and modern paintings. Works for Museums, associations,
dealers and private clients.

————————————— MARNES-LA-COQUETTE —————————————

MME ARIANE BORDES
1 rue Porte-Blanche, 92430 Marnes-la-Coquette ■ Telfax: 47 01 01 92 ■ Mon-
Fri 10:00-18:00 ■ Prices medium ■ Professional discount
Restoration of oil paintings on all surfaces (wood, canvas, paper, copper).
All periods.

————————————————— SENLIS —————————————————

ALAIN BOUCHARDON
3 rue de Lavarande, 60300 Senlis ■ Tel: 44 53 10 15 ■ Mon-Fri 8:00-
12:00/13:30-17:00 and by appointment ■ Prices medium
Restoration of paintings on canvas and on wood. Re-mounting, re-consti-
tution of wood elements, transposition.

Restoration of Parasols and Umbrellas
Restauration de parasols et parapluies

PEP S
223 rue Saint-Martin, 75003 Paris ■ Tel: 42 78 11 67 ■ Mon 9:00-19:00/Tues-
Fri 13:30-18:30 ■ Jocelyne Marcourt speaks English ■ Prices low
Restoration of all parasols and umbrellas, old and recent. Custom re-
covering of umbrellas, large and small. Sale of selected models, specializing in umbrellas for weddings.

Restoration of Porcelain,
Faience and Ceramics
Restauration de porcelaine, faïence et céramique

————————————————— VIII —————————————————

♛ MME MONIQUE LEROY
58 rue de Londres, 75008 Paris ■ Tel: 43 87 17 88 ■ Tues-Fri by appointment ■ Mme Leroy speaks English
A master at her craft. Madame Leroy restores porcelain for the top Antique
Dealers, Christies and Sothebys, the Louvre and the Center of Archeological Restoration of Florence.Expert to the Cour d'Appel, Paris.

JEAN-PIERRE ROYER

20 rue de Chabrol, 75010 Paris ■ Tel: 47 70 46 74 ■ Mon-Fri 9:00-12:00 ■ Eric Royer speaks English

Restoration of art objects in porcelain, faience, terra cotta, crystal, pate de verre (Gallé, Daum). Engraving on crystal. Repair of glass and ceramic. Restoration of antique bronzes, chiseling, mounting, remounting and restauration of crystal chandeliers. Electrification.

XI

MME DANIELE HUGUET LHERMINE

173 rue du Faubourg Saint-Antoine, 75011 Paris ■ Tel: 43 42 39 46 ■ Mon-Fri 9:00-18:00 ■ Prices medium

Restoration of broken or incomplete ceramic. Research into materials and colours. Invisible repairs. Firm estimates. Ask for Sophie Muguet

---
XVII

ATELIER SOUCHET

18 rue Biot, 75017 Paris ■ Tel: 45 22 53 47 ■ Tues-Fri 11:00-17:30 ■ Fabien Souchet speaks English ■ Prices medium to high

Restoration of faience, porcelain, enamel, terra cotta, old dolls.

XVIII

YVES MEROVIL

19 rue Marc Seguin, 75018 Paris ■ Tel: 46 07 01 55 ■ Mon-Fri 8:30-17:30 ■ English spoken

Repair and restoration of porcelain, terra cotta, ceramics. Gilding of objects in wood. High quality work.

XX

MME ORLANDA AGOSTINHO

18 rue Henri-Chevreau, 75020 Paris ■ Tel: 46 36 28 26 ■ Mon-Fri 10:00-12:00/14:00-17:00 by appointment ■ Prices medium ■ 20% professional discount to bearers of "TOUT PARIS GUIDE"

Restoration of art objects, sculpture, faience, porcelain, terra cotta, archaeological ceramics.Courbevoie

ATELIER LUMONT

12 rue Cacheux, 92400 Courbevoie ■ Tel: 47 89 56 90 ■ By appointment ■ Prices medium

Restoration of faience, porcelain, bisquit, terra cotta, ivory collages, plaster. Master Artisan.

Restoration of Silver
Restauration d'orfèvrerie

ATELIER RIOT

24 rue de la Folie-Mericourt, 75011 Paris ■ Tel. 47 00 34 47 ■ Mon-Fri 8:30-12:00/13:30-18:00 ■ Jeanne Privat speaks English ■ Prices medium

Restoration of all metal objects, silver, bronze and pewter. Specialty: silver. Restoration and re-gilding of furniture bronzes, chandeliers, clocks.

CHASTEL COUTELIER ORFEVRE

190 bd Haussman, Paris 75008 ■ Tel: 45 63 20 59 ■ Mon 13:30-18:00/Tues-Fri 9:45-12:30/13:30:18:45/Repair of cutlery, replacement of knife blades.

Restoration and repair of objects in silver and pewter. Sale of cutlery, pocket and hunting knives, good selection of table knives and professional cooking knives.

MAURICE CHEVALIER

26 rue des Gravilliers, 75003 Paris ■ Tel: 42 74 18 11 ■ Mon-Fri 8:00-12:00/13:00-17:00 ■ English spoken ■ Prices medium

Repair of objects in silver.

COURTOIS

20 rue de Montmorency, 75003 Paris ■ Tel: 48 87 50 79 - Fax: 48 87 48 08 ■ Mon-Fri 9:00-17:00 ■ Prices medium ■ Professional discount

Restoration and repair of all objects in gold, silver, pewter and bronze. Gilding and silver plating. Master Artisan.

COUTELLERIE DE PASSY

17 rue de l'Annonciation, Paris 75016 ■ Tel. 42 24 77 46 ■ Tues-Sat 10:00-13:00/13:30-18:30

Repair and replating of silver since 1922.

EPPE FRERES

5 rue Chapon, 75003 Paris ■ Tel: 48 87 78 65 ■ Mon-Fri 8:00-12:00/13:30-18:00 ■ Guy Eppe speaks English ■ Prices medium

Gilding and silver plating of all metals, silverware and jewellery. Antique patinas, silver plating of cutlery. Nickle plating.

MADELEINE NOE

2 passage Saint-Sebastien, 75011 Paris ■ Tel: 43 55 62 07 ■ Mon-Fri 8:30-12:00/13:00-18:00

Restoration and replating of silver. Small production of silver trays and goblets.

LES ORFEVRES DE SEVIGNE

2 passage Saint-Sebastien, Paris 75011 ■ Tel. 47 00 15 32 ■ Mon-Fri 8:30-12:30/13:30-17:30 ■ Prices medium ■ Professional discount

Restoration of special silver objects, as well as bronze. Repair and re-silvering of cutlery.

Restoration of Sculpture
Restauration de sculpture

BENOIT LAFAY

4 Villa Chalets, 94110 Arcueil ■ Tel: 49 85 11 58 - Fax: 49 85 94 82 ■ By appointment ■ Benoît Lafay speaks English ■ Prices medium

Restoration of sculpture: stone, wood, plaster, terra cotta with or without polychrome. Restoration of monumental exterior stone. Clients include the National Museums, Historic Monuments and private clients.

ARNAUD VILLENEUVE

3 square des Frères-Farman, 92100 Boulogne-Billancourt ■ Tel: 46 03 78 32 ■ By appointment ■ Arnaud Villeneuve speaks English ■ Prices medium ■ 5 to 10% professional discount

Restorer of sculptured works of art. Restoration of polychromed wood, stone, marble, terra cotta, plaster.
Works for the National Museums and private clients.

Restoration of Bronze
Restauration de bronze

BRONZE DECORATION ETIENNE ET DORE

4 passage Josset, 75011 Paris ■ Tel: 43 55 33 42 - Fax: 43 55 13 17 ■ Mon-Fri 9:00-12:00/13:30-18:30 ■ Prices medium to high ■ Professional discount

Repair and restoration of all objects in bronze. Custom creation and reproduction of bronzes of all periods. Restoration of chandeliers and replacement of missing crystal.

ATELIER COUSTE

3 passage Rauch, 75001 ■ Tel: 43 79 71 01 ■ Mon-Fri 8:00-12:00/13:00-17:00 ■ Prices medium to high ■ Professional discount

Restoration of all art bronze: clocks, furniture bronzes, chandeliers, candelabra. Everything.

MARLENE EDITH DUPONT

8 passage de la Bonne-Graine, 75011 Paris ■ Tel: 47 00 60 52 - Fax: 48 05 37 70 ■ Mon-Fri 8:00-12:00/13:00-17:00/Fri closing 16:00 ■ Georges Michelson-Dupont speaks English ■ Prices high ■ Professional discount

Restoration and copies of XVII, XVIII and XIX century lighting and bronze objects. Mercury gilding, chiselling and mounting. Creation of all types of lighting. Catalogue in 3 languages.

GILBON ET COROLLER

4 rue de Cotte, 75012 Paris ■ Tel: 43 43 94 55 - Fax: 43 43 96 87 ■ Mon-Fri 9:00-12:30/14:00-18:00 ■ English spoken ■ Prices high ■ Professional discount

Restoration of all metal objects of all periods: crystal chandeliers, electrification, statues (all sizes), clocks, all metal furniture, patinas, chiselling, mounting.
Custom creation for National Museums and major corporations.

FERNANDO MOREIRA

8 bd de Ménilmontant, 75020 Paris ■ Tel: 43 72 91 72 - Fax: 43 79 11 48 ■ Mon-Fri 8:00-17:00/Sat by appointment ■ Fernando Moreira speaks English ■ Prices high ■ 10 to 20% professional discount

Restoration and repair of XVIII and XIX century art bronze and furniture bronzes. Bronze gilding, antique patinas, chiselling and mounting. Restoration of ivory.

PEYRUSEIGT

35 rue Rousselet, 75007 Paris ■ Tel: 42 73 09 02 ■ Mon-Fri 6:45-12:30/13:45-19:30 ■ Prices medium to high ■ Professional discount

Restoration of all decorative bronze objects, lighting and electrification. Restoration and reproduction of furniture locks, furniture bronzes.

MAISON SCHMITT

41 rue du Faubourg-du-Temple, 75010 Paris ■ Tel: 42 08 05 43 - Fax: 42 08 49 92 ■ Mon-Fri 8:00-12:30/14:00-18:30 ■ English spoken ■ Professional discount

Restoration of all bronze of all periods. Custom reproduction of bronze objects and furniture bronzes. Mercury gilding and silver plating.

TOULOUSE

10 rue Beautreillis, 75004 Paris ■ Tel: 48 87 82 85 ■ Mon-Fri 8:00-12:00/14:00-18:00/Fri closing 15:00 ■ Prices high

Restoration of art objects in bronze: clocks, sconces, andirons, crystal chandeliers, furniture bronzes.
Restorer of historic monuments.

Wood Carvers
Sculpteurs sur bois

──────────── III ────────────

JEAN RENOUVEL

3 rue Elzévir, 75003 Paris ■ Tel: 42 72 15 28 ■ Mon-Fri 8:00-12:00/14:00-18:00 ■ Prices medium

Wood carving: boiseries (wood panelling), chairs and consoles. Fabrication and restoration.

VINCENT MOUCHEZ

106 rue de Montreuil, 75011 Paris ■ Tel: 43 73 22 47 ■ Mon-Fri 9:00-18:30
■ Prices medium

Carving of ornaments in wood. Wood panelling, wainscoting, copies of antique furniture and chairs. Creation and restoration.

—————————————————————— XVII ——————————————————————

BOISERIES DE SAINT LOUIS

12 place du Maréchal-Juin, 75017 Paris ■ Tel: 45 34 86 30 - Fax: 45 34 86 50
■ Mon-Fri 9:30-18:00 ■ English spoken ■ Prices medium ■ Professional discount

Specialists of modular panels in solid oak, with and without wainscoting. For residential use: libraries, entrance halls, corridors. For contract use: offices, art galleries, hotels, restaurants, exhibition halls and all public spaces.

—————————————————— PARIS SUBURBS ——————————————————

👑 FANCELLI

31 rue Marcel-Bourdarias, 94140 Alfortville ■ Tel: 43 75 47 87 - Fax: 43 75 24 72 ■ Mon-Fri 7:30-12:00/13:30-17:30/Fri closing 17:00 ■ Jean-Pierre and Michel Fancelli speak English ■ Prices high ■ Professional discount

One of the best in France. Fine wood carving of panelling, fireplaces, doors and gates, parquets, windows, lanterns and chandeliers in wood, frames. Sculpture of wood ornaments and statuary, chairs and armchairs. Restoration and creation. Work experience: the National Museums and Châteaux of France, the Palaces of Versailles, Fontainebleau and Compiègne, Notre-Dame de Paris. The Corcoran Gallery, Washington D.C.

👑 AU VIEUX TEMPS
GEORGE SAVIGNY

136 av. Aristide-Briand, 92220 Bagneux ■ Tel: 46 65 14 56 - Fax: 46 65 36 62
■ Mon-Fri 8:00-12:00/14:00-19:00 ■ Prices medium ■ 20% professional discount

One of the great master craftsmen. Fireplaces, wood panelling, doors, parquets. Extraordinary collection of antique boiseries (wood panelling) and sculptured wood objects.

👑 JEAN-CLAUDE TREHERNE

272 av. d'Argenteuil, 92600 Asnières ■ Tel: 47 99 06 41 - Fax: 47 94 27 67
■ Mon-Fri 8:30-12:30/13:30-17:30 ■ English spoken ■ Prices medium to high
■ Professional discount

One of France's best known specialists in millwork. Custom doors, exterior and interior. Wood panelling. An interesting museum collection of antique carved wood and decorative door and window hardware.

Icons
Icônes

---XIII---

ATELIER SAINT LUC
36 bd Arago, 75013 Paris ■ Tel: 43 31 10 22 ■ Mon-Fri by appointment ■ Didier Gulmann speaks English ■ Prices medium

Painting of icons in the traditional manner with a double layer of 24ct gold leafing. On order.

---XX---

MR. FREDERIC COCAULT
5 rue Ernest-Lefèvre, 75020 Paris ■ Tel: 40 31 54 23 ■ Tues-Sat 10:00-19:00 ■ Lydia Manic speaks English ■ Prices medium to high

Restoration of icons, antique gilding and conservation of polychrome on wood.

---MONTREUIL---

MME ISABELLE CLEMENT
Bât B, 33 rue Fernand-Combette, 93100 Montreuil ■ Tel: 48 70 87 97 ■ Mon-Sat by appointment ■ Prices medium

Restoration of Greek, Russian and Byzantine icons.

Lithography
Lithographie

ATELIER DE LITHOGRAPHIE "LA BETE A CORNES"
91 rue La Condamine, 75017 Paris ■ Tel: 42 67 52 32 ■ By appointment ■ English spoken ■ Prices medium ■ Professional discount

Complete lithography studio: creations of original lithographs on stone and hand printed.

ATELIER POINT & MARGE
35 av. Général-Pierre-Billotte, 94000 Créteil ■ Tel: 43 77 96 16/45 40 81 64 ■ Mon-Fri by appointment ■ Jorge de Sousa-Noronha speaks English ■ Prices medium to high ■ 10 to 20% professional discount

Art lithography. Expert in contemporary lithography and estampes. Works directly with artists and edits the "Cahiers de l'Estampe Contemporain".

Miniatures
Miniatures

MME MICHELE BOURDESSOL

18 rue de l'Abreuvoir, 75018 Paris ■ Tel: 42 54 98 35 ■ By Appointment ■
Prices high

Painter of miniatures on ivory and other noble materials. Portraits. Restoration. International clientele.

ZERO FIGURE

38 rue de Seine, 75006 Paris ■ Tel: 43 26 85 91 ■ Mon-Sat: afternoons ■
English spoken ■ Prices medium

1900-1930 art objects, Chinese porcelain, Bohemian crystal, Opaline: all in miniature.
Expert in antique miniatures.

Restoration of Posters
Restauration d'affiches

BRIGITTE BUSSIERE

43 rue de l'Arbre-Sec, 75001 Paris ■ Tel: 47 03 32 58 - Fax: 40 15 96 60 ■
Mon-Fri 9:30-12:30/14:30-18:30 by appointment ■ English spoken ■ Prices
medium ■ Professional discount

High quality and complete restoration of posters. Bleaching and linen backing. Expertise and evaluation.
Sale of posters specializing in tourism and sports.

PATRICE DASSONVILLE

14 rue Daru, 75008 Paris ■ Tel: 42 67 53 64 - Fax: 42 89 03 22 ■ Every day
8:30-23:00 by appointment ■ English spoken ■ Prices medium ■ Professional discount

Excellent restoration of old and contemporary posters.
Linen backing. Works mainly for the Museums.

L'ATELIER

106 av. Marguerite-Renaudin, 92140 Clamart ■ Telfax: 46 48 95 91 ■ Mon-
Fri 9:00-12:30/14:00-19:30 ■ English, Italian and Spanish spoken ■ Prices
medium ■ Professional discount

Restoration of all types of posters. Very high quality. Works for Museums,
Cinemas, collectors and dealers.
Expertise and estimations.

ART FOUNDRIES

Fonderies d'Art

──────────── III ────────────

MEGAFONTE FRANCE

147 rue du Temple, 75003 Paris ■ Tel: 42 71 79 00 - Fax: 42 71 79 01 ■ Mon-Thurs 9:30-18:00/Fri 9:00-15:00 ■ Evelyne Sitbon speaks English ■ Prices medium ■ Professional discount

Casting of all metals, gold, silver, bronze, brass and pewter. Delivered rough or finished as ordered. Work in precious metals for the jewellers of Paris and non-precious metals for haute-couture accessories.

──────────── IV ────────────

♕ ENTREPRISE TOULOUSE

10 rue Beautreillis, 75004 Paris ■ Tel: 48 87 82 85 ■ Mon-Fri 8:00-12:00/14:00-18:00

Chiseling of bronze and work in all metals. Restoration of precious art objects. Work experience: Paul Getty Museum, the Louvre, Château de Versailles, the treasures of the cathedrals.

──────────── XII ────────────

MME FRANCE MARIE LEHE

47 rue de Lyon, 75012 Paris ■ Tel: 43 43 40 49 - Fax: 43 43 14 18 ■ Mon-Fri 8:30-17:30 ■ Prices medium

Foundry for ornaments in bronze and brass. Sand casting and lost wax process.

──────────── XVII ────────────

FONDERIE D'ART DUCROS

1 rue Baron, 75017 Paris ■ Tel: 42 29 22 39 ■ Mon-Fri 8:00-12:00/12:30-18:30 ■ Prices medium

Casting of sculpture in bronze, in limited numbered editions, using the lost wax process. Restoration and mounting of bronzes.

──────────── XX ────────────

MEILLEUR

32 rue des Amandiers, 75020 Paris ■ Tel: 43 66 45 13 - Fax: 43 66 45 43 ■ Mon-Fri 8:30-19:00 by appointment ■ Catherine Meilleur and Claude Delorme speak English ■ Prices high to very high ■ Professional discount

Founders of bronze and wrought iron in decoration and architecture. Work experience: Bibliothèque Nationale in Paris, Palais de Fontainebleau, Palais de Compiègne, the lanterns of the Conseil d'Etat and the Palais Royal.

BLANCHET LANDOWSKI

57 av. Gambetta, 93170 Bagnolet ■ Tel: 43 61 16 41 - Fax: 48 97 17 37 ■ Mon-Fri 8:00-12:00/13:00-17:30/Fri closing 16:30■English spoken■Prices high

This foundry specializes in statuary using both sand casting and the lost wax process. They do the final chiseling as well as the finishing. Their work experience includes the restoration of major historic bronze statues in France as well as casting for well known contemporary sculptors. Also the Dome of Les Invalides, Préfecture de Bobigny, doors at the Louvre.

FLEURANT

Chemin du Halage, Z.I., 78270 Bonnières-sur-Seine■ Tel: 30 98 90 11 ■ Mon-Fri 8:30-12:00/13:30-18:00 ■ Alain Brieu speaks English ■ Prices high

Bronze foundry. Casting, sand and lost wax, to final patinas. Original works of art and limited numbered editions. Realisations for artist-sculptors.

FONDERIE CLEMENTI

29 rue du Lieutenant-Batany, 92190 Meudon ■ Tel: 45 34 56 32 - Fax: 45 34 73 35■Mon-Fri 7:30-12:30/13:30-17:00■English spoken■Prices high

Specialty in statuary, using the lost wax process. Clients include: Miro (Galerie Maeght), Artcurial, Musée Bourdelle.

ARTISAN'S SUPPLIES

Fournitures pour artisans

ART ET CONSERVATION

33 av. Trudaine, 75009 Paris ■ Tel: 48 74 95 82 - Fax: 42 80 35 38 ■ Mon-Fri 13:00-18:30 ■ Prices medium

Products and materials used for restoration and conservation of works of art. Catalogue in French language available upon request.

BHV - BAZAR DE L'HOTEL DE VILLE

52 rue de Rivoli, 75004 Paris ■ Tel: 42 74 90 00 - Fax: 42 74 96 79 ■ Mon-Sat 9:30-19:00/Wed evening until 22:00 ■ Prices reasonable

A very large department store with a basement wonderland of everything imaginable for the artisan, handyman, gardener, etc. If it exists, you'll find it here. Don't hesitate to explore the upper floors for more treasures for the woodworker, the framer, and other decorative accessories.
Maybe the best of its kind in the world.

DECORS BURACH

212 rue du Faubourg-Saint-Antoine, 75012 Paris ■ Telfax: 43 72 12 18 ■ Mon-Fri 8:30-12:00/14:00-18:30/Sat 8:30-12:00 ■ English spoken ■ Prices medium

All wood materials for ebenistes and carpenters. Mouldings and hand turned articles in wood for furniture restoration.

DUGAY

92 rue des Rosiers, 93400 Saint-Ouen ■ (In the Marché aux Puces) ■ Tel: 40 11 87 30 - Fax: 40 12 26 32 ■ Thurs-Mon 9:00-18:00 ■ Prices reasonable ■ Professional discount

Nearly 2,000 different products for artisans, ebenistes, gilders, painters of trompe l'œil, restorers of furniture and marble.

L'ECLAT DE VERRE

2 bis rue Mercœur, 75011 Paris ■ Tel: 43 79 23 88 - Fax: 43 79 23 34 ■ Tues-Sat 9:30-13:00/14:00-19:00 ■ Prices medium ■ 15 % professional discount

Everything for the framer: 500 different models of mouldings (baguettes). Papers for mattes and backing. Art papers. They will cut and assemble frames on the spot. Everything supplied for painting on porcelain.

ETS JULLIEN

42 rue Saint-Jacques, 75005 Paris ■ Tel: 43 54 52 56 - Fax: 43 26 16 77 ■ Mon-Fri 8:30-12:00/13:30-18:00/Fri 8:30-17:00 ■ Discount after 10 dozen

Best selection of leather for book binding.

LEPRINCE DE PARIS

19 rue de Cléry, 75002 Paris ■ Tel: 42 36 59 10 - Fax: 40 26 34 78 ■ Mon-Fri 9:00-18:00 ■ English spoken ■ Prices medium ■ 5 to 15% professional discount

Products for artisans and artists: 400 varieties of silk for silk screening, wide width silk for theatre applications, colors for tinting and painting on silk. Printing on fabric.

RELMA

6 rue Danton, 75006 Paris ■ Tel: 43 25 40 52 - Fax: 43 26 52 94 ■ 3 rue des Poitevins, 75006 Paris ■ Mon-Fri 8:30-12:00/14:00-18:00 ■ English spoken ■ Prices medium ■ Professional discount

Best selection of papers, canvases, leathers, for book binding, leather working, packaging, framing.

ROUGIER ET PLE

13 bd des Filles-du-Calvaire ■ Tel: 42 72 82 91 - Fax: 42 76 03 90 ■ Mon-Sat 9:30-18:30 ■ English spoken ■ Prices reasonable

Everything for the artisan and the artist: the professional and the amateur. Special attention is focussed on simplified products for the amateur. Graphic arts, Beaux Arts, restoration, hobbies and crafts. A very large section is devoted to children's crafts.

TEXLIBRIS

34 rue du Sentier, 75002 Paris ■ Tel: 42 33 86 97 - Fax: 42 36 36 67 ■ Mon-Fri 9:00-13:00/14:00-18:00 ■ English spoken ■ Prices medium ■ Professional discount

Manufacturer of cloth in over 300 colors and weaves, marbled papers (hand and machine made/printed), flocked paper, PVC paper, wood grain printed papers for: book binding, stationary, box manufacturing, framing. Acid free adhesive tape.

─────────────── OUTSIDE PARIS ───────────────

DYNACHOC

6 rue Victor-Carmignac, 94110 Arcueil ■ Tel: 46 65 32 10 - Fax: 45 47 94 77 ■ Mon-Fri 8:45-12:45/13:45-17:45 ■ Pierre Voidet speaks English ■ Discounts depend on quantity

Tools: mallets, small hammers in natural wood, compressed wood, leather, rubber.

ARTIST'S SUPPLIES

Fournitures pour artistes

ADAM MONTPARNASSE

11 bd Edgar-Quinet, 75014 Paris ■ Tel: 43 20 68 53 - Fax: 43 21 23 72 ■
Mon 9:30-12:30/13:30-19:00/Tues-Sat 9:30-19:00 ■ English spoken ■ Prices
medium ■ 10% professional discount

Products for the artist and the restorer. Mouldings and hand turned elements
for furniture restoration. Technical books.

ARTES
BEAUX-ARTS

26 rue Vavin, 75006 Paris ■ Tel: 43 26 94 99 - Fax: 43 54 61 69 ■ Mon-Sat
10:00-19:00 ■ English spoken ■ Prices medium

Complete line of supplies for the artist. Best known brands of colors in oils,
aquarelles, acrylics, gouaches, vinyls, pigments. Brushes, easels, canvas
and stretchers.
Paints for silk screening and porcelain. Supplies for calligraphy. Papers.
Framing supplies. Canvas stretched on order. Porcelain firing. Fixing of silk
screens. Art books.

ART ET JOIE

74 rue de Maubeuge, 75009 Paris ■ Tel: 48 78 27 72 - Fax: 40 16 14 66 ■
Mon-Fri 9:30-18:30 ■ Prices medium ■ 10% professional discount on purchases over 1,000 francs

All supplies for Beaux Arts and artisans. Books and art papers.

ARTISTE PEINTRE

54 bd Edgar-Quinet, 75014 Paris ■ Tel: 43 22 31 71 - Fax: 43 22 41 79 ■
27 rue Gabrielle, 75018 Paris ■ Tel: 42 52 89 02 ■ Mon-Sat 9:30-19:00 ■
English spoken ■ Prices low to medium ■ 10% professional discount

Manufacturers of canvas. All artists supplies, wholesale and retail. Brushes, all colors in oils, aquarelles, pastels, gouaches, acrylics. Everything for
the painter.

DUGAY

92 rue des Rosiers, 93400 Saint-Ouen ■ (In the Marché aux Puces) ■ Tel:
40 11 87 30 - Fax: 40 12 26 32 ■ Thurs-Mon 9:00-18:00 ■ Prices reasonable ■ Professional discount

Nearly 2,000 products for artists, artisans, gilders, restorers of furniture
and marble, painters of trompe l'œil.

PAPETERIE DU PONT LEGENDRE

57 rue Legendre, 75017 Paris ■ Tel: 47 63 69 90 - Fax: 47 63 92 40 ■ Mon-
Fri 9:30-18:00 ■ English spoken ■ Prices medium ■ Professional discount

Products for the Beaux Arts and graphic artist.

PARIS AMERICAN ART

4 rue Bonaparte, 75006 Paris ■ Tel: 43 26 79 85 - Fax: 43 54 33 80 ■ Tues-Sat 10:00-13:00/14:00-18:30 ■ Jo Diamond speaks English ■ Prices medium to high ■ Professional discount

All material for artists: oils, pastels, aquarelles, crayons, brushes, papers, classic canvases, easels, books.

LA REGLE D'OR

10 rue Gassendi, 75014 Paris ■ Tel: 43 20 06 05 ■ Tues-Sat 9:30-12:30/13:30-18:45 ■ Emmanuel Delivet speaks English ■ Prices low ■ Professional discounts

All products for the Beaux Arts. Colors (fine and extra fine). Oils, aquarelles, gouaches, acrylics, pastels, brushes, pigments, canvases, stretchers. 76 different choices of prepared or raw canvases. Supplier to the National Museums.

SENNELIER

3 quai Voltaire, 75007 Paris ■ Tel: 42 60 72 15 - Fax: 42 61 00 69 ■ Mon-Sat 9:00-18:00 ■ English spoken ■ Prices medium to high

Full selection of artists' materials: paints, pastels, aquarelles, crayons, art papers, canvases for the artist, the graphic artist and designer.

———————————— **OUTSIDE PARIS** ————————————

LA THEIERE DE BOIS

5 bis rue Exelmans, 78000 Versailles ■ Tel: 39 53 72 85 ■ Mon-Sat 9:30-18:00 ■ English spoken ■ Prices medium ■ Professional discount

Full line of supplies for artists. Framing services and a training studio in framing.

HELIOLITHE

22 rue Honoré-Oursel, 94290 Villeneuve-le-Roi ■ Tel: 45 97 26 07 - Fax: 49 61 57 06 ■ Mon-Fri 8:30-12:30/13:30-18:00 ■ English spoken ■ Prices medium ■ Will discuss professional discount

Everything to do with design: design tables, accessories and equipment for the graphic artist and designer, chairs, illuminated tables, drawing boards.

BATHROOMS
Salles de bains

III

JACOB DELAFON
Hôtel du Grand Veneur ■60 rue de Turenne, 75003 Paris ■Tel: 40 27 04 50 -
Fax: 48 04 91 50 ■Mon-Fri 9:30-18:30/Sat 10:00-18:30 ■Prices medium to
high
Everything for bathroom installations.

IV

A L'EPI D'OR
17 rue des Bernardins, 75005 Paris ■Tel: 46 33 08 47 ■Tues-Sat 11:00-19:00
■ Prices medium to high ■ Professional discounts
Antique style bathrooms and bathroom fittings. Creations and re-editions.

VI

BEAUTE DIVINE
40 rue Saint-Sulpice, 75006 Paris ■ Tel: 43 26 25 31 ■ Tues-Sat 10:00-
18:00 ■ Prices medium
Bathroom accessories, old and contemporary. Lighting, decorative objects.

X

BAIN & DECOR
37 rue du Paradis, 75010 Paris ■Tel: 48 24 98 80 - Fax: 48 24 08 19 ■Mon-
Fri 9:30-12:30/13:30-18:30/Sat by appointment ■ Jean Pierre Van Beek
speaks English ■ Prices medium to very high ■ Professional discount
Representation of several French manufacturers of everything for the bathroom: from tiling to marble and granite, lighting, faucets, furniture, modular
showers.

XI

CASCADE
26 bd Richard-Lenoir, 75011 Paris ■ Tel: 48 06 14 79 - Fax: 43 38 34 79 ■
Mon-Sat 9:00-19:00 ■ Evelyne Coquet speaks English ■ Prices high ■ 25%
professional discount
Creators of their own high quality line of bathrooms and accessories, including hydro-massage showers, furniture, decorative hardware in crystal and
bronze.

AUX SALLES DE BAINS "RETRO"

29-31 rue des Dames, 75017 Paris ■ Telfax: 43 87 88 00 ■ Mon-Sat 11:00-19:00 by appointment ■ Vera Beboutoff speaks English ■ Prices low to high ■ 10% professional discount

Fully restored antique bathtubs, basins, faucets, bathroom lighting and accessories

J. DELEPINE

104 bd de Clichy, 75018 Paris ■ Tel: 46 06 89 70 - Fax: 42 23 63 82 ■ English spoken ■ Prices medium to very high ■ Professional discount

Complete bathroom installations. From the simple to the extraordinary. Inventor of the cascade faucet. Bathtubs and accessories in faux finishes. Excellent choice of faucets.

DIDIER MARAUT

111 rue du Docteur-Bauer, 93400 Saint-Ouen ■ Tel: 40 10 90 03 - Fax: 40 11 65 22 ■ Mon-Fri 9:00-18:99 ■ Didier and Michel Maraut speak English ■ Prices high ■ 10% professional discount

XIX to early XX century bathrooms and accessories.

BILLIARDS

Billards

————————— V —————————

BILLARDS SOULIGNAC

43 rue Claude-Bernard, 75005 Paris ■ Tel: 43 31 49 75/Atelier: 39 56 25 45
■ Tues-Fri 10:00-13:00/16:00-18:00/Sat I0:00-12:00/16:00-18:00 ■ English
spoken ■ Prices medium to high

Fabrication of billiard tables and games. Restoration and sale of old billiard
tables.

————————— VII —————————

BILLARDS PROUST

50 rue de Babylone, 75007 Paris ■ Tel: 47 53 73 03 - Fax: 45 50 35 53 ■
Tues-Sat 10:30-18:30 ■ English spoken ■ Prices medium

Billiard tables and accessories. Repair of cues and felt. Games in wood, old
and new.

————————— XVII —————————

BILLIARDS - FRANCK CREATIONS

3 av. des Ternes, 75017 Paris ■ Tel: 40 54 02 07 ■ Mon-Sat 10:30-
13:00/14:00-20:00 ■ Frank Teboul and Marylène Lemaitre speak English ■
Prices low ■ Professional discount

Custom fabrication of billiard tables and accessories.

DECOR D'AUTREFOIS

2 rue Le Châtelier, 75017 Paris ■ Tel: 47 66 46 03 - Fax: 40 53 80 47 ■ Mon-
Fri 10:00-13:00/Afternoons by appointment ■ Some English spoken ■ Prices
medium ■ 15% professional discount

Billiard tables and accessories.

————————— VERSAILLES —————————

ROYAL BILLARDS

14 rue Montbauron, 78000 Versailles ■ Tel: 30 21 21 58 - Fax: 30 21 21 55
■ Mon-Sat 9:30-12:30/13:30-19:00 ■ English spoken ■ Prices high ■ 15% professional discount

Sale and repair of high quality billiard tables and accessories. Distributor for
Chevillotte.

BOOK BINDING AND RESTORATION
Reliure et restauration

ATELIER AMELINE

320 rue Saint-Honoré, 75001 Paris ∎ Tel: 42 60 50 65 ∎ Wed-Fri 9:30-12:00/14:00-18.30 ∎ Prices medium to high

Deluxe contemporary bindings. Leathers and papers hand dyed and air-brushed. Full bindings and half bindings.
Gives classes on Mondays and Tuesdays.

JEAN-BERNARD ALIX

52 rue Saint-André-des-Arts, 75006 Paris ∎ Tel: 43 54 28 17 ∎ English spoken ∎ Prices high

High quality classic and comtemporary bindings for original editions.

ROGER BUISSON

4 rue d'Aligre, 75012 Paris ∎ Tel: 43 07 19 25 ∎ Mon-Fri 9:00-18:00 ∎ Prices medium

Restoration of old books, XVI-XIX century. Some binding.

ALAIN DEVAUCHELLE

98 rue du Faubourg-Poissonnière, 75010 Paris ∎ Tel: 48 78 67 12 ∎ Mon-Fri 9:00-17:00 ∎ Prices high

Superb quality classic book binding using old style techniques. Restoration of antique books.

SUN EVRAD

La Celle-les-Bordes, 78720 Dampierre ∎ Tel: 34 85 22 85 ∎ English spoken ∎ Prices low to medium ∎ Every day by appointment

Very high quality and unique comtemporary bindings. Modern structures and constructions based on individual needs of each book. Unique and beautifully painted leather work.

JEAN DE GONET

8 rue Edouard-Lecroy, 75011 Paris ∎ Tel: 43 38 06 57 - Fax: 43 38 22 25 ∎ Mon-Fri 9:00-13:00/14:00-18:00/Fri closing 17:00 ∎ Jean de Gonet speaks English ∎ Prices medium to high

Very contemporary binding using RIM technique (reticulated injected mould). This creates a more supple spine so that the book will remain open without damaging it while photocopying or during reference. It also affords long lasting protection. Ideal method for protection of old works in museums, libraries, etc.

MME CLAUDE HONNELAITRE

14 rue du Cardinal-Lemoine, 75005 Paris ■ Tel: 43 54 89 88 ■ Mon-Fri 9:00-13:00/14:00-18:00/Sat pm by appointment ■ Prices reasonable to high

Excellent quality comtemporary binding, using classic techniques. Bindings follow book themes and are intricately worked, exquisitely embossed.

JEAN KNOLL

6 place Corneille, 92100 Boulogne ■ Tel: 46 21 58 14 ■ Every day by appointment ■ English spoken ■ Prices medium to high

High quality contemporary book binding in simple original styles.

JEHANNE LAEDERICH

22 bd Edgar-Quinet, Bât. B, 75014 Paris ■ Tel: 43 20 92 32 ■ Mon-Fri 9:00-12:00/14:00-18:00/Sat by appointment ■ English spoken ■ Prices medium

Classic and contemporary bindings, restoration of antique bindings, parchment bindings (monastery technique). Gives classes. Holder of the Gold Medal of Master Artisan.

ALAIN LOBSTEIN

5 rue Félix-Faure, 75015 Paris ■ Tel: 45 58 31 25 ■ Mon-Fri 9:00-19:00/Sat 9:00-13:00 ■ Gertrude Delacour speaks English ■ Prices high

Classical and original styles of book binding.
Expert in the restoration of books damaged by fire or flood.

DANIEL MERCHER

18 rue Visconti, 75006 Paris ■ Tel: 43 26 40 41 ■ Mon-Fri 10:00-12:00/14:00-18:00 ■ English spoken ■ Prices medium to high

Contemporary bindings of xx century books. Style oriented towards surrealism and dadaism for original editions.

REGINE MUNIER

1 rue du Pont-de-Lodi, 75006 Paris ■ Tel: 43 26 87 96 ■ Mon 14:00-17:00/Tues-Thurs 10:00-12:00/14:00-17:00 ■ Prices medium

Classic, modern and contemporary styles of binding.
Gives classes.

LUCILLE OLIVER RELIEURE

45 rue Madame, 75006 Paris ■ Tel: 45 48 38 06 ■ Mon 14:30-19:00/Tues-Fri 10:00-12:00/14:30-19:00 ■ English spoken ■ Prices low to high

Classic and contemporary bindings in leather and fabric.
Makes beautiful cases for bibliophiles. Gives classes in the mornings.

RELIEURE SUR COUR
BRIGITTE BLANC

46 rue Monsieur-le-Prince, 75006 Paris ■ Tel: 44 07 28 71 ■ Mon/Thurs 14:30-19:00/Tues-Wed/Fri-Sat 10:00-13:00/14:30-19:00 ■ English spoken ■ Prices medium

All kinds of binding, classic and contemporary, but especially finely worked contemporary. Special occasion books, such as birthdays, weddings, anniversaries, retirements, visitors books, bound memorabilia of all kinds.

FLORENT ROUSSEAU

34 rue Ballu, 75009 Paris ■ Tel: 45 26 70 58 ■ Mon-Fri 9:30-12:00/14:00-18:00
■ Professional discount for minimum of 10 books

Classic and contemporary book binding, embossing and gold leafing, restoration. Art papers. Japanese binding. Visitors and special occasion books. Special.

CLAUDIE SEGUIER

20 rue Berthe, 75018 Paris ■ Tel: 42 55 72 79 ■ English spoken ■ Prices medium

Top quality classic and contemporary binding.

Gold leafing on books
Dorure sur reliure

♔ LA FEUILLE D'OR

7 rue de La Tour d'Auvergne, 75009 Paris ■ Tel: 42 82 17 36 ■ Mon-Fri 8:30-12:30/14:00-18:30 ■ Pascale Therond speaks English ■ Prices medium

Specializes in gold leafing by hand, on leather bound books. Restoration of gold leafing on old books. Gold leafing of designs on modern and contemporary bindings. Titles. Unique models and in small series. Gold leafing on leather for furnishing and leather-covered objects.
Very high quality work.

♔ ATELIER CAMILLE BERTHAUX

4 rue René-Hamon, 94800 Villejuif ■ Tel: 46 78 66 32 ■ Mon-Fri 9:00-12:00/14:00-18:00 by appointment ■ Camille Berthaux speaks English ■ Prices low to high

Very high quality gold leafing on leather, especially titles and decoration on book bindings. Titles harmonious with the text and the quality and style of the binding.

BOOK SELLERS

Librairies

In contrast with the United States, books in France fall within the domain of the arts and are not sold in the same way. With few exceptions, Paris book shops are small, cozy and often dusty and crowded.

Walk into any of the small book shops of Paris and, chances are, you will find a passionate lover of books who can tell you not only the contents of any of his books, but the exact and intimate details of the author's life, the provenance of the book and when, where and how it received its beautiful binding.

Books represent, as clearly as the design and decoration of a home, the character of the owner. As in the shape and form of a house, the colors of the interior, the furniture, the draperies, and the pictures on the wall, books are a window into an individual's soul.

There are literally thousands of English language books, beautifully bound, as well as those in French, in the book shops of Paris. Take the time to browse, and don't forget the book stalls along the banks of the Seine. They make a pleasant diversion on a balmy Spring day in Paris. You never know what you will come up with.

This section of the TOUT PARIS SOURCE GUIDE begins with the antique and rare books and then moves into the specialized areas. You will also find many of the most renowned antique book dealers under the Fine Arts section.

The editors have tried to select the best of the book shops dealing in subjects of interest to the designer, the architect and the discriminating individual.

Antique and Rare

II

LIBRAIRIE MARCO POLO

25 rue Saint-Marc, 75002 Paris ■ Tel: 42 96 82 83 ■ Mon-Fri 9:30-12:00/14:00-18:30 ■ François Roux-Dessarps speaks English ■ Prices: medium

Antique books, particularly illustrated books, of the XIX century.

III

CARNAVALETTE

2 rue des Francs-Bourgeois, 75003 Paris ■ Tel: 42 72 91 92 ■ Mon-Sun 10:30-18:30 ■ Dominique Franciosi speaks English ■ Prices medium ■ 10% professional discount

Antique books and newspapers of the XIX century, essentially satirical in nature. Specialty: original lithographs by the caricaturist SEM. Original antique engravings of the XIX century.

IV

LA VOUIVRE

11 rue Saint-Martin, 75004 Paris ■ Tel: 42 72 37 82 - Fax: 42 72 02 83 ■ Sale by correspondence ■ Brigitte Mathieu speaks English ■ Prices medium

Literature from the end of the XIX and early XX century. History books. Also offers research service. Catalogues on order.

LIBRAIRIE ROSTAIN

3 rue de l'Ave-Maria, 75004 Paris ■ Tel: 42 74 50 18 ■ Tues-Sat afternoons ■ Patrice Rostain speaks English ■ Prices medium ■ 10 to 15% professional discount

Antique books, original editions, paintings, engravings.

V

L'ALBERTINE

9 rue Maître-Albert, 75005 Paris ■ Tel: 43 29 39 20 ■ Tues-Sat 14:30-19:00 ■ Christine Mafart speaks English ■ Prices medium ■ 10% professional discount

Antique and modern books: literature, history, beaux-arts. Antique and modern prints (not contemporary). Portrait engravings of the XVI to early XX century by the French. Flemish, German, Italian, Spanish and English schools. Other engravings, organized by period and theme.

⚜ LIBRAIRIE DE L'ABBAYE

27 rue Bonaparte, 75006 Paris ■ Tel: 43 54 89 99 - Fax: 43 29 81 69 ■ Tues-Sat 10:00-12:30/14:00-19:00 and by appointment ■ Régine Bernard speaks English ■ Prices medium to high

Antique books on bibliophilism. Illuminated manuscripts of the XVI-XVIII centuries. Autographs and manuscripts, autographed musical scores, small format books, autographed manuscripts.
Stock: 5,000 volumes, 30,000 autographs.
Jacques-Henri Pinault is an expert before the Court of Appeals, Paris.

BENELLI

244 rue Saint-Jacques, 75005 Paris ■ Tel: 46 33 73 51 - Fax: 40 51 01 39 ■ Mon-Fri 11:30-18:30 ■ A little English spoken ■ Prices medium ■ 10% professional discount

Antique books through the XIX century. Expert to the Cour d'Appel, Paris.

LIBRAIRIE MICHEL BOUVIER

14 rue Visconti, 75006 Paris ■ Tel: 46 34 64 53 - Fax: 40 46 91 40 ■ By appointment ■ Michel Bouvier speaks English ■ Prices medium

Antique, rare and precious books. Old documents.
Qualified expert.

LIBRAIRIE CLAUDE BUFFET

7 rue Saint-Sulpice, 75006 Paris ■ Tel: 43 26 61 79 ■ Tues-Sat 10:30-12:30/14:30-18:30 ■ Blanche Buffet speaks English ■ Prices medium

French literature from XIX and XX centuries. Original editions and rare works no longer in print. They will research works on request.

RENE CLUZEL

61 rue de Vaugirard, 75006 Paris ■ Tel: 42 22 38 71 - Fax: 45 44 79 66 ■ Tues-Sat 14:30-18:30/Mornings by appointment ■ René Cluzel speaks English ■ Prices medium

Rare and precious old and modern books, Original editions of literature, books on painters, illustrated books, travel, curiosa, erotica, esoterica, philosophy. Bibliographies. Beautiful bindings.

CHRISTIAN GALANTARIS

15 rue des Saints-Pères, 75006 Paris ■ Tel: 47 03 49 65 - Fax: 42 60 42 09 ■ Mon-Fri 10:00-12:30/14:30-18:30 ■ Christian Galantaris speaks English ■ Prices medium to high

Antique collectible books. Expert to the Court of Appeals. Organisation of public sales of books internationally.

LIBRAIRIE LE FELL

16 rue de Tournon, 75006 Paris ■ Tel: 43 26 52 89 - Fax: 43 54 24 17 ■ Tues-Sat 10:00-13:30/14:30-19:00 ■ Jean-Marie Le Fell speaks English ■ Prices medium ■ Professional discount

Antique books on Paris, the history of Paris, maps of Paris. Old photographs 1850 to 1980. Mediaeval manuscripts, mediaeval illuminations. Antique books on various subjects (XVI to XIX century).

FERNAND MARTINEZ

97 rue de Seine, 75006 Paris ■ Tel: 46 33 08 12 ■ Mon-Sat 9:45-18:30 ■ Anne-Claude Bonaventure speaks English ■ Prices medium ■ 10% professional discount

Antique prints, engravings and original lithographs on France and other countries. Old maps, some old books and framed engravings.

NEUF MUSES

41 quai des Grands Augustins, 75006 Paris ■ Tel: 43 26 38 71 - Fax: 43 26 06 11 ■ Mon-Fri 14:00-18:30/Mornings and Sat by appointment ■ Alain Nicolas speaks English ■ Prices medium ■ Professional discount

Antique books, autographs and manuscripts. Qualified expert.

JEAN MOREL

19 rue du Vieux-Colombier, 75006 Paris ■ Tel: 45 44 43 26 - Fax: 35 59 73 41 ■ By appointment ■ Jean Morel speaks English ■ Prices medium ■ 10% professional discount

Rare and precious books, manuscripts, documents, expertise on inheritance, insurance appraisals.
Qualified expert.

LE PONT TRAVERSE

62 rue de Vaugirard, 75006 Paris ■ Tel: 45 48 06 48 ■ Tues-Sat 12:00-19:00 ■ Prices medium

Rare books of poetry, literature, beaux-arts. Original and out of print editions.

♛ LIBRAIRIE PINAULT

36 rue Bonaparte, 75006 Paris ■ Tel: 46 33 04 24 - Fax: 43 29 81 09 ■ Tues-Sat 10:00-12:00/14:00-19:00 ■ English spoken ■ Prices medium to high ■ Professional discount

A marvellous collection of rare books, manuscripts, illuminated documents from the XV to the XX centuries.

LIBRAIRIE HISTORIQUE TEISSEDRE

102 rue du Cherche-Midi, 75006 Paris ■ Tel: 45 48 03 91 - Fax: 45 44 35 52 ■ Mon-Fri 10:00-12:00/13:30-19:00 ■ M. Teissedre speaks English ■ Prices medium ■ 10% professional discount

XVIII, XIX and XX century books on history from antiquity to the present day, military arts, genealogy.

———————————————— VII ————————————————

♛ LIBRAIRIE DE LATTRE

56 rue de l'Université, 75007 Paris ■ Tel: 45 44 75 30 - Fax: 45 44 83 53 ■ Mon-Fri 10:30-13:00/14:00-19:00 ■ Marché Vernaison, Marché aux Puces, ■ 99 rue des Rosiers, 93400 Saint-Ouen ■ Tel: 40 12 68 89 ■ Sat-Mon 9:30-18:00 ■ Dominique and Marie-Ange de Lattre speak English ■ Prices medium ■ 10% professional discount

Extraordinary collection of posters and books of the XIX and XX centuries. Theatre and film publicity, advertising, illustrations. Old books on the beaux-arts, travel, fashion, children's books.

VIII

♛ LIBRAIRIE AUGUSTE BLAIZOT

164 rue du Faubourg-Saint-Honoré 75008 Paris ■ Tel: 43 59 36 58 - Fax: 42 25 90 27 ■ Tues-Sat 9:30-12:30/14:00-18:30 ■ Claude Blaizot speaks English ■ Prices medium to high ■ 10% professional discount

Antique & modern books, original editions, illustrated books. Specialty: rare and precious editions of French literature. Beautiful bindings, classical and very special contemporary.

JADIS ET NAGUERE

166 rue du Faubourg-Saint-Honoré, 75008 Paris ■ Tel: 43 59 40 52 - Fax: 45 62 93 54 ■ Mon-Fri 11:00-19:00/Sat 14:00-19:00 ■ English spoken

Books of XVI to XX centuries, beautifully bound. Bibliophilism. Watercolours, Art Nouveau & Art Deco drawings and engravings.

LES JOURS ANCIENS

57 rue de Rome, 75008 Paris ■ Tel: 45 22 68 86 ■ Mon-Fri 11:30-18:30 ■ Michel Fournier speaks English ■ Prices medium

Antique books and documents.

LIBRAIRIE LARDANCHET

100 rue du Faubourg-Saint-Honoré, 75008 Paris ■ Tel: 42 66 68 32 - Fax: 49 24 07 87 ■ Mon-Sat 10:00-19:00 ■ Bertrand Meaudre speaks English ■ Prices high

Antique and modern books, documents on the beaux-arts. Superbly bound.

LIBRAIRIE HENRI PICARD ET FILS

126 rue du Faubourg-Saint-Honoré, 75008 Paris ■ Tel: 43 59 28 11 - Fax: 43 59 04 02 ■ Mon-Sat 10:00-12:30/14:00-19:00 ■ Christian Picard speaks English ■ Prices medium ■ 10% professional discount

Founded in 1860. High quality antique and modern books, engravings and prints. Books of bibliophilism.

IX

♛ LIBRAIRIE FRANÇOIS AND RODOLPHE CHAMONAL

5 rue Drouot, 75009 Paris ■ Tel 47 70 84 87 - Fax: 42 46 35 47 ■ Mon-Fri 9:00-18:30/Sat 9:00-12:00 call first on Sat ■ Prices low to high ■ Professional discount

Rare and precious books from the XV to late XIX centuries, mainly in French. Specializing in marine, voyages, medicine, science, gastronomy. Beautiful bindings.

GERARD GANET

10 passage Verdeau, 75009 Paris ■ Tel: 42 46 31 15 - Fax: 40 22 97 63 ■ Mon-Sat 10:00-13:00/15:00-19:00 ■ Gérard Ganet speaks English ■ Prices medium ■ 10 to 20% professional discount

Antique books and decorative prints (hunt scenes, flowers, birds, marine). Old maps, topography — illustrated books, maps, views.

AU VIEUX DOCUMENT

6 bis rue de Châteaudun, 75009 Paris ■ Tel: 48 78 77 84 ■ Mon-Fri 11:00-18:00 ■ Foucauld Bachelier speaks English ■ Prices medium ■ 10% professional discount

Antique and modern books: literature, beaux-arts, travel, leisure, sports, gastronomy. Framing for old engravings and prints.

————————————— **XI** —————————————

LIBRAIRIE ALCANDRE

46 rue Léon-Frot, 75011 Paris ■ Tel: 40 09 13 73 ■ Mon-Fri 14:00-20:00 and by appointment ■ Catherine Severo speaks English ■ Prices medium ■ 10% professional discount

Literature of XIX and XX centuries: original editions, illustrated editions. Works on theatre, poetry, criticism. Will research on request.

FRANCOIS VALLERIAUX

98 bd Voltaire, 75011 Paris ■ Tel: 47 00 50 43 ■ Mon-Fri 14:00-19:00/Sat 11:00-19:00 ■ François Valleriaux speaks English ■ Prices medium

They specialize in rare & antique books: erudition, architecture & urbanism, ethnology, folklore, arts & crafts, as well as books on other subjects.

————————————— **XII** —————————————

LES FLEURS DU MAL

24 rue Chaligny, 75012 Paris ■ Tel: 43 40 63 34 ■ Mon-Sat 14:30-20:00 ■ Thierry Valin speaks English ■ Prices low ■ 10% professional discount on presentation of TOUT PARIS SOURCE GUIDE

Antique and second hand books.

————————————— **XIV** —————————————

JACQUES LEVY

46 rue d'Alésia, 75014 Paris ■ Tel: 43 27 08 79 ■ Mon-Sat afternoons ■ Jacques Levy speaks English

Old books, documents and judaica.

————————————— **XV** —————————————

LIBRAIRIE RECHERCHES

238 rue de la Croix-Nivert, 75015 Paris ■ Tel: 45 32 42 72 ■ Mon-Sat 10:30-13:00/15:00-19:00 ■ Prices medium ■ 10% professional discount

Antique books and out of print editions.

PAGES VOLANTES

7 rue Auguste-Bartholdi, 75015 Paris ■ Tel: 40 59 88 46 ■ Tues-Sat 12:00-19:00 ■ Prices medium

Antique and modern books. Specialty: research on out of print books and specialized subjects. Beautiful old illustrated children's books. Liliane Reutsch and Pascale Celereau claim to be the Sherlock Holmes of out of print editions.

LIVRES DE A TO Z

3 rue des Moines, 75017 Paris ■ Tel: 42 29 49 19 ■ Tues-Sat 10:30-13:00/14:00-19:00 ■ Béatrice Bablon speaks English ■ Prices medium ■ 10 to 20% professional discount

Antique books of the XIX and XX centuries: literature, beaux-arts, history. Research service offered free.

———————————— VERSAILLES ————————————

LIBRAIRIE ANCIENNE ET MODERNE

30 rue de la Paroisse, 78000 Versailles ■ Tel: 39 50 43 75 ■ Mon 16:00-19:00/Tues-Sat 11:00-12:00/16:00-19:00/Sun 11:00-12:00/17:00-19:00 ■ Prices medium ■ 10% professional discount

Antique & modern books and engravings.

LIBRAIRIE GALERIE LEFEBVRE

38 rue de la Paroisse, 78000 Versailles ■ Tel: 39 50 44 84 - Fax: 30 24 66 36 ■ Tues-Sat 14:30-19:00

Old and rare books, on painting and sculpture, architecture, Versailles, furniture, the hunt, gastronomy.
Illustrated books in limited editions.

———————————— MAISONS-LAFFITTE ————————————

A LA NEF DES FOUS

8 av. Sully, 78600 Maisons-Laffitte ■ Tel: 34 93 90 22 - Fax: 34 93 90 23 ■ Daily 10:00-19:00 by appointment ■ F.G. Hunold speaks English ■ Prices high ■ 10% professional discount

Antique, rare and precious books. Illustrated books.
High quality bindings.

Architecture, Fine Arts & Décoration

LIBRAIRIE ABENCERAGE

177 rue Jeanne-d'Arc, 75013 Paris ■ Tel: 47 07 30 32 - Fax: 47 07 30 67 ■ Mon-Sat 10:00-12:30/15:00-18:30 ■ Prices medium

Old books and reference works on Islam and the Arab World concerning beaux-arts, architecture, decoration and design.

▩ LES EDITIONS DE L'AMATEUR

5 rue de Montholon, 75009 Paris ■ Tel: 45 23 13 44 - Fax: 45 23 59 89 ■ Mon-Fri 9:00-18:00/ Fri closing 17:00 ■ Librarian: M. Isidoro ■ English, German and Spanish spoken ■ Prices medium ■ Professional discount with ID

Valuable reference resources for architects, interior designers and art collectors. Specialized works on ebenisterie, furniture, the period 1900 to 1930. Haute Epoque (XVII, XVIII, XIX centuries). Books that contain everything to do with the art market, i.e. latest prices, appraisals, state of the market, auctions, etc.

Some English publications. Catalogues available and sales by correspondence.

LIBRAIRIE DE L'AMEUBLEMENT ET DE LA DECORATION

23 rue Joubert, 75009 Paris ■ Tel: 42 82 09 21 - Fax: 40 16 43 65 ■ Mon-Sat 10:00-19:00/Sat closed 18:00 ■ Danielle Tetard and Olivier Wittwer speak English ■ Prices medium

Excellent collection of contemporary books on woods, furniture styles, interior architecture and design, antiques, art objects and collectibles. Sale by correspondence and free catalogue available on request. If they don't have it they will know where to find it. Extremely helpful.

LIBRAIRIE DES ANTIQUAIRES

Le Louvre des Antiquaires (street level) ■ 2 place du Palais-Royal, 75001 Paris ■ Tel: 42 61 56 79 ■ Tues-Sat 11:00-19:00 ■ English spoken ■ Prices medium ■ Professional discount

Books on antiques, collectibles, decoration, XVIII and XIX century furniture, art objects, art deco. Most in French, a few in English.

ARCHIVES LIBRAIRIE

52 rue Mazarine, 75006 Paris ■ Tel: 43 54 12 64 - Fax: 40 46 84 22 ■ Mon-Sat 16:00-19:00/Tues-Fri 11:00-12:30/16:00-19:00 ■ Jean-Dominique Carre speaks English ■ Prices medium to high ■ Professional discount

XX century books, all documentation and samples of architecture, decorative arts, beaux-arts. 2 or 3 catalogues available every year.

GALERIE ARENTHON

3 quai Malaquais, 75006 Paris ■ Tel: 43 26 86 06 - Fax: 43 26 62 08 ■ Mon-Fri 8:30-12:30/15:00-19:00/Sat closed 18:00 ■ English and Italian spoken ■ Prices medium ■ Professional discount

XX century illustrated books, reference books on artists, documentation on engravings, engravings and posters.

JEAN-LOUIS BARBERY

2 rue des Grands-Degrés, 75005 Paris ■ Tel: 43 25 33 76 ■ Tues-Sat 13:00-19:00 ■ Annick Barbery speaks English ■ Prices medium ■ 10% professional discount

XIX and XX century books and prints. Books on the beaux-arts: painters, engravers, architecture, fabrics, etc. Original editions.

Antique and modern prints: architecture, views, artists' engravings. Japanese prints.

LIBRAIRIE DU CAMEE

70 rue Saint-André-des-Arts, 75006 Paris ■ Tel: 43 26 21 70 - Fax: 43 29 38 88 ■ Mon-Sat 14:00-19:00 ■ Prices medium

Old and contemporary books on trades, artisanat, decoration, architecture, decorative arts, beaux-arts.

LIBRAIRIE DU COMPAGNONNAGE

2 rue de Brosse, 75004 Paris ■ Tel: 48 87 88 14 - Fax: 48 04 85 49 ■ Mon-Fri 11:00-18:30/Sat 14:00-18:00 ■ Prices medium ■ Professional discount

Works on the specialized building trades, restoration and decoration. "How to" books on every discipline including artisanat and architecture. Sale by correspondence. Catalogue upon request.

LIBRAIRIE DU COMPAGNONNAGE (MUSEUM)

10 rue Mabillon, 75006 Paris ■ Tel: 43 26 25 03 ■ Mon-Fri 14:00-18:00

This museum representing the building trades, stone masons, master carpenters, roofers, plumbers, zinc workers, carpenters, ebenistes and metal workers displays the qualifying models "chefs-d'œuvre" of apprentices who then become members of the Guilds (Compagnons).
Some books on these trades are available in French.

LIBRAIRIE JULLIEN CORNIC

29 av. Matignon, 75008 Paris ■ Tel: 42 68 10 10 - Fax: 42 65 18 19 ■ Mon-Sat 9:00-19:00 ■ Prices medium ■ Professional discount

Rare and precious antique books on decoration, gardens, beaux-arts, photography, fashion. Illustrated books of artists and art exhibit catalogues. Research service for out of print books.

LIBRAIRIE DU CYGNE

17 rue Bonaparte, 75006 Paris ■ Tel: 43 26 32 45 - Fax: 43 26 92 68 ■ Mon-Fri 10:00-12:00/14:30-19:00 and by appointment ■ Prices medium ■ 10% professional discount

Old books on decorative arts, books of fabric samples, drawings and decorative panels.

LIBRAIRIE EDITORIALE

10 rue de l'Abbaye, 75006 Paris ■ Tel: 43 29 21 45 ■ Mon-Fri 9:00-12:30/14:00-17:00

Outlet for all the works produced by the National Museums: books, posters, catalogues, models, reproductions.
Catalogue available and sale by correspondence.

F.M.R.
FRANCO MARIA RICCI

12 rue des Beaux-Arts, 75006 Paris ■ Tel: 46 33 96 31 - Fax: 43 25 79 06 ■ Tues-Sat 10:00-13:00/14:30-19:00 ■ English spoken ■ Prices medium ■ 10% professional discount

Contemporary books on architecture, art, design and decoration.

♛ BIBLIOTHEQUE FORNEY

1 rue Figuier, 75004 Paris ■ Tel: 42 78 14 60 ■ Tues-Fri 13:30-20:30/Sat 10:00-20:00 ■ English spoken

The beautiful old Hotel de Sens. Extensive collection of works on architecture, applied arts. decorative arts, interior decoration, gardens and landscaping. Fabulous collection of antique books. Favorite research hangout for the dedicated professional and students of art, decoration, design and architecture.

LIBRAIRIE HACHETTE

24 bd Saint-Michel, 75006 Paris ∎ Tel: 43 25 98 71 - Fax: 46 34 17 31 ∎ Mon-Sat 10:00-19:00 ∎ Some English spoken ∎ Prices medium ∎ Professional discount

Recent works of Hachette and other publishers on the beaux-arts, including art books, some works on European decorative arts, renaissance and art deco.

LIBRAIRIE LECOINTRE OZANNE

9 rue de Tournon, 75006 Paris ∎ Tel: 43 26 02 92 - Fax: 46 33 11 40 ∎ Tues-Sat 10:00-19:00/Sat closing 18:00 ∎ English spoken ∎ Prices medium ∎ Professional discount

Books dating from the beginning of the XIX century to just prior to the second world war, specializing in architecture and decorative and applied arts. In all languages.

LIBRAIRIE LEONCE LAGET
VERONIQUE DELVAUX

76 rue de Seine, 75006 Paris ∎ Tel 43 29 90 04 - Fax: 43 26 89 68 ∎ Mon 14:00-18:30/Tues-Fri 9:00-12:00/Sat by appointment ∎ Prices medium to high

Excellent collection of rare old and contemporary editions on the history of art, ancient and modern, from the beginning to now: architecture, painting, sculpture, costumes, ceramics, beaux-arts and applied arts.

LIBRAIRIE MAEGHT

42 rue du Bac, 75007 Paris ∎ Tel: 45 48 45 15 - Fax: 42 22 22 83 ∎ 12 rue Saint-Merri, 75004 Paris ∎ Tel: 42 78 43 44 - Fax: 42 78 27 61 ∎ Tues-Sat 10:00-13:00/14:00-19:00 ∎ Prices from a postcard to a Braque lithograph for FF100,000.00 ∎ 10 to 30% professional discount

Beautiful books on art, large collection of catalogues of exhibitions of these two establishments plus the Foundation Maeght. Art editions, lithographs, modern and contemporary artists' posters, Braque, Chagall, Miro, Calder, Giacometti, Leger and others. Monographs and engravings.

♛ LIBRAIRIE DU MUSEE DES ARTS DECORATIFS

107 rue de Rivoli, 75001 Paris ∎ Tel: 42 96 21 31 ∎ Mon-Sun 10:00-19:00 ∎ Antoinette Baraev speaks English and is extremely helpful. If she doesn't have it, she'll find it for you.

A treasure house for the period 1900 to 1930 and all other periods covering architecture, design, furniture, plastic arts, beaux-arts, fabric designs, decorative hardware, table arts, gardens - all possible areas of decoration. Sale by correspondence.

NOTE: Just next door you will find the Bibliotheque (Library) of the Musée des Arts Décoratifs. It is the repository of just about everything in the vast history of French decoration. You are perfectly welcome to use the facility for research as long as you provide ID.

LIBRAIRIE F. DE NOBELE

35 rue Bonaparte, 75006 Paris ∎ Tel: 43 26 08 62 - Fax: 40 46 85 96 ∎ Mon-Fri 9:00-12:00/14:00-19:00 ∎ Prices low to very high ∎ Professional discount

Antique and modern books on the arts: architecture, painting, applied arts, furniture, decoration...

LIBRAIRIE LE PETIT PRINCE

121 bd Saint-Michel, 75005 Paris ■ Tel: 43 54 45 60 ■ Mon-Sat 9:30-19:00
■ English spoken

Books for collectors: XVII to XIX century books on the beaux-arts and related subjects.

GALERIE DE LA SORBONNE

52 rue des Écoles, 75005 Paris ■ Tel: 43 25 52 10 ■ Mon-Sat 10:30-19:30
■ English spoken ■ Prices medium ■ Professional discount

Extensive collection of second hand books on architecture of all schools, particularly XX century, famous architects from Haussmann to the great masters of today. They also have other sections.

LIBRAIRIE VISIONS

184 bd Saint-Germain, 75006 Paris ■ Tel: 45 48 77 91 ■ Mon-Sat 10:30-19:00
Excellent collection of art books at reasonable prices.
Books on painting, sculpture, drawing, decorative arts, photography.

XXᵉ SIECLE ET SES SOURCES

4 rue Aubry-le-Boucher, 75004 Paris ■ Tel: 42 78 15 49 - Fax: 42 78 47 90
■ Tues-Fri 10:30-12:30/14:30-18:30/Sat 14:30-18:30 ■ Alain Blondel speaks English ■ Prices medium ■ 10% professional discount on old books

Antique and recent reference books, reviews and documention on art, architecture and decoration between 1870 and the present day.

Arms & Military

ARMES ET COLLECTIONS

19 av. de la République, 75011 Paris ■ Tel: 47 00 68 72 - Fax: 40 21 68 72
■ Tues-Sat 10:00-19:00 ■ English spoken ■ Prices medium ■ Professional discount

Vast collection of books, of which 75% are in English, on arms, uniforms, conflicts, military and utilitarian vehicles. Video cassettes on planes, wars, elite forces.

LIBRAIRIE PIERRE PETITOT

234 bd Saint-Germain, 75007 Paris ■ Tel: 45 48 05 27 ■ Mon-Fri 9:30-12:30/14:30-19:00 ■ Danyela Petitot speaks English ■ Prices medium

Antique and out of print books on the military arts: arms, artillery, decorations, fortifications, 1870-1971 War, regimental history, military uniforms, French Army memorabilia...

Cartoons and Comic Strips

L'AGE D'OR

59 & 61 rue Raymond-Losserand, 75014 ■ Tel: 42 79 89 89 ■ Tues-Sat 15:30-19:30 ■ Prices high ■ 5 to 10% professional discount

Old comic strips and all old works for children, albums, documents and illustrated books 1920-1960.

Jean-Louis Duriez is President of the Chambre Européenne Syndicale des Antiquaires Réunis et Experts en Bandes Dessinées et Papiers Anciens, la "C.E.S.A.R."

ALBUM

6 rue Dante, 75005 Paris ■ Tel: 43 54 67 09 ■ Tues-Sat 10:00-20:00 ■ English spoken ■ Prices medium ■ Professional discount

American comic books and English language comic strips from the sixties to the present, movie magazines and books on cinema.

AUX LIVRES D'ALESIA

13 rue Daval, 75011 Paris ■ Tel: 47 00 98 77 ■ Mon-Sat 14:30-19:00 ■ Prices medium ■ Professional discount

Interesting collection of 1920 to the present American and French comic strips, children's books and books on scouting.

LIBRAIRIE ROLAND BURET

6 passage Verdeau, 75009 Paris ■ Tel: 47 70 62 99 - Fax: 42 46 00 75 ■ Tues-Fri 12:15-18:45 ■ Prices high

Cartoon art: old comic strips and original cartoon cells.

FANTASMAK

17 rue de Belzunce, 75010 Paris ■ Tel: 48 78 72 44 ■ Tues-Sat 15:30-19:00

1950's and 1960's comic strips. Old detective and mystery novels. Cinema posters.

LIBRAIRIE NATION

4 bd de Charonne, 75020 Paris ■ Tel: 43 73 01 04 - Fax: 43 70 42 93 ■ Mon-Sat 10:00-19:00 ■ Gilles and Marc speak English ■ Prices average ■ Professional discount

Substantial collection of French cartoons and comic strips. Original cells and drawings, quite often signed by the author. They also bind comic strips and have them autographed at no extra charge. Occasionally have on offer cartoons from other countries.

ODYSSEE

160 av. Parmentier, 75010 Paris ■ Tel: 42 40 10 68 ■ Mon-Fri 11:00-19:30/Sat 14:30-19:30 ■ Prices low ■ 25 to 30% professional discount and 10% for a FF250 purchase for anyone carrying the TOUT PARIS SOURCE GUIDE

Second-hand books, rare and out of print.

Specialties: comic strips, detective and mystery novels, science fiction, fantastic stories; psychoanalysis, psychology, pedagogy; contemporary literature.

Cinema

LIBRAIRIE ATMOSPHERE
7 rue Francis-de-Pressencé, 75014 Paris ■ Tel: 45 42 29 26 ■ Mon-Sat 14:00-20:00
Large collection of cinema posters.

AUX FILMS DU TEMPS
8 rue Saint-Martin, 75004 Paris ■ Tel: 42 71 93 48 - Fax: 42 71 94 84 ■ Mon 14:00-19:30/Tues-Sat 11:30-19:30 ■ English spoken ■ Prices medium ■ Professional discount
Old and recent books in English and French on all aspects of the cinema, photos and posters. Sale by correspondence.

CINEDOC
45-53 Passage Jouffroy, 75009 Paris ■ Tel: 48 24 71 36 ■ Mon-Sat 10:00-19:00 ■ English spoken ■ Prices medium ■ Professional discount
A vast collection of 16,000 movie posters from the beginning of cinema to the present. Photos of the stars, books and reviews.

Contemporary

ABBEY BOOKSHOP
29 rue de la Parcheminerie, 75005 Paris ■ Tel: 46 33 16 24 ■ Mon-Sat 11:00-20:00 ■ Brian Spence and staff speak English ■ Prices medium
Books from all parts of Canada, especially Quebec: English, American - new and out of print. Bibliographic research and sale by correspondence. Orders taken for all Canadian, Quebecois, and Anglo-American works.

BRENTANO'S
37 av. de l'Opéra, 75002 Paris ■ Tel: 42 61 52 50 - Fax: 42 61 07 61 ■ Mon-Sat 10:00-19:00 ■ English spoken ■ Prices medium ■ Professional discount
Excellent English/French language bookshop with all the latest. Good selection of current books on the beaux-arts, antiques, decoration, history, current affairs, current biography. Most of the books on antiques, furniture and decoration are in French. The latest American magazines and a special department for English language videos and audio cassettes. A touch of Fifth Avenue in Paris.

F.M.R.
FRANCO MARIA RICCI
12 rue des Beaux-Arts, 75006 Paris ■ Tel: 46 33 96 31 - Fax: 43 25 79 06 ■ Tues-Sat 10:00-13:00/14:30-19:00 ■ Yves Dantoing speaks English
Special art editions, broad collection of works in French,English and Spanish on architecture, artists and painting.

FLAMMARION

19 rue Racine, 75006 Paris ■ Tel: 43 29 12 52 - Fax: 43 26 47 81 ■ Mon-Fri 9:30-13:00/14:15-18:30■ English spoken ■ Prices medium ■ Professional discount

The retail outlet for this large publisher, distributor. They also operate the bookshops in several of the Paris Museums, including the Musée des Arts Décoratifs (Museum of the Decorative Arts) on the rue de Rivoli. Their publications include every aspect of architecture and design as well as a broad range of other subjects. There are only a few works in English.

FNAC FORUM

1 rue Pierre-Lescot, 75001 Paris ■ Parking Forum des Halles, Sud, Porte Berger ■ Tel: 40 41 40 00 - Fax: 40 41 40 86■ Mon-Sat 10:00-19:30■ Marie-Edith Gillette speaks English ■ Prices medium

A supermarket of bookstores. Run on the same principles as an American chain, there is, in this location, a good collection of works on the beaux-arts as well as a vast general offering in all other subject areas.

GALIGNANI

224 rue de Rivoli, 75001 Paris ■ Tel: 42 60 76 07 - Fax: 42 86 09 31 ■ Mon-Sat 10:00-19:00 ■ English spoken ■ Prices medium ■ Professional discount

Anglo-American-French book store with an excellent and broad collection on all subjects. The latest works of fiction and non-fiction. Their beaux-arts section is international with many works in English. Sale by correspondence to all countries.

GALLIMARD

15 bd Raspail, 75007 Paris ■ Tel: 45 48 24 84 - Fax: 42 84 16 97 ■ Mon-Sat 10:00-19:00 ■ English spoken ■ Prices medium ■ Professional discount

Fine selection of works on the beaux-arts and decoration in the French language. Mme Cheenne is the specialist.

GIBERT-JEUNE

5 place Saint-Michel, 75005 Paris ■ Tel: 43 25 70 07 - Fax: 43 26 25 34 ■ Mon-Sat 9:00-19:30■ English spoken ■ Prices medium ■ Professional discount

This well known Latin Quarter institution for students of all ages has a special section devoted to decoration and the beaux-arts. Well worth exploring as you will find works in English and a splendid collection in the French language.

LIBRAIRIE LA HUNE

170 bd Saint-Germain, 75006 Paris ■ Tel: 45 48 35 85 - Fax: 45 44 49 87 ■ Mon-Sat 10:00-23:45■ English spoken ■ Prices medium ■ Professional discount

Ask for Mr Pajaud. He runs the section on architecture, decorative arts, graphics, interior design with works in many languages, including English.

W. H. SMITH

248 rue de Rivoli, 75001 Paris ■ Tel: 44 77 88 99 - Fax: 42 96 83 71 ■ Mon-Sat 9:30-19:00 ■ Everyone speaks English ■ Prices medium ■ Professional discount

35,000 titles in English as well as a good selection of English and American magazines. Well organized stacks include books on interior design, architecture, furniture, antiques.

SHAKESPEARE & CO.

37 rue de la Bûcherie, 75005 Paris ■ Tel: 43 26 96 50 ■ Open 7 days a week from noon to midnight ■ English spoken

This famous old landmark dates back to the traditions of Sylvia Beech, publisher of James Joyce and good friend of the expatriate writers of the 1920s and 1930s. George, the proprietor and his acolytes can help you find your way through the stacks and lead you to whatever they have in the fields of design, architecture, furniture, etc.
The shop holds the best collection of Hemingway, Joyce, Fitzgerald and others of the period. One thing is certain, the collection is highly volatile, changing every week with new acquisitions in English and French. George also holds a "salon" every Sunday afternoon at 16:00 hours. Don't miss it. You never know what you might find and whom you may encounter.

TEA AND TATTERED PAGES

24 rue Mayet, 75006 Paris ■ Tel: 40 65 94 35 - Fax: 39 50 33 76 ■ English spoken ■ Prices reasonable

Second-hand English books. American tea room with American and English gifts such as quilts and teapots.

Gastronomy and Oenology

LIBRAIRIE GOURMANDE

4 rue Dante, 75005 Paris ■ Tel: 43 54 37 27 - Fax: 43 54 31 16 ■ 7 days a week 10:00-19:00 ■ English spoken ■ Prices medium ■ Professional discount
From the XVI century to today, books on food and wine.
Some in the English language.

LIBRAIRIE REMI FLACHARD

9 rue du Bac, 75007 Paris ■ Tel: 42 86 86 87 ■ Mon-Fri 10:30-12:30/14:30-18:30 ■ Prices high ■ Professional discount

Antique and recent works on gastronomy and oenology from the XV century to the present.

LA LIBRAIRIE DES GOURMETS

98 rue Monge, 75005 Paris ■ Tel: 43 31 16 42 - Fax: 43 31 60 32 ■ Mon 13:00-19:00/Tues-Sat 10:30-19:00 ■ English spoken ■ Prices average ■ Professional discount to students of the Ecole Ritz and Cordon Bleu

Recent works and re-editions of books from 200 BC to the present. From Apicius to the great chefs of today.

History

BOUTIQUE DE L'HISTOIRE

24 rue des Écoles, 75005 Paris ■ Tel: 46 34 03 36 - Fax: 43 26 83 96 ■ Mon 14:00-19:00/Tues-Sat 9:00-19:00 ■ Pierre and Michelle Borella speak English ■ Prices medium

New and second-hand books on history from all parts of the world. Will sell by correspondence.

EDITION LIBRAIRIE LA TABLE D'EMERAUDE

8 rue des Trois-Portes, 75005 Paris ■ Tel: 43 25 40 32 - Fax: 40 51 02 67 ■ Mon-Sat 10:30-12:30/14:30-18:30 ■ George Staune speaks English ■ Prices medium

Antique books, especially dealing with the history of religions and esoterism.

LIBRAIRIE HISTORIQUE CLAVREUIL

37 rue Saint-André-des-Arts, 75006 Paris ■ Tel: 43 26 71 17 - Fax: 43 54 95 37 ■ Tues-Sat 9:00-12:00/14:00-19:00/Sat closing 18:00 ■ English spoken ■ Prices average ■ Professional discount

This splendid old book shop specializes in the history of France from the VI century to the end of the XIX century.
Books in all languages date from the XV century.
They will undertake heraldic research. They have a good selection of works on the beaux-arts. They also specialize in the military arts, relating to the French revolution and the Napoleonic wars.

Orientalism

LIBRAIRIE ORIENTALISTE PAUL GEUTHNER

12 rue Vavin, 75006 Paris ■ Tel: 46 34 71 30 - Fax: 43 29 75 64 ■ English spoken ■ Mon-Fri 9:15-12:00/13:00-18:00/Wed closed 19:00

Antique books on archaeology, linguistics, history of religions, ethnology of: the Mediterranean, Caucasian Central Asia, India, Tibet, the Far East, Black Africa, the Americas, the Hebraic and Islamic worlds.

Sciences

BERNARD MAILLE

3 rue Dante, 75005 Paris ■ Tel: 43 25 51 73 ■ Mon-Fri 14:00-18:00 ■ Bernard Maille speaks English ■ Prices medium ■ 10% professional discount to bookstores

Antique books on the exact sciences (mathematics, physics, chemistry), natural science, medecine. Catalogues published in all these categories.

FABRICE BAYARRE

21 rue de Tournon, 75006 Paris ■ Tel: 43 54 91 99 - Fax: 43 54 58 78 ■ Fabrice Bayarre speaks English ■ Prices medium ■ 10% professional discount

Antique books on the sciences and medicine.

L'INTERSIGNE LIVRES ANCIENS

66 rue du Cherche-Midi, 75006 Paris ■ Tel: 45 44 24 54 - Fax: 45 44 50 55 ■ Mon-Fri 11:00-19:00/Sat 11:00-14:00 ■ Alain and Nevine Marchiset speak English ■ Prices medium ■ 10% professional discount

Antique books, documents concerning the sciences, medicine, philosophy, Freemasonry, occult sciences, curiosities. Orders by correspondence. Five new illustrated catalogues per year upon request.

Sports

LIBRAIRIE DES ALPES

6 rue de Seine, 75006 Paris ■ Tel: 43 26 90 11 - Fax: 44 07 03 66 ■ Tues-Fri 10:30-12:30/14:30-19:00/Sat 10:00-17:00 ■ Elise Vibert-Guigue and Véronique du Chatelier speak English ■ Prices medium

Old and recent books, engravings and posters on alpinism and speleology. First editions of works by Jules Verne.

"LE SPORTSMAN"

7 bis rue Henri-Duchêne, 75015 Paris ■ Tel: 45 79 38 93 ■ Friday 11:00-20:00 and by appointment ■ Prices high

Antique documentation on sports: books, reviews, photos, programmes, posters, etc.

Voyages

CHARLES BLACKBURN

27 rue Pierret, 92200 Neuilly-sur-Seine ■ Tel: 47 22 82 30 - Fax: 40 88 35 13 ■ Charles Blackburn speaks English and Japanese ■ Prices high ■ 10% professional discount

Antique and rare books, photos and engravings on voyages to the Far East, Japan, South East Asia, China and the Pacific Basin.

LIBRAIRIE DUDRAGNE

86 rue de Maubeuge, 75010 Paris ■ Tel: 48 78 50 95 - Fax: 48 74 14 04 ■ Mon-Fri 9:00-13:00/14:00-18:00/Sat by appointment ■ Patrick Dudragne speaks English ■ Prices medium ■ 5 to 10% professional discount

XVI to XIX century books and engravings on voyages to all parts of the world. Maps and atlas of this period. Decorative prints.

LIBRAIRIE LEPERT ET SCHELER

42 rue Jacob, 75006 Paris ■ Tel: 42 61 42 70 - Fax: 42 61 46 03 ■ Wed-Sat 15:00-18:00 and by appointment ■ Lucie Scheler speaks English ■ Prices medium

Antique and rare editions specializing in voyages to all parts of the world.

LA TROISIEME VEILLE

40 rue Milton, 75009 Paris ■ Tel: 40 16 13 87 ■ Tues-Sat 10:00-13:30/15:00-19:30 ■ Michel Sarlin speaks English ■ Prices medium ■ 10% professional discount

Antique and modern books especially on voyages.

CARPETS AND TAPESTRIES
Tapis et tapisseries

II

CASA LOPEZ

34 Galerie Vivienne, 75002 Paris ■ Tel: 42 60 46 85 - Fax: 49 27 99 17 ■
Mon-Sat 10:30-19:00 ■ Bernard Magniant speaks English ■ Prices medium ■ Professional discount

Interesting decorative carpets and rugs. Original creations of Bernard Magniant and executed by artisans.

JULES FLIPO

49 bis rue Sainte-Anne, 75002 Paris ■ Tel: 47 03 44 77 - Fax: 47 03 47 57
■ Some English spoken ■ Prices medium to high ■ Professional discount

A specialist in the creation of original carpets and rugs for over 100 years. Original creations of Manuel Canovas and Patrick Frey. Large choice of carpets in all fibers for residential and contract use. Custom and stock. Colette Sarrat is extremely helpful.

TOULEMONDE-BOCHART

10 rue du Mail, 75002 Paris ■ Tel: 40 26 68 83 ■ English, Spanish and German spoken ■ Prices medium to high ■ Professional discount

Tapestries in original designs by Andrée Putman, Jean-Jacques Baume, Christian Duc, Didier Gomez, Hilton Macconico, Pascal Morgue, Hélène Yardley. Some of these are on permanent exhibit at the Cooper Hewitt Museum in New York and regularly shown at the Musée des Arts Décoratifs in Paris.

III

ARTIS FLORA

75 rue Vieille-du-Temple, 75003 Paris ■ Tel: 48 87 76 18 - Fax: 48 87 98 60
■ Mon-Sat 9:00-19:00 ■ Jean-François Gravier speaks English ■ Prices high
■ 20% professional discount

Reproductions of antique tapestries, hand woven, as well as machine woven, and printed giving an antique patina. They are hand finished and the process takes approximately 3-5 months. Decorative cushions and table throws.

🏠 BRAQUENIE

111 bd Beaumarchais, 75003 Paris ■ Tel: 48 04 30 03 - Fax: 48 04 30 39 ■
Mon-Fri 9:00-18:00 ■ English spoken ■ Prices high ■ Professional discount

XIX century Aubusson tapestries and reproductions of the XVIII century. Choice of 5,000 documents from the XVIII and XIX centuries from which to choose Jacquard woven carpets and wall to wall carpeting. Wall to wall carpeting is 70cms wide (28") and can be ordered in small and large quantities. Custom colors 54 yard minimum. Carpets and rugs are usually 3.50m wide and 4.85m long (44"X62"). They have some art deco designs for custom orders and will work with you and make your own designs. Mr. Jacques Gaultier is the expert.

VI

TAPIS BOUZNAH

55 bd Raspail, 75006 Paris ■ Tel: 42 22 52 26 ■ Mon-Sat 9:30-19:00/Sun 10:00-14:00 ■ Messrs Bouznah and Khan speak English ■ Prices medium ■ 10 to 20% professional discount

Antique and modern carpets from Iran, the Caucasus and Turkey. Cleaning and repair services.

CODIMAT

63-65 rue du Cherche-Midi, 76006 Paris ■ Tel:45 48 79 67 - Fax:45 48 79 25 ■ Mon-Fri 8:30-12:00/13:30-18:00/Fri closing 17:00 ■ English spoken ■ Prices medium ■ Professional discount

Contemporary carpets machine-made to customers design and wall to wall carpets to measure.

GALERIE DIURNE

45 rue Jacob, 75006 Paris ■ Tel: 42 60 94 11 - Fax: 43 43 44 07 49 ■ Mon 14:00-19:00/Tues-Fri 11:00-13:00/14:00-19:00/ ■ Sat 11:00-19:00 ■ Shawn Doubiago speaks English ■ Prices medium to high ■ 20% professional discount

Remarkable custom creations by Marcel Zelmanovitch made in Katmandu, in all sizes.

♛ ROBERT FOUR

28 rue Bonaparte, 75006 Paris ■ Tel: 43 29 30 60 - Fax: 43 25 33 95 ■ Mon 14:00-19:00/Tues-Sat 10:00-19:00 ■ English and German spoken ■ Prices medium to high ■ Professional discount

Contemporary tapestries of artists: Sonia Delaunay, Magritte, Klee, Picasso, Douanier Rousseau, Folon, Miotte, Toffoli, made in Aubusson. Antique French carpets and tapestries. Restoration.

KILIM

21 rue Dauphine, 75006 Paris ■ Tel: 44 07 29 52 ■ Mon-Sat 10:30-20:00 ■ Runi Olmez and Frederic Bertin speak English ■ Prices low ■ 20% professional discount

Oriental carpets and kilims. Mostly old.

VII

GALERIE AFSARI

67 av. de Suffren, 75007 Paris ■ Tel: 45 66 45 48 - Fax: 45 67 30 76 ■ Tues-Sun 11:00-19:00 ■ Siyamak Afsari speaks English ■ Prices medium

Antique Oriental and European carpets, kilims and tapestries.

♛ GALERIE CHEVALIER

17 quai Voltaire, 75007 Paris ■ Tel: 42 60 72 68 - Fax: 42 86 99 06 ■ Mon 14:00-18:00/Tues-Fri 10:00-13:00/14:00-19:00/ ■ Sat 11:00-19:00 ■ English spoken ■ Prices high

The best of antique carpets and tapestries, European and Oriental. Restoration and cleaning. The Chevalier brothers are extraordinarily knowledgable. Qualified experts.

LAURENT TAPIS

101 av. de la Bourdonnnais, 75007 Paris ■ Tel: 45 50 40 21 ■ Mon 14:30-19:30/Tues-Sat 10:30-19:30 ■ Mr. Laurent speaks English ■ Prices medium ■ Professional discount

Antique and contemporary oriental carpets. Repair and washing.

TAI PING CARPETS

30 rue des Saints-Pères, 75007 Paris ■ Tel: 42 22 96 54 - Fax: 45 44 28 92 ■ Mon-Fri 9:00-13:00/14:00-18:30/Sat 14:00-19:00 ■ English spoken ■ Prices high ■ Professional discount

Carpets and rugs by contemporary creators as well as custom made carpets to your design. Wall to wall carpeting.

☷ TISCA

46 rue de Grenelle, 75007 Paris ■ Tel: 42 22 84 23 - Fax: 42 22 88 61 ■ English spoken ■ Prices medium to high ■ Professional discount

Contemporary custom carpets, tapestries, and carpeting made to measure. Special editions of carpets designed by well known artists and designers as well as made to your own design. Machine made and hand tufted.

——————————— VIII ———————————

ARTCURIAL

9 av. Matignon, 75008 Paris ■ Tel:42 99 16 16 - Fax: 43 59 29 81 ■ Tues-Sat 10:15-19:15 ■ English spoken ■ Prices high

Numbered editions of designs of the great contemporary artists woven into carpets.

BOCCARA

184 rue du Faubourg-Saint-Honoré, 75008 Paris ■ Tel: 45 53 84 63 - Fax: 42 56 50 44 ■ Tues-Sat 10:30-13:00/14:00-18:30 ■ Jacqueline Boccara speaks English ■ Prices high to very high

Antique European tapestries of the XV to XVIII century. Restoration.

☷ CENTRE FRANÇAIS DES TAPIS D'ORIENT

217 rue du Faubourg-Saint-Honoré, 75008 Paris ■ Tel: 45 61 12 95 - Fax: 53 76 05 16 ■ Tues-Sat 10:30-12:30/14:00-19:30 ■ Shiva Sabet speaks English ■ Prices high ■ 20 to 30% professional discount

Specialty: Antique Oriental carpets.

COROT EDITIONS D'ART

65 av. des Champs Elysées, 75008 Paris ■ Tel: 42 25 36 59 - Fax: 42 25 65 76 ■ Mon-Thurs 10:00-18:00 ■ Raymond Corot speaks English ■ Prices medium ■ Professional discount

Exclusive contemporary tapestries by well known artists, numbered and signed. Also reproductions of antique tapestries.

HADJER ET FILS

102 rue du Faubourg-Saint-Honoré, 75008 Paris ■ Tel: 42 66 61 13 - Fax: 42 66 66 03 ■ Mon-Sat 10:30-19:00 ■ Reynold Hadjer speaks English ■ Prices medium to high ■ 10% professional discount

Antique European and Oriental carpets and tapestries. Restoration, expertise.

HENIDE TAPIS

25 rue La Boétie, 75008 Paris ■ Telfax: 42 65 62 30 ■ Mon-Fri 9:30-12:00/14:00-18:30 ■ Mr. de Leon speaks English ■ Prices medium to high ■ Professional discount

Antique Oriental and European carpets, antique tapestries, tapestries of contemporary artists. Atelier of restoration. Qualified expert.

LEFORTIER-POTIGNON

54 rue du Faubourg-Saint-Honoré, 75008 Paris ■ Tel: 42 65 43 74 ■ Mon-Fri 10:00-12:30/14:00-18:30 ■ English spoken ■ Prices high ■ Professional discount

French and Flemish tapestries of the XVI, XVII and XVIII centuries. Expert to the Cour d'Appel, Paris.

ROBERT MIKAELOFF

23 rue La Boétie, 75008 Paris ■ Tel: 42 65 24 55 - Fax: 49 24 05 16 ■ Mon-Sat 9:00-12:00/14:00-19:00 ■ Robert and Albert Michaeloff speak English ■ Prices very high ■ Professional discount

Beautiful carpets and tapestries. Qualified expert.

♛ YVES MIKAELOFF

10 rue Royale, 75008 Paris ■ Tel: 42 61 64 42 - Fax: 49 27 07 32 ■ Mon-Sat 10:00-19:00 ■ Yves Mikaeloff and Nicolas Joly speak English ■ Prices very high ■ Professional discount

One of the greatest collections of European and Oriental carpets and tapestries. Qualified expert.

PERSEPOLIS

95 bd Haussmann, 75008 Paris ■ Tel: 42 65 32 60 ■ Mon 14:00-19:00/Tues-Sat 10:00-19:00 ■ English spoken ■ Prices medium to high ■ Professional discount

Excellent collection of Persian and European carpets.

PRESTIGE DE PERSE

122 bd Haussmann, 75008 Paris ■ Tel: 45 22 05 48 - Fax: 43 87 53 32 ■ Mon-Fri 10:30-18:30 ■ Farhad and Farideh Ahi speak English ■ Prices medium ■ 5 to 10% professional discount

Antique Oriental carpets. Antique French carpets (Aubusson and Savonnerie). French and Flemish tapestries. Antique embroidery and fabrics.

---------------------------**IX**---------------------------

TAPIS AMSTERDAM

96 rue d'Amsterdam, 75009 Paris ■ Tel: 45 26 72 94 - Fax: 48 74 40 99 ■ Mon-Sat 9:30-19:00 ■ Jean-Pierre and Nicole-France Benichou speak English ■ Prices medium ■ 25% professional discount

Oriental carpets, antique and modern, reproductions, cleaning.

LES ATELIERS DE LA TAPISSERIE FRANÇAISE

4 rue de Clichy, 75009 Paris ■ Tel: 42 85 13 00 - Fax: 40 23 95 90 ■ Mon-Fri 10:00-19:00/Sat 14:00-18:00 ■ Patrick Wheeler speaks English ■ Prices low ■ Professional discount

Jacquard woven tapestry reproductions of XV to XIX centuries: Aubusson, Gobelin, Flanders.

ERIC BAKERDJIAN

10 rue Choron, 75009 Paris ■ Tel: 48 78 93 39 ■ Mon-Fri 9:00-17:30 ■ Eric Bakerdjian and Gaby Douzmanian speak English ■ Prices medium ■ 10 to 20% professional discount

Antique Oriental and European carpets. Aubusson and Flemish tapestries from the XVI to XIX centuries.

GERARD HADJER

22 rue Drouot, 75009 Paris ■ Tel: 48 24 96 67 - Fax: 44 79 05 06 ■ Tues-Sat 14:00-19:00 and by appointment ■ Gérard Hadjer speaks English ■ Prices high ■ Professional discount

Carpets, kilims and tapestries from Europe and the Orient.
Editions of carpets. Restoration. Qualified expert.

———————————————— X ————————————————

CNA TAPIS

Douane Centrale (Central Customs) ■ 18, rue Yves-Toudic, 75010 Paris ■ Tel: 42 08 54 30 - Fax: 48 03 19 73 ■ Mon-Fri 8:00-12:00/13:30-17:30 ■ Yves Mille speaks English ■ Prices medium

Wholesale and in bond Oriental and Far Eastern carpets.

DJADDA AND COMPANY

Douane Centrale (Central Customs) ■ 11 rue Léon-Jouhaux, 75010 Paris ■ Tel: 42 40 22 55 - Fax: 42 40 59 70 ■ Mon-Fri 9:00-17:00 ■ Homeira Jadda speaks English ■ Prices medium ■ Prices wholesale on presentation of TOUT PARIS GUIDE

Oriental carpets and kilims from Iran, Turkey, China, India, Pakistan. Will ship.

SAM LAIK

Douane Centrale (Central Customs) ■ 18 rue Yves-Toudic, 75010 Paris ■ Tel: 42 41 13 63 - Fax: 42 41 99 90 ■ Mon-Fri 9:00-17:30 ■ Philippe Laik speaks English ■ Prices high ■ 30% professional discount

Custom carpets by contemporary designers hand loomed to measure. Kilims, sisal floor covering and wall to wall.

ROHAN

Douane Centrale (Central Customs) ■ 11 rue Léon-Jouhaux, 75010 Paris ■ Tel: 42 45 32 51 - Fax: 42 45 33 80 ■ Mon-Fri 8:30-17:30 ■ Rohan and Mohamad Chafai speak English ■ Prices low ■ 10 to 20% professional discount

Large selection of Persian and Caucasian carpets and textiles. Sold in bond.

SABET PERSEPOLIS

Douane Centrale (Central Customs) ■ 18 rue Yves-Toudic, 75010 Paris ■ Tel: 42 41 31 95 - Fax: 42 41 96 20 ■ Mon-Fri 8:00-18:00/Sat 8:00-12:00 ■ Shiva Sabet speaks English ■ Prices medium ■ 10% professional discount
Oriental carpets from Iran, China, Turkey, Afghanistan, India, Pakistan. Sold in bond.

FRANCE SAMIN

Douane Centrale (Central Customs) ■ 11 rue Léon-Jouhaux, 75010 Paris ■ Tel: 42 08 25 97 - Fax: 42 08 25 50 ■ Mon-Fri 9:00-18:00 ■ English spoken ■ Prices low ■ Professional discount
Old and recent Persian carpets, some Afghan and Russian. Sold in bond.

TAPIS VOLANT

Douane Centrale (Central Customs) ■ 11 rue Léon-Jouhaux, 75010 Paris ■ Tel: 40 18 37 66 - Fax: 44 52 96 87 ■ Mon-Fri 9:00-18:00 ■ Prices low
Oriental carpets of all origins (Iran, Pakistan, China) Sold in bond. Cleaning, repair.

TEHRANEX

Douane Centrale (Central Customs) ■ 11 rue Léon-Jouhaux, 75010 Paris ■ Tel: 42 00 18 68 - Fax: 42 06 87 14 ■ Mon-Fri 9:30-12:00/14:30-17:00 ■ Rahim Nafisspour speaks English ■ Prices medium to very high
Oriental carpets of all origins.

---------------------- **XI** ----------------------

LA CORNE D'OR

15 rue Jean-Macé, 75011 Paris ■ Tel: 43 79 28 66 - Fax: 43 56 33 25 ■ Mon-Fri 14:00-19:00 ■ Prices medium ■ Professional discount
Oriental carpets.

---------------------- **XII** ----------------------

CARRE BASTILLE TAPIS

74 rue du Faubourg-Saint-Antoine, 75012 Paris ■ Tel: 43 45 48 86 - Fax: 43 45 00 70 ■ Mon 14:00-19:00/Tues-Fri 10:00-19:00/Sat 10:00-19:30 ■ Patrick Sarfati speaks English ■ Prices medium to high ■ Professional discount
Old carpets from Iran, Turkey, Caucasus, India, Pakistan.
Contemporary avant garde designs from Nepal in exclusivity.

NISSIM

32 rue du Faubourg-Saint-Antoine, 75012 Paris ■ Tel: 43 43 78 00 - Fax: 43 43 82 12 ■ Mon-Sat 10:00-19:30 ■ Guy and Philippe Nissim speak English ■ Prices medium ■ 5 to 20% professional discount
Rare, antique Oriental carpets of all origins in sizes up to 35 square meters. Contemporary carpets in exclusive designs.

KILIMI

36 av. des Gobelins, 75013 Paris ■ Tel: 42 41 27 74 - Fax: 42 02 42 24 ■ Mon-Sat 10:00-19:00 ■ English Spoken ■ Prices low to medium ■ 20 to 40% professional discount

Antique and modern Oriental carpets and kilims.
Small furniture upholstered in antique kilims. Repairs.

AUX TRESORS DE LA PERSE

1 av. Paul Déroulède, 75015 Paris ■ Tel: 45 67 38 28 ■ Thurs-Sun 10:00-19:00 ■ Morteza Kafi speaks English ■ Prices low ■ 20% professional discount

Oriental carpets, especially Persian, some from Pakistan, Turkey, China.

GALERIE CARDO

61 av. Kléber, 75116 Paris ■ Tel: 47 27 08 45 - Fax: 47 27 88 21 ■ Mon-Sat 10:00-19:00 ■ Masoud & Yahya Moghadaszadeh speak English ■ Prices medium

Antique and recent Persian carpets in wool and silk. Kilims, Persian and Chinese art objects.

MOMTAZ TAPIS

17 rue de la Tour, 75116 Paris ■ Tel: 42 15 09 09 - Fax: 42 15 06 43 ■ Mon 14:00-19:00/Tues-Sat 10:00-19:00 ■ Patrick and Philippe Momtaz speak English ■ Prices high ■ 15% professional discount

Specialists in Oriental carpets in silk and in large dimensions. Restoration and estimates.

TAPIS POINCARE

88 av. Raymond-Poincaré, 75116 Paris ■ Tel: 45 00 67 26 - Fax: 45 00 23 41 ■ Mon-Sat 10:00-19:00 ■ Albert Bellaiche speaks English ■ Prices medium ■ 20% professional discount

Oriental carpets of all origins., recent, old and antique. Non-slip liners. Cleaning and restoration of carpets and tapestries.
French crystal chandeliers.

MONA

40 bd Gouvion-Saint-Cyr, 75017 Paris ■ Tel: 45 72 28 55 ■ Mon-Sat 10:00-12:00/14:00-19:00 ■ Mahmood Masghati speaks English ■ Prices medium

Oriental carpets, objects, glass, ceramics.

SOPEXIM

21 rue Ruhmkorff, 75017 Paris ■ Tel: 45 74 08 34 - Fax: 45 74 60 20 ■ Mon-Sat 10:00-19:00 ■ Sevket Ozmen and Attila Altan speak English ■ Prices medium ■ 30 to 50% professional discount

Carpets and kilims: Persian, Turkish, Afghan, Chinese, Pakistani. Furniture covered in antique kilims.
Wrought iron furniture and objects. Old pottery.

──────────VERSAILLES──────────

LANGTON & GRIFF

23 rue du Général-Leclerc, 78000 Versailles ■ Tel: 30 21 66 25 ■ Tues-Sat 10:30-12:30/14:00-19:00 ■ Paula and Nicolas Sargenton speak English ■ Prices medium ■ 30 to 40% professional discount

Oriental carpets and kilims, antique and contemporary. Restoration and cleaning.

────────── OUTSIDE PARIS ──────────

♔ MANUFACTURE DES TAPIS DE COGOLIN

Bd Louis-Blanc, 83311 Cogolin ■ Tel: 94 54 66 17 - Fax: 94 54 47 93 ■ Mon-Fri 8:30-12:00/14:00-18:00 ■ English spoken

Carpets woven to order in any size and colour.
Hand woven, hand tufted, hand knotted.

♔ MANUFACTURE PINTON

Savonneries d'Aubusson at Felletin (Creuse) ■ 36 rue des Jeuneurs, 75002 Paris ■ Tel: 40 26 54 69 - Fax: 42 21 35 62 ■ Mon-Fri 9:00-12.30/14:00-18:30 ■ English spoken

This is the cradle of French tapestry making. Custom short pile Aubusson carpets and Savonnerie tapestries in contemporary designs by some of the great artists, Calder, Delaunay, Miro, Vasarely. Custom re-editions of antique designs and made to measure contemporary.

♔ MANUFACTURE DE TAPIS CONTEMPORAIN LEDEVE

Hôtel de Ville, 34702 Ledève ■ Tel: 67 88 86 00 ■ Mon-Fri

Contemporary custom carpets. Art Deco and your design.
This is the manufacturer of the Art Deco carpets of the luxury liner "Normandy".

Tapestries - Restoration & Reproduction

♛ MAISON BROCARD

1 rue Jacques-Cœur, 75004 Paris■Tel: 42 72 16 38 - Fax: 42 72 04 77■Mon-Fri 9:00-12:00/14:00-17:00 ■ Marie Brocard speaks English ■ Prices high

Restoration, historic reconstitution and copying of antique embroideries and tapestries.

HENRIETTE GUICHARD

8 rue des Pyramides, 75001 Paris■Tel: 42 60 40 40 ■Mon-Sat 11:00-18:30 ■ English spoken ■ Prices medium to high ■ Professional discount

Restoration of tapestries and Aubusson carpets of all periods. Reproduction and custom designs of canvases for needlepoint, as well as all supplies. Will make screens and cushions.

HOSSEIN AMINIAN

7 rue de Verneuil, 75007 Paris■ Tel: 40 21 08 16 - Fax: 56 44 04 98 (Bordeaux)■ By appointment

Restoration and cleaning of antique Oriental carpets and tapestries. Qualified expert.

DELARUE-TURCAT

94 rue du Bac, 75007 Paris■Tel: 45 48 56 74 - Fax: 45 48 02 42■Tues-Fri 10:15-12:30/14:15-19:00/■Sat 10:30-12:30/14:30-19:00■Norbert Delarue speaks English ■ Prices medium to high ■ Professional discount

Restoration and cleaning of antique tapestries and carpets.

♛ AU JARDIN D'ISPAHAN

9 rue de Bassano, 75116 Paris■Tel: 47 20 38 95 - Fax: 47 23 67 60■Mon-Fri 9:00-18:00/Fri closing 17:00 ■ English spoken ■ Professional discount

One of the best restorers of carpets and tapestries.

Tapestry and Embroidery
Custom Work and Materials

ATELIER D'ANAIS

23 rue Jacob, 75006 Paris ■Tel: 43 26 68 00■Tues-Fri 10:00-12:00/14:00-18:00/Sat 14:00-18:00 ■ Anne-Marie Giffard speaks English ■ Prices high

Prepared canvases and supplies for needlework.

MAISON SHOKKOS

27 rue d'Assas, 75006 Paris■Mon 14:00-19:00/Tues-Fri 10:30-12:00/14:00-19:00■Prices medium to high ■ Professional discount

Restoration of old tapestries. Custom antique reproductions and contemporary designs. Canvases prepared for all types of needlepoint. All materials available.

TAPISSERIES DE LA BUCHERIE

3 rue du Haut-Pavé, 75005 Paris ■ Tel: 40 46 87 69 ■ Mon-Sat 10:00-19:00
■ Dominique Siegler speaks English ■ Prices medium to high ■ Professional discount

Needlepoint classes in English and French.
1,000 documents from the Middle Ages to Loire tapestries to the present. Top quality custom work with hand dyed wools. Pillows, screens, panels. Speciality: custom panels for churches and cathedrals. Estimates provided. Everything for needlepoint, custom made or "do it yourself". All types of kits and materials.

TAPISSERIES DE FRANCE

25 rue Paul-Fort, 75014 Paris ■ Tel: 45 41 77 92 ■ Mon-Fri 10:00-18:30/Sat by appointment ■ Prices medium ■ Professional discount

Custom preparation of canvases for tapestry and needlepoint of old and contemporary designs, middle ages, rural panels, "mille fleurs", for chairs, armchairs, sofas. They will make to order or you can "do it yourself".

VOISINE

12 rue de l'Eglise, 92200 Neuilly ■ Tel: 46 37 54 60 - Fax: 46 24 23 28 ■ Tues-Sat 10:00-19:00 ■ English spoken ■ Prices medium ■ Professional discount

All kits for embroidery and tapestry.

CHAIRS
Sièges

——— V ———

DANIEL PIERRE

22 rue des Boulangers, 75005 Paris ■ Tel: 43 54 15 11 ■ Mon-Fri 8:30-12:30/13:30-18:00 ■ Prices medium to high ■ Professional discount

Specialist in the restoration of antique chairs.
Works for the best antique dealers.

——— VI ———

ETAT DE SIEGE

1 quai de Conti, 75006 Paris ■ Tel: 43 29 31 60 - Fax: 43 29 84 97 ■ 21 av.de Friedland, 75008 Paris ■ Tel: 42 56 64 75 - Fax: 45 61 29 47 ■ Mon 14:00-19:00/Tues-Sat 11:00-19:00 ■ English spoken ■ Prices high ■ 10% professional discount

Specialist in chairs, from Louis XIII to today. Other locations in Paris: 94 rue du Bac, 75007 Paris and 45 rue de Lyon, 75012 Paris.

——— IX ———

CLAUDE BERNARD HUBERT

21 rue Joubert, 75009 Paris ■ Tel: 48 74 25 08 ■ Mon-Fri 9:00-13:00/15:00-17:00 ■ 78 rue des Rosiers, 93400 Saint-Ouen ■ Tel: 40 12 44 27 ■ Every day 10:00-17:30 ■ Prices high to very high ■ 8 to 10% professional discount

Fabrication of chairs in all classic styles. Restoration and upholstery.

——— XI ———

LA CHAISERIE DU FAUBOURG

26 rue de Charonne, 75011 Paris ■ Tel: 43 57 67 51 ■ Mon-Sat 9:00-12:30/14:00-19:00 ■ Prices medium to high ■ Professional discount

Fabrication of chairs, sofas, beds, in classic styles. Repair and restoration. Caning.

HESPERIDES DREAMS

1 passage Rauch, 75011 Paris ■ Tel: 43 72 66 44/43 72 50 13 - Fax: 43 72 50 17 ■ Mon-Fri 8:00-18:00 ■ Annick Ledily speaks English ■ Prices high ■ 15% professional discount

Hervé Delarue's designs of chairs and sofas to measure.

STRAURE

95 rue du Faubourg-Saint-Antoine, 75011 Paris ■ Tel: 43 47 20 50 ■ Mon-Fri 8:00-12:00/13:15-17:00 ■ Prices medium ■ 5 to 10% professional discount

Specialist in restoration and fabrication of chairs. Very high quality.

TAPISSERIE MENDES

41 rue Basfroi, 75011 Paris ■ Tel: 40 09 08 41 ■ Mon-Sat 8:00-12:00/13:00-19:00 ■ Prices medium ■ 10% professional discount

Restoration and custom fabrication of sofas and chairs.Full upholstery service.

CHRISTIAN WERDMULLER

27 rue Titon, 75011 Paris ■ Tel: 43 71 96 30 - Fax: 43 71 94 60 ■ Mon-Fri 8:00-12:00/13:00-18:00 ■ Christian Werdmuller speaks English ■ Prices high to very high ■ 10% professional discount

Custom made chairs and sofas in all styles. Creations and copies of old. Restoration of antique chairs. Full upholstery service. Works for the National Museums, the Mobilier National, professionals of decoration and private individuals.

——————————————— **XII** ———————————————

ATELIER LE VESTIBULE

20 bis rue de la Gare de Reuilly, 75012 Paris ■ Tel: 40 04 92 80 ■ Mon-Fri 9:30-18:00/Sat by appointment ■ Sylvia Telfser speaks English ■ Prices medium ■ 10% professional discount

This upholsterer has a stock of restored chairs for sale. Restoration and complete upholstery service.

CHEZ L'ARTISAN

71 rue de Charenton and 73 av. Ledru-Rollin, 75012 Paris ■ Tel: 43 43 48 20 ■ Mon-Fri 9:00-13:00/14:00-19:00 ■ Prices low ■ 25% professional discount

Fabrication of chairs, armchairs and sofas in all styles. Upholstery.

SIEGES ET MEUBLES AMBOISE

16 passage du Chantier, 75012 Paris ■ Tel: 44 75 00 44/43 55 95 53 - Fax: 44 75 00 66 ■ Mon-Sat 10:00-12:00/14:00-19:00 ■ Atelier Amboise, 4 rue de la Main-d'Or, 75011 Paris ■ Mon-Sat 8:00-12:00/14:00-18:00 ■ Prices medium ■ 10% professional discount

Fabrication of chairs, sofas and banquettes to measure. Restoration.

——————————————— **XIII** ———————————————

DAPHNE CREATION

25 bd Arago, 75013 Paris ■ Tel: 34 74 03 67 - Fax: 34 74 04 08 ■ Mon-Fri by appointment ■ Bruno Fanget speaks English ■ Prices medium ■ Professional discount

Manufacturer of chairs, armchairs and sofas for private and commercial use. Custom made convertible sofas.

SEE ALSO ANTIQUE FURNITURE RESTORATION

MEILLEUR

32, rue des Amandiers
75020 Paris

Tel 43 66 45 13
Fax 43 66 45 43

DECORATIVE HARDWARE
Serrurerie décorative

French Decorative Hardware has a tradition going back to Roman times. The most beautiful designs of levers, knobs, surface locks, cremones and espagnolettes began in the middle ages, continued on through the XVIII, XIX and into the XX century. Exquisite originals in excellent condition still grace the great homes and chateaux of Europe. Skilled designers, chiselers and gilders have drastically declined in numbers, but there are still enough of them to meet the demands of the most discriminating clients.

——————————————— I ———————————————

FONTAINE

190 rue de Rivoli, 75001 Paris ■ Tel: 42 61 51 53 - Fax: 42 61 04 13 ■ Mon-Fri by appointment ■ Geneviève Berton speaks English ■ Prices medium ■ 10 to 20% professional discount

Company founded in1740. Small museum collection of decorative hardware. Specialists in mortise locks and magnetic card-operated locks. Stock of antique hardware available for sale. In many cases one of a kind. Special collection of everything from door knockers to espagnolettes in styles from the middle ages to Art Deco. All finishes available over solid brass.

——————————————— IV ———————————————

SERIE RARE

14 rue des Ecouffes, 75004 Paris ■ Tel: 44 59 81 71 - Fax: 44 59 81 90 ■ Mon-Fri 12:00-19:00 ■ Marie-Luce Podva speaks English ■ Prices medium ■ 30% professional discount

Small and original collection of door and furniture hardware in contemporary designs. Matching drapery hardware. Catalogue upon request.

——————————————— V ———————————————

LA QUINCAILLERIE

4 bd Saint-Germain, 75005 Paris ■ Tel: 46 33 66 71 - Fax: 43 29 80 58 ■ Mon-Fri 10:00-13:00/14:00-19:00 ■ Philippe Goldsztain speaks English ■ Prices high ■ 15% professional discount

Distributor of contemporary hardware, designed by architects and designers, for windows, doors and furniture. Will custom make any design. Bathroom accessories.

BRASS

4 rue Papillon, 75009 Paris ■ Tel: 45 23 44 45 - Fax: 42 47 11 58 ■ Mon-Fri 8:30-17:00 ■ Stephane Aksakow speaks English ■ Prices medium to high ■ 30% professional discount

Large choice of brass hardware for doors, windows and furniture, as well as letter boxes and curtain rods.
Catalogues available.

RAYMOND SCHMITT

41 rue du Faubourg-du-Temple, 75010 Paris ■ Tel: 42 08 05 43 - Fax: 42 08 49 92 ■ Mon-Fri 8:30-12:30/13:30-18:30 ■ English spoken ■ Prices medium ■ Professional discount

Specialist in custom decorative hardware for furniture. Finishes in gold or silver. Restoration and reproduction of bronzes from models. No catalogue. Only custom work.

RENNOTTE

161 Faubourg-Saint-Antoine, 75011 Paris ■ Tel: 43 43 39 58 - Fax: 43 41 50 27 ■ Mon-Fri 9:00-12:30/14:00-18:30 ■ Some English spoken ■ Prices medium to high ■ Professional discount

The largest collection of hardware for furniture in Paris. Catalogue upon request.

SCHMIDT

15/17 passage de la Main-d'Or, 75011 Paris ■ Tel: 48 06 57 19 - Fax: 48 06 62 22 ■ Mon-Fri 8:30-18.00 ■ Fernande Schmidt speaks English and Spanish ■ Prices medium to high ■ Professional discount

Founded in 1928. Large selection of door, window and furniture hardware. Wide choice of finials for staircases as well as lighting and showcases. Decorative work in brass for shops, offices and homes. Two price levels. Catalogue upon request.

LEJEUNE FRERES

209 rue du Faubourg-Saint-Antoine, 75011 Paris ■ Tel: 43 72 27 37 - Fax: 43 72 99 26 ■ Mon-Fri 9:00-12:00/14:00-18:00/Sat closing 17:00 ■ Some English spoken ■ Prices medium ■ 20% professional discount

200 years of experience making decorative hardware for furniture, knobs, levers, keys and keyholes in many finishes. Lower cost line.

"AUX BRONZES DE STYLE"

74 rue du Faubourg-Saint-Antoine, 75012 Paris ■ Tel: 43 43 36 36 - Fax: 43 43 46 50 ■ Mon-Fri 9:00-19:00/Sat 10:00-19:30 ■ Lydie Claisse speaks English ■ Prices medium to high ■ 20% professional discount

Manufacturer of bronzes for furniture. Bronze lighting, lamps, lanterns and chandeliers, small tables. Some decorative hardware. Restoration of bronze and copies of antique models. Middle range.

ETS GARNIER

30 bis bd de la Bastille, 75012 Paris ■ Tel: 43 43 84 85 - Fax: 43 46 13 76
■ Mon-Fri 9:00-12:30/13:30-18:00 ■ Francis Vernhol and Richard Mertz
speak English ■ Prices medium to high ■ 20% professional discount

Remy Garnier founded the company in 1834. One of the finest collections
of decorative hardware of all periods. Everything for doors and windows.
Reliable for large projects. Restoration of antique hardware.

———————————————————— **XX** ————————————————————

MEILLEUR

32 rue des Amandiers, 75020 Paris ■ Tel: 43 66 45 13 - Fax: 43 66 45 43 ■
Mon-Fri 8:30-19:00 by appointment ■ Catherine Meilleur and Claude
Delorme speak English ■ Prices high to very high ■ Professional discount

Highest quality custom made decorative hardware for windows and doors
in bronze with a large choice of finishes. Good selection of faucets in exclusive designs. All types of lighting and small tables. Master artisan and
member of the Grands Ateliers.

DECORATIVE FINISHERS OF METAL
Décorateurs sur métaux

BETTENCOURT FRERES

12 rue St-Gilles, 75003 Paris ■ Tel: 42 72 34 04 - Fax: 42 72 83 02 ■ Mon-Fri 7:30-12:00/13.30-17:15 ■ Frédéric Lebas speaks English ■ Prices medium ■ Professional discount

Excellent quality varnishing, gold varnishing, nickel and gun metal, bronze patinas, vert-de-gris, all patinas for statues. Restoration of metal objects, such as clocks. Restoration and re-plating of silver as well as reproduction of objects in metal.

🏰 MAISON MAHIEU

15 impasse des Primevères, 75011 Paris ■ Tel: 43 55 88 25 - Fax: 48 06 92 99 ■ Mon-Fri 8:00-12:00/13:00-17:00 ■ Claude Kern and Edith Maurette speak English ■ Prices high ■ 10% professional discount

Mercury gilding, gold plating by electro-plating, all finishes: silver, bronze, antique patinas. Restoration of bronze objects. The best. Top quality workmanship.

TEXIER

2 rue de la Roquette, 75011 Paris ■ Tel: 47 00 70 59 - Fax: 43 38 14 25 ■ Mon-Fri 8:00-12:00/13:00-18:00 ■ Prices low to medium ■ 15% professional discount

Gilding on metal: electro-plating, silver plating, patinas.
Work on historic monuments.

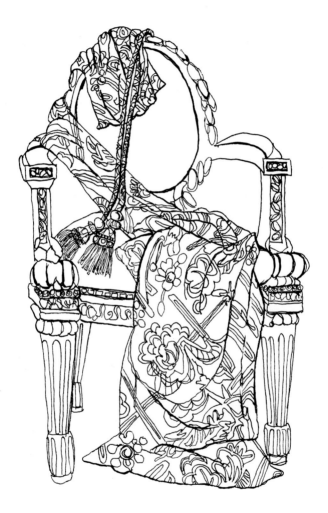

CENTRE DE DOCUMENTATION DES EDITEURS DE TISSUS D'AMEUBLEMENT

THE FABRIC FORUM

35, rue Danielle Casanova, 75001 Paris

Tel 42 86 04 05   Fax 42 86 05 25

FABRICS

Tissus

The Fabric Forum

Founded in 1912, this attractive center displays the latest work of the leading creators and editors of French furnishing fabrics and trimmings.

Here, professionals and their clients can see for themselves the great variety, as well as the beauty and charm, of the world of French fabrics.

Here, you will find a friendly staff of qualified experts who can provide a marvellous overview of the latest creations. They can provide samples and introduce you to the sources.

Here, in this convenient location, you can browse through the entire panorama of the world of French fabrics.

The Fabric Forum is located in the heart of Paris just off the place Vendôme and the rue de la Paix.

Hours: Monday to Friday 10:00-18:30 except during August.

THE FABRIC FORUM
35 rue Danielle Casanova, 75001, Paris
Tel: 42 86 04 05 - Fax: 42 86 05 25

Fabric Editors

G.P. & J. BAKER

6 bis rue de l'Abbaye, 75006 Paris ■ Tel: 43 25 73 44 - Fax: 43 54 22 78 ■
Tues-Sat 9:30-18:30 ■ English spoken

Prints, jacquards, satins, silks, cottons, wallpaper.

CREATION BAUMANN

48 rue de Grenelle, 75007 Paris ■ Tel: 45 49 08 22 - Fax: 45 49 31 22 ■
Mon-Fri 9:00-12:30/14:00-17:30 ■ English spoken

Large collection of sheers. Flame resistant fabrics.
A new "living" collection. Prints, jacquards, blinds, interior automatic blinds,
self adhesive fabrics for walls.

BISSON BRUNEEL

15 rue du Mail, 75002 Paris ■ Tel: 42 21 30 51 - Fax: 42 21 41 24 ■ Mon-
Fri 9:00-18:00/Sat 11:00-18:00 ■ Karine Bruneel speaks English

Contemporary designs, jacquards, plaid-throws, sheers.

BOUSSAC TISSU D'AMEUBLEMENT

27 rue du Mail, 75002 Paris ■ Tel: 42 21 83 00 - Fax: 42 33 57 87 ■ Mon-
Fri 9:00-18:00/Sat 11:00-18:00 ■ Philippe Derazey speaks English

Prints, solids, jacquards.

♕ BRAQUENIE & CIE

111 bd Beaumarchais, 75003 Paris ■ Tel: 48 04 30 03 - Fax: 48 04 30 39
■ Mon-Fri 9:00-18:00 ■ English spoken

Superb quality fabrics. Large collection based on old documents. Carpets
in jacquard designs, rugs, Aubusson tapestries, needlepoint. All can be custom made.

♕ BURGER-BORDERIEUX

39 rue des Petits-Champs, 75001 Paris ■ Tel: 42 97 46 19 - Fax: 43 07 76 05
■ Mon-Fri 9:00-17:30 ■ Marie-Noëlle speaks English

Specialty: printed fabrics from XVIII century documents using 200 year old
cylinders. Silks, velvets. Remarkable selection of Toiles de Jouy (39" wide).

MANUEL CANOVAS

6 rue de l'Abbaye, 75006 Paris ■ Tel: 43 29 91 36 - Fax: 45 04 04 83 ■ Mon-
Fri 9:00-18:30 ■ English spoken

Jacquards, prints from old documents and contemporary, stripes, solids,
ottomans. 2,500 references.

CASAL

40 rue des Saints-Pères, 75007 Paris ■ Tel: 44 39 07 07 - Fax: 40 49 09 54
■ Mon-Fri 9:30-13:00/14:00-18:00 ■ Dominique Bage speaks English

Contemporary fabrics: jacquards, structured designs, silks, ottomans, toiles.
Specialty: coordinates.

CHANEE-DUCROCQ

6 rue du Mail, 75002 Paris ■Tel: 42 60 82 01 - Fax: 45 08 12 19 ■ Mon-Fri 10:00-17:45

Upholstery fabrics for chairs: tapestries, jacquards, velvets.

COMOGLIO

22 rue Jacob, 75006 Paris ■ Tel: 43 54 65 86 - Fax: 40 51 70 56 ■ Tues-Fri 10:00-18:30/Mon-Sat 10:00-13:00/14:30-18:30 ■ English spoken

Specialty: re-edition of XVIII and XIX century prints, particularly Indian and Persian motifs.

COTONNIERE D'ALSACE/LES EDITIONS PAULE MARROT

16 rue de l'Arcade, 75008 Paris ■ Tel: 42 65 76 02 - Fax: 47 42 83 16 ■ Mon-Fri 9:30-17:00

Specialty: cottons, prints, Toiles de Jouy, contemporary designs.

DESCHEMAKER

22 rue du Mail, 75002 Paris ■ Tel: 42 33 35 80 - Fax: 42 33 73 11 ■ Mon-Fri 9:00-18:00 ■ Philippe Coupe and Nathalie Clement speak English

Velvets, jacquards and prints. Beautiful line of contemporary sofas and arm chairs.

DESTOMBES

35 rue du Sentier, 75002 Paris ■ Tel: 42 33 61 05 - Fax: 42 33 04 09 ■ Mon-Fri 9:00-12:30/13:30-17:30 ■ English spoken

Tapestries, velvets, silk blends, jacquards.

EDITIONS DOLLFUS MIEG

3 rue de Furstemberg, 75006 Paris ■ Tel: 40 46 94 82 - Fax: 48 87 23 83 ■ Mon-Sat 10:00-19:00 ■ Pierre-Laurent Durantin and Sylviane Descamps speak English

Prints, jacquards, solids.

ETS R. DRIOT-GRADI

52 rue Marcelin-Berthelot, 94140 Alfortville ■ Tel: 43 78 31 73 - Fax: 43 78 48 11 ■ Mon-Fri 9:00-12:30/13:30-18:00 ■ Dominique Lafourcade and Myriam Guessous speak English

Furnishing fabrics, tapestries, velvets and sheers.

ETAMINE

3 rue Jacob, 75006 Paris ■ Tel: 43 25 70 65 - Fax: 43 25 92 76 ■ Mon-Sat 9:30-13:00/14:00-18:30 ■ Marilyne Rioult and Chrystelle Thouan speak English

Complete range of furnishing fabrics and wall paper.

EURO-HOME DIFFUSION (EHD)

116 rue du Bac, 75007 Paris ■ Tel: 40 49 03 03 - Fax: 40 49 00 96 ■ Mon-Sat 10:00-13:00/14:00-18:30 ■ English spoken

Modern and classic designs: silks, silk blends, prints, jacquards, velvets. Over 2,000 references.

FADINI BORGHI

8 rue Chabanais, 75002 Paris ■ Tel: 47 03 40 66 - Fax: 42 60 47 29 ■ Mon-Sat 9:30-18:00 ■ English spoken

Specialty: re-edition of documents from Louis XIII through Empire.

FARDIS

6 bis rue de l'Abbaye, 75006 Paris ■ Tel: 43 25 73 44 - Fax: 43 54 22 78 ■ Tues-Sat 9:00-18:00 ■ English spoken

Prints, jacquards, satins, silk blends, cottons, wallpaper.

LA FILANDIERE-CHRISTIAN LANZANI

84 avenue Ledru-Rollin, 75012 Paris ■ Tel: 43 41 01 01 - Fax: 43 40 05 76 ■ Mon-Fri 8:30-18:00 ■ English spoken

Specialty: tapestries for upholstery and wall panels, hand and machine woven. Wide width jacquards, velvets, damasks, silk weaves.

CHRISTIAN FISCHBACHER
EURODRAP

3 impasse Bon-Secours, 75011 Paris ■ Tel: 43 70 97 60 - Fax: 43 70 26 99 ■ Mon-Fri 9:00-18:00 ■ English spoken

Sheers, solids, chintz, moires, upholstery fabrics in classic and contemporary designs.

ROBERT FOUR

28 rue Bonaparte, 75006 Paris ■ Tel: 43 29 30 60 - Fax: 43 25 33 95 ■ Mon 14:00-19:00/Tues-Sat 10:00-19:00 ■ English spoken

Tapestries, carpets, restoration.

PIERRE FREY

2 rue de Furstemberg, 75006 Paris ■ Tel: 46 33 73 00 - Fax: 42 96 85 38 ■ Mon-Sat 10:00-12:00/14:00-18:30 ■ English spoken

Prints, jacquards, toiles, damasks.

GAMME-VEREL DE BELVAL

4 rue de Furstemberg, 75006 Paris ■ Tel: 43 26 17 89 - Fax: 42 96 99 46 ■ Mon-Sat 10:30-18:30 ■ Didier Dresco speaks English

Specialty: natural silks.

ATELIER VINCENT HAMELIN S.A.

25 rue du Mail, 75002 Paris ■ Tel: 42 33 66 75 - Fax: 45 08 49 88 ■ Mon-Fri 9:00-18:00 and by appointment ■ François Lesage and Anne-Mieke Matteoda speak English

Embroidered upholstery fabrics and restoration of antique embroidered fabrics.

HAMOT

75 rue de Richelieu, 75002 Paris ■ Tel: 42 96 62 04 - Fax: 42 96 07 04 ■ Mon-Fri 9:00-12:30/14:00-18:00 ■ English spoken

Tapestries in wool and cotton for chairs. Prints and velvets.

HOULES (TRIMMINGS)

18 rue Saint-Nicolas, 75012 Paris ■ Tel: 43 44 65 19 - Fax: 64 24 71 76 ■ Mon-Fri 8:30-17:30 ■ English spoken

Trimmings: braids, tassels, tie-backs, cords, woven accessories. Drapery hardware, upholstery tools.

LES IMPRESSIONS EDITIONS

3 rue Jacob, 75006 Paris ■ Tel: 43 25 70 65 - Fax: 43 25 92 76 ■ Mon-Sat 9:30-13:00/14:00-18:30 ■ English spoken

Specialty: solids in a wide variety of weaves. Prints, wide width wall upholstery fabrics, satins and taffetas in stripes and checks.

JAB

155 bd Haussmann, 75008 Paris ■ Tel: 43 59 92 50 - Fax: 43 59 92 52 ■ Mon-Fri 9:00-17:30 ■ English spoken

Prints, solids, silk blends, jacquards, sheers.

JAC DEY

1 rue de Furstemberg, 75006 Paris ■ Tel: 43 26 41 55 - Fax: 35 98 17 52 ■ Mon-Sat 10:00-18:30 ■ English spoken

Specialty: prints.

JERO

95 av. de la Bourdonnais, 75007 Paris ■ Tel: 47 53 70 63 - Fax: 47 53 73 80 ■ Mon-Fri 9:15-13:30/14:00-18:00 Fri closed at 16:00 ■ Isabelle Desche speaks English

Furnishing fabrics, sofas, accessories.

TISSU LAUER-TAPIS DE COGOLIN

5 avenue de l'Opéra, 75001 Paris ■ Tel: 42 61 63 52 - Fax: 42 61 03 50 ■ Mon-Fri 9:00-12:00/14:00-18:00 ■ English spoken

Toiles, prints, jacquards, sheers.

FRANÇOIS LAURAY

3 rue d'Aboukir, 75002 Paris ■ Tel: 40 26 70 41 - Fax: 40 26 69 87 ■ Mon-Fri 9:30-18:00 ■ Agnes Queros speaks English

Furnishing fabrics, prints, fire resistant fabrics.

♚ LELIEVRE

13 rue du Mail, 75002 Paris ■ Tel: 42 61 53 03 - Fax: 42 61 49 99 ■ Mon-Fri 9:00-18:00/Fri closing 17:00 ■ English spoken

In every sense, the most complete line of French furnishing fabrics, from the classics to the contemporary.
Wide width fabrics, silks, velvets, damasks, jacquards.

MARITAC-TEXUNION

31 bd Bourdon, 75004 Paris ■ Tel: 48 87 72 13 - Fax: 48 87 23 83 ■ Mon-Fri 9:00-11:45/14:00-17:30

Prints, cottons, satins, cotton toiles, linen/cotton weaves.

CREATIONS METAPHORES

7 place de Furstemberg, 75006 Paris ■ Tel: 46 33 03 20 - Fax: 48 91 87 23 ■ Mon-Sat 10:30-13:00/13:30-19:00 ■ Olivier Nourry and Sophie Pelletier speak English

Furnishing fabrics and wallpaper.

NOBILIS

29 rue Bonaparte, 75006 Paris ■ Tel: 43 29 21 50 - Fax: 43 29 77 57 ■ Mon-Sat 9:30-18:30 ■ English spoken

Large selection of prints, stripes, damasks, silks.

O.A.L.- AMELIE PREVOT

24 rue Feydeau, 75002 Paris ■ Tel: 45 08 47 77 - Fax: 42 36 28 69 ■ Mon-Fri 9:00-12:30/13:30-17:30

Wide selection of furnishing fabrics.

J. PANSU

42 rue du Faubourg-Poissonnière, 75010 Paris ■ Tel: 42 46 72 45 - Fax: 42 46 66 85 ■ Mon-Fri 8:30-12:30/14:00-18:00 ■ English spoken

Prints, solids, wide width blends, velvets.
Antique and reproduction tapestries by appointment.

LA PASSEMENTERIE NOUVELLE (CLAUDE DECLERC)

15 rue Étienne-Marcel, 75001 Paris ■ Tel: 44 76 90 70 - Fax: 42 33 13 75 ■ Mon-Fri 9:00-18:00

Trimmings: braids, tassels, cords.

LES PASSEMENTERIES DE L'ILE-DE-FRANCE

11 rue Trousseau, 75011 Paris ■ Tel: 48 05 44 33 - Fax: 30 35 75 39 ■ Mon-Thurs 9:00-17:30/Fri 9:00-17:00 ■ English spoken

Trimmings: tassels, braids, cords.

EDMOND PETIT

23 rue du Mail, 75002 Paris ■ Tel: 43 33 48 56 - Fax: 40 26 24 56 ■ Mon-Fri 9:00-18:00 ■ Jean François Petit and Chris Koning speak English

Classic French styles: damasks, silks, velvets, jacquards.
Trimmings. Flame resistant fabrics. Theatre curtains.

♛ PRELLE & CO.

5 place des Victoires, 75001 Paris ■ Tel: 42 36 67 21 - Fax: 42 36 90 39 ■ Mon-Fri 9:00-12:30/14:00-18:00 ■ Guillaume Verzier and Cecile Verzier speak English ■ Prices very high

Highest quality silks and other fabrics. Superb custom reproductions of antique fabrics and silks. Museum quality. Founded in 1752.

REYMONDON (TRIMMINGS)

13 rue Richard-Lenoir, 75011 Paris ■ Tel: 43 56 21 30 - Fax: 43 56 89 78 ■ Mon-Fri 8:30-12:30/13:30-17:00/Fri closing 16:00

Trimmings: braids, tassels, cords.

♚ L. RUBELLI

6 bis rue de l'Abbaye, 75006 Paris ■ 11-13 rue de l'Abbaye, 75006 Paris ■ Tel: 43 54 27 77 - Fax: 43 54 97 32 ■ Mon-Sat 9:00-12:45/14:00-18:00 ■ English spoken

Complete line of furnishing fabrics: prints, jacquards, silks, damasks, velvets. Tops in designs and colors and magnificent quality.

SAHCO HESSLEIN

17 rue du Mail, 75002 Paris ■ Tel: 40 26 23 86 - Fax: 40 26 58 60 ■ Mon-Thurs 8:30-17:45/Fri 8:30-16:45 ■ Astrid Lenormand speaks English

Contemporary designs: solids, jacquards, prints, sheers.

SAT CREATIONS

Successeurs d'Albert Tronc ■ 25-27 rue du Mail, 75002 Paris ■ Tel: 45 08 07 60 - Fax: 42 36 51 48 ■ Mon-Fri 8:30-17:45 ■ Martine Doreau speaks English

Furnishing fabrics: satins, velvets, jacquards, silks, taffetas, moires, Toiles de Jouy.
Specialist: wide width solids, and the best selection of wide width Toiles de Jouy.

SOULEIADO-ETS CHARLES DEMERY

78 rue de Seine, 75006 Paris ■ Tel: 43 54 15 13 - Fax: 43 54 84 45 ■ Mon-Sat 10:00-19:00 ■ English spoken

Specialty: printed country cottons.

♚ TASSINARI ET CHATEL

26 rue Danielle Casanova, 75002 Paris ■ Tel: 42 61 74 08 - Fax: 42 60 37 15 ■ English spoken

Embroidered silks: the best.

TASSINARI ET CHATEL
CHOTARD COLLECTION

26 rue Danielle Casanova, 75002 Paris ■ Tel: 42 61 74 08 - Fax: 42 60 37 15

Jacquards, prints, solids, velvets.

TISSUS L'ABEILLE

234 rue du Faubourg-Saint-Antoine, 75012 Paris ■ Tel: 44 93 14 14 - Fax: 43 72 19 12 ■ Mon-Fri 9:00-12:30/14:00-18:00 ■ Guy and Catherine Balzarotti speak English

Satins, prints, chintz, damasks, velvets.

URGE

96 av. Ledru-Rollin, 75011 Paris ■ Tel: 43 55 39 50 - Fax: 47 00 04 65 ■ Mon-Fri 8:30-17:15 ■ English spoken

Prints, cottons, satins, velvets, solids, blackouts, everything.

VERASETA

18 rue des Petits-Champs, 75002 Paris ■ Tel: 42 97 52 62 - Fax: 40 20 95 27 ■ Mon-Fri 8:30-12:15/13:45-18:00/Fri closing 17:00 ■ Pierre Lorton speaks English

Specialty: natural silks in taffetas, failles, satins, damasks. Excellent quality.

VOGHI

21 rue Bonaparte, 75006 Paris ■ Tel: 43 54 85 44 - Fax: 40 51 83 59 ■ Mon-Sat 10:00-18:30 ■ English spoken

Printed Kashmirs. Special collection.

ZIMMER ET ROHDE

2 rue du Bouloi, 75001 Paris ■ Tel: 42 33 15 15 - Fax: 42 33 68 15 ■ Mon-Fri 8:00-18:00 ■ Philippe Jariel speaks English

Classic and contemporary fabrics.

ZUMSTEG-VEREL DE BELVAL

4 rue de Furstemberg, 75006 Paris ■ Tel: 43 26 17 89 - Fax: 42 96 99 46 ■ Didier Dresco speaks English

Specialty: Cotton jacquards.

NOTE: The prices in the showrooms of the Editors represented in the Fabric Forum range from modest to astronomical. The choice of fabrics and trimmings is almost infinite. Non-professionals are also welcome to both the Fabric Forum and the Showrooms. Discounts are, of course, available to the professionals.

Fabric Specialties

AUVER A SOIE S.A.
ETABLISSEMENT L. BOUCHER

102 rue Réaumur, 75002 Paris ■ Tel: 42 33 52 92 - Fax: 42 33 14 44 ■ Sun-Fri 8:30-17:00 ■ Jean-Marie Boucher speaks English ■ Prices high ■ Professional discount

Manufacturer of silk threads for all use: embroidery, tapestry, sewing, weaving. Other threads: metallic, chenille, rayon and natural silk.

GRIFFINE

37 rue du Capitaine-Guynemer, 92090 Paris La Défense ■ Tel: 47 88 51 30 - Fax: 47 88 87 81 ■ Mon-Fri 8:00-18:00 ■ Jean Aran and Marie-Anne Morer speak English ■ Prices medium ■ 5% professional discount

Coated fabrics.

GEORGES LE MANACH

31 rue du Quatre-Septembre, 75002 Paris■Tel: 47 42 52 94 - Fax: 47 42 02 04 ■Mon-Fri 9:00-12:00/14:00-17:45■English spoken■Prices medium to very high ■Professional discount

Manufacturers of silk since 1830. They have 4,000 designs, of which 300 are currently available. The others can be made to order. There are approximately 100 prints available from XVIII and XIX century documents.

SIMONNOT ET GODARD

33 rue Vivienne, 75002 Paris ■ Tel: 42 33 94 60 - Fax: 40 39 06 95 ■ Mon-Fri 9:00-12:00/13:30-17:30 ■ Benjamin and François Simonnot speak English ■ Prices high

High quality cotton in regular and wide widths. Wools, silks.

TOILES DE MAYENNE

9 rue de Mézières, 75007 Paris ■ Tel: 45 48 70 77 - Fax: 45 49 28 91 ■ 1 rue des Graviers, 92200 Neuilly-sur-Seine ■ Tel: 47 22 94 48 ■ Factory: Fontaine-Daniel, 53101 Mayenne ■ Tel: 43 00 34 80 - Fax: 43 00 35 75 ■ Tues-Sat 10:00-13:30/14:30-18:30 ■ English spoken ■ Prices low to medium ■ Professional discount

Large selection of furnishing fabrics, especially cotton toiles in solids and prints. Wide widths. Mail or fax orders for custom draperies and sheers, bedspreads, cushions.

─────────────── **OUTSIDE PARIS** ───────────────

ILE DE FRANCE

66 rue du Chalons, 59202 Tourcoing ■ Tel: (16) 20 25 99 40 - Fax: (16) 20 26 47 62 ■ English spoken

Custom fabrics of all types for Editors and the contract market: minimum 150 yards.

FRABELEX

6 rue Volta, 94140 Alfortville ■ Tel: 49 77 66 47 - Fax: 49 77 00 30 ■ Mon-Fri 9:00-18:00 ■ English spoken ■ Professional discount

Upholstery fabrics for walls and furniture in classic and contemporary styles: damasks, satins, jacquards, satin stripes, unshrinkable toiles.

SOFIEPI

93 Grande-Rue, Pavillon 2, 78240 Chambourcy ■ Tel: 30 74 17 91 - Fax: 30 74 44 13 ■ Mon-Fri 8:00-12:00/14:00-18:00 ■ English spoken ■ Prices low to medium ■ Professionals only

Felts: wide width for conference tables, billiard tables, exhibition stands. Flame resistant fabrics for wall coverings.

Fabric: Embroidered

☖ HAMELIN-LESAGE

25-27 rue du Mail, 75002 Paris ■ Tel: 42 33 66 75 - Fax: 45 08 49 88 ■ Mon-Fri 9:00-18:00 ■ English spoken ■ Prices medium to high ■ Professional discount

Top quality embroidered fabrics designed by François Lesage for furniture, draperies, table throws, bed hangings, screens and other uses.

Fabric: Painted and Printed

♛ MARYVONNE DE FOLLIN

21 rue Ernest-Deloison, 92200 Neuilly ■ Tel: 47 22 38 51 ■ By appointment
■ English spoken ■ Prices medium to high

Paintings on silk for ceiling and wall panels, upholstery, cushions, ottomans.

♛ GEORGES KRIVOSHEY

46 rue Albert-Thomas, 75010 Paris ■ Tel: 40 40 04 35 - Fax: 42 45 88 30 ■
By appointment ■ English Spoken ■n Prices high

Atelier for printing on textiles. Reproductions of all motifs: antique and contemporary designs adapted for all projects. Printing on velvet, silk, leather. Specialty: Artisanal work of quality in the highest tradition. Reproduction of motifs of the Renaissance, XVII, XVIII centuries using techniques of those periods.

Fabric: Antique

LES INDIENNES-TISSUS ANCIENS

10 rue Saint-Paul, 75004 Paris ■ Tel: 42 72 35 34 - Fax: 42 72 78 85 ■ Mon-Sat 14:30-19:00/Sun & mornings by appointment ■ English spoken ■ Prices high ■ 12 to 20% professional discount

Antique fabrics: XVI, XVII, XVIII centuries. Kashmir shawls: XVIII, XIX centuries. Objects of art.
Mme Virginie David organizes antique textile auctions at the Drouot auction rooms. Museum quality. Qualified expert.

MLLE JULIETTE NICLAUSSE

50 rue La Bruyère, 75009 Paris ■ Tel: 48 74 11 49 ■ By appointment ■ Interpreter recommended

Amazing collection of museum level upholstery fabrics of the XV, XVI, XVII, XVIII centuries.

♛ TRIMMINGS
Passementerie

Trimmings go back to the time of Adam and Eve. When men and women began to adorn themselves, they started a trend which has never slackened. In the annals of art history, we find trimmings on the fringes of the Venus of Lespugue (15,000 BC) on display in the Museum of Man in Paris. All ancient cultures show visual records of the use of tassels, feathers, pompons, cords, braids and fringes. From China through India, Egypt, the South Pacific and Ancient America, we find strings of beads, feather ornaments, decorative shells and elaborately painted masks. Today, Haute Couture and Haute Décoration would not be what they are without the "trimmings". They are an essential part of decoration for walls, draperies, chairs, cushions, carpets, etc. For the most elegant, the most tasteful, French trimmings are simply the best.

HOULES (TRIMMINGS)
18 rue Saint-Nicolas, 75012 Paris ■ Tel: 43 44 65 19/64 24 55 00 - Fax: 64 24 71 76 ■ Mon-Fri 8:30-17:30 ■ Gilles Drapanaski and Virginie Wittmer speak English ■ Prices high ■ Professional discount
Superb collection and choice of trimmings, braids, tassels, tie-backs, cords, all woven accessories. Drapery hardware and upholstery tools.

PASSEMENTERIE DU MARAIS
6 bd des Filles-du-Calvaire, 75011 Paris ■ Tel: 47 00 56 82 ■ Tues-Sat 9:30-12:45/14:00-18:15 ■ English spoken ■ Prices low to high ■ 5 to 10% professional discount
Special selection of braids and fringes for lampshades.

LA PASSEMENTERIE NOUVELLE (CLAUDE DECLERC)
15 rue Etienne-Marcel, 75001 Paris ■ Tel: 42 36 30 01 - Fax: 42 33 13 75 ■ Mon-Fri 9:00-18:00 ■ Prices high ■ Professional discount
Excellent collection of everything in trimmings.

LES PASSEMENTERIES DE L'ILE-DE-FRANCE

11 rue Trousseau, 75011 Paris ■ Tel: 48 05 44 33 - Fax: 48 05 04 36/
30 35 75 39 ■ Mon-Fri 9:00-17:30/Fri closing 17:00 ■ English spoken

Outstanding and complete collection of trimmings.

REYMONDON (PASSEMENTERIE)

13 rue Richard-Lenoir, 75011 Paris ■ Tel: 43 56 21 30 - Fax: 43 56 89 78 ■
Mon-Fri 8:30-12:30/13:30-17:00/Fri closing 16:00 ■ Prices high ■ Professional
discount

This is a "must see". Fabulous collection of trimmings.

DRAPERY HARDWARE
Tringles à rideaux

HOULES

18 rue Saint-Nicolas 75012 Paris ■ Tel: 43 44 65 19 - Fax: 64 24 71 76 ■ Mon-Fri 8:30-17:30 ■ English spoken ■ Prices medium to high ■ Professional discount

Large choice of high quality decorative drapery hardware. The floor above has one of the most extraordinary collections of trimmings.

MARIN ET TULLET

7 rue de Monceau, 75008 Paris ■ Tel: 42 25 09 10 - Fax: 42 25 81 04 ■ Mon-Fri 8:00-18:00 ■ Michel Bourdon speaks English ■ Prices high ■ 20% professional discount

They have the reputation of being the best for drapery hardware. Large selection of curtain rods in wood, brass and wrought iron in classic and contemporary styles. Decorative hardware for furniture and trimmings.

SITRA

95 rue du Faubourg-Saint-Antoine, 75011 Paris ■ Tel: 43 43 88 88 - Fax: 43 41 80 82 ■ Mon-Fri 8:30-18:00 ■ Prices low to high ■ Professional discount

Drapery rods in brass, wood and iron in every shape and style. Large selection of interior and exterior blinds, shades and awnings.

GENERAL HARDWARE
Quincaillerie

BHV - BAZAR DE L'HOTEL DE VILLE

52 rue de Rivoli, 75004 Paris ■ Tel: 42 74 90 00 - Fax: 42 74 96 79 ■ Mon-Sat 9:30-19:00/Wed until 22:00 ■ Prices reasonable

There are thousands of good hardware stores in and around Paris, but for convenience and economy the editors suggest a visit to BHV. There, you will find a vast hardware supermarket of every hardware item you can imagine. Begin in the basement and work your way up from general hardware and garden supplies, through architectural elements, a complete wood working shop, decorative hardware and drapery hardware. Don't miss it.

FIREPLACES & ACCESSORIES
Cheminées et accessoires

A.B.J. CHEMINEES

Marché aux Puces ■ Marché Dauphine, 140 rue des Rosiers, Allée 1, Stand 105 and 4 rue Lécuyer, 93400 Saint-Ouen ■ Tel: 40 11 44 78 - Fax: 40 12 87 44 ■ Mon-Fri 9:00-18:00 ■ Prices medium ■ Professional discount

Antique fireplaces of every period and every style in stone, marble, wood. Installation services.

Versailles parquet, antique wood panelling (boiseries), statues in stone and marble. Wrought iron and other architectural elements.

CAMUS

Marché aux Puces ■ 88 rue des Rosiers et 5 rue Eugène-Lumeau, 93400 Saint-Ouen ■ Tel: 40 10 88 59/43 44 14 02 - Fax: 40 11 82 17 ■ Mon-Sun 10:00-19:00 ■ English spoken ■ Prices medium ■ 5 to 10% professional discount

XVIII and XIX century wood, marble and stone fireplaces. Versailles parquet, boiseries (wood panelling) and architectural elements. Restoration and installation.

DIGIART

Marché aux Puces ■ Marché Vernaison, 105 rue des Rosiers, Allée 1/3, Stand 14 ■ Tel: 40 11 61 34/40 12 68 95 - Fax: 40 12 12 60 ■ Sat-Mon and by appointment ■ Gilles Zoi speaks English ■ Prices medium ■ 10 to 20% discount

Marble fireplaces and consoles. Lighting, clocks, mirrors and other decorative objects.

JEAN LAPIERRE

58 rue Vieille-du-Temple, 75003 Paris ■ Tel: 42 74 07 70 - Fax: 42 74 37 60 ■ Mon-Sat 11:00-19:00 ■ Michel David speaks English ■ Prices medium ■ 5 to 20% professional discount

Antique fireplaces in stone and wood from all periods. Stone, flagstone, terra cotta tiles, oak doors, stone framwork for doors and windows, parquet, and diverse architectural elements.

♛ ANDREE MACE

266 rue du Faubourg-Saint-Honoré, 75008 Paris ■ Tel: 42 27 43 03 - Fax: 44 40 09 63 ■ Mon-Sat 9:00-12:30/14:00-18:30 ■ English spoken ■ Prices medium to high ■ Professional discount

Extraordinary collection of fireplaces in stone, marble and wood. Statues, fountains, columns from the Gothic period to the XX century. And much more.

PIERRE MADEL

4 rue Jacob, 75006 Paris ■ Tel: 43 26 90 89 - Fax: 40 46 07 09 ■ Tues-Fri 15:00-19:00/Sat 11:00-12:00/15:00-19:00 ■ English spoken ■ Prices medium ■ 10% professional discount

Antique iron and bronze accessories for the fireplace.

JEAN MAGNAN CHEMINEES
241 rue de la Croix-Nivert, 75015 Paris ■ Tel: 48 42 35 32 ■ Tues-Sat 14:00-19:00/to 22:00 by appointment ■ Prices medium
Manufacturer of contemporary fireplaces and accessories, barbecues, grills, bread and pizza ovens.

PROVINCES DE FRANCE
59 rue de Maubeuge, 75009 Paris ■ Tel: 48 78 34 22 ■ Tues-Sat 10:00-12:30/14:00-19:00 ■ Prices medium to high ■ Professional discount
Special collection of 200 models of cast iron back plates for fireplaces.

FRAMES & FRAMING

Cadres & Encadreurs

Frames

———————————— VI ————————————

GEORGES BAC
35 rue Bonaparte, 75006 Paris ■ Tel: 43 26 82 67 - Fax: 46 34 51 58 ■ Mon 14:00-18:30/Tues-Sat 10:00-12:00/14:00-18:30 ■ English spoken ■ Prices high ■ 10% professional discount

XVI to XVIII century gilded frames. Specialty: Louis XV.

———————————— VIII ————————————

♛ CADRES LEBRUN
155 rue du Faubourg-Saint-Honoré, 75008 Paris ■ Tel: 45 61 14 66 - Fax: 45 61 00 65 ■ Mon-Fri 14:30-19:00 ■ English spoken ■ Prices high ■ 10% professional discount

Antique gilded frames from the XV to the XIX centuries.
Mirrors, consoles, barometers.

MAISON EDOUARD GROSVALLET
126 bd Haussmann 75008 Paris ■ Tel 45 22 19 68 ■ Mon-Fri 9:30-12:00/14:30-18:00 ■ English and Spanish spoken

Antique mirrors, consoles and frames of all styles.

Framing

———————————— II ————————————

ALTUGLAS
10 rue du Mail, 75002 Paris ■ Tel: 42 36 38 74 ■ Mon-Fri 9:00-12:30/14:00-18:30 ■ Prices medium to high

Custom made items in plexiglas for the presentation of art objects. Table frames, columns, boxes.

———————————— III ————————————

CHARLOTTE
9 cité Dupetit-Thouars, 75003 Paris ■ Tel: 42 77 85 15 - Fax: 42 77 85 80 ■ Mon-Fri 14:00-18:00 and by appointment ■ Charlotte speaks English ■ Prices low

Framing of watercolors, gouaches, engravings, lithographs, canvases, tapestries.

V

APARTELIER

47 rue Censier, 75005 Paris ■ Tel: 43 36 14 74 ■ Tues-Sat 9:30-12:30/14:00-19:00/ Sun by appointment ■ Jacques Maréchal speaks English ■ Prices medium

Framing, restoration: paintings, engravings, art objects.

ATELIER CHRISTIAN DE BEAUMONT

11 rue Frédéric-Sauton, 75005 Paris ■ Tel: 43 29 88 75 - Fax: 40 51 88 06 ■ Tues-Sat 11:00-13:00/15:00-19:00 ■ English spoken ■ Prices high ■ 15% professional discount

Creation and fabrication of frames, stands and accessories of presentation for decorative objects. Creation of furniture and accessories in unique editions.

ATELIER MARTINE RAMA

62 rue du Cardinal-Lemoine, 75005 Paris ■ Tel: 46 34 09 54 - Fax: 46 33 07 78 ■ Tues-Sat 10:30-13:00/14:00-19:00 ■ English spoken ■ Prices medium ■ 10% professional discount

Framing in gold and copper leafing, trompe l'œil. Specialist in framing for hotels and offices.

L'ENCADREMENT

40 rue des Ecoles, 75005 Paris ■ Tel: 43 26 83 16 ■ Tues-Sat 9:30-13:00/14:00-18:30 ■ Bertrand and Joselyne Gaudiat speak English ■ Prices medium ■ Professional discount

Framing & restoration of paintings. All styles of frames: Italian, Dutch, French: Louis XV. Restoration of frames.

UNE IMAGE EN PLUS

19 rue Saint-Séverin, 75005 Paris ■ Tel: 43 25 83 85 ■ Mon-Sat 10:00-24:00 ■ Prices medium

Framing of art posters, postcards, film posters, concert posters and photos of stars.

VI

ART DE L'ENCADREMENT

9 rue de l'Odéon, 75006 Paris ■ Tel: 40 51 70 61 ■ Mon-Fri 9:00-12:00/13:00-17:00 ■ Prices medium ■ 15 to 20% professional discount

Framing of paintings, drawings, engravings. Old style and modern frames.

JEAN ESTEVE

3 rue Jacques-Callot, 75006 Paris ■ Tel: 43 54 19 10 - Fax: 46 34 67 03 ■ Tues-Sat 9:30-12:30/14-18:30 ■ Prices medium ■ 15 to 25% professional discount

Framing. Restoration of frames, paintings, engravings, pastels.

HAVARD PERE ET FILS

123 bd du Montparnasse, 75006 Paris ■ Tel: 43 22 34 87 - Fax: 43 20 42 87
■ Mon-Fri 9:00:12:30/14:00-18:30 ■ Prices high ■ Professional discount
Custom frames. Gilding. Restoration of paintings.

ERIC JAQUEMET

19 rue du Dragon, 75006 Paris ■ Tel: 42 22 20 37 ■ Tues-Sat 10:00-
13:00/14:00-19:00 ■ Eric Jaquemet speaks English ■ Prices medium ■ 10%
professional discount

Framing in all styles and designs. Subcontracting: restoration of paintings,
papers, sculpture, gilding.

ATELIER GUILLAUME MARTEL

2 rue du Regard 75006 Paris ■ Tel: 45 49 02 07 ■ Tues-Sat 9:00-11:45/14:30-
19:00

Custom framing in unusual and original designs. Classic style frames, particularly XVII century. Leafing in gold, copper, silver, platinum and aluminium.

THE PARIS AMERICAN ART CO.

4 rue Bonaparte, 75006 Paris ■ Tel: 43 26 09 93 - Fax: 43 54 33 80 ■ Tues-
Sat 10:00-13:00/13:45-18:30 ■ Danielle Lévêque speaks English ■ Prices
medium to high ■ Professional discount

Gilded frames in classic styles. Restoration. Modern frames. Antique frames,
mirrors, frames for miniatures, engravings, drawings and paintings. Framing.

VII

CADRES LAPOLI

45 rue Vaneau, 75007 Paris ■ Tel: 42 22 57 96 - Fax: 42 84 07 51 ■ Tues-
Sat 14:30-18:30 ■ Prices medium to high ■ Professional discount
Custom frames in French, Italian and Dutch styles. Restoration of gilded
wood (bois doré).

OISEAUX BLEUS

23 rue Augereau, 75007 Paris ■ Tel: 47 05 94 58 ■ Tues-Sat 10:00-
12:30/14:30-19:00 ■ Monique Lazou speaks English ■ Prices medium ■ Professional discount

Framing of drawings, engravings, watercolors, paintings. Presentation of
objects. Old style hand washing for drawings and engravings.

VIII

ATELIER CLAIRE DE GRAMONT

6 rue d'Astorg, 75008 Paris ■ Tel: 42 65 08 14 - Fax: 42 66 61 29 ■ Mon-Fri
9:30-18:00 ■ English spoken ■ Prices low ■ 10% professional discount
Framing of canvases, works on paper, engravings, watercolors. Copies of
antique wood frames, gilded, resin and stencilled frames. Restoration of
frames. Does much work for contemporary artists. Only acid free paper used.
Fast service.

BERTHELOT

184 rue du Faubourg-Saint-Honoré, 75008 Paris ■ Telfax: 45 63 34 07 ■ Mon-Fri 9:15-18:30/Sat 9:30-12:30/14:30-18:00 ■ English spoken ■ Prices medium ■ 10% professional discount

Frames and framing in classic styles. Reproduction of antique style frames. Gold leafing of frames and all objects in wood. Limited editions and reproductions of classic sculpture in bronze.

PHILIPPE MULER

24 rue de la Ville-l'Evêque, 75008 Paris ■ Tel: 42 65 43 38 - Fax: 42 65 08 13 ■ Tues-Fri 14:00-19:00/Sat 10:00-13:00 ■ Philippe Muler speaks English ■ Prices very high ■ 10% professional discount

Specialty: mounting of all types of art works. Antique frames, non-reflective glass, anti-ultra-violet glass, plexi-glass. Chemical free mattes and backings. High quality. Restoration of frames and old mountings.

RAPID CADRE

7 rue du Commandant-Rivière, 75008 Paris ■ Tel: 42 56 06 08 - Fax: 42 56 80 58 ■ Mon-Fri 9:30-18:30 ■ Marie-France Paul-Reynaud speaks English ■ Prices medium ■ 10 to 20% professional discount

Framing of posters, paintings, engravings.
Old style hand color washing. Rapid service.

—————————————— IX ——————————————

ATELIER 29

29 passage Verdeau, 75009 Paris ■ Tel: 42 46 60 76 ■ Mon-Fri 10:00-19:00
Frames of all styles for paintings, drawings and engravings.

—————————————— X ——————————————

P.M. ROUSSEAU

Anciennement Ets Piéton ■ 105 rue La Fayette, 75010 Paris ■ Tel: 48 74 21 23 - Fax: 45 26 25 29 ■ Mon-Fri 8:00-12:00/14:00-18:00 ■ Pierre-Marie Rousseau speaks a bit of English ■ Prices medium ■ 5 to 10% professional discount

Fabrication of XIX century style frames in gilded wood.
Expertise and restoration of antique frames.

—————————————— XI ——————————————

BENEDETTI ESTEVE

80 rue de Charonne, 75011 Paris ■ Tel: 43 71 21 35 - Fax: 43 67 63 34 ■ Tues-Fri 9:00-12:00/14:00-19:00/Sat 9:00-12:00/15:00-18:00 ■ Jane-Renée Estève speaks English ■ Prices medium ■ Professional discount

Framing in all styles of paintings, lithographs, drawings.
Restoration of objects (fans, masks) and frames, gold and silver leafing.

CENTRE DE L'ENCADREMENT ET DU BOIS DECORATIF

76 bd Richard-Lenoir, 75011 Paris ■ Tel: 43 57 47 25 - Fax: 43 55 09 95 ■ Mon-Sat 9:00-18:00

Wide range of accessories for framing. Restoration of frames and paintings as well as first class framing.

METAL

172 rue de Charonne, 75011 Paris ■ Tel: 43 79 08 02 - Fax: 43 79 16 90 ■ Mon-Fri 8:30-12:30/13:30-17:30 ■ George Stein speaks English ■ Prices medium ■ Professional discount

Framing for art galleries, museums, expositions, advertising agencies, architects. Framing for hotels and offices. Specialty: framing with non-acid materials. Classic and contemporary.

MARTINE ZWOLINSKI

33 rue Amelot, 75011 Paris ■ Tel: 43 55 63 80 - Fax: 43 55 52 20 ■ Mon-Fri 9:00-12:00/14:00-18:00/Sat 9:30-12:30 ■ Laurent and Karine Zwolinski speak English ■ Prices low ■ Professional discount

Framing, mirrors for boutiques.

XII

BOIS EXTREME

27 rue Claude-Decaen, 75012 Paris ■ Tel: 43 45 86 82 - Fax: 43 45 71 73 ■ Mon-Fri 9:00-18:00

An interesting line of framing elements, custom framing in all styles.

CLAUDE GALATRY

43 rue de la Gare de Reuilly, 75012 Paris ■ Tel: 43 07 24 92 ■ Mon-Sat 9:00-12:00/14:00-18:00 ■ Prices medium ■ 20% professional discount

Framing. Fabrication of frames, especially for miniatures, round and oval. Hand color washing.

XIII

♛ ALOT

101 rue de Patay, 75013 Paris ■ Tel: 45 82 80 32 - Fax: 44 24 51 90 ■ Mon-Fri 8:00-18:00/Sat 8:00-12:00 ■ Prices medium ■ Professional discount

Framing. All types of gilding on wood. Wood carving.
Restoration of all objects and furniture in gilded wood (bois doré).
Specialist in French gilded furniture of the XVII and XVIII centuries.
Qualified expert.

ARTEM

15 rue Boussingault, 75013 Paris ■ Tel: 45 88 74 83 ■ Mon-Fri 9:15-12:00/14:00-19:00 ■ Prices low ■ Professional discount

Framing of all kinds. Frames made in wood and aluminium.
Art supplies.

XV

LES ATELIERS D'ANNE-MARIE

29 rue Oscar-Roty, 75015 Paris ■ Tel: 45 58 12 22 ■ Mon-Fri 10:00-14:00/15:30-20:00 ■ Anne-Marie Villette speaks English ■ Prices low to medium ■ 10 to 30% professional discount

Framing, sale of lithographs.

BADIA-ENCADREMENT

55 rue Blomet, 75015 Paris ■ Tel: 42 73 00 82 ■ Tues-Sat 9:30-12:30/14:00-19:00 ■ Prices low ■ 20% professional discount for purchases over 6,000 francs.

Gilding, framing all styles, restoration of paper, paintings. Fabrication of mounts for art objects.

MARIE-LAURE DE LAPEROUSE

24/31 rue Violet, 75015 Paris ■ Tel: 45 75 00 08 ■ Tues-Sat 10:00-14:00/15:00-19:00 ■ Charles McClay speaks English ■ Prices medium

Framing & restoration of frames. Frames for paintings, mounting of collectibles, fans, stamps, pipes, butterflies.

AGNES CADRILLAGE SAULEAU

15 rue de l'Abbé-Groult, 75015 Paris ■ Tel: 42 50 19 40 ■ Tues-Sat 10:30-12:30/14:30-19:00 ■ Agnès Sauleau speaks English ■ Prices medium ■ 10% professional discount

Framing in classic and contemporary styles.

--------------------------------- XVI ---------------------------------

GALERIE COROT

8 rue Corot, 75016 Paris ■ Tel: 42 88 46 80 ■ Tues 10:00-12:30/15:00-19:00/Wed-Sat 10:00-19:00 ■ Prices medium ■ 20% professional discount

Classical & modern framing. Restoration of paintings, old engravings, charcoal drawings and pastels.

LA MAISON DU CADRE

96 rue de la Tour, 75116 Paris ■ Tel: 45 04 75 73 - Fax: 45 04 75 79 ■ Mon-Sat 9:30-19:30 ■ Hinda Zerbib speaks English ■ Prices medium to high ■ 10% professional discount

Antique frames. Gilding. Fabrication of frames in all styles and all types of framing. Restoration of antique frames, gilding. Restoration of paintings, pastels, engravings. High quality work and materials.

C. LARRIVE ET J.L. VERDIE

21 rue du Bois-le-Vent, 75016 Paris ■ Tel: 45 25 02 74 ■ Tues-Sat 10:00-12:30/14:00-19:00 ■ Jean-Louis Verdie speaks English ■ Prices high ■ Professional discount

Traditional framing in classic styles. Old style hand color washing. Gilding, restoration of gilded wood (bois doré).

MIREILLE MATHIEU

50 rue de l'Assomption, 75016 Paris ■ Tel: 42 88 50 51 ■ Tues-Sat 10:00-13:00/14:30-19:00 ■ Mireille Mathieu speaks English ■ Prices medium to high ■ Professional discount

Studio and boutique of framing. Restoration of engravings, frames, gilding.

THELLIER

64 rue de Longchamp, 75116 Paris ■ Tel: 47 04 32 83 - Fax: 47 27 66 02 ■
Tues-Sat 10:00-12:30/14:30-19:00 ■ Philippe-Louis Mexler speaks English
■ Prices medium ■ Professional discount

All kinds of gilding and framing, restoration.
Excellent quality.

--- XVII ---

ATELIER DU BOIS DORE

80 av. des Ternes, 75017 Paris ■ Tel: 45 74 67 58 - Fax: 44 74 72 49 ■ Mon-
Sat 9:00-12:30/14:00-19:00 ■ English spoken ■ Prices medium to high ■ Professionals only

Choice of 1,500 antique frames. 300 moulding styles for reproductions of
antique frames. Framing. Restoration of gilded wood (bois doré). Creation
in very limited editions of furniture and objects in gilded wood.

BERENGERE POLACK

27 rue de Chazelles, 75017 Paris ■ Tel: 46 22 70 93 - Fax: 47 98 33 89 ■
Tues-Sat 10:00-19:00 ■ Patricia Inman speaks English ■ Prices medium ■
Professional discount

Framing, book binding, art objects.

--- XVIII ---

LA BAGUETTE DE BOIS

44 rue Lepic, 75018 Paris ■ Tel: 46 06 36 80 - Fax: 42 54 54 92 ■ Tues-Sat
9:00-18:30 ■ Prices medium ■ 10% professional discount

Something special. Wonderful selection of antique frames. Framing in all
styles from classic through modern.

--- XIX ---

PEINTRES SANS FRONTIERES

2 av. Moderne, 75019 Paris ■ Tel: 42 38 05 82 - Fax: 42 00 42 25 ■ Mon-Fri
9:30-13:30/14:30-18:30 ■ Pierre Estrada speaks English ■ Prices low ■ Professional discount

Framing of all kinds.

--- XX ---

ESPACE 20

22 villa Riberolle, 75020 Paris ■ Tel: 43 79 78 14 ■ Mon-Sat 9:00-12:00/14:00-
17:00 ■ Prices medium ■ 20% professional discount

Framing of paintings and drawings. Specialty: photographic framing.

GALERIE 20
ETIENNE LEROY-PIERRE LEROY
288 rue des Pyrénées, 75020 Paris ▪ Tel: 43 66 83 88 ▪ Tues-Wed-Fri-Sat
10:00-12:30/Thurs and Sun 11:00-13:30 ▪ Prices medium ▪ 20% professional
discount
Framing, restoration. Custom glass cases (vitrines) for objects. Specialty:
old paintings. Also photo retouching.

—————————————— NEUILLY ——————————————

ROBERT DUVIVIER
30 rue de Sablonville, 92200 Neuilly ▪ Tel: 47 22 25 90 - Fax: 46 43 01 49
▪ Tues-Sat 8:00-12:00/14:00-19:00 ▪ Miss Duvivier speaks a little English ▪
Prices medium to high
Reproduction frames of all styles, Louis XIV to contemporary. Restoration
and gilding of all sculptured wood items (bois doré). Excellent quality work.

CONTEMPORARY FURNITURE
Meubles contemporains

──────────── **I** ────────────

EMILIO ROBBA "LA MAISON"

47 rue Etienne-Marcel, 75001 Paris ■ Tel: 42 36 66 48 - Fax: 40 26 48 23 ■ Mon-Sat 10:00-19:00 ■ English spoken ■ Prices medium to high ■ Professional discount

Contemporary furniture in interesting original designs. Tables in wrought iron and glass, decorative hardware with marine theme. Furniture in traced leather. Slip covers and linens. Everything in white, cream and beige. Will do custom colours.

──────────── **VI** ────────────

COOPERATIVE LOZERIENNE

1 bis rue Hautefeuille, 75006 Paris ■ Tel: 43 26 93 99 - Fax: 44 07 00 43 ■ Tues-Sat 11:00-19:00 ■ Prices medium ■ 5% professional discount

Custom furniture in solid woods, chairs and objects in wood. This is a cooperative group of artisans who make furniture, crafts and also good things to eat.

NOBILIS

29 rue Bonaparte, 75006 Paris ■ Tel: 43 29 12 71 - Fax: 43 29 77 57 ■ English spoken ■ Prices medium ■ Professional discount

Their own exclusive line of contemporary furniture, lamps and fabrics.

──────────── **VII** ────────────

ABSOLUTE

22 bis rue des Saints-Pères, 75007 Paris ■ Tel: 42 96 18 03 - Fax: 42 86 83 61 ■ Mon-Fri 10:00-19:00/Sat 11:00-19:00 ■ 10 to 12% professional discount

Contemporary Californian style furniture designed for Absolute. A good choice of accessories.

ETAMINE

63 rue du Bac, 75007 Paris ■ Tel: 42 22 03 16 - Fax: 43 25 92 76 ■ Mon 13:00-19:30/Tues-Sat 10:00-19:30 ■ Laurence Millet speaks English ■ Prices medium ■ Professional discount

Etamine's exclusive line of contemporary furniture, lamps, tables, consoles, coffee tables, curtain rods in wrought iron and wood. Trimmings, together with their great fabric collection.

LIGNE ROSET

189 bd Saint-Germain, 75007 Paris ■ Tel: 45 48 54 13 - Fax: 45 44 01 20 ■ Mon-Sat 10:00-19:00 ■ English spoken ■ Prices medium to high

Large choice of contemporary furniture, chairs, carpets and accessories.

BAGUES

37 av. Pierre-1er-de-Serbie, 75008 Paris ■ Tel: 47 20 61 17 - Fax: 40 70 06 76 ■ Mon-Sat 10:00-19:00 ■ English spoken ■ Prices high ■ Professional discount
High quality contemporary furniture, lighting, mirrors and decorative objects.

BESSON RIVE DROITE

46 av. Marceau, 75008 Paris ■ Tel: 47 20 75 35 - Fax: 47 30 15 62 ■ Mon-Fri 10:00-18:00
Small line of contemporary furniture and sofas, wallpapers, fabrics, rugs. Also at 39 rue Bonaparte, 75006 Paris.

PROTIS

153 rue du Faubourg-Saint-Honoré, 75008 Paris ■ Tel: 45 62 22 40 - Fax: 45 62 57 71 ■ Mon-Fri 9:15-19:00/Sat 10:00-13:00/14:30-18:30 ■ Georges Assouline speaks English ■ Prices medium ■ 15% professional discount
Contemporary furniture: sofas, bookcases, tables, chairs, desks, for the office and the home.

GUY STEPHANE

225 rue du Faubourg-Saint-Honoré 75008 Paris ■ Tel: 46 22 21 52 ■ Mon 15:00-19:00/Tues-Sat 10:00-19:00 ■ Prices medium ■ Professional discount
Contemporary furniture, sofas, chairs, mirrors, lighting, decorative objects.

MARINA DE BOURBON

112 bd de Courcelles, 75017 Paris ■ Tel: 47 63 42 01 - Fax: 40 53 96 50 ■ Mon-Sat 10:30-19:30 ■ English spoken ■ Prices medium to high ■ Professional discount
Nice mixture of contemporary and antique furniture, lighting and decorative objects.

Rattan furniture
Meubles en rotin

DECOUVERTE

245 rue du Faubourg-Saint-Antoine, 75011 Paris ■ Tel: 43 72 85 61 - Fax: 43 72 24 86 ■ Mon-Sat 10:30-13:00/14:00-19:30 ■ English spoken ■ Prices medium ■ 10 to 15% professional discount
Contemporary rattan furniture, for home and office.

ROTIN D'AUJOURD'HUI

65 av. Gambetta, 75020 Paris ■ Tel: 46 36 90 32 - Fax: 44 62 09 11 ■ Tues-Sat 9:30-12:00/14:00-19:00 ■ Prices medium
Custom fabrication and repair of rattan furniture.

CUSTOM CONTEMPORARY FURNITURE

Meubles contemporains sur mesure

---------------- **V** ----------------

ATELIER CHRISTIAN DE BEAUMONT

11 rue Frederic Sauton, 75005 Paris ■ Tel: 43 29 88 75 - Fax: 40 51 88 06
■ Tues-Sat 11:00-13:00/15:00-19:00 ■ English spoken ■ Prices high ■ 15%
professional discount

Creation and fabrication of furniture and lighting, frames, accessories for presentation of decorative collectibles.

---------------- **VI** ----------------

MEUBLES ANTOINE SCHAPIRA

Ebéniste ■ 74 bd Raspail, 75006 Paris ■ Tel: 45 48 22 80 - Fax: 42 84 15 22
■ Tues-Sat 10:30-13:00/14:00-19:00 ■ Prices high ■ Professional discount

Creation and fabrication of all styles of contemporary and classical furniture in the tradition of the French artisan.

LAURE WELFLING

30 rue Jacob, 75006 Paris ■ Tel: 43 25 17 03 - Fax: 43 56 72 15 ■ Mon-Sat
11:00-19:00 ■ Laure Welfling speaks English ■ Prices high ■ 5 to 10% professional discount

Creation of a wide choice of custom contemporary furniture and lighting.

---------------- **VII** ----------------

MARIE-CHRISTINE DE LA ROCHEFOUCALD
ELINAS L.R.

16 rue de l'Université, 75007 Paris ■ Tel: 42 86 02 40/42 61 22 22 - Fax:
42 60 21 17 ■ Mon-Sat 11:00-19:00 ■ English spoken ■ Prices medium to high
■ Professional discount

Original creations of Marie-Christine de la Rochefoucald:table bases of piles of antique books made of painted wood, painted cabinets, armchairs upholstered in tapestry, small sofas, lighting, cushions, tablecloths bordered in velvet. Special editions of aged fabrics.

---------------- **XII** ----------------

EBENISTERIE SEGRANSAN

74 rue du Faubourg-Saint-Antoine, 75012 Paris ■ Tel: 43 43 97 25 - Fax:
43 43 96 07 ■ Mon-Fri 8:00-12:00/14:00-18:00 ■ Patrice Dizière speaks
English ■ Prices medium ■ 5 to 10% professional discount

Creator of custom centemporary furniture. Work experience includes the Elysée Palace and the the Opera House of Lyon.

JOSEPH KARAM

61 av. Raymond-Poincaré, 75116 Paris ■ Tel: 44 05 09 21 - Fax: 44 05 09 20
■ Mon-Sat 10:00-19:00 ■ English spoken ■ Prices high ■ Professional discount

Custom creations of contemporary furniture: sofas, table bases, tric-tracs, desks and pedestal tables.

GALERIE L'ANCIEN & LE NOUVEAU

Jean-Louis Dainaut ■ 3 rue Cyrano-de-Bergerac, 75018 Paris ■
Tel: 42 58 25 69 ■ Tues-Fri 15:00-19:30/Sat 10:00-19:30/Sun 15:00-19:30
■ Prices medium ■ 20 to 30% professional discount

Creation and fabrication of the gallery's own designs in furniture, ceramics, figurines and bookshelves.

Plexiglass

ALTUGLAS

Michel Selim ■ 10 rue du Mail, 75002 Paris ■ Tel: 42 36 38 74 ■ Mon- Fri
9-12:30/14:00-18:00 ■ Prices medium to high ■ Professional discount

Custom creation of furniture and objects in plexiglass.

Display Cabinets
Vitrines

VITRINES VENDOME

81 rue des Archives, 75003 Paris ■ Tel: 42 72 58 38 - Fax: 42 72 65 59 ■
Mon-Fri 9:00-12:00/13:00-18:00 ■ English spoken ■ Prices high 20% professional discount

High quality display cabinets for the home, for stores, hotels, museums, galleries. All dimensions. Installation.

CUSTOM REPRODUCTION FURNITURE

Reproduction de meubles sur mesure

——————————— XI ———————————

ATELIERS DE BRIMBOIS

5 cité Beauharnais, 75011 Paris ■ Tel: 43 71 76 30 - Fax: 43 71 74 84 ■ Mon-Fri 8:00-11:45/13:00-18:30 ■ Janine Robineau speaks English ■ Prices high ■ Professional discount

Reproduction of XVIII to XX century style furniture, specializing in marquetry.

DEGROOTE ET MUSSY

12 passage de Taillandiers, 75011 Paris ■ Tel: 48 05 13 91 ■ Mon-Fri 8:30-19:00 ■ Christiane Mussy speaks English ■ Prices medium to high ■ Professional discount

Custom furniture in all classic styles.

NOUVEAUX MEUBLES D'ART

179 rue du Faubourg-Saint-Antoine, 75011 Paris ■ Tel: 43 07 24 75 - Fax: 43 07 42 47 ■ Mon-Sat 8:00-12:00/14:00-18:00 ■ Jean-Paul Bart speaks English ■ Prices medium to high ■ Professional discount

Top quality custom reproductions of antique furniture.

BERNARD RIMOLDI

3 passage Rauch, 75011 Paris ■ Tel: 43 79 78 59 ■ Mon-Fri 8:00-12:00/14:00-18:00/Sat 8:00-12:00 ■ Prices medium ■ Professional discount

All classic styles of furniture custom made to order.

RINCK

8 passage de la Bonne-Graine, 75011 Paris ■ Tel: 47 00 42 67 - Fax: 43 55 89 54 ■ Mon-Fri 8:00-12:00/14:00-18:00 ■ Prices medium to high ■ Professional discount

High quality cabinet maker of furniture in contemporary and classic styles. Boiseries. Specialist in Art Deco.

SIEGES ANDRY

24 rue de Lappe, 75011 Paris ■ Tel: 43 55 16 62 - Fax: 47 00 45 57 ■ Mon-Fri 9:00-19:00 ■ Hervé Charpentier speaks English ■ Prices high ■ Professional discount

Fabrication of furniture in classic styles. Reproductions in small quantity or by series.

STEFANSEN

2 rue de la Roquette, 75011 Paris ■ Tel: 48 05 25 51 - Fax: 47 00 27 41 ■ Mon-Fri 8:00-18:30/Sat-Sun by appointment ■ Joel Stefansen speaks English ■ Prices medium ■ 10 to 20% professional discount

Highest quality creation of furniture in marquetry styles of the XVII and XVIII centuries. Decorative wood panels in marquetry and decorative objects. Meilleur Ouvrier de France.

XII

JEAN-LUC FAUCHEUX

19 rue Claude-Tillier, 75012 Paris ■ Tel: 43 48 86 91 ■ Mon-Fri 8:00-18:00 ■ Prices medium

Copies of all antique furniture styles to measure.

L.O.R.D.

10 rue de Toul, 75012 Paris ■ Tel: 43 40 50 20 - Fax: 43 46 80 23 ■ Mon-Fri 9:00-18:00 ■ English spoken ■ Prices high ■ Professional discount

Successors to Jansen. A unique atelier of artisans who make furniture, wood panelling, bronzes, painting, upholstering. A complete service.

XV

ERIC LAURENT-LASSON

159 rue Saint-Charles, 75015 Paris ■ Tel: 45 54 65 22 - Fax: 44 25 18 65 ■ Mon-Fri 8:00-17:00 ■ Diane Laurent-Lasson and Jean-Michel Reginster speak English ■ Prices medium ■ 20% professional discount

Hand made copies of XVII and XVIII century furniture and chairs. Upholstery and wall upholstery.

XVI

JEAN-MARC DESLOUBIERES

105 rue Lauriston, 75116 Paris ■ Tel: 45 53 24 91 - Fax: 47 27 07 03 ■ Mon-Fri by appointment ■ English spoken ■ Prices medium ■ Professional discount

Fabrication to measure of antique furniture.

SAINT-OUEN

BENOIT MARCU

7 rue Madeleine, 93400 Saint-Ouen ■ Tel: 40 11 15 23 ■ Mon-Sat 8:30-12:30/13:30-17:30 ■ Prices medium ■ Professional discount

Creation of copies of antique furniture of the XVII and XVIII centuries.

OUTSIDE PARIS

☖ PATRICK VASTEL

143 rue du Général-Leclerc, 50110 Tourlaville, Cherbourg ■ Tel: (16) 33 22 46 07 - Fax: (16) 33 22 96 26 ■ Mon-Fri 9:00-12:00/13:30-18:30/Sat by appointment ■ English spoken ■ Prices medium ■ Professional discount

Custom re-creation of period furniture. Expert to the Cour d'Appel. One of the best.

ETS PIERRE COUNOT BLANDIN

B.P.1, 88350 Liffol-le-Grand ■ Tel: (16) 29 06 62 40 - Fax: (16) 29 06 78 04 ■ Mon-Fri by appointment ■ Jean-Pierre Duhoux and Philippe Counot speak English ■ Prices high ■ Professional discount

High quality reproduction of antique furniture and chairs, including Art Deco.

M.H.R.

3 square Copernic, 78150 Le Chesnay ■ Tel: 39 63 37 84 - Fax: 39 63 37 70 ■ Every day by appointment ■ Gerry Gay and Corinne Nogues speak English ■ Prices medium ■ 10% professional discount

Manufacturing and repair of furniture for hotels, motels and restaurants. Reupholstering.

GARDEN, TERRACE AND LANDSCAPE DESIGNERS

Paysagistes et aménagement de jardins et terrasses

---------------------------------- I ----------------------------------

JARDINS D'AMSTERDAM

59 rue d'Amsterdam, 75001 Paris ■ Tel: 42 81 02 63 - Fax: 48 74 06 81 ■ Mon-Sat 8:00-20:30 ■ Prices medium

Conception and installation of city gardens, terraces and patios, indoor and outdoor. Flowering plants and trees.

---------------------------------- II ----------------------------------

LES JARDINS DE DEMETHER

56 bis rue du Louvre, 75002 Paris ■ Tel: 48 39 35 72 - Fax: 49 37 09 70 ■ Prices medium ■ 5 to 15% professional discount

Design, creation and maintenance of terrace gardens, interior gardens and aquatic gardens.

---------------------------------- IV ----------------------------------

LES JARDINS DU TROUBADOUR

10 rue des Lions Saint-Paul, 75004 Paris ■ Tel: 42 77 81 85 - Fax: 42 77 35 95 ■ Mon-Fri 9:00-20:00 by appointment ■ Marie-Thérèse Le Menestrel speaks English ■ Prices medium

Design, planting and maintenance of city gardens, balconies, terraces and interior gardens.

---------------------------------- XI ----------------------------------

FRANÇOIS CHARMOY

3 rue Titon, 75011 Paris ■ Tel: 40 09 29 67 - Fax: 40 09 96 85 ■ Mon-Fri 10:00-19:00 ■ François Charmoy speaks English ■ Prices high ■ Professional discount

Conception and execution of terraces and gardens, following ecological principles.

---------------------------------- XIII ----------------------------------

DOMINIQUE BOYER

5 place Pinel, 75013 Paris ■ Tel: 45 84 56 99 - Fax: 45 83 50 02 ■ Mon-Fri 9:30-18:30 ■ Jacqueline Boulanger speaks English ■ Prices medium ■ 20 to 30% professional discount

Advisers on gardens, landscapes and environments.

MICHEL VIOLLET

8 rue Albert-Bayet, 75013 Paris ■ Telfax: 45 35 86 16 ■ Mon-Fri by appointment ■ Marie-Clotilde Bonfils and Michel Viollet speak English ■ Prices medium

Study and diagnosis of landscapes and gardens for installation, maintenance and rehabilitation.

XIV

SERGE EYZAT

7 rue Fermat, 75014 Paris ■ Tel: 43 22 51 31 - Fax: 40 50 10 12 ■ Mon-Fri 9:00-18:00 ■ Serge Eyzat speaks English ■ Prices medium

Planning and execution of parks, gardens, green spaces, sports parks. Planning, counsel, control, maintenance and rehabilitation of landscapes and gardens. Extensive experience abroad.

XV

SOCIETE AGENCE D'AMENAGEMENT D'ESPACES VERTS

124 rue du Théâtre, 75015 Paris ■ Tel: 45 78 65 46 - Fax: 45 78 65 47 ■ Mon-Fri 8:00-19:00 ■ Annick Blanchet speaks English ■ Prices medium

Creation of interior and exterior gardens. Planting and maintenance of terraces and patios.

XVI

PARIS VERT

7 rue des Pâtures, 75016 Paris ■ Tel: 42 88 43 12 - Fax: 42 88 90 50 ■ Mon-Fri 7:30-19:30 ■ Prices medium

Creation and planting of green spaces. They specialize in planting of terraces and interior gardens. Also design and install lighting for gardens and terraces.

XVII

LES JARDINS DE PARIS

9 passage Cardinet, 75017 Paris ■ Tel: 40 31 52 20 - Fax: 39 19 80 75 ■ Mon-Fri 8:00-18:00 ■ Prices medium ■ 5 to 10% professional discount

Planning, installation and maintenance of green spaces, terraces and patios. Sale and rental of indoor plants. Custom fabrication and installation of trellises and planters.

XVIII

BERTRAND PAULET

49 rue des Poissonniers, 75018 Paris ■ Tel: 42 64 42 67 - Fax: 42 64 04 96 ■ Mon-Fri 9:00-18:00 ■ English spoken ■ Prices medium

Landscape designer, conception and installation of gardens and terraces.

HERMES

182 av. Charles-de-Gaulle, 92200 Neuilly-sur-Seine ■ Tel: 46 24 50 12 - Fax: 46 24 66 41 ■ Tues-Sat 9:00-19:30 ■ Prices medium to high ■ Professional discount

Landscaping of gardens, terraces and patios. Complete installations with green and flowering plants.

Fountains - Manufacture & Installation
Fontaines - Fabrication et installation

——————— V ———————

ARBRE A PLUMES

48 bd Saint-Germain, 75005 Paris ■ Tel: 43 29 07 77 - Fax: 46 34 29 96 ■ Tues-Sat 12:00-19:00 ■ Professional discount

Interior fountains in closed circuit designed by artisans. Unique creations or production.

——————— IX ———————

PROVINCES DE FRANCE

59 rue de Maubeuge, 75009 Paris ■ Tel: 48 78 34 22 ■ Prices medium to high

Excellent selection of cast iron garden fountains in classic designs. A large selection of rustic cast iron garden furniture, tables, consoles, lanterns.

——————— XIV ———————

A L'EAU VIVE

82 rue de la Tombe-Issoire (Angle rue d'Alésia), 75014 Paris ■ Tel: 43 22 42 28 - Fax: 43 22 03 83 ■ Tues-Sat 13:00-19:30 ■ Gilles Toussaert speaks English ■ Prices medium ■ 10% professional discount

Fabrication and installation of interior fountains for individuals and businesses. Creations by Guy Lartigue and F. Taillandier. Sculpture. Renovation of old fountains.

——————— OUTSIDE PARIS ———————

FRIGEBRICE

139 av. d'Argenteuil, 92600 Asnières-sur-Seine ■ Tel: 47 93 62 56 - Fax: 40 86 14 81 ■ Mon-Fri 8:00-12:00/13:00-17:00/Fri closing 16:00 ■ Stéphane Rose speaks English ■ Prices medium ■ Professional discount

Manufacturer of fountains, cold water and hot and cold. Maintenance and repair of fountains of all brands.

LES NOUVELLES FONTAINES

2 rue Colonel-Fabien, 94110 Arcueil ■ Tel: 46 63 45 27 - Fax: 46 63 45 66
■ Mon-Fri 8:00-19:00 ■ René Massan speaks English ■ Prices medium

Conception, fabrication and installation of decorative fountains for the interior and exterior. Complete turn-key service.

SDF

124 bis av. de la République, 94120 Fontenay-sous-Bois ■ Tel: 43 94 03 28 -
Fax: 43 94 36 45 ■ Mon-Fri 9:00-18:00 ■ Didier Dumaine speaks English ■
Prices medium ■ Professional discount

Conception and design of luminous fountains and cascades. Private and monumental installations. Clients include: hotels at Euro-Disney, hotels and palaces throughout the world.

Garden supplies and outdoor furniture
Fournitures et meubles de jardin

——————————— IV ———————————

LE JARDIN SAINT-PAUL

24 quai des Célestins, 75004 Paris ■ Tel: 42 78 08 89 - Fax: 42 78 40 98 ■
Mon-Sat 9:30-18:30 ■ Michel Boucher speaks English ■ Prices medium ■ Professional discount

Garden furniture in the styles of Napoleon III and 1900s in teak, cast aluminium and wrought iron. Statuary, urns, lamps and lanterns, fountains, pumps, tables, benches and carousel horses.

——————————— VII ———————————

JARDINS DE PLAISANCE

72 bd de la Tour-Maubourg, 75007 Paris ■ Tel: 45 55 98 52 - Fax: 45 50 38 32
■ Tues-Sat 8:30-19:30/Mon April-July ■ Jean-Pierre Boullanger speaks English ■ Prices medium to high ■ 10 to 15% professional discount

Garden furniture in teak and aluminium. Contemporary and classic styles. Fountains and cast iron Medici vases, pottery and wooden parasols.

PASSWORLD FRANCE

11 bd de la Tour Maubourg, 75007 Paris ■ Tel: 45 55 45 65 - Fax 45 55 20
56 ■ Mon-Fri 9:00-19:00 ■ Pascal Boucard speaks English ■ Prices medium
to high ■ Professional discount

Garden furniture and exterior decorations.

TECTONA

3 av. de Breteuil, 75007 Paris ■ Tel: 47 35 70 70 - Fax: 47 35 37 66 ■ Mon-
Sat 10:00-19:00 ■ Aubert Lacroix and Geneviève Murith speak English ■
Prices medium to high ■ Professional discount

High quality garden furniture in teak. Parasols: round, rectangular and square. Croquet games. Garden shelters and gazebos in wood. Folding furniture in metal and teak.

DAMBLEMONT

67 rue de Provence, 75009 Paris ■ Tel: 47 03 34 83 - Fax: 42 61 68 95 ■
Mon-Fri 9:30-18:30 by appointment only ■ Bruno Caron speaks English ■
Prices high ■ 5 to 15% professional discount

Garden furniture in teak and painted white or green moabi. Eight different
lines of chairs, tables, armchairs and benches from designs of the XVII century to the 1920s. Made by compagnons.

Lattice and Trellis
Treillage

SAINT-DENIS

PASCAL WAUTHY

30 rue de la Légion-d'Honneur, 93200 Saint-Denis ■ Tel: 48 13 00 22 - Fax:
30 40 77 59 ■ Mon-Sat 8:00-20:00 ■ Francesca Salerno speaks English ■
Prices medium ■ Professional discount

Lattice for interior and exterior decoration. Partitions for balconies, facades
of any height. Plant supports, pergolas.

Sports Installations
Installations sportives

3 S, SURFACES SYNTHETIQUES SPORTIVES

52 rue d'Auteuil, 75016 Paris ■ Telfax: 45 20 51 02 ■ Mon-Fri 9:00-18:30 ■
Prices medium ■ Professional discount

Installation of artificial turf for sports facilities. Tennis courts, football and hock-
ey fields. Wide experience with installations at Wimbledon and in Australia.

HUBERT DE VACHON

12 rue Pouchet, 75017 Paris ■ Tel: 44 85 97 05 - Fax: 44 85 05 69 ■ Mon-
Fri 9:00-17:00 ■ Hubert de Vachon speaks English ■ Prices medium ■ 20 to
30% professional discount

Landscape architect specializing in the creation of Golf Courses. Also general landscape design and installation.

LUD ESPACE

4 rue des Nations-Unies, 92160 Antony ■ Tel: 40 96 13 35 - Fax: 40 96 12 11
■ Mon-Fri 8:00-18:00 ■ English spoken ■ Prices medium

Installation and maintenance of outdoor recreational facilities, toboggan runs,
swings, etc.

GENEALOGISTS
Généalogistes

III

MME ANNE-SOPHIE CHEVALIER

81 rue de Turbigo, 75003 Paris ■ Tel: 48 04 55 03 ■ Every day by appointment ■ Anne-Sophie Chevalier speaks English ■ Prices medium

Genealogy research and history, genealogical trees.

XV

CABINET LIGNIERES

78 rue Cambronne, 75015 Paris ■ Tel: 45 66 89 19 ■ Mon-Sat 9:00-20:00 ■ Hervé Lemoine-Lignières and Laetitia Guggenheim speak English ■ Prices medium to high

Genealogical and historical research. Identification of family crests, family trees, family portraits, silver or china. Research of patrimony and heraldic designs.

MME GENEVIEVE MORANT

85 bd Pasteur, B.P. 211, 75015 Paris ■ Tel: 43 21 55 33 ■ By appointment ■ Prices medium

Genealogy: research and genealogical tableaux prepared. Judicial services: all procedures for name changes, adjunction to surnames, rights of and to nobility.

XIX

CABINET GENEALOGIQUE
MYRIAM PROVENCE

4 rue Vincent-Scotto, Boîte No. 58, 75019 Paris ■ Tel: 42 40 58 26 - Fax: 42 45 46 35 ■ Prices medium ■ Professional discount

Covering all France and French territories: specialty in historical and family research: research into ancestors, descendents, family histories, history of homes, villages or enterprises, research into bibliographies, transcription of family texts and drawing of family trees and heraldry.

KITCHEN ACCESSORIES
Accessoires de cuisine

———————————— I ————————————

DEHILLERAN

18 rue Coquillière, 75001 Paris ■ Tel: 42 36 53 13 - Fax: 45 08 86 83 ■ Mon 8:00-12:30/14:00-18:00/Tues-Sat 8:00-18:00 ■ English spoken ■ Prices medium to high ■ Professional discount

Very high quality kitchen utensils of professional level. Superb collection of copper pots and pans.

———————————— II ————————————

A. SIMON

36 rue Etienne-Marcel and 48 rue Montmartre, 75002 Paris ■ Tel: 42 33 71 65 - Fax: 42 33 68 25 ■ Mon-Sat 8:30-18:30 ■ English spoken ■ Prices medium to high ■ Professional discount

For the amateur and the professional, everything for cooking and serving food and drink. Marvellous quality.

LIBRARY SHELVES AND CLOSETS
Bibliothèques et rangements

---------------------------------- VIII ----------------------------------

CESAM

169 bd Haussmann, 75008 Paris ■ Tel: 45 61 04 16 - Fax: 45 63 46 07 ■ Tues-Fri 10:00-19:00/Sat 10:00-12:30-14:00-19:00 ■ English and Spanish spoken ■ Prices high ■ Professional discount

Bookshelves and closets, custom and stock. Very high quality.

---------------------------------- XIV ----------------------------------

PRISM ALL

211 bd Raspail, 75014 Paris ■ Tel: 43 20 37 53 - Fax: 43 22 75 42 ■ Tues-Sat 9:00-18:00 ■ Prices medium ■ 20 to 30% professional discount

Modular shelves for libraries and glass display cabinets.

---------------------------------- XVII ----------------------------------

DE LONG EN LARGE

124 rue de Courcelles, 75017 Paris ■ Tel: 42 27 64 71 - Fax: 42 27 31 57 ■ Mon 14:30-19:00/Tues-Sat 9:30-19:00 ■ Prices medium to high ■ Professional discount

Custom made shelves and bookshelves and built-in units.

---------------------------------- SURESNES ----------------------------------

NEVES

99 rue des Bas-Rogers, 92150 Suresnes ■ Tel: 46 97 80 80 - Fax: 46 97 80 70 ■ Mon-Fri 8:00-12:00/13:00-17:30 ■ Anne Laurent speaks English ■ Professional discount

Manufacturer of modular units for closets, dressing rooms, room dividers, library shelving and offices.

---------------------------------- OUTSIDE PARIS ----------------------------------

INPLACARDS

Rue André-Citroën, 78140 Vélizy-Villacoublay ■ Tel: 34 65 35 70 ■ Wed-Fri 11:00-20:00/Sat-Sun 10:00-20:00 ■ Jean-Michel Legras speaks English ■ Prices high ■ Professional discount

Sliding and pivoting doors, room dividers, closets and dressing rooms. Made to measure.

Delisle

4, rue du Parc-Royal - 75003 Paris
Téléphone : (1) 42 72 21 34 - Téléfax : (1) 42 72 04 79

LIGHTING
Luminaires

---------- III ----------

♨ DELISLE

4 rue du Parc-Royal, 75003 Paris ■ Tel: 42 72 21 34 - Fax: 42 72 04 79 ■ Mon-Fri 9:00-12:00/14:00-18:00 and by appointment ■ Jean-Michel Delisle speaks English ■ Prices high ■ 20% professional discount

The very highest quality reproductions of classic designs from the Renaissance to contemporary in bronze and wrought iron. Ceiling lamps, suspension lamps, chandeliers, indoor lanterns, sconces, table and desk lamps, standing lamps, outdoor lighting. Collection of 4,000 models to choose from as well as designs to order. Some beautiful small furniture. Clients include: Fine Arts Museum, San Francisco, Plaza Athenee and Essex House Hotels in New York, the Riggs National Bank and State Department in Washington, D.C., the Beverly Wilshire Hotel in Beverly Hills. Member of the Comite Colbert.

DUTRUC-ROSSET

12 rue Béranger, 75003 Paris ■ Telfax: 42 72 13 31 ■ Mon-Fri 9:00-12:30/13:30-18:00 ■ François Xavier Dutruc-Rosset speaks English ■ Prices high

Specialties: Articulated and extensible lighting, Adjustable office and standing lamps. Traditional and halogen lighting. Chandeliers. Styles: Louis XVI, Regency, Contemporary, Rustic, English. Lampshades: paper, fabric, pleated, silk. Restoration and custom work.

PETITOT

10 rue du Vert-Bois, 75003 Paris ■ Tel: 42 78 09 08 - Fax: 42 72 67 23 ■ Mon-Fri 8:30-12:00/13:00-18:00/Fri closing 16:00 ■ Gérard Petitot speaks English ■ Prices very high

Bronze lighting in classic styles: French renaissance, Louis XIV, Louis XV, Louis XVI, Empire, Rustic, 50s and contemporary. Ceiling and suspension lamps, chandeliers, lanterns, sconces, table and floor lamps, halogen, outdoor.
Restoration, repair and custom work.

---------- IV ----------

ARLUMIERE

8 av. Victoria, 75004 Paris ■ Tel: 42 71 23 42 - Fax: 42 71 87 50 ■ Tues-Sat 10:00-19:00 ■ Serge Franck speaks English ■ Prices medium to high ■ 10 to 20% professional discount

Representatives of 80 international suppliers of lighting. Specialty: all types of halogen lamps, standing, desk and wall lamps. Large choice of Murano glass.

DRIMMER

30 bd Saint-Germain, 75005 Paris ■ Tel: 46 33 60 22 - Fax: 40 51 78 45 ■ Mon-Fri 9:00-13:00/14:00-18:00 ■ Harry Follman speaks English ■ Prices medium ■ Professional discount

All types of lamps in retro-romantic, traditional and contemporary designs. Two new collections each year.
All types of lampshades and lampshade frames.

LUMIERE DE L'ŒIL

4 rue Flatters, 75005 Paris ■ Tel: 47 07 63 47 ■ Tues-Fri 14:00-19:00/Sat 11:00-17:00 ■ English spoken ■ Prices low

Restoration of antique lighting 1850-1925, oil lamps, gas lamps, into working condition. Electrification and wiring to halogen. Beaded fringes made to measure.
Specialist in lighting work for historic monuments, museums, theatre and cinema. Hundreds of lamps for sale.

VII

MONTAGNIER

24 rue de Grenelle, 75007 Paris ■ Tel: 45 48 16 41 - Fax: 42 84 01 10 ■ Mon-Fri 9:00-12:30/14:30-18:30 ■ English spoken ■ Prices high ■ Professional discount

High quality ceiling and suspension lamps, crystal chandeliers, interior lanterns, sconces, exterior lighting.
Styles: Louis XIV, Louis XV, Louis XVI, Empire, Art Deco.
Restoration and repair. Custom work.

VOLT ET WATT ASSOCIES

29 bd Raspail, 75007 Paris ■ Tel: 45 48 29 62 - Fax: 45 48 54 17 ■ Mon-Sat 10:00-19:00 ■ Bruno-Jean Herbin, Erick Boronat speak English ■ Prices medium ■ Professional discount

Contemporary lighting by young French creators. Classics of the xx century.

VIII

BAGUES

37 av. Pierre 1er de Serbie, 75008 Paris ■ Tel: 47 20 61 17 - Fax: 40 70 06 76 ■ Mon-Sat 10:00-19:00 ■ English spoken ■ Prices high ■ Professional discount

For the last century, one of the best known creators of superb quality lighting in all styles as well as occasional furniture. Objects.

DOME

182 bd Haussmann, 75008 Paris ■ Tel: 45 62 74 47 - Fax: 45 62 83 72 ■ Tues-Sat 10:30-19:00 ■ Chantal Clair speaks English ■ Prices high ■ 15% professional discount

Contemporary and custom lighting.

VERONESE

184 bd Haussmann, 75008 Paris ∎ Tel: 45 62 67 67 - Fax: 42 25 79 66 ∎
Mon-Fri 9:00-12:30/14:00-18:30/Sat 10:00-12:30/14:00-18:30 ∎ Danielle
Chauvelin speaks English ∎ Prices high ∎ 10% professional discount

Special creations working with architects and decorators of high quality crystal chandeliers.

2D/VERRE LUMIERE

53 rue du Rocher, 75008 Paris ∎ Tel: 43 87 44 21 - Fax: 44 70 03 83 ∎ Mon-Fri 14:00-19:00 ∎ English spoken ∎ Prices medium to high ∎ Professional discount

High quality contemporary and original adaptation of glass for lighting. Wall, table and desk lamps, standing lamps and halogen standing lamps. Some lamps in blown glass. Will work off plan to make original creations. Work experience includes custom designed lamps for the Elysee Palace.

———————————— X ————————————

THIOLON ECHALIER

8 rue Legouve, 75010 Paris ∎ Tel: 42 38 0559 - Fax: 42 38 22 33 ∎ Mon-Fri 8:00-12:00/13:15-17:00 ∎ English spoken ∎ Prices medium ∎ Professional discount

Specialist in picture lighting, antique and modern styles. Lighting for tapestries, display cases and shelf units.

———————————— XI ————————————

ART ET STYLE

172 rue de Charonne, 75011 Paris ∎ Tel: 40 09 09 00 - Fax: 40 09 77 55 ∎
Mon-Fri 9:00-12:00/14:00-18:00 ∎ Phillippe Thibaut speaks English ∎ Prices high

Bronze lighting in all styles, sconces, table lamps, ceiling lamps, lanterns, crystal chandeliers. Occasional tables, consoles. Restoration and repair.

ARTISAN BRONZIER

17 rue Trousseau, 75011 Paris ∎ Tel: 47 00 92 45 - Fax: 47 00 95 16 ∎ Mon-Sat 9:00-19:00 ∎ English Spoken ∎ Prices high

Lighting and furniture in bronze.

BRINGAS ET FILS

8 rue Froment, 75011 Paris ∎ Tel: 47 00 74 74 ∎ Mon-Fri 9:00-12:30/14:00-18:30 ∎ Didier-Jacques Bringas speaks English ∎ Prices medium to high ∎ Professional discount

Custom made crystal chandeliers, bronze wall sconces, lamps, objects and occasional furniture. Restoration.

BRONZES ET LUMIERE
CATHERINE ANDRE-TOUPET

5 rue Saint-Bernard, 75011 Paris ∎ Tel: 43 70 72 78 ∎ Mon-Fri 9:00-17:00 ∎ Prices medium ∎ 10% professional discount

Makes and restores bronze art objects, lighting. Copies of antique styles. Restoration of patinas.

MARLENE EDITH DUPONT

8 passage de la Bonne-Graine, 75011 Paris ■ Tel: 47 00 60 52 - Fax: 48 05 37 70 ■ Mon-Fri 8:00-12:00/13:00-17:00/Fri closing 16:00 ■ George Michelson-Dupont speaks English ■ Prices medium to high ■ Professional discount

They make very high quality bronze lighting and objects.
Styles of XVII, XVIII and XIX century. Restoration of lighting, clocks and bronzes. Catalogue available in 3 languages.

LES LUMINAIRES LUCIEN GAU

2 rue de la Roquette, 75011 Paris ■ Tel: 48 05 22 11 - Fax: 48 05 09 33 ■ Pascal Gau speaks English ■ Prices medium ■ Professional discount

Major collection of period style halogen lighting fixtures.
Classic styles of all types of lighting: Louis XIII to Louis XVI, Empire, rustic, Art Nouveau, Art Deco, the 1950s, contemporary and Dutch. Contemporary lighting. Low voltage spotlight systems and lighting for pictures.

JACQUES CHARPENTIER

41 rue de Lappe, 75011 Paris ■ Tel: 43 55 62 33 - Fax: 48 07 22 94 ■ Mon-Fri 9:30-18:00 ■ Thierry Charpentier speaks English, Hervé Charpentier speaks German ■ Prices medium ■ Professional discount

First Empire, modern, contemporary and English wall lamps, table, desk lamps and standing lamps. Custom work.

FOURCOUX-PRINCE

24 passage Gustave-Lepeu, 75011 Paris ■ Tel: 43 71 09 78 - Fax: 43 71 88 16 ■ Mon-Fri 9:00-12:00/13:45-18:00 ■ Christine Prince speaks English ■ Prices medium to high

Copies of chandeliers, wall, table and desk lamps of the styles of Louis XIV, Louis XV, Louis XVI, First Empire and contemporary. High quality.

K. S. LUMINAIRE DECORATIF

92 av. Phillippe-Auguste, 75011 Paris ■ Tel: 43 71 22 15 - Fax: 43 71 88 13 ■ Tues-Sat 10:00-12:00/14:00-19:00 ■ Mme Fuli Kass speaks English ■ Prices medium ■ 15% professional discount

Specializes in importation of lighting in Murano glass.
Custom lampshades.

LUSTRA DECORS

22 rue de la Roquette, 75011 Paris ■ Tel: 43 55 84 16 ■ Mon-Fri 8:30-12:00/13:30-18:00 ■ Mr. Marchat speaks English ■ Prices medium ■ Professional discount

Major contract contemporary lighting specialists. Bracket lamps, free standing, desk and floor lamps. Halogen floor lamps. Work from drawings and blue prints. Work experience includes the White House in Washington, D.C., the Beverly Wilshire Hotel and the U.S. Ambassadors' residences in London, Paris and Brussels.

RAYNAUD

1 passage Etienne-Delaunay/172 rue de-Charonne, 75011 Paris ■ Tel: 43 79 59 37 - Fax: 43 79 75 02 ■ Mon-Fri 9:00-12:00/13:00-17:30 ■ Gisèle Renouard speaks English ■ Prices medium ■ Professional discount

Over 600 models of traditional styles, from Louis XIV to contemporary, rustic and English. Ceiling and suspension lamps, chandeliers, indoor lanterns, wall lamps, table and desk lamps, standing lamps, halogen standing lamps, luminous sculptures. Restoration, repair and work off plans.

TISSERANT LUMINAIRE D'ART

9 rue Saint-Sébastien, 75011 Paris ■ Tel: 47 00 37 37 - Fax: 48 06 59 51 ■ Mon-Fri 8:00-12:00/13:00-17:30 ■ M. Bernard and Antoine Tisserant speak English ■ Prices very high ■ Professional discount

High quality lighting in all styles from French Renaissance through Art Nouveau and Art Deco to the 1950s and contemporary. Ceiling and suspension lamps, indoor lanterns, chandeliers, wall, table, desk and standing lamps. Halogen standing lamps. Decorative bronze work. Restoration, repairs. Research department and picture library available to architects and decorators.

—————————————— XII ——————————————

ATELIER A. DEBLANGEY

5 rue de Capri, 75012 Paris ■ Tel: (province) 51 54 27 22 ■ Thurs and Sat 14:00-19:00 by appointment ■ English spoken ■ Prices medium ■ Professional discount

Top quality copies of Dutch style chandeliers, from one storey to the largest three storey, for hotels, castles, historic monuments, offices and individuals. Top of the range solid bronze table lamps in the styles of Louis XIII and Louis XIV.

GOURDON

28 rue Nicolaï, 75012 Paris ■ Tel: 43 07 16 18 - Fax: 43 40 24 41 ■ Mon-Fri 10:00-12:00/14:00-19:00 ■ Phillippe Gourdon speaks English and Italian

Custom contemporary designs for lighting manufacturers and for architectural projects.

KOBIS ET LORENCE

67 rue de Reuilly, 75012 Paris ■ Tel: 43 41 40 70 - Fax: 43 44 97 49 ■ Mon-Thurs 7:30-12:00/13:00-17:30/Fri closing 13:00 ■ English spoken ■ Prices medium

Working in close collaboration with architects and designers, this company specializes in custom lighting for hotels, cafes and restaurants. Styles include 1900, 1930, and contemporary. Recent work experience includes Hilton Hotel in Paris, the Mamounia Hotel in Marrakech.

—————————————— XIV ——————————————

ATELIER JEAN PERZEL

3 and 15 rue de la Cité-Universitaire, 75014 Paris ■ Tel: 45 88 77 24 - Fax: 45 65 32 82 ■ Mon-Sat 9:00-12:00/14:00-18:00 ■ Prices medium to high ■ Professional discount

The 1930s specialist. Excellent original, signed and copyrighted designs since 1931. Ceiling lamps, suspension, wall, table and desk lamps. Halogen standing lamps, outdoor lighting. Restoration and repairs.

MAX LE VERRIER

30 rue Deparcieux, 75014 Paris ■ Tel: 43 22 62 95 ■ Mon-Fri 9:00-12:00/14:00-17:30 ■ Prices medium to high

The company was founded in 1919 by Max Le Verrier, a bronze sculptor, designer and worker in decorative casting. In addition to the bronze sculptures – animals, figures and decorative objects for desks – their specialty is also small objects and luminous sculptures in the 1930s style in decorative cast iron and signed by well known artists. Specialty: art deco lamps.

———————————————— **XV** ————————————————

MAUFACTOR

76 rue de l'Amiral-Roussin, 75015 Paris ■ Tel: 42 50 99 72 - Fax: 42 50 96 80 ■ Mon-Fri 9:00-18:00 ■ English spoken ■ Prices medium to high

High quality contemporary lamps: table, desk, standing.
Wall lamps, lighting for pictures, Large choice of halogen floor lamps. Custom designs for prototypes. Production in large quantity possible for offices, hotels.

———————————————— **XVI** ————————————————

GALERIE SAN MARCO

25 bis rue Franklin, 75116 Paris ■ Tel: 45 53 56 72 - Fax: 45 53 85 10 ■ Mon-Sat 10:00-19:00 ■ Prices medium ■ 20% professional discount

"Venetien glass". Chandeliers, sconces, standing lamps, candelabra, mirrors, consoles, sculptures, glasses, flacons, decorative objects, vases, lamps. All exclusively in Murano glass.

MARTINE KLOTZ
DECORS LUMINEUX

9 rue de Belloy, 75116 Paris ■ Tel: 47 27 92 64 - Fax: 47 27 27 90 ■ Mon-Fri 8:30-12:30/13:30-17:30 ■ Martine Klotz speaks English ■ Prices very high ■ 10% professional discount

Specialist in restoration and improvement of antique lighting and crystal chandeliers by disguising wiring with trompe-l'œil. Lighting for pictures. Specialist in indirect lighting.

———————————————— **XVII** ————————————————

JEAN DURST

49 rue Pierre-Demours, 75017 Paris ■ Tel: 47 63 54 58 - Fax: 47 63 39 50 ■ Tues-Sat 10:00-13:00/14:30-19:00 ■ Jean Durst speaks English ■ Prices medium to high ■ 10% professional discount

Makes lighting in bronze and crystal in copies of old styles. Mounting of lamps, custom lampshades and restoration of all types of antique lighting.

TRAK

1 rue Théodule-Ribot, 75017 Paris ■ Tel: 47 66 32 92 - Fax: 47 66 32 04 ■ Mon-Fri 9:00-12:00/13:00-18:00 ■ Anne-Chantal Reau speaks English ■ Prices high

Custom creation of halogen and contemporary lighting.
Illuminated mirrors.

DARIC

9 bd Ney, 75018 Paris ■ Tel: 40 34 01 39 - Fax: 40 34 94 04 ■ Mon-Fri 8:30-12:00/13:00-17:30 ■ Phillippe Daric and Eric d'Humieres speak English ■ Prices medium ■ 30% professional discount

Incandescent lamps for bathrooms: ceiling, walls and shelves. Wide variety of contemporary lighting. Spots for shops and homes. Flexible strip lighting for shelves.

POTENTIEL

10 bis rue Muller, 75018 Paris ■ Tel: 42 23 14 04 - Fax: 42 54 02 63 ■ Mon-Fri 9:00-20:00 ■ Gilles Beaumont speaks English ■ Prices high ■ 30% professional discount

Contemporary lighting: suspension and wall lamps, halogen standing lamps, projectors. Special wall lamps for bathrooms. Original custom designs.

AUTOGRAPHE

82 rue d'Aubervilliers, 75019 Paris ■ Tel: 40 35 20 05 - Fax: 40 35 50 59 ■ Mon-Fri 8:30-12:30/13:30-17:30/Fri closing 16:00 ■ Patricia Cotie speaks English ■ Prices medium ■ 20 to 30% professional discount

Contemporary architectural lighting. Wall, ceiling and suspension lamps, table and desk lamps. Picture lighting and standing lamps. Good designs. Custom work.

ATEA

14 rue Soleillet, 75020 Paris ■ Tel: 44 62 03 05 - Fax: 44 62 03 06 ■ Mon-Fri 9:00-12:00/13:00-17:00 ■ Pierre Scholtes speaks English ■ Prices high ■ Professional discount

Decorative and architectural contemporary lighting in unusual designs. Table, desk, wall and suspension lamps.
Light fittings for pictures and halogen standing lamps.

♔ CHARLES

Showroom: 18-20 rue Soleillet, 75020 Paris ■ Tel: 43 49 51 50 - Fax: 43 49 61 08 ■ Gallery: 34 rue Bonaparte, 75006 Paris ■ Tel: 43 25 60 04 ■ Chrystiane Charles speaks English ■ Prices high ■ Professional discount

Remarkable selection of a broad range of unusual and original designs in styles ranging from Louis XIV to today.
Every work hand-crafted by designers and artisans who have been at their trade for four generations. Everything from chandeliers to lanterns, classic sconces, standing and halogen floor lamps to sculptured decorative table lamps.
Custom designs for fashion pace-setters. Restoration and repair. Don't miss.

♛ MEILLEUR

32 rue des Amandiers, 75020 Paris ■ Tel: 43 66 45 13 - Fax: 43 66 45 43 ■
Mon-Fri 9:00-18:00 ■ Catherine Meilleur speaks English ■ Prices high ■ Professional discount

One of the very best custom creators of classic and contemporary style lighting. Chandeliers, lamps, lanterns, beautifully chiselled bronze sconces, contemporary, standing, articulated floor lamps in their own copyrighted designs.

Good selection of tables in bronze. Custom designs and creation of unique models.

OUTSIDE PARIS

AMBIANCE LUMIERE

65 quai Auguste-Blanqui, 94141 Alfortville ■ Tel: 43 68 45 22 - Fax: 43 75 75 01 ■ Mon-Fri 10:00-12:30/13:30-18:00 ■ English spoken ■ Prices medium to high ■ Professional discount

Festive lighting products. Fairy lights for decorating shop windows. Illumination of monuments. Decorative lighting for casinos and discotheques. Will work closely with architects and designers on major projects.

Parts and accessories for lighting

GIRARD SUDRON

47 rue des Tournelles, 75003 Paris ■ Tel: 44 59 22 20 - Fax: 42 74 7072 ■
Mon-Fri 8:30-17:30/Fri closing 17:00 ■ Elizabeth Carre speaks English ■
Prices medium ■ Professional discount

5,000 different components for lighting fixtures, as well as light bulbs, lighting glassware, candle bulbs, halogen lamps. 100 years of expertise.

JANVIER

17 rue Pastourelle, 75003 Paris ■ Tel: 42 72 14 11 - Fax: 42 72 54 19 ■ Mon-Fri 8:00-12:30/13:30-17:30 ■ Jean-Marc Finck speaks English ■ Prices medium ■ Professional discount

Accessories for lighting in decorative bronze and wrought iron. Over 100,000 stampings for lighting and furniture.

Figures, animals, bookends, etc. Furniture hardware in unfinished bronze. Custom work.

PARIS CHAINES

25 rue Saint-Sébastien, 75011 Paris ■ Tel: 47 00 14 74 - Fax: 47 00 08 22
■ Mon-Fri 8:30-12:00/13:30-17:30 ■ Prices medium ■ Professional discount

Lighting fixture fittings. All components including chains, thoughs, bowls, etc. Founded in 1850, the company can fill large orders quickly with quality products.

SWAROVSKI

15 bd Poissonnière, 75002 Paris ■ Tel: 44 76 15 15 - Fax: 44 76 15 00 ■ Mon-Fri 9:00-12:00/13:30-17:00/Fri closing 16:00 ■ English spoken ■ Prices medium to high

The world's leader in the production of cut crystal elements for chandeliers and lighting. Classic and contemporary. For lighting manufacturers.

G S INDUSTRIES

47 bd du Colonel-Fabien, 94200 Ivry-sur-Seine ■ Tel: 47 33 31 20 - Fax: 47 93 00 84 ■ Mon-Fri 8:30-17:30 ■ Alain Brunon speaks English ■ Prices high to very high ■ 5 to 20% professional discount

Decorative light bulbs in original shapes and finishes. High quality.

Antique lighting
Luminaires anciens

DES LAMPES

9 rue de Verneuil, 75007 Paris ■ Tel: 40 20 02 58 - Fax: 40 20 08 36 ■ Mon 14:00-19:00/Tues-Sat 11:00-19:00 ■ Antoine Pialoux and Jean Meoule speak English ■ Prices medium ■ Professional discount

Beautiful antique lamps and lampshades.

A. COLIN MAILLARD

11 rue de Miromesnil, 75008 Paris ■ Tel: 42 65 43 62 ■ Mon 14:00-18:30/Tues-Fri 10:30-12:30/14:00-18:30/Sat 14:00-18:30 ■ Pierre-Jacques Chauveau speaks English ■ Prices high ■ 15 to 20% professional discount

Antique lamps and lampshades made to order.

MEILLEUR

32, rue des Amandiers
75020 Paris

Tel 43 66 45 13
Fax 43 66 45 43

LAMPSHADES

Abat-jour

III

GEORGES FICHET

26 rue Saint-Gilles, 75003 Paris ■ Tel: 42 72 32 65 ■ Tues-Sat 9:30-12:30/14:00-18:30 ■ Some English spoken ■ Prices medium ■ Professional discount

Made to measure lampshades. Restoration of all types of lighting. They sell antique lamps which they have restored.

DANIEL SCHMIDT

37 bd Beaumarchais, 75003 Paris ■ Tel: 42 72 67 45 - Fax: 42 72 16 33 ■ Tues-Fri 9:00-13:00/14:30-18:30/Sat 9:00-13:00 ■ Daniel Schmidt speaks English ■ Prices medium ■ 20% professional discount

All styles of lampshades to measure. Very careful finish and quick delivery. Creation of original models and good selection of bases.

IV

ABAT-JOUR BOUCHADEAU

13 rue de l'Arsenal, 75004 Paris ■ Tel: 42 72 86 95 - Fax: 42 72 14 19 ■ Mon-Fri 9:00-12:00/14:00-18:00/Fri closing 17:00 ■ Some English spoken ■ Prices medium to high

Custom lampshades in all forms, all fabrics and papers.

PAUL-EMILE

10 rue de Jarente, 75004 Paris ■ Tel: 48 87 21 21 ■ Mon-Fri 10:00-12:30/14:00-18:00 ■ English spoken ■ Prices medium ■ 10% professional discount

Lampshades made to measure. Simple and complex mounts.
Repair of antique lamps.

VI

ISABELLE ROUTIER

9 rue de Savoie, 75006 Paris ■ Tel: 46 33 36 58 - Fax: 44 07 18 66 ■ Mon-Fri by appointment ■ Isabelle Routier speaks English ■ Prices medium to high ■ Professional discount

All styles of lampshades made by hand. Mounting of lamps. Custom creations of lamps and lampshades.

VII

ANTICA

38 rue de Verneuil, 75007 Paris ■ Tel: 42 61 28 86 ■ Tues-Sat 10:00-18:30 ■ Arlette Clerin speaks English ■ Prices high ■ 10% professional discount

Custom lampshades in all shapes and in all materials, including hand sewn silk in classic old styles.

MJMS

3 rue Saint-Dominique, 75007 Paris ■ Tel: 45 44 03 37 - Fax: 45 48 29 91
■ Mon-Fri afternoons by appointment ■ Marie-Joseph Maze-Sencier speaks
English ■ Prices medium ■ Professional discount

All kinds of hand made lampshades, classic and contemporary. Will also
make from your fabric.

------------------------------ X ------------------------------

ANNICK CARUSO

10 rue de Lancry, 75010 Paris ■ Tel: 42 41 10 93 ■ Mon-Thurs 9:00-17:30/Fri
8:30-16:00 ■ Prices low ■ Professional discount

Lampshades to measure. Classic and contemporary styles, hand painted.
Objects mounted as lamps. Oriental vases available as bases.

------------------------------ XI ------------------------------

ABAT-JOUR BLANCO

9 rue Saint-Sébastien, 75011 Paris ■ Tel: 43 55 73 57 ■ Tues-Sat afternoons
■ Prices medium

Lampshades made to measure. Restoration.

PASSEMENTERIE DU MARAIS

6 bd des Filles-du-Calvaire, 75011 Paris ■ Tel: 47 00 56 82 ■ Tues-Sat 9:30-
12:45/14:00-18:15 ■ English spoken ■ Prices low to high ■ 5 to 10% professional discount

Exclusively supplies for making lampshades: from frames ("carcasses"), to
all types of fabrics, braids, fringes, everything. They will mount and electrify your bases using silk covered wiring. They will also advise on "how to".

------------------------------ XII ------------------------------

PLAS DUCLEROIR ABAT-JOUR

8 rue Dagorno, 75012 Paris ■ Tel: 43 43 42 98 - Fax: 43 45 50 65 ■ Mon-
Fri 9:30-12:30/13:30-18:30/Saturdays Oct-April ■ Gilles Plas speaks English ■ Prices medium ■ Professional discount

Fabrication of all types of lampshades: classic to contemporary, stretched
fabric, pagoda shapes, skirts. Fully lined. Hand and machine made. Residential and contract work in quantity for hotels, offices, etc.
Lamps in unbreakable resin for the hotel market.

------------------------------ XIV ------------------------------

RUYS

63 rue de l'Ouest, 75014 Paris ■ Tel: 43 22 93 81 ■ Tues-Sat 10:30-
12:30/15:00-19:00 ■ Prices high ■ Professional discount

Lampshades made to measure.
Repair of lamps and halogens of all types.

XV

ALEXANDRE

74 rue Fondary, 75015 Paris ■ Tel: 45 75 21 26 ■ Tues-Sat 10:00-19:00 ■ Prices medium to high ■ Professional discount

Alexandre has created over 100 original and unique custom creations of lampshades in the last 10 years. They will work from your ideas or their own. Contemporary and especially classic styles.

ABAT-JOUR JEANINE BAUDIN

27 rue Franklin, 75016 Paris ■ Telfax: 47 27 17 21 ■ Tues-Sat 10:00-19:00 ■ Madame Garnier speaks English ■ Prices medium to high ■ Professional discount

Madame Garnier has models to help you in your choice for made to measure lampshades. Very wide selection of shapes and fabrics: silk, chintz, suede, taffeta, marbleized and reptile fabrics and the best of braids. Will mount and electrify your bases. Some lamps for sale.

BEL OMBRE

32 rue Gustave-Courbet, 75116 Paris ■ Tel: 47 27 96 57 ■ Mon: 14:30-18:30/Tues-Sat 10:00-12:00/14:00-19:00 ■ Catherine Roumilhac speaks English ■ Prices medium ■ Professional discount

Wonderful choice of beautiful lampshades available in all styles. They also make to order and will mount and electrify your bases.

SEMAINE

20 rue Nicolo, 75016 Paris ■ Telfax: 45 20 06 69 ■ Tues-Sat 10:30-19:00 ■ English spoken ■ Prices low to medium ■ Professional discount

Marie-France Petit specializes in pleated lampshades and has a large selection of colours available in chintz. She also carries some toiles in stripes and checks for a more country look.

XVII

A BATIGNOLLES-JOUR

66 place Docteur Félix-Lobligeois, 75017 Paris ■ Tel: 40 25 01 35 - Fax: 40 25 01 33 ■ Mon 14:00-18:30/Tues-Fri 10:00-18:30/Sat 10:00-13:00 ■ Prices medium to high ■ 10% professional discount

Lampshades made to measure. Lighting and bronze sculptures exclusively by Felix Agostini. Mounting of objects as lamps. Leather, velvet and silk covering of small furniture, boxes and objects.

CARVAY

3 av. de Villiers, 75017 Paris ■ Tel: 47 63 56 32 ■ Mon-Sat 9:30-12:30/14:00-18:45 ■ Prices medium ■ 10 to 50% professional discount

Residential and contract lampshades in paper, stretched or pleated fabric, pagoda shapes, skirts. Mounting of lamps.

IMPROMPTU

8 rue Gustave-Flaubert, 75017 Paris ■ Tel: 42 27 62 99 ■ Tues-Sat 10:00-12:30/14:00-19:00 ■ Dominique Henriot speaks English ■ Prices high ■ 15% professional discount

Custom lampshades of all types: paper, fabric, hand pleating. Restoration and electrical mounting of old lamps.

———————————— **XVIII** ————————————

MARTINE ABAT-JOUR

4 rue Androuet, 75018 Paris ■ Tel: 42 55 54 83 ■ Mon-Sat 9:30-12:30/14:00-19:00/Wed 9:30-12:30 ■ Prices modest to high ■ 30% professional discount

Quality made to measure lampshades in a wide choice of beautiful fabrics. Mounting of lamps. Lamps, vases and candles.

THE PALANCAR COMPANY LTD

PALANCAR
the Maxi-media Company presents
its multi-media publications for 1995-1996

1995: The TOUT PARIS SOURCE GUIDE TO
THE ART OF FRENCH DECORATION
Watch for the exciting new CDROM

1996: The television series, "THE COMPAGNONS"
"The Great Artisans of Europe"

1996: The TOUT PARIS GUIDE TO FRENCH
PRET-A-PORTER
Also on CDROM

1996: The TOUT PARIS GUIDES FOR THE
BUSINESSMAN
With CDROM

1996: SHODATA

The exciting new database for the television
professional. Every film or tape ever produced
anywhere in the world. Full details on contents,
casts, producers, writers, directors. sales, prices, etc.

Database, catalogues and CDROM

THE PALANCAR COMPANY LTD.
The Courtyard, 12 Hill Street,
St. Helier, Jersey, C.I.

LINEN - HOUSEHOLD AND TABLE
Linge de maison et de table

—————————————— IV ——————————————

MERIDIEM

9 quai de Bourbon, 75004 Paris■Tel: 46 33 21 27 - Fax: 44 07 25 92■Tues-Fri 13:00-19:00/Sat 10:30-19:00 ■ Ann Halvorsen speaks English ■ Prices medium■20% professional discount

Custom made household linens for table, bath and bedroom. Linen and blends of cotton and linen in natural colours.

POURPRE

28 quai d'Orléans, Ile Saint-Louis, 75004 Paris ■ Tel: 43 54 27 17 - Fax: 43 54 27 79■Mon-Fri 9:00-12:00/14:00-18:00■Dominique Charles speaks English ■ Prices high ■ 10 to 30% professional discount

Creation of fine table and bed linens: linen, cotton, organdi and embroidered organza. Throws for sofas, cushions, slip covers, mats. Custom and personalized work possible. Objects for the table and decoration: glassware, porcelain, cutlery in resin and metal, napkin rings, knife-rests, candle holders, vases, lamps.

—————————————— VI ——————————————

MANUEL CANOVAS

5 rue de Furstemberg, 75006 Paris ■ Tel: 43 26 89 31 - Fax: 40 46 07 70■ Mon 11:00-18:30/Tues-Sat 10:00-18:30 ■ English spoken ■ Prices high

Household linens. Sheets and duvet/comforter covers.Tablecloths, napkins, table sets, household perfumes, dishes.

—————————————— VII ——————————————

DESCAMPS

115 rue Saint-Dominique, 75007 Paris■Tel: 45 51 58 64 - Fax: 45 50 26 71 ■44 rue de Passy, 75016 Paris ■ Tel: 42 88 10 01 - Fax: 45 20 50 29■Mon-Sat 10:00-19:00■English spoken■Prices medium ■ 10% professional discount

Wide range of good quality household linen. Descamps has outlets in almost every Arrondissement in Paris.

VIS A VIS BOUTIQUE

16 rue du Pré-aux-Clercs, 75007 Paris ■ Tel: 42 84 38 31 - Fax: 42 22 52 59 ■ Mon-Fri 10:30-19:00 ■ Showroom same address by appointment (Stair B/4th floor)■ Aurélie Menesguen speaks English■Prices high ■ 10 to 20% professional discount

Household and table linen. Custom designs in 30 colors of linen. No minimum quantity. Blinds and shades in linen and muslin.

COLIN LINGE - BOUTIQUE DU LIN

10 rue des Saussaies, 75008 Paris ■ Tel: 42 65 45 60 ■ Mon-Fri 10:00-18:30/Sat Nov-March ■ 10 to 15% professional discount

All household linens. Blankets in cashmere, alpaca, mohair, camel hair. Pure linen toiles sold by the metre.
Embroidery by hand and by machine.

AGNES COMAR

7 avenue George-V, 75008 Paris ■ Tel: 49 52 01 89 - Fax: 49 52 01 67 ■ Mon-Sat 10:30-13:00/14:00-19:00 ■ English spoken ■ Prices medium to high

Contemporary designs of high quality household and table linen.

👑 FRETTE

48 rue du Faubourg-Saint-Honoré, 75008 ■ Tel 42 66 47 70 - Fax: 42 66 98 98 ■ Mon-Sat 10:00-18:00 ■ English spoken ■ Prices medium to high ■ 10% professional discount

Excellent quality and wide range of table and household linens.

👑 PORTHAULT

18 av. Montaigne, 75008 Paris ■ Tel: 47 20 75 25 - Fax: 40 70 09 26 ■ English spoken ■ Prices medium to very high ■ 10% professional discount

Beautiful linens for the table and the household. Fine linen for children and a good choice of gift items.

LA MAISON REVE

29 rue Marbeuf, 75008 Paris ■ Tel: 43 59 02 46 - Fax: 45 61 22 29 ■ Mon-Sat 10:00-19:00 ■ Anne and Caroline de Tilly speak English ■ Prices high

Attractive collection of table and household linens.
Household gifts.

AFT

10 rue du Colonel-Rozanoff, 75012 ■ Tel: 44 67 09 67 - Fax: 44 67 09 60 ■ Mon-Sat 10:00-19:00 ■ Christelle Doniguian speaks English ■ Prices medium ■ Professional discount

All household linens, table, bed, bath. Linen and furniture for babies. Supplier of linens for hotels and restaurants.

BROD WAY FRANCE

71 rue Fondary, 75015 Paris ■ Tel: 45 77 18 53 - Fax: 45 77 26 83 ■ Mon-Fri 10:00-19:00 ■ Joséphine Bouqueneur speaks English ■ Prices medium

Embroidery by machine, also hand guided, of household linens and furnishing fabrics for sofas and draperies.
Will work on small quantity orders.

CHATELAINE

170 av. Victor-Hugo, 75116 Paris ■ Tel: 47 27 44 07 - Fax: 47 27 19 85 ■
Tues-Fri 9:30-18:30/Sat 9:30-12:30/14:30-18:30 ■ Prices high ■ Professional discount

All household linens. Layettes and children's clothes 0 to 12 years. Custom household linens, made to measure at no extra charge. Alterations free of charge.

♕ PENELOPE

"Fond de la Cour" ■ 19 av. Victor-Hugo, 75116 Paris (Courtyard) ■ Tel: 45 00 90 90 - Fax: 40 64 16 82 ■ Mon-Fri 9:30-12:30/14:30-18:30

A gathering of remarkable women who hand craft some of the most beautifully embroidered linen in the world.
Large choice of household and table linen, layettes, embroidered towels, tablecloths, sheets embroidered to match their mohair blankets, gadgets and table sets.
Specialty: Custom made tablecloths and napkins in exclusive designs. Superb quality. Designs to match your antique china, crystal or any idea you may have. Penelope is a non-profit organization which organizes this group of skilled women.

♕ NOEL

1 av. Pierre-1er-de-Serbie, 75116 Paris ■ Tel: 40 70 14 63 - Fax: 40 70 05 25 ■ Mon-Sat 10:00-19:00 ■ English spoken ■ Prices high ■ 30 to 40% professional discount on large orders

Hand and machine embroidered table and household linen of the highest quality. Custom orders to the client's design or the designs of Noël. 1,300 designs in their archives to choose from.

CLAIRE DE DONZY

33 rue de Chazelles, 75017 Paris ■ Tel: 47 66 84 30 - Fax: (16)77 27 06 54 ■ Mon-Fri 8:00-12:00/13:30-19:00 ■ Frederic Palais speaks English

Table linen. Specialists of stain-resistant and non-iron tablecloths in 100% polyester. Solids and prints. Napkins in 100% cotton.

—————————————————————— OUTSIDE PARIS ——————————————————————

SIRETEX

14 rue Kléber, 93100 Montreuil ■ Tel: 49 88 92 70 - Fax: 49 88 92 02 ■ Mon-Fri 8:30-18:00 ■ Gérard Szenik speaks English

Manufacturers of household linen. Towelling 400 gms/m² and 525 gms/m². Towels in all sizes, robes/dressing gowns. Bed linen in all dimensions. Tablecloths in American percale.

Antique Linen

FUCHSIA

Village Saint-Paul, 2 rue de l'Ave-Maria, 75004 Paris ■ Tel: 48 04 75 61 ■
Every day 12:00-19:00 ■ Prices very high ■ 15% discount

Antique table and household linen as well as lace, collectibles and 1900s
fashion.

SOURIS VERTE

Village Saint-Paul, 23 rue Saint-Paul, 75004 Paris (Courtyard) ■ Tel:
42 74 79 76 ■ Thurs-Mon 11:00-19:00 ■ Prices medium ■ 20% professional
discount

Lace, buttons and braids. Old tablecloths and napkins.
Decorative household objects.

———————————— XVI ————————————

GALERIE ACANTHE

18 rue Cortambert, 75116 Paris ■ Tel: 45 03 15 55 ■ Tues-Sat 11:00-
13:00/14:00-19:00 ■ English spoken ■ Prices medium ■ 10 to 20% professional discount

Antique linen, furniture and collectibles.

———————————— MARCHÉ AUX PUCES ————————————

Marché Serpette

MONIQUE LARDE - Allée 1, Stand 28

Tel: 40 10 02 21

Antique household linen, lace and antique clothes.

Marché Vernaison

L'ARLEQUIN - Allée 7, Stands 128-128 bis

Tel: 40 11 16 38

Old linen, lace, decorative objects and fashion.

FRANCINE - Allée 7, Stands 121-123,140 bis

Tel: 40 10 93 36/40 12 05 58

Old table and household linen, fabrics, objects and 1900s fashion.

IRMA - Allée 9, Stand 200

Tel: 40 10 08 57

Old linen, buttons, lace and glassware.

MIRRORS
Miroirs

— VI —

THE PARIS AMERICAN ART CO.
2 rue Bonaparte, 75006 Paris ■ Tel: 43 26 09 93 - Fax: 43 54 33 80 ■ Tues-Sat 10:00-13:00/13:45-18:30 ■ Danielle Leveque speaks English ■ Prices medium to high ■ Professional discount
Mirrors in gilded antique frames. Gilded frames in classic styles. Restoration. Mirrors in modern frames. Antique frames, frames for miniatures, engravings, drawings and paintings.

MANUEL NAVARRO
15 rue Saint-Sulpice, 75006 Paris ■ Tel: 46 33 61 51 ■ Tues-Sat 14:30-19:00 ■ Prices medium ■ 15% professional discount
Antique gilded wood mirrors of the XVII to the XIX century. Gilded wood decorative ornaments.

— VIII —

MAISON EDOUARD GROSVALLET
126 bd Haussmann, 75008 Paris ■ Tel 45 22 19 68 ■ Mon-Fri 9:30-12:00/14:30-18:00 ■ English and Spanish spoken
Antique mirrors, consoles and frames of all styles.

⚜ CADRES LEBRUN
155 rue du Faubourg-Saint-Honoré, 75008 Paris ■ Tel: 45 61 14 66 - Fax: 45 61 00 65 ■ Mon-Fri 14:30-19:00 ■ English spokenPrices high ■ 10% professional discount
Antique mirrors from the XV to the XIX centuries. Antique gilded frames from the XV to the XIX centuries.

— XI —

MARTINE ZWOLINSKI
33 rue Amelot, 75011 Paris ■ Tel: 43 55 63 80 - Fax: 43 55 52 20 ■ Mon-Fri 9:00-12:00/14:00-18:00/Sat 9:30-12:30 ■ Laurent and Karine Zwolinski speak English ■ Prices low ■ Professional discount
Framed mirrors for boutiques. Framing services.

— VII —

ATELIER DU BOIS DORE
80 av. des Ternes, 75017 Paris ■ Tel: 45 74 67 58 - Fax: 44 74 72 49 ■ Mon-Sat 9:00-12:30/14:00-19:00 ■ English spoken ■ Prices medium to high ■ Professionals only
Antique mirrors and framing for mirrors. Choice of 1,500 antique frames. 300 moulding styles for reproductions of antique frames. Framing. Restoration of gilded wood (bois doré).

LA GALERIE DES GLACES

138 rue des Rosiers, 93400 Saint-Ouen ■ Tel: 40 11 17 52 - Fax: 45 22 52 99 ■ Fri 9:00-12:00/Sat 8:30-18:30/Sun-Mon 10:00-18:30 ■ Roger Cuperty speaks English ■ Prices reasonable ■ 20% professional discount

All styles of antique mirrors in gilded wood and gilded plaster. Gilded bronze decorative objects.

LES MIROIRS DE FRANCE

109 rue des Rosiers, 93400 Saint-Ouen ■ Tel: 40 10 25 29 ■ Fri 9:00-12:00/Sat-Sun 9:30-18:00 ■ Prices low ■ 40% professional discount

Mirrors in gilded wood XVIII and XIX centuries.

MARIE-EVE ROSENTHAL

Marche Serpette, Allée 4, Stand 13 ■ 110 rue des Rosiers, 93400 Saint-Ouen ■ Tel: 40 12 04 85 - Fax: 39 69 46 21 ■ Prices medium ■ Professional discount

One of the best selections of antique gilded wood mirrors in Paris. All periods, all styles, all sizes.

PACKING & SHIPPING
Emballage & Transport

ART TRANSIT
Marché aux Puces, Marché Biron, Allée 1, Stand 63■Tel: 40 12 24 97■Fri-Mon 9:00-19:00■English spoken
Packing and shipping service.

NOUVELLE ATLANTIC
62 rue Mirabeau, 94200 Ivry-sur-Seine ■ Tel: 46 72 74 36 - Fax: 46 70 71 45
■Mon-Sat 8:00-12:00/13:00-18:00■Umberto Siani and Agnès Delest speak English■Prices medium
Specialists in packing fine art and antiques. Regular weekly groupings to all international destinations.
Customs agents. Can also provide complete containers 20' × 40'. Correspondents in all the major ports of the world. Documents prepared in English.

BURLINGTON FINE ART TRANSPORT
2 bd de la Libération, 93200 Saint-Denis ■ Tel: 48 09 43 95 - Fax: 48 09 45 75
■ Mon-Fri 8:30-12:15/13:30-17:30 ■ Pierre Gosse and Michèle Gobeaut speak English■Prices medium
Expert packing and shipping by sea and air. All export and import clearances arranged.

CAMARD
Marché aux Puces ■ 140 rue des Rosiers, 93400 Saint-Ouen ■ Tel: 40 12 84 45■Fri-Mon 9:00-19:00■Prices medium
Packing and shipping service direct from the Flea Market to all parts of the world.

ANDRE CHENUE ET FILS
5 bd Ney, 75018 Paris■Tel: 40 37 46 62 - Fax: 40 37 22 28■Mon-Fri 8:30-12:15/13:30-17:15 ■ English spoken ■ Prices average
Experts in the packing and shipping of fine works of art and antiques. They work extensively with the Museums of Paris.

DESBORDES
14 rue de la Véga, 75012 Paris ■ Tel: 44 73 84 96/44 73 84 84 - Fax: 43 42 51 48 ■ Mon-Fri 8:00-12:00/14:00-18:00 ■ Annnick Farina, Christine Iglesias and Gordon Claye speak English ■ Prices medium
Packing and shipping of antiques and works of art to all destinations.

EMERY WORLD-WIDE
Tel: 48 62 36 40/48 62 85 85 - Fax: 48 62 50 75■Mon-Fri 9:00-12:00/14:00-17:30■English spoken■Prices medium
A large, efficient American company well established in Europe. Shipping to all destinations.

ALAN FRANKLIN TRANSPORT

2 rue Etienne Dolet, 93400 Saint-Ouen ■ Tel: 40 11 50 00 - Fax: 40 11 48 21
■ Mon-Thurs 8:30-17:30/Fri 7:30-17:30/Sat 8:30-17:30/Sun 10:00-17:00 ■ Stuart Mardon and Nadège Mardon speak English ■ Prices medium

Transport of antiques, paintings, sculpture and works of art by road throughout Europe. Air freight shipments worldwide and sea freight consignments via the U.K.

HEDLEY'S HUMPERS

1 impasse Simon, 93400 Saint-Ouen ■ Tel: 40 10 94 00 - Fax: 48 13 07 08
■ Mon-Fri 8:00-19:00/Sat 8:00-18:00/Sun 11:00-18:00 ■ English spoken

Service of expert packing and shipping of fine art and antiques, directly from the Flea Market and elsewhere to all parts of the world by air, sea and road. Weekly containers.

INTERNATIONAL ART TRANSPORT

54 av. Lénine, 94250 Gentilly ■ Tel: 41 17 41 17 - Fax: 49 85 91 31 ■ Mon-Fri 9:00-12:30/13:30-17:30 ■ Carol Farra and Anne-Marie Verdanet speak English. ■ Prices medium

Packing and shipping antiques and works of art. Export documents arranged.

EMBALLLAGES LENORMAND

53-55 rue de Verdun, BP 24, 93161 Noisy-le-Grand Cedex ■ Tel: 43 03 38 73 - Fax: 43 04 33 99 ■ Mon-Fri 7:30-12:00/13:00-17:00 ■ Prices medium ■ 10% professional discount

Specialists in packing of furniture and art objects.International movers and shippers.

UPS - UNITED PARCEL SERVICE

87 av. de l'Aérodrome, BP 39, 94310 Orly ■ Tel: 48 92 50 00 - Fax: 48 92 50 52
■ Mon-Fri 8:00-19:00 ■ English spoken

The best known American small package express, door-to-door, air shipping service to America and 100 other countries. Very reliable and very fast. Maximum weight 150 lbs.

TABLE ARTS
Arts de la table

French tableware falls primarily into three sectors: porcelain and earthenware, crystal and glass and silver.

France is the world's leader in tableware exports. The United States is the biggest and best customer. There is an excellent reason for this. France has always been admired for tableware of elegance, beauty and tradition. Tableware, once the exclusive province of royalty and the upper classes has, since the middle of the XVIII century, become a symbol of prosperity.

The origins of tableware can be traced back to the earliest history of man. Table utensils and food vessels are amply illustrated in what we know of ancient Egyptian and Persian civilizations and the Chinese undoubtedly pre-dated both of these.

Paris, the ever manageable city, has a concentration of tableware suppliers on the rue de Paradis in one of the older and most charming neighborhoods of Paris. You can visit the showrooms of the manufacturers and even if they only sell to professionals, a non-professional can make choices, obtain prices and be directed to the showroom where purchases can be made. Many of the merchants offer good discounts which others in higher rent areas cannot do. Make certain you ask for your detaxe. It will very likely offset the price of shipping what you buy.

Crystal and Glass
Cristal et verre

French history can trace the beginning of glass centers in France to the XII century. We know that the production and utilization of glass goes back a long time before that, but it is to the French province of Lorraine that we owe much of the credit for the beautiful glass and crystal as it exists today. They were so good at their craft, that these Lorrainers attracted the attention of the Kings of France, and it was the Cristalleries Saint-Louis who first discovered the technique of making flawless crystal.

The most renowned of the crystal manufacturers in France are: Baccarat, Daum, Lalique, Saint-Louis.

In addition to the expensive and beautiful crystal made by the producers mentioned above, you can also find good quality factory made product from Verreries Cristalleries d'Arques. Their production is enormous and they are the international leader in their field.

For hand blown glass, the principal source is the Verrerie de Biot. If you find yourself in the hills above Cannes on a pleasure trip, the glassworks in Biot are worth a visit.

CRYSTAL

———————————— II ————————————

♕ DAUM

4 rue de la Paix, Paris 75002 ■ Tel. 42 61 25 25 - Fax: 40 20 96 71 ■ Mon-Sat 10:00-19:00 ■ English spoken ■ Prices high ■ Professional discount
The superb Daum crystal, some good porcelain and unusual glass furniture.

———————————— VIII ————————————

♕ LES CRISTALLERIES DE SAINT-LOUIS

13 rue Royale, Paris 75008 ■ Tel. 40 17 01 74 - Fax: 40 17 03 87 ■ Mon-Sat 9:30-18:30 ■ English spoken ■ Prices high to very high ■ 20% professional discount
A wonderland of hand made French crystal glasses, decanters, flasks, trays, crystal works of sculpture. The showroom also carries some porcelain and the silver from their sister company, Puiforcat.

♕ LALIQUE

11 rue Royale, Paris 75008 ■ Tel. 42 65 33 70 - Fax: 42 65 59 06 ■ Mon-Sat 9:30-18:30 ■ English spoken ■ Prices high ■ Professional discount
Fabulous examples of the fine art of blown and cut crystal. Glasses, goblets, decanters, flasks, everything in the art of crystal, including tables and decorative objects. In addition they have a collection of fine French porcelain and some silver.

🏰 BACCARAT

30 bis rue de Paradis, 75010 Paris ■ Tel: 47 70 64 30 - Fax: 48 24 29 01 ■
Mon-Fri 9:30-18:30/Sat 10:00-12:30/14:00-18:00 ■ English spoken ■ Prices
high to very high

In the same splendid building where the marvellous Baccarat Crystal Museum displays 2,000 works of crystal art, blown and hand cut since 1764, there
is a retail shop where you can buy crystal services, decorative pieces,
vases, chandeliers. A choice of 1,500 references.

GLASSWARE

VERRERIE ET CRISTALLERIE D'ARQUES

6 place des Etats-Unis, 75016 Paris ■ Tel: 47 23 31 34 - Fax: 47 20 22 84
■ Mon-Fri 9:30-18:00 ■ English spoken ■ Prices low to medium ■ Professional
discounts on large orders

One of the world's best known producers of glassware in various price
ranges.

ART GLASS

CARAN DESIGN

3 rue du Pont Louis-Philippe, 75004 Paris ■ Tel: 48 04 30 40 ■ Tues-Sat
11:00-19:00 ■ Carola Londeix speaks English ■ Prices medium ■ 20% professional discount

Blown glass for the table and the home. Glasses, vases, salad bowls, candlesticks, flacons.

GALERIE DONYA QUIGUER

1 rue Sainte-Croix-Bretonnerie, 75004 Paris ■ Tel: 48 04 72 55 ■ Tues-Sat
13:00-19:00 ■ English spoken ■ Prices medium ■ 10% professional discount

Contemporary blown glass. Unique pieces.

GALERIE LE SUD/LES MAITRES VERRIERS

23 rue des Archives, 75004 Paris ■ Tel: 42 78 42 37 ■ Tues-Sat 10:30-19:00
■ Sebastien Aschero speaks English ■ Prices medium to high ■ 10% professional discount

Blown glass by the Masters (Maîtres Verriers) Novaro, Pierini, Guillot, Fievet,
Dreutler, Marion, Monod, Guittet, Durand-Gasselin, Schamschula, Luzoro, Lepage,
Baquere, Deniel, Pertshire and others. Decorative objects in Murano glass.

VERRE ET ROUGE

19 rue de Miromesnil, Paris 75008 ■ Telfax: 42 65 75 05 ■ Mon-Fri 10:00-
19:00/Sat during December ■ Christiane Follias speaks English ■ Prices
medium ■ 10 to 20% professional discount

Engraving on blown glass. Personalized engraving of monograms, names,
text, logos of companies, crests. Large choice of paper weights, flacons,
flasks, vases and lamps by the great contemporary Masters.

VERREGLASS

32 rue de Charonne, 75011 Paris ■ Tel: 48 05 78 43 ■ Tues-Sat 12:30-19:00 ■ Claudius Breig speaks English ■ Prices low to medium ■ Professional discount
1920-1960 glass. Some lighting and wrought iron.

—————————— X ——————————

MME FABIENNE PICAUD

35 rue du Retrait, 75020 Paris (Bldg in Courtyard) ■ Tel: 47 97 10 78 ■ Every day by appointment ■ English spoken ■ Prices medium to high
Fabienne Picaud is the glass artist. Unique art objects in blown glass. Sculpture, goblets, vases, perfume flacons, lighting.

—————————— OUTSIDE PARIS ——————————

JEAN-PIERRE BAQUERE

5 rue Bouin, 92700 Colombes ■ Tel: 47 86 09 49 - Fax: 47 85 83 47 ■ Mon-Sat 9:30-17:00 and by appointment ■ Jean-Pierre Baquere and Isabelle Emmerique speak English ■ Prices low ■ 3 to 7% professional discount
Blown glass creations decorated in gold leaf, platinum and palladium. Series of 50 made in a year. Hand made perfume bottles. Restoration of glass.

Porcelain and Earthenware
Porcelaine et faïence

Porcelain from China was already present in France in the XVI century.

Porcelain first reached Europe from China through Italy. Venice, established by Marco Polo as the major trading centre with the Far East, was very likely the first European city to have ever seen porcelain or fine china. The secrets for producing porcelain were eventually discovered almost simultaneously by craftsmen in France and Germany in the XVII century.

At this time, Louis Poterat, of Rouen, discovered the secret formula and technique and the first French porcelain was produced. There are now approximately 30 porcelain manufacturers in France. All of them have their outlets in Paris and most are active in the export market.

Earthenware was already an established art before the secrets of porcelain were discovered, but it was not until the XVI century that the Italian technique of "Majolica" was developed (scenery painted on white opaque enamel).

French earthenware is produced mainly in the northern part of France and in the Loiret.

The earthenware produced by artisans with hand painted scenery is made in Provence. Moustiers is an important center.

---I---

♛ MANUFACTURE NATIONALE DE SEVRES
4 place André-Malraux, Paris 75001 ■ Tel. 47 03 40 20 - Fax: 47 03 40 20 ■ Mon-Fri 11:00-18:00 ■ English spoken ■ Prices high
All beautiful Sèvres porcelain. Not restricted to the professional.

---IV---

♛ QUIMPER FAIENCE
84 rue Saint-Martin, Paris 75004 ■ Tel: 42 71 93 03 ■ Mon-Sat 11:00-19:00
Wonderful collection of faience from Quimper.

VI

🏛 SÉGRIÈS

13 rue de Tournon, Paris 75006 ■ Tel. 46 34 62 56 - Fax: 46 34 67 65 ■ Mon-Sat 11:00-19:00 ■ English spoken ■ Prices medium to high ■ Professional discount

Manufacturing studio in Moustiers, Sainte-Marie-de-Provence. Magnificent faience for personalized table settings, complete tableware services and decorative objects. Museum re-editions and customized table settings.

LE CHAMBRELAIN

11 av. de la Motte-Picquet, 75007 Paris ■ Tel: 45 55 03 45 ■ Mon-Fri 9:00-12:30/14:00-19:30 ■ Prices high ■ Professional discount

Hand made porcelain. Classes in porcelain painting offered by professionals.

🏛 DRAGESCO CRAMOISAN

13 rue de Beaune, 75007 Paris ■ Tel: 42 61 18 20 - Fax: 42 85 40 37 ■ Mon-Fri 10:30-12:30/13:00-19:00/Sat 14:30-19:00 ■ English spoken ■ Prices high to very high ■ 10 to 20% professional discount

Museum quality XVIII and XIX century French porcelain.
Glassware from the XVI to the XVIII centuries.
Qualified expert.

LE GRAND TOURNÉ

Headquarters: 40390 Saint-Martin-de-Seignanx ■ Tel: 59 56 10 28 - Fax: 59 56 17 21 ■ Showroom: 184 rue de l'Université, 75007 Paris ■ Tel: 45 51 36 26 ■ Mon-Fri 8:00-12:00/14:00-18:00 ■ Bernard de Sisteron speaks English ■ Prices very high ■ 20% professional discount

Manufacturer of hand painted Limoges fine porcelain.
Hand printed fabrics in exclusive designs.
Appointed to the Royal European Courts.

🏛 BERNARDAUD

11 rue Royale, Paris 75008 ■ Tel. 47 42 82 66 - Fax: 49 24 06 35 ■ Mon-Sat 9:30-18:30 ■ English spoken ■ Prices medium to very high

Superb designs in porcelain. Also a vast line from Daum, Lalique, Baccarat, and silver place settings.

🏛 JEAN-LOUIS COQUET

11 rue Royale, 75008 Paris ■ Mon-Fri 9:00-18:00 ■ Mr. Sellers speaks English ■ Prices High

Manufacturer of Limoges porcelain. Custom colours and forms possible. Professionals only.

🏛 LA FAIENCERIE DE GIEN

18 rue de l'Arcade, Paris 75008 ■ Tel. 49 24 07 77 ■ Tues-Sat 10:00-19:99 ■ Prices medium to high

Faience of Gien and tableware.

☙ TRESORS DU PASSE

131 rue du Faubourg-Saint-Honoré, 75008 Paris ■ Tel: 42 25 05 39 ■ Tues-Sat 14:30-19:30/Mornings by appointment ■ Prices high ■ Professional discount

XVIII century French porcelain and faience. Chinese porcelain, Famille Verte and Famille Rose and East India Company porcelain of the XVII & XVIII centuries.

☙ VILLEROY ET BOCH

21 rue Royale, Paris 75008 ■ Tel. 42 65 81 84 - Fax: 49 24 96 18 ■ Mon-Sat 10:00-18:15 ■ English spoken ■ Prices medium to high ■ 10% professional discount

Porcelain and fine bone china. Crystal and silver. Gifts.

——————————————— **X** ———————————————

APILCO

17 bis rue de Paradis, 75010 Paris ■ Tel: 42 46 36 28 - Fax: 48 24 04 85 ■ Mon-Fri 8:30-12:30/14:00-18:00 ■ English and German spoken ■ Prices medium

Outlet for Porcelaines F. Deshoulières. For professionals only. Specialists in porcelain for hotels and restaurants.

☙ ROBERT HAVILAND & C. PARLON

47 rue de Paradis, 75010 Paris ■ Tel: 42 46 04 90 - Fax: 48 24 99 35 ■ Mon-Fri 9:30-12:30/14:00-18:30 ■ English spoken ■ Prices high to very high ■ Professional discount

Superb hand made Limoges porcelain. Traditional and contemporary styles. Custom designs. For professionals only. Non-professionals can make selections and secure prices and addresses of nearest retail outlets.

PORCELAINES JAMMET SEIGNOLLES

19 rue de Paradis, 75010 Paris ■ Tel: 45 23 25 49 - Fax: 42 46 61 65 ■ Mon-Fri 9:00-12:00/14:00-18:00 Fri closing 17:00 ■ English spoken ■ Prices medium to high

Limoges porcelain, particularly in contemporary designs. For professionals only. Private clients welcome to make selection, secure prices and be directed to the retailer for purchase.

PORCELAINE LAFARGE

17 bis rue de Paradis, 75010 Paris ■ Tel: 45 23 19 89 - Fax: 48 24 66 76 ■ Mon-Fri 9:30-12:30/14:00-18:00 ■ English spoken

For professionals only. Limoges porcelain. Non-professionals are welcome in the showroom to make selections, secure prices and are then directed to the retailer.

PORCELAINES RAYNAUD

32 rue de Paradis, 75010 Paris ■ Tel: 47 70 94 89 - Fax: 42 46 70 76 ■ Mon-Fri 9:00-18:00 ■ English spoken ■ Prices high

Manufacturer of Limoges porcelain. Showroom for professionals only. Retail buyers can make selections to purchase at outlets.

PORCELAINES DE SOLOGNE

30 bis rue de Paradis, 75010 Paris ■ Tel: 45 23 15 86 - Fax: 42 46 05 12 ■ Mon-Fri 9:00-12:30/14:00-17:30 ■ English spoken ■ Prices high

Manufacturer of Limoges porcelain. Professionals only.

SOLAFRANCE

34 rue de Paradis, 75010 Paris ■ Tel: 47 70 92 96 - Fax: 45 23 14 44 ■ Mon-Fri 9:00-12:00/13:00-17:30 ■ English spoken

For professionals only. Representation of several manufacturers of porcelain, crystal and silver. Some of their own editions of porcelain and glassware lines.

Non-professionals can make their choice and be directed to retail outlet.

—————————————————— **OUTSIDE PARIS** ——————————————————

CERAMIQUE DE VINCENNES

Atelier, 21 rue du Midi, 94300 Vincennes ■ Tel:43 98 31 55 - Fax: 43 98 37 64 ■ Thierry Cheyrou and Dominique Paramythiotis speak English ■ Prices medium to high ■ 20% professional discount

Manufacturers of high quality porcelain, faience and silver sold under their trade mark "Palais Royal Paris". The knives have porcelain handles. They will custom produce special series.

CUSTOM CREATIONS

MME ANNIE FRANCE DANG

10 rue Montgallet, 75012 Paris ■ Tel: 43 07 92 71 ■ Mon-Fri 9:00-12:00/14:00-18:30 ■ Prices medium to very high ■ 6% professional discount

Creation of special decoration on porcelain and glass.
Decors in fine gold engraving. Custom reproductions.

DINER DE GALA
CHANTAL MIRABAUD

Atelier, 8 Villa Laugier, 75017 Paris ■ Tel: 42 67 73 14 - Fax: 44 15 97 55 ■ Mon-Fri 10:00-18:30/Sat by appointment ■ Edouard Mirabaud speaks English ■ Prices medium ■ 30 to 40% professional discount

Painting on crystal and porcelain, exclusive creations and made to order. Custom design of tole, decorative objects, lamps and a small line of furniture.

Ceramics
Céramiques

--------------------------------- I ---------------------------------

JEANNE GAMBERT DE LOCHE

147 Galerie de Valois, 75001 Paris ■ Tel: 42 96 04 65 ■ Mon-Sat 15:00-18:00
■ English spoken ■ Prices medium ■ 10% professional discount
Ceramics of the 1940s to 1960s: Vallauris, Daum, Schneider, pate de verre, crystal and other decorative objects.

--------------------------------- V ---------------------------------

ARTISANAT REALITE

6 rue Le Goff, 75005 Paris ■ Tel: 43 54 59 59 ■ Tues-Sat 11:00-19:30 ■ Raymond Sauvaire speaks English ■ Prices high
Contemporary ceramic art.

--------------------------------- VI ---------------------------------

FANCE FRANCK

47 rue Bonaparte, 75006 Paris ■ Tel: 43 26 15 99 ■ By appointment only ■ English spoken ■ 10 to 20% professional discount
Unique works in porcelain, stoneware, terra cotta. Panels and pottery.

LEFEBVRE ET FILS

24 rue du Bac, 75006 Paris ■ Tel: 42 61 18 40 - Fax: 42 86 91 58 ■ Georges and Louis Lefebvre speak English ■ Prices medium to high ■ Professional discount
Extraordinary antique European ceramics of the XVI to the XIX centuries. Expert to the Cour d'Appel, Paris.

LA MAISON IVRE

38 rue Jacob, 75006 Paris ■ Tel: 42 60 01 85 ■ Tues-Sat 10:30-19:00 ■ Jacques Nobecourt speaks English ■ Prices medium ■ Professional discount
Large selection of pottery hand made by French artisans.
Varnished clay pots, art ceramics, stoneware. Everything for the table, Provence style, including table linen.

MME ULRIKE WEISS

12 passage des Taillandiers, 75011 Paris ■ Tel: 47 00 24 47 - Fax: 47 00 24 47 ■ By appointment ■ Ulrike Weiss speaks English ■ Prices medium ■ Professional discounts possible
Cermaic products for the table and for decoration. Unique and humorous character. Development of ceramic designs for industrial production.

LA COUR DES POTIERS

62 allée Montfermeil, 93340 Le Raincy ■ Tel: 42 81 00 16 ■ Mon-Sat 9:00-19:30 ■ Claude Bermann speaks English ■ Prices low ■ Professional discount

Ceramic products made to order: decorative murals, bas reliefs, objects, statues, animals, lighting, dishes. Tiling for kitchens and bathrooms. Restoration of exterior ceramic installations.

Silversmiths
Orfèvres

Surprisingly, the use of silver for eating utensils owes its origins to the Indians of North and South America. Silver had been used at least 5,000 years before Christ for ornamental purposes and was considered by the Egyptians to be more precious than gold.

The Conquistadores, after they had pillaged the Inca and Aztec civilizations of most of their gold, turned their attention to silver and loaded their galleons with tons of it in massive ingots.

Charles V of Spain caused the first vulgarization of the precious metal and created the first "argenterie", producing plates and table utensils which then found their way through trading channels to the other royal and upper class households of Europe.

Much of the older silver plate and utensils created by the artisans of the time did not survive. The Kings would often have the metal melted down to finance their wars or have their own court craftsmen create new designs in the style of their own epoch.

I

GEORG JENSEN

239 rue Saint-Honoré, 75001 Paris ■ Tel: 42 60 07 89 - Fax: 49 27 83 36 ■ Mon-Sat 10:00-12:30/13:30-18:30 ■ English spoken ■ Prices high
Superb collection of cutlery and objects in contemporary designs of silver, plated silver and stainless steel.

III

ESCHWEGE

42 rue Meslay, 75003 Paris ■ Tel: 42 78 51 94 - Fax: 42 78 47 63 ■ Mon-Fri 8:30-12:30/13:30-17:30 ■ Prices medium ■ Professional discount
Custom fabrication, restoration and repair of silver, pewter and objects in other metals. Classic silver and plated silver place settings and objects.

ETAINS DU MARAIS

26 rue des Gravilliers, 75003 Paris ■ Tel: 42 78 73 70 - Fax: 42 78 11 16 ■ Mon-Fri 9:00-12:00/13:00-18:00 ■ Stephane Dodin speaks English ■ Prices medium ■ Professional discount
Silver, pewter, silver plate, stainless steel.
Custom fabrication, repair, restoration, re-silvering.

FRANCIA ORFEVRERIE

24 rue Béranger, 75003 Paris ■ Tel: 48 87 23 77 - Fax: 48 87 57 15 ■ Mon-Fri 8:30-12:00/13:30-17:30 ■ Veronique Walcour speaks English ■ Prices medium ■ Professional discount

Silver table settings, baptismal cups, children's cutlery.
Silver and silver plate. Custom fabrication.

♛ MARISCHAEL

4 rue de Saintonge, 75003 Paris ■ Tel: 42 78 07 63 ■ Mon-Sat 8:00-12:00/14:00-18:00 ■ English spoken ■ Prices high ■ Professional discount

Everything for the table in solid silver and plated silver.
XVIII and XIX century silver. Custom creations in contemporary designs.
Restoration of fine silver.

PATRICK PAILLOUX

14 rue au Maire, 75003 Paris ■ Tel: 42 77 82 53 ■ Mon-Fri 9:00-17:00 ■ Prices medium

Custom fabrication of silver and restoration of antique silver.

ROUGE PULLON

189 rue du Temple, 75003 Paris ■ Tel: 48 87 62 90 - Fax: 44 78 03 83 ■ Mon-Fri 8:30-12:00/13:30-17:30 ■ Prices medium to high ■ Professional discount

Manufacturer of silver for the table. Everything. Solid silver and plated silver. Custom fabrication, repair and restoration.

TETARD FRERES

12 rue Portefoin, 75003 Paris ■ Tel: 44 59 71 90 - Fax: 44 59 71 91 ■ Mon-Fri 9:00-17:30 ■ Frederic Pignot and Isabelle Laucournet speak English ■ Prices medium ■ 5 to 15% professional discount

Custom fabrication of objects in silver, vermeil and gold.
Re-edition of museum pieces. Silver place settings, everything for the table, gifts.

VOGLUX

3 rue de Saintonge, 75003 Paris ■ Tel: 42 72 67 51 ■ Mon-Fri 9:00-17:30 ■ Prices medium ■ 10 to 15% professional discount

Manufacturer of silver tableware, cups and plates for baptisms, champagne buckets and gifts. Re-silvering of cutlery.

––––––––––––––––––– IV –––––––––––––––––––

♛ PLASAIT

9 place des Vosges, 75004 Paris ■ Tel: 48 87 77 66 ■ Mon-Fri 9:00-17:30 ■ Prices Medium ■ 10 to 15% professional discount

Creation of silver for the table, decoration, gifts, bridal registry, births, baptisms, business and courtesy gifts. Cups and trophies. Restoration and repair. Small Museum of unique silver objects.

🏰 CHRISTOFLE

9 rue Royale, 75008 Paris ■ Tel. 49 33 43 00 - Fax: 49 33 43 07 ■ Mon-Sat 9:45-18:30 ■ English spoken ■ Prices medium to high ■ 15% professional discount on large orders

A name known the world over and well deserved. Their huge selection includes both solid and plated silver.

Other CHRISTOFLE outlets:

24 rue de la Paix, 75002 Paris ■ Tel: 42 65 62 43 ■ 95 rue de Passy, 75016 Paris ■ Tel: 46 47 51 27 ■ 17 rue de Sèvres, 75006 Paris, Tel: 45 48 16 17

🏰 ODIOT ORFEVRE

7 place de la Madeleine, 75008 ■ Tel: 42 65 00 95 - Fax: 42 66 49 12 ■ Mon-Fri 9:30-18:30/Sat 10:00-13:00/14:15-18:30 ■ Olivier Gaube du Gers speaks English ■ Prices high ■ 25% professional discount

Creation of silver for the table. Enormous collection in solid silver, antique and contemporary. Collectors items.

🏰 PETER CREATIONS

191 rue du Faubourg-Saint-Honoré, 75008 Paris ■ Tel: 45 63 88 00 - Fax: 45 61 03 93 ■ Claude Peter and Elisabeth Dumaine speak English ■ Prices medium to high ■ Professional discount

Extraordinary custom cutlery. Top of the line: knife handles in semi-precious stones with solid silver mounts, forks and spoons in solid silver. Every day collection, knife handles in specially treated wood for the dishwasher. All table arts.

🏰 PUIFORCAT ORFEVRE

2 av. Matignon, 75008 Paris ■ Tel. 45 63 10 10 - Fax. 42 56 27 15 ■ Mon-Sat 9:30-18:30 ■ English spoken ■ Prices medium to high ■ Professional discount

One of the largest collections of solid and plated silver. They also carry Limoges porcelain, some crystal and a collection of table linens.

Other location

22 rue François-Ier, Paris 75008 ■ Tel. 47 20 74 27 - Fax: 47 20 01 62 ■ Tues-Sat 9:30-18:30

IX

COUZON

31 rue Victor-Massé, 75009 Paris ■ Tel: 49 95 98 02 - Fax: 49 95 97 63 ■ Outside Paris: Tel: 73 51 69 80 - Fax: 73 51 23 51 ■ Mon-Fri 9:00-17:00 ■ Alain Poujol speaks English ■ Prices medium to high ■ Professional discount

Manufacturer of silverware, high quality stainless steel flatware and holloware, cookware and kitchen utensils.

ALGORITHME

9 rue des Trois-Bornes, 75011 Paris ■ Tel: 48 05 53 53 - Fax: 48 05 53 52 ■ Mon-Fri 9:30-12:30/14:00-18:00 ■ Carole Bultel speaks English ■ Prices medium ■ Professional discount

Fabrication and editions of articles of table arts and decoration in plated silver, specially created by contemporary designers.

ATELIER BLETTON

1 passage Saint-Sébastien, 75011 Paris ■ Tel: 47 00 85 98 ■ Mon-Fri 9:00-12:00/14:00-17:00 ■ Prices low

Fabrication and restoration of silver. Trays, platters, coffee-pots, tea-pots, goblets, tankards and flatware.

👑 ERCUIS SAINT-HILAIRE

11 chemin de la Montagne, 94510 La Queue-en-Brie ■ Tel: 49 62 23 62 - Fax: 49 62 23 69 ■ Mon-Fri 9:00-18:00 ■ Isabelle Rigail and Isabelle Ferrer speak English ■ Paris Showroom: 32 rue de Paradis, 75011 Paris ■ Tel: 45 23 17 94 - Fax: 48 00 95 02 ■ Mon-Fri 9:00-12:30/13:30-18:00 ■ English spoken ■ Prices medium to high ■ Professional discount possible

Manufacturers of excellent quality silver plated tableware.

PIERRE MEURGEY

20 bd des Filles-du-Calvaire, 75011 Paris ■ Tel: 48 05 82 65 - Fax: 48 05 71 05 ■ Mon-Fri 8:30-12:00/13:30-18:00/Sat 8:30-12:00 ■ English spoken ■ Prices medium

Custom creations in plated silver. Pierre Meurgey holds the record in the "Guinness Book of Records" for making the world's largest fork – 86 inches.

MAISON MOSSLER

20 bd des Filles-du-Calvaire, 75011 Paris ■ Tel: 48 05 50 28 - Fax: 40 21 75 13 ■ Mon-Sat 10:00-19:00 ■ English spoken ■ Prices medium to high ■ Professional discount

Manufacturer of silver, solid and plated, for all uses.
Restoration, repair, re-silvering. Also carries good selection of porcelain. Bridal registry.

ORFEVRERIE DU MARAIS

1 passage Etienne-Delaunay, 75011 Paris ■ Tel: 43 71 25 04 - Fax: 43 71 20 48 ■ Mon-Fri 8:30-18:30 ■ François Cadoret speaks English ■ Prices high ■ Professional discount

Fabrication of silver tableware. Restoration and repair.

SCHWARTZ ORFEVRE

24 rue de la Folie-Méricourt, 75011 Paris ■ Tel: 47 00 76 02 ■ Mon-Fri 9:00-19:00 ■ Jacques Schwartz speaks English ■ Prices medium

Fabrication of silver articles used for religious purposes: chalices, patons and ciboria.
Repairs of all silver.

XVI

AUGER

13 av. d'Eylau, 75116 Paris ■ Tel: 45 53 34 25 - Fax: 54 70 98 07 ■ Mon-Fri 8:30-17:30 ■ Janine Manderville speaks English ■ Prices medium ■ 10% professional discount

Antique silver and jewellery. Silversmiths since 1774.
Custom fabrication of everything in silver. Repair of cutlery.

XVIII

THIERRY LEFEVRE-GRAVE
24 rue Durantin, 75018 Paris ■ Tel: 42 23 65 60 ■ By appointment ■ Thierry Lefevre-Grave speaks English ■ Prices medium to high ■ Professional discount
Creation of art objects in silver: jewellery, furniture, statuary.

Recognizing Silver

Prior to the French Revolution, hallmarks ("poinçons") on French crafted silver were complex, but provided a virtual identity card of its origin. The hallmark gave a precise geographic origin, the date of fabrication, the name of the Master and the establishment where it was created. Pieces pre-dating 1790 should always show 4 hallmarks. After the revolution, in 1797, the system was simplified. XIX century silver should show three hallmarks, the losange of the master, the pompom of guarantee and the title of the company.

For the amateur silver hunter, there are two methods recommended, using the hand and the nose. First, pick up the piece and judge its heft. A little practise and you can become pretty good at it. Compare it with a piece you already have and know well. Then memorize how it feels.

For the really skilled amateur there is a sworn-by technique. Silver does give off a distinctive odor and once you have committed this smell to your memory you will never forget it. Try it for yourself. Take a linen handkerchief, or even the bottom of a cotton shirt, and rub it on the silver. It will give off its distinctive and familiar smell. Also, you can rub the silver vigorously with the palm of your hand, a little saliva might help as well. Then put your nose to it. If the distinctive odor is not present, BEWARE!

Antique silver

———————— I ————————

♔ A. CHANTAL

12 rue Richepanse, 75001 Paris ■ Tel: 42 61 28 11 ■ English spoken ■ Prices
high to very high ■ Professional discount

Specialist in XVIII and XIX century silver.

———————— IV ————————

ARGENTERIE DES FRANCS-BOURGEOIS

17 rue des Francs-Bourgeois, 75004 Paris ■ Tel: 42 72 04 00 - Fax:
42 72 08 24 ■ Mon-Sat 10:30-19:00 ■ Jean-Pierre de Castro and
Isabelle Pinguet speak English ■ Prices low to medium ■ Professional discount

Antique silver, retro and contemporary. Solid and plated silver.

———————— VII ————————

A LA MINE D'ARGENT

108 rue du Bac, 75007 Paris ■ Tel: 45 48 70 68 - Fax: 45 49 06 55 ■ Mon-
Fri 10:00-19:00/Sat 11:00-18:00 ■ Daniel Chifman and Simona Kletzkine
speak English ■ Prices medium ■ 10% professional discount

Antique solid silver. Plated contemporary silver, porcelain and crystal.
Repair of knives and re-silvering.

———————— VIII ————————

ELEONORE

18 rue de Miromesnil, 75008 Paris ■ Tel: 42 65 17 81 ■ Mon-Fri 10:30-
12:00/14:00-18:30 ■ Prices medium to high ■ 10% professional discount

Exceptional collection of XVIII and XIX century silver.

♔ KUGEL

279 rue Saint-Honoré, 75008 Paris ■ Tel: 42 60 19 45 - Fax: 42 61 06 72 ■
English spoken ■ Prices high ■ Professional discount

One of the great collections of silver, XV to XIX century.

———————— OUTSIDE PARIS ————————

FAUCILLE D'OR

5 rue de Baillage, 78000 Versailles ■ Tel: 39 53 12 10 ■ Tues-Sun 10:30-
13:00/14:30-19:00 ■ English spoken ■ Prices medium to high ■ 5% professional discount

Antique silver.
Qualified expert.

Pewter
Etain

XI

FLOR'

35 rue de Paradis, 75010 Paris ■ Tel: 48 24 47 28 ■ English spoken ■ Prices medium ■ Professional discount

This outlet represents the production of:

Les Etains de la Fontaine

Les Etains de l'Abbaye et Anjou

Les Etains à la Rose

Les Etains du Prince (paintings on pewter tablets)

Les Etains du Grand Duc

Les Etains à La Licorne

All these manufacturers are from the region of Angers and Lyon. One of the best collections.

XIX

CREDOR

14 rue Manin, 75019 Paris ■ Tel: 42 08 42 47 - Fax: 47 42 30 45 ■ Mon-Fri 8:30-18:30 ■ Nicole Mongeal speaks English ■ Prices medium to high

Manufacturer of pewter. Speciality: tea services and soup tureens in polished pewter. All items for table arts, lamps, clocks. Will make to order.

See Antique Dealers and the Markets.

General

🏰 DEHILLERAN

18 rue Coquillière, 75001 Paris ■ Tel: 42 36 53 13 - Fax: 45 08 86 83 ■ Mon 8:00-12:30/14:00-18:00/Tues-Sat 8:00-18:00 ■ English Spoken ■ Prices medium to high ■ Professional discount

High quality professional kitchen utensils. Marvellous selection of copper serving dishes, pots and pans.

MURIEL GRATEAU BOUTIQUE

130-133 Galerie de Valois, Jardins du Palais-Royal, 75001 Paris ■ Tel: 40 20 90 30 - Fax: 42 96 12 32 ■ Mon 14:00-19:00/Tues-Sat 11:00-19:00 ■ English spoken ■ Prices medium to high ■ Professional discount

XIX century French faience, Murano glass, embroidered and plain table linens in a choice of 66 colors.

LA VIE DE CHATEAU

17 rue de Valois, 75001 Paris ■ Tel. 49 27 09 82 ■ Mon-Sat 13:00-19:00 ■ Prices high ■ Professional discount

Antique table services.

PORTO SANTO

7 rue du Vingt-neuf Juillet, 75001 Paris ■ Tel: 42 86 97 81 ■ Mon-Sat 10:00-19:00 ■ Prices medium to high ■ Professional discount

Faience and table linen from Portugal.

🏰 A. SIMON

36 rue Etienne-Marcel and 48 rue Montmartre, 75002 Paris ■ Tel: 42 33 71 65 - Fax: 42 33 68 25 ■ Mon-Sat 8:30-18:30 ■ English spoken ■ Prices medium to high ■ Professional discount

One of the highlights of Paris for the cook, professional or amateur. A vast selection of both high quality cookware, utensils and ceramics, porcelain, crystal and glass. Treasures you never even thought of. Feast your eyes on their copper. If you are looking for great quality knives and restaurant quality cookware, just cross the street to their professional showroom.

BONEGA

40 rue des Francs-Bourgeois, 75003 Paris ■ Tel: 48 87 79 21 - Fax: 48 87 73 66 ■ Mon-Fri by appointment ■ Pierre Messbauer and Genevieve Maillot speak English ■ Prices high ■ Professional discount

Hand embroidered table cloths. Dishes and table settings in mother-of-pearl with semi-precious stones, goblets, platters and trays in lacquer, eggshell lacquer, lacquer on silver. Exclusive furniture and objects in lacquer and eggshell.

IV

SERIE RARE EDITIONS

14 rue des Ecouffes, 75004 Paris ■ Tel: 44 59 81 71 - Fax: 44 59 81 90 ■ Mon-Fri 14:00-19:00 ■ Some English spoken ■ Professional discount

Original collection of knife-rests, trivets, candelabra and frames in decorative bronze. A small line of unusual door knobs in various bronze finishes.

INTERIEURS RIVE GAUCHE

37 bd Saint-Germain, 75005 Paris ■ Tel: 46 33 61 40 - Fax: 43 29 95 00 ■ Mon-Sat 10:00-13:00/14:30-19:30 ■ Prices medium ■ 10 to 20% professional discount

Table arts from the XVIII century to the 1950's. Porcelain, faience, glass, crystal, silver. Some lighting, small furniture, paintings. Marriage lists.

TAIR MERCIER

7 bd Saint-Germain, 75005 Paris ■ Tel: 43 54 19 97 - Fax: 43 25 57 22 ■ Tues-Fri 11:00-19:00/Sat 11:00-13:00/14:30-19:00 ■ Judith Tair Mercier speaks English ■ Prices medium

Custom designs of contemporary table arts products.

LA TUILE A LOUP

35 rue Daubenton, 75005 Paris ■ Tel: 47 07 28 90 - Fax: 43 36 40 95 ■ Tues-Sat 10:30-19:30/Sun 10:30-13 ■ Marie-France Joblin speaks English ■ Prices medium ■ 5% professional discount

Table arts, traditional French artisan objects, ceramics, cutlery, pottery, glass.

LA CASA PASCAL

15 rue d'Assas, 75006 Paris ■ Tel: 42 22 96 78 - Fax: 45 49 43 83 ■ Mon 14:00-19:00/Tues-Sat 10:00-19:00 ■ English spoken ■ Prices low ■ 10% professional discount

White Limoges porcelain, some with decorative finish. Glassware, cutlery, lamp bases, decorative perfume boxes.

DAULIAC SUBRA ANTIQUITES

112 rue du Cherche-Midi, 75006 Paris ■ Tel: 42 22 14 16 ■ Tues-Sat 10:30-19:30 ■ Prices medium ■ 20% professional discount

1920-1940 table arts, bathroom accessories, lighting, silver, small furniture. Qualified expert.

FORMELLE

115 rue du Cherche-Midi, 75006 Paris ■ Tel: 42 22 18 37 ■ Tues-Sat 10:00-19:00/Friday closing 20:00 ■ Michel Fourmy speaks English ■ Prices medium ■ 20% professional discount

Table arts and candles.

PORTOBELLO

56 rue Notre-Dame-des-Champs, 75006 Paris ■ Tel: 43 25 74 47 ■ Tues-Sat 11:00-13:00/14:00-19:00 ■ Catherine Remoissenet speaks English ■ Prices low

Antique linen and table arts, decorative objects, mirrors, lamps, engravings and paintings.

REGIS DHO DIFFUSION

92 bd Raspail, 75006 Paris ■ Tel: 45 44 00 13 - Fax: 42 84 25 04 ■ Tues-Sat 11:00-19:30 ■ Serge Gonda speaks English ■ Prices high ■ 20% professional discount

Exclusive line of crystal, hand painted porcelain, printed terry cloth, bronze gift items.

SOULEIADO

78 rue de Seine, 75006 Paris ■ Tel: 43 54 15 13 - Fax: 43 54 84 45 ■ Mon-Sat 10:00-19:00 ■ English Spoken ■ Prices medium ■ Professional discount

Beautiful provincial style fabrics, table cloths, table sets and porcelain.

TORVINOKA

4 rue Cardinale, 75006 Paris ■ Tel: 43 25 09 13 - Fax: 40 51 89 46 ■ Mon 14:30-19:30/Tues-Sat 10:00-19:30 ■ Françoise Schryne speaks English ■ Prices medium ■ 10% professional discount on furniture

Contemporary table arts, objects, glasses, dishes, table settings, tole. Animal figures in porcelain and glass. Exclusive furniture line designed by Alvar Aalto of Finland.

––––––––––––––––––––––––– VII –––––––––––––––––––––––––

AUX ARMES DE FRANCE

4 rue de Babylone, 75007 Paris ■ Tel: 45 48 05 06 ■ Tues-Sat 10:30-18:30 ■ Prices medium

Silver, porcelain de Saxe, jewellery, plated silver, crystal. Repairs of knives and silver.

DINERS EN VILLE

27 rue de Varenne, 75007 Paris ■ Tel: 42 22 78 33 - Fax: 45 44 87 25 ■ Mon 14:00-19:00/Tues-Sat 11:00-19:00 ■ English spoken ■ Prices medium to very high ■ 10% professional discount

Large selection of porcelain, faience, antique and contemporary silver, crystal and table linens.

LAURE JAPY ET CIE

34 rue du Bac, 75007 Paris ■ Tel: 42 86 96 97 - Fax: 48 33 48 93 ■ Mon-Sat 10:30-19:00 ■ English spoken ■ Prices medium ■ Professional discount

Everything for the table. Linen, crystal, porcelain, silver, lighting, candles.

SIECLE

24 rue du Bac, 75007 Paris ■ Tel:47 03 48 03 - Fax: 47 03 48 01 ■ Mon-Sat 10:30-13:00/14:00-19:00 ■ English spoken ■ Prices low to high ■ 10 to 20% professional discount

Beautiful and original creations for the table, especially the table linen and cutlery collections. Linen, silk, silver, crystal, rare wood, shagreen, mother-of-pearl.
Marriage lists.

--- VIII ---

AU BAIN MARIE

10 rue Boissy-d'Anglas, 75008 Paris ■ Tel: 42 66 59 74 - Fax: 42 66 45 08 ■ Mon-Sat 10:00-19:00 ■ English spoken ■ Prices medium to high ■ Professional discount

Linen and tableware. Exclusive designs of dinner services.Bridal registry.

BRODERIES DE FRANCE

37 bis rue de Ponthieu, 75008 Paris ■ Tel: 43 59 60 73 ■ Mon-Sat 9:00-21:00 ■ Prices medium ■ 15% professional discount

Hand embroidered linen, crystal, silver plated table settings and trays, Limoges porcelain.

CARTIER

51 rue Francois-Ier, Paris 75008 ■ Tel: 40 74 61 83 - Fax: 40 74 01 61 ■ Mon-Fri 9:00-19:00 ■ English spoken ■ Prices high

An attractive table arts department with a selection of well known names in English bone china, French porcelain, crystal and silver. Marriage lists.

CHRISTIAN DIOR

30-32 av. Montaigne, 75008 Paris ■ Tel: 40 73 53 40 - Fax: 47 20 00 60 ■ Mon-Sat 10:00-18:30/Tues-Fri 9:30-18:30 ■ English spoken ■ Prices high

Special exclusive lines of tableware, objects for the home and gifts. Beautiful dinner services like the new deco design bone china "Rayures 55" and the classic 1972 ecological line of platters. Exclusive services in hand made porcelain with special themes, the "Harlequin" crystal line, trays in plexi and fabric, faience with "Jardin à la Française" theme. Frames in plated silver, wood and marquetry. Marriage lists.

HERMES

24 rue du Faubourg-Saint-Honoré, 75008 Paris ■ Tel: 40 17 47 17 - Fax: 40 17 47 18 ■ Mon-Sat 10:00-13:00/14:30-18:30/Tues-Fri 10:00-18:30 ■ All languages spoken ■ Prices high

Exclusive lines of Limoges porcelain, Saint-Louis crystal and table settings. Marriage lists.

MEDIONI CHAMPS-ELYSEES

112 rue La Boétie, 75008 Paris ■ Tel: 42 25 93 39 - Fax: 45 62 29 04 ■ Mon-Sat 10:15-19:00 ■ Henri Medioni speaks English ■ Prices high to very high ■ 15 to 20% professional discount

Wide selection of high quality table arts. Porcelain, crystal, silver, pate de verre.

♛ PETER CREATIONS

191 rue du Faubourg-Saint-Honoré, 75008 Paris ■ Tel: 45 61 18 00 - Fax: 45 61 03 93 ■ Mon 13:30-18:30/Tues-Fri 10:00-18:30/ ■ Sat 10:00-13:00/14:00-18:30 ■ Claude Peter and Elisabeth Dumaine speak English ■ Prices medium ■ 20% on exclusive Peter models

The knife specialist. Knives for the table, kitchen, sport and toilette (razors, scissors...). Manufacturer of high quality table settings. Table arts: silver, plated silver, porcelain, crystal. Exclusive models for use in dishwasher. Gifts. Very high quality.

VIF ARGENT

27 rue Jean-Mermoz, 75008 Paris ■ Tel: 42 66 14 25 ■ Mon-Sat 11:00-19:00 ■ Michèle Duprat speaks English ■ Prices medium ■ Professional discount

Hand painted porcelain, crystal, glassware, silverware, table linen, gadgets and articles for the bar.

————————————— X —————————————

ARTS CERAMIQUES

15 rue de Paradis, 75010 Paris ■ Tel: 48 24 83 70 - Fax: 47 70 64 73 ■ Tues-Sat 10:00-18:00 ■ English spoken ■ Prices medium to very high ■ Professional discount

Faience re-editions of Luneville, Rouen, Moustiers.
Porcelain and crystal of the top brands. Silver and plated silver of Ercuis. Contemporary knives with coloured handles by Scof.

AURELIA PARADIS

21 bis rue de Paradis, 75010 Paris ■ Tel: 42 47 07 00 - Fax: 48 00 92 85 ■ Mon-Sat 9:30-18:45 ■ English spoken ■ Prices medium to high ■ Professional discount

Large selection of the great manufacturers of crystal, porcelain, lighting, objects, gifts. Marriage lists.

CRISTALLERIE PARADIS

17 rue de Paradis, 75010 Paris ■ Tel: 48 24 72 15 - Fax: 44 79 01 08 ■ Mon-Sat 10:00-19:00 ■ English spoken ■ Prices low to high ■ 15% professional discount

Limoges porcelain, crystal of Baccarat and Saint-Louis, silverware, gifts. Their own editions of Limoges boxes. Marriage lists.

EDITIONS PARADIS

29 rue de Paradis, 75010 Paris ■ Tel: 45 23 05 34 - Fax: 45 23 23 73 ■ Mon-Sat 10:00-19:00 ■ English, German and Spanish spoken ■ Prices medium to high ■ Professional discount

An extensive collection of the top brands of crystal, porcelain, lighting, objects, gifts. Marriage lists.

FLOR'

35 rue de Paradis, 75010 Paris ■ Tel: 48 24 47 28 ■ Mon-Fri 10:00-18:00 ■ English spoken ■ Professional discount

Faience from Moustiers and pewter.

FONCEGRIVE

36 rue du Paradis, 75010 Paris ■ Tel: 42 47 18 25 - Fax: 42 47 08 03 ■ Tues-Sat 9:30-18:30 ■ English spoken ■ Prices medium to high ■ Professional discount possible

Porcelain of Herend, Royal Doulton, Minton, Richard Ginori and Royal Albert. Murano glass of Nason. Department of gift items. Marriage lists.

LIMOGES-UNIC

12 and 58 rue de Paradis, 75010 Paris ■ Tel: 47 70 26 65 - Fax: 45 23 18 56 ■ Mon 10:00-13:00/14:00-18:30/Tues-Sat 10:00-18:30 ■ Michèle Bruneau (#12) and Anne Lecomte (#58) speak English ■ Prices medium to high ■ 10% professional discount

Large collection of porcelain, crystal, silverware and gifts.

LUMICRISTAL

22 bis rue de Paradis, 75010 Paris ■ Tel: 47 70 27 97 - Fax: 45 23 23 73 ■ Mon-Sat 9:30-19:00 ■ English spoken ■ Prices medium to high ■ Professional discount

Top brands of porcelain and crystal, Puiforcat silver.

MADRONET

34 rue de Paradis, 75010 Paris ■ Tel: 47 70 34 59 - Fax: 45 23 18 56 ■ English and Spanish spoken ■ Prices medium to high ■ Professional discount

Large selection of porcelain and crystal, silver by Christofle and Ercuis, stainless steel place settings by Rosenthal.

REINE PARADIS

40 rue de Paradis, 75010 Paris ■ Tel: 47 70 30 11 - Fax: 47 70 00 27 ■ English, Italian and Spanish spoken ■ Prices medium to very high ■ Professional discount

Good collection of porcelain and crystal, expecially Lalique, Daum and Baccarat.

LA TISANIERE

21 rue de Paradis, 75010 Paris ■ Tel: 47 70 22 80 ■ 35 rue de Paradis, 75010 Paris ■ Tel: 47 70 40 69 ■ Mon-Sat 9:45-18:30 ■ English spoken ■ Prices low to medium ■ Professional discount

5,000 different models of white Limoges porcelain, oven proof and decorative. Re-editions, in collaboration with the Musée Condé, of XVIII century Porcelaine de Chantilly:
"La Brindille", "L'Œillet" and "Kakiemon".

---------------------------------- **XII** ----------------------------------

CONSTANCE MAUPIN

11 rue du Docteur-Goujon, 75012 Paris ■ Tel: 43 07 01 28 ■ Mon 15:00-19:00/Tues-Sat 10:00-13:00/14:30-19:30 ■ Constance Maupin speaks some English ■ Prices medium ■ Professional discount

Specialist in antique table arts and everything remotely concerned with the decor of the dining room: dishes, glassware, decorative objects, paintings, linen and small furniture. Custom and coordinated linen, faience and porcelain.

MADAME EST SERVIE

75 av. de Wagram, 75017 Paris ■ Tel: 47 64 10 16 ■ Patrick Mery speaks English ■ Prices high ■ 10% professional discount

XIX century services in faience, sometimes XVIII century, most often English. Unusual cutlery, lamps in wrought iron, wood and glass. Custom lampshades.

L'ORFEVRIER

87 av. des Ternes, 75017 Paris ■ Tel: 45 74 15 86 - Fax: 45 74 07 04 ■ Mon 14:00-19:30/Tues-Sat 10:00-19:30 ■ English spoken ■ Prices medium ■ Professional discount

Manufacturer of silver plated table arts: trays, platters, cutlery, goblets, chafing dishes, lamps, everything. Porcelain and crystal.

LA TABLE EN FETE

73 place Docteur Félix-Lobligeois, 75017 Paris ■ Tel: 46 27 75 49 ■ Tues-Sat 10:00-12:00/14:00-19:00 ■ Some English spoken ■ Prices medium ■ Professional discount

Old and antique table settings. Dishes, glasses, solid and plated silver cutlery and objects.

Candles
Bougies

POINT A LA LIGNE

67 av. Victor-Hugo, 750 I6 Paris ■ Tel: 45 00 96 80 - Fax: 45 00 84 95 ■ Mon-Sat 10:00-19:00 ■ English spoken ■ Prices High ■ Professional discount

Perfumed candles for decoration. All classic candles for table arts. Two new collections each year.

Also at:

25 rue de Varenne, 75007 Paris ■ Tel: 42 84 14 45 ■ Mon-Sat 10:00-19:00

Manufacturer:

POINT A LA LIGNE

Z.I., 21 rue Jean-Perrin, 33600 Pessac ■ Tel: 56 36 42 11 - Fax: 56 36 63 43 ■ Mon-Fri 7:30-18:30

VEILLEUSES FRANÇAISES

12 rue Félix-Faure, 94400 VITRY-SUR-SEINE ■ Tel: 46 80 86 83 - Fax: 46 82 34 61 ■ Mon-Fri 8:00-16:30/Fri closing 16:00 ■ Michel Cardosi speaks English ■ Prices medium ■ 10% professional discount for orders of over 5,000 pieces

Oil lamps and their accessories. Decorative candles of unusual design for household and religious purposes (Shabath, Buddhist and Yoga meditation).

UPHOLSTERERS
Tapissiers

"Tapissiers" in France occupy a very special place in the decorating hierarchy. They are, first of all, artisans in the true sense of the word, having learned a difficult and demanding trade. Their skills include just about everything to do with decorating and they can provide valuable advice and assistance in finding artisans in other trades to work on a project.

IV

♕ JEAN RABHI
51 rue Saint-Louis-en-l'Ile, 75004 Paris ■ Tel: 43 54 30 38 - Fax: 40 46 81 61 ■ Mon-Sat 9:00-18:00 ■ English spoken ■ Prices medium ■ Professional discount
Wall and furniture upholstery. All types of window treatments. Good and reliable. Work abroad.

PHILIPPE WYTERS
51 rue Saint-Louis-en-l'Ile. 75004 Paris ■ Tel: 43 54 35 12 ■ Mon-Fri 9:00-18:00 ■ Prices medium ■ Professional discount
Specialists in the upholstery of chairs and restoration.

V

DAT
4 rue des Carmes, 75005 Paris ■ Tel: 46 33 61 24 - Fax: 40 46 84 64 ■ Mon-Fri 8:00-18:30 ■ Bruno Brocard speaks some English ■ Prices medium ■ 10 to 15% professional discount
Upholstery of chairs and sofas.

THEODOR
14 rue de Pontoise, 75005 Paris ■ Tel: 46 33 00 08 - Fax: 40 46 09 92 ■ Mon-Fri 9:00-13:00/14:00-19:00 ■ Jean-Claude Théodore speaks English ■ Prices medium to high
All types of upholstery.

VI

ROBERT SEIGNEUR
6 rue des Quatre-Vents, 75006 Paris ■ Tel: 43 26 92 41 - Fax: 45 44 87 74 ■ Mon-Fri 8:00-18:00 ■ Prices high
Upholstery of furniture and walls. Window and bed treatments.

TAPISSERIE 27

27 quai des Grands-Augustins, 75006 Paris ■ Tel: 43 26 17 85 - Fax: 43 54 67 28 ■ Mon 12:00-18:30/Tues-Fri 9:00-18:30/Sat 12:00-18:00 ■ Prices medium ■ 15% professional discount
Specialists in the upholstery of XVIII and XIX century chairs.

──────────────── **VIII** ────────────────

👑 HIRAM DECORATION
PHILIPPE POIRIER

172 bd Haussmann, 75008 Paris ■ Tel: 43 54 30 38 - Fax: 40 46 81 61 ■ Mon-Sat 9:30-18:30 ■ Philippe Poirier speaks English ■ Prices medium ■ Professional discount
High quality wall upholstery, invisible and with braids and cords. All window treatments. Work abroad.

──────────────── **XI** ────────────────

JEAN BINDER

6 rue de la Folie-Méricourt, 75011 Paris ■ Tel: 47 00 87 89 ■ Mon-Fri 8:00-12:00/14:00-18:00 ■ Jean Binder speaks English ■ Prices medium to high ■ 10% professional discount
Meticulous wall upholstery and upholstery of chairs.Window treatments.

JACQUELINE BRAJON

8 cité Industrielle, 75011 Paris ■ Tel: 43 79 40 47 ■ Mon-Fri 9:00-18:00 ■ Prices medium
Furniture upholstery and window treatments.

CREATIONS MOURRA

102 rue de Charonne, 75011 Paris ■ Tel: 43 71 03 07 - Fax: 43 71 34 28 ■ Mon-Fri 8:30-19:00 ■ Prices medium ■ 10 to 15% professional discount
Wall upholstery and upholstery of classic and contemporary chairs. Window treatments.

👑 DANIEL DELAPLACE

13 av. Parmentier, 75011 Paris ■ Tel: 43 79 68 97 - Fax: 43 79 67 03 ■ Prices medium to high ■ Professional discount
Top quality upholstery of walls and furniture. All window treatments.

PIERRE FROUIN

4 rue Chanzy, 75011 Paris ■ Tel: 43 71 54 44 ■ Mon-Sat by appointment ■ Prices medium ■ Professional discount
Upholstery of chairs, sofas, bed-heads and walls.Window treatments.

LECRUX

35 rue Saint-Maur, 75011 Paris ■ Tel: 43 38 23 56 ■ Mon-Fri 8:00-17:30 ■ Jean-David Lecrux speaks English ■ Prices medium ■ 10 to 15% discount
Specialist in upholstery of chairs and sofas.

─────────── **XII** ───────────

CLAUDE LUCAS
58 rue Crozatier, 75012 Paris ■ Tel: 43 07 50 40 ■ Mon-Sat by appointment
Upholsterer of walls and chairs, both antique and new. Window treatments.

─────────── **XV** ───────────

VICTOR BEMBARON
7 rue du Hameau, 75015 Paris ■ Tel: 42 50 20 00 ■ Mon-Fri 10:00-12:30/14:00-18:30
All types of upholstery and caning of chairs. Window and bed treatments.

ATELIER JEROME PAVIE
216 rue de la Croix-Nivert, 75015 Paris ■ Tel: 45 32 51 99 - Fax: 40 45 01 84 ■ Mon-Fri 10:00-12:30/15:00-19:00/Sat by appointment ■ Jérôme Pavie speaks English ■ Prices medium ■ 5 to 10% professional discount
Upholstery of chairs, sofas and walls. Window treatments.

─────────── **XVI** ───────────

♚ REMY BRAZET
22 rue des Belles-Feuilles, 75116 Paris ■ Tel: 47 27 20 89 - Fax: 47 55 68 90 ■ Mon-Fri 8:30-18:00 ■ Rémy Brazet speaks English ■ Prices high ■ Professional discount
Wall upholstery. Specialist in upholstery of antique chairs. All types of window treatments.
Work experience: National Museums, Château de Fontainebleau, Château de Malmaison, Château de Pau. Member of the Grands Ateliers.

CLAUDE GOUHIER
30 bd Exelmans, 75016 Paris ■ Tel: 45 25 08 53 ■ Mon 16:00-18:30/Tues-Sat 9:30-18:30 ■ Prices medium
Upholstery of chairs and walls. Window treatments.

─────────── **XVII** ───────────

PHILIPPE & CORNELIA CONZADE
99 rue Jouffroy-d'Abbans, 75017 Paris ■ Tel: 47 63 57 45 - Fax: 40 54 92 81 ■ Mon-Fri 9:00-19:00 ■ Cornélia Conzade speaks English ■ Prices medium ■ 10 to 15% professional discount
Upholstery in the traditional manner. Window treatments.

SALVATORE MOTISI
100 rue Lemercier, 75017 Paris ■ Tel: 46 27 40 54 - Fax: 46 27 71 60 ■ Mon-Fri 9:00-12:00/14:00-19:00 ■ Prices medium ■ 10% professional discount
Upholstery of chairs and sofas. Specialist in the traditional style for antique chairs and armchairs.

---XVIII---

♕ FONTAINE-LALANDRE

10 rue Coysevox, 75018 Paris ■ Tel: 42 26 13 30 ■ Mon-Fri 8:00-12:00/13:00-19:00 ■ Prices high ■ Professional discount

Upholstery of antique chairs, armchairs and sofas, XVII and XVIII centuries, for top antique dealers and private clients.

---XX---

♕ ETS RAYMOND DROUARD

4 rue Albert-Marquet, 75020 Paris ■ Telfax: 43 48 79 71 ■ Mon-Fri 9:00-12:00/13:00-17:00 ■ Michel Brunet and Jean-Claude Holgard speak English ■ Prices high ■ Professional discount

Top quality wall upholstery, stretched, pleated or floating, with and without braid. Restoration and upholstery of chairs and sofas. All types of window finishes. Work experience in England, U.S. and Switzerland.

PHAM TAPISSIER

7 rue du Capitaine-Ferber, 75020 Paris ■ Tel: 40 31 03 70 ■ Mon-Fri 8:00-12:00/14:00-16:00 ■ English spoken ■ Prices medium ■ 10 to 15% professional discount

Good quality upholstery: walls, antique and contemporary chairs and sofas. Cushions and window treatments.

♕ PASCAL SCHRICKE-HERVE BAROUKHEL

30 rue de la Réunion, 75020 Paris ■ Tel: 43 48 25 91 - Fax: 43 73 12 57 ■ English spoken ■ Prices medium to high ■ Professional discount

Upholstery of chairs in the traditional manner. Wall upholstery, invisible and with braid on request. Window treatments. Work abroad.

---BOULOGNE---

ENTREPRISE GUILLON-ARIENTI

13 rue d'Aguesseau, 92100 Boulogne-Billancourt ■ Tel: 46 05 78 81 ■ Tues-Sat 10:30-12:30/15:30-20:30 ■ Onar Metin speaks English

Wall upholstery and window treatments. Upholstery of chairs and sofas. Window and bed treatments.

IDEA DECORATION

131 ter rue du Château, 92100 Boulogne-Billancourt ■ Tel: 46 05 98 10 - Fax: 41 10 81 16 ■ Tues-Sat 10:00-12:00/14:00-19:00 ■ Jean-Pierre Laurent speaks English ■ Prices medium ■ 10% professional discount

Traditional upholstery of walls and chairs. Window treatments. Dropped ceilings of PVC with a lacquer look, painted on request.

WALLPAPERS
Papiers peints

I

PRELLE

5 place des Victoires, 75001 Paris ■ Tel: 42 36 67 21 - Fax: 42 36 90 39 ■ English spoken ■ Prices high

Very special selection of wallpapers by Mauny.

VI

BESSON

32 rue Bonaparte, 75006 Paris ■ Tel: 40 51 89 64 ■ Tues-Sat 9:30-18:30 ■ 46 av. Marceau, 75008 Paris ■ 47 20 75 35 ■ English spoken ■ Prices medium

Lines from Frey, Canovas, Etamine. They specialize in coordinates of wallpapers and fabrics.

ETAMINE

3 rue Jacob, 75006 Paris ■ Tel: 43 25 70 65 - Fax: 43 25 92 76 ■ Mon-Sat 9:30-13:00/14:00-18:30 ■ Marilyne Rioult and Chrystelle Thouan speak English ■ Prices medium ■ Professional discount

Excellent selection of wallpapers to coordinate with their fabrics.

FARDIS

6 bis rue de l'Abbaye, 75006 Paris ■ Tel: 43 25 73 44 - Fax: 43 54 22 78 ■ Tues-Sat 9:00-18:00 ■ English spoken ■ Prices medium ■ Professional discount

Their own interesting designs of wallpaper and fabrics.

PIERRE FREY

2 rue de Furstemberg, 75006 Paris ■ Tel: 46 33 73 00 - Fax: 42 96 85 38 ■ Mon-Sat 10:00-12:00/14:00-18:30 ■ English spoken ■ Prices medium to high

Superb collection of wallpapers, coordinated with fabrics.

MANUEL CANOVAS

6 rue de l'Abbaye, 75006 Paris ■ Tel: 43 29 91 36 - Fax: 45 04 04 83 ■ Mon-Fri 9:00-18:30 ■ English spoken ■ Prices medium to high

Beautiful selection of their own wallpapers and fabrics.

NOBILIS

29 rue Bonaparte, 75006 Paris ■ Tel: 43 29 21 50 - Fax: 43 29 77 57 ■ Mon-Sat 9:30-18:30 ■ English spoken ■ Prices medium to high ■ Professional discount

A very good selection of wallpapers and coordinates.

♛ ZUBER

55 quai des Grands-Augustins, 75006 Paris ■ Tel: 43 29 77 84 ■ Mon-Sat 10:00-18:00 ■ English spoken ■ Prices medium to high ■ Professional discount

For over 100 years, Zuber has been a leader in the production of wallpapers. Their lines include panoramas, mosaics and especially Empire styles.

———————————— XV ————————————

MERIGUET-CARRERE

84 rue de l'Abbaye-Groult, 75015 Paris ■ Tel: 48 28 48 81 - Fax: 45 32 57 84 ■ Mon-Fri 8:00-12:00/14:00-18:00 ■ English spoken ■ Prices high

Restoration of antique wallpapers, trompe l'œil and gilding. His work experience includes the historic monuments of France including the Palace of Versailles.

Wallpaper Consultant

———————————— VII ————————————

CAROLLE THIBAUT-POMERANTZ

54 rue de l'Université, 75007 Paris ■ Tel: 42 22 83 41 ■ By appointment ■ Carolle Thibaut-Pomerantz speaks English ■ Prices high ■ Professional discount

A specialist in French XVIII and XIX century and Art Deco wallpapers.

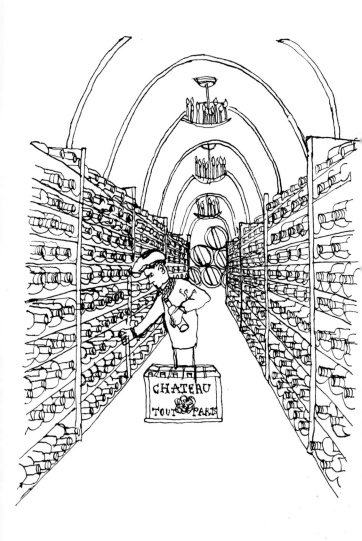

WINE CELLAR EQUIPMENT
Équipement de cave

―――――――――― IV ――――――――――

LESCENE-DURA

63 rue de la Verrerie, 75004 Paris ■ Tel: 42 72 08 74 - Fax: 42 76 09 69 ■
Tues-Sat 9:30-19:00 ■ Prices reasonable ■ 10% professional discount
Articles for the wine cellar and the bar. Accessories for wine tasting. Special armoires for wine storage.

―――――――――― X ――――――――――

L'ESPRIT ET LE VIN

32 rue de Paradis, 75010 Paris ■ Tel:48 24 20 80 - Fax: 48 24 06 56 ■ Mon-Fri 8:00-18:00 ■ Headquarters - La Ville aux Nonains, 28250 Senonches ■ Tel: 37 53 53 06 - Fax: 37 37 73 90 ■ Jean-Loup Ravinet speaks English ■ Prices medium to high ■ Professional discount
Over 150 items for serving and tasting wine, from cork screws to carafes and a good selection of special wine glasses.

―――――――――― XI ――――――――――

LA CAVE BACCHUS

106 av. Philippe-Auguste, 75011 Paris ■ Tel: 43 72 00 55 - Fax: 43 72 91 71 ■ Mon-Fri 9:00-12:00/14:00-18:00 ■ English spoken ■ Prices medium to high ■ 15% professional discount
Custom and stock armoires for wine storage. Wide selection of special wine dispensing equipment for restaurants and hotels. An exciting new refrigerated wine barrel. They also build and equip complete wine cellars for restaurants, hotels and private individuals.

―――――――――― XIV ――――――――――

AU CHENE LIEGE

74 bd Montparnasse, 75014 Paris ■ Tel: 43 22 02 15 - Fax: 42 79 81 23 ■ Tues-Sat 9:30-12:30/13:45-18:30 ■ Prices medium ■ Professional discount
A large assortment of articles for serving wine. Accessories for the bar, decanters, glasses. The cork specialists.

―――――――――― XV ――――――――――

EUROCAVE

48 rue de Vouille, 75015 Paris ■ Tel: 48 56 08 12 - Fax 48 56 08 18 ■ Mon-Fri 9:00-19:00/Sat 9:00-12:00/14:00-18:00 ■ English spoken ■ Prices medium ■ Professional discount
Large stock and made to order temperature controlled armoires for wine. Sizes from 50 to 2,800 bottles. Catalogue in English available upon request.

―――――――――― OUTSIDE PARIS ――――――――――

L'ATELIER DU VIN

Route de Chejoix, 60120 Breteuil-sur-Noye ■ Tel: 44 07 07 11 - Fax: 44 07 16 00 ■ English spoken ■ Prices medium
Accessories for wine cellars, for serving wine, tasting, storage and bottling of wine.

THE MARKETS OF PARIS

Les marchés de Paris

The wonderful markets of Paris, which include the Village Suisse, all of the markets of the Marché aux Puces, the Village Saint-Paul, the Village Saint-Honoré and others, can present a picture of confusion to the first time visitor.

In contrast to the Marché aux Puces, the Village Suisse is a well manicured enclave in the midst of an elegant residential area in the heart of Paris. Many of the top antique dealers from the Carre Rive Gauche and the Louvre des Antiquaires have shops here which display their wares in a more casual atmosphere. Make this a must.

The Marché aux Puces (Flea Market), the largest of them all, is actually a vast, sprawling expanse at the Porte de Clignancourt on the edge of Paris which houses a conglomeration of many different markets, each with its own distinctive character. It is a truly exciting experience.

The Village Saint-Paul in the Marais has a wide variety of collectibles. The Village Saint-Honoré has several interesting dealers in silver and a few dealers in furniture of the XVIII and XIX centuries. They are both worth a look if you have the time.

The editors have selected those markets and individual merchants whose wares may best suit the needs of the professional or the individual looking for something special.

The markets of Paris are always a delight and for the skilled treasure hunter, there is no better reward than a surprise discovery. You will be astonished at how many of the people in these markets speak English.

Le Village Suisse

The Village Suisse has a vast variety of antique furniture, art and art objects of value as well as a lot of brocante. It is well worth a visit. You can expect to find a bargain now and then but generally prices are quite high. Don't forget to negotiate and if you are buying authentic antiques and art be sure to demand a certificate.

Most merchants will offer a professional discount.

The market is open Thursday, Friday, Saturday, Sunday and Monday from 11:00 to 19:00. Remember, lunch is considered sacred so most merchants will close from 12:30-13:30.

Le VILLAGE SUISSE

78 av. de Suffren and 54 av. de La Motte-Picquet, 75015 Paris - Tel: 47 34 13 82 - Fax: 44 49 02 20

Contact: Mr. Michel d'Istria

PLACE DE GENEVE

1. GALERIE DE VILLIERS
Tel: 45 66 06 52
Art Books, deluxe editions, estampes, framing.

2. ADAM
Tel: 45 67 23 99
Antiquities, decorative objects.

3. MAISON HAYE
Tel: 45 67 49 85
Furniture, curiosities, art objects, especially chairs.

4. ROSE-MARIE GATEAU
Tel: 43 06 21 82
XVIII & XIX century furniture and art objects.

5. LE GRENIER DE GRAND-MERE
Tel: 47 83 32 84
Restoration of antique furniture, XVII and XIX century.

6. SUFFREN ANTIQUITES
Tel: 47 83 21 10
XIX century furniture and art objects.

8. ROGER SAGET
Tel: 43 06 26 39
Antiques, art objects.

9. SPINELLA
Tel: 45 66 56 62
Furniture & glass.

11. CONTE ANTIQUITES
Tel: 47 83 41 83 - Fax: 42 60 14 72
XVIII & XIX century furniture & art objects.

12. LE COIN REVE
Tel: 47 34 07 29
XVIII century antiques, furniture & art objects.

13. CORINNE ANTIQUITES
Tel: 43 06 47 03
Small antique art objects, curiosities.

PLACE DE LAUSANNE

16/18. MAISON HAYE
Tel: 45 67 49 85
Antique furniture, chairs, fireplace accessories, curiosities.

19. MARCHAND D'OUBLI
Tel: 43 06 84 41
XVII & XVIII century antiques.

20/21. LA GRANDE ROUE
Tel: 45 66 42 38 - Fax: 48 85 31 36
Jacques Perquis
XVIII to XX century furniture, lighting, paintings, art objects and curiosities.

23. SIGRID
Tel: 45 67 41 43
Sigrid Julicher
Furniture, art objects & paintings of the XVII & XVIII century.

PLACE DE BERNE

28. CATHERINE HIRSCH
Tel: 45 66 00 09 - Fax: 40 68 76 97
Furniture & art objects of the XVIII & XIX centuries. Qualified expert.

29/30. L'ECUYER
Tel: 45 66 78 36
Antiques & art objects.

32.   CHRISTIANE DANIEL
Tel: 45 67 59 55
Ceramics, faiences, art objects.

33.   ERIC SAGET
Tel: 43 06 07 22
Antique furniture & art objects.

34/35. GALERIE DE MARS
Tel: 47 83 45 18 - Fax: 42 61 32 41
Michel Ottin
Regional natural wood furniture of the XVIII century. Paintings of the XIX century, art objects.

36/37. ANTONIN RISPAL
Tel: 47 83 72 34
Art Nouveau & Art Deco.

38.   LA FILLE DU PIRATE
Tel: 47 34 06 76
Antique arms, antique scientific instruments, antique marine items.

39.   GERALDINE
Tel: 40 56 02 23
Antique furniture and art objects.

──────────────**PLACE DE LUCERNE**──────────────

45/51/52. MICHEL D'ISTRIA
Tel: 43 06 47 87 - Fax: 44 49 02 20
Antique furniture and objects. Qualified expert.

49.   ROXANE
Tel: 45 66 51 56
Roxane Sabatrier
XVIII & XIX century paintings, curiosities.

50.   HENRI SELOIN
Tel: 45 66 42 87
Decorative objects.

54.   CHARLOTTE HALLER
Tel: 47 83 40 66
Decorative items.

55.   JEAN-PAUL DE VOLDERE
Tel: 45 66 54 53
Antique paintings & art objects.

56. **ANCELLE**
Tel: 43 06 21 99
Restoration of old photographs, antique frames.

57. **MICHEL BOZON**
Tel. 45 67 44 44 - Fax: 44 18 95 44
XIX century antique drawings, engravings, paintings & art objects.

58. **GALERIE F. PRISTON**
Tel: 43 06 62 32
Art of Asia.

───────────── **ALLEE DE FRIBOURG** ─────────────

42/43/44. MAISON HAYE
Tel: 40 65 95 80
XVII, XVIII & XIX century furniture & art objects.

45. **MICHEL D'ISTRIA**
Tel: 43 06 47 87 - Fax: 44 49 02 20
Antique furniture and objects. Qualified expert.

46. **JEANINE KUGEL**
Tel: 47 34 62 74
International expert on Viennese bronzes.

47. **ALMANDINE**
Tel: 45 49 23 43
Antique silver & antique jewellery.

48. **AUX VIEUX FRIBOURG**
Tel: 47 34 91 97
XVIII century furniture & art objects.

───────────── **GRANDE ALLEE** ─────────────

26. **CATHERINE HIRSCH**
Tel: 45 67 46 29
Antiques & art objects.

27/27 SYLVAIN ROCHAS
Tel: 47 34 15 47
XVIII, XIX century furniture in natural woods.
Panelling and glass of the XVIII century.
Mirrors and pier glasses. Restoration of antique furniture.

40/41. REGIS AERNOUTS
Tel: 47 34 85 10
Antiques, decorative objects.

71/72. HUGUETTE RIVIERE
Tel: 44 49 91 82
Specialist in Napolean III furniture and art objects.

88. JEAN-PAUL LECLERC
Tel: 45 67 98 24
XIX century English and French furniture.

89/90. A. and J. BESREST
Tel: 45 67 59 61
XVIII & XIX century furniture and art objects.

91. LA VIEILLE EUROPE
Tel: 43 06 61 87
Antique furniture and decorative items.

92. MELODIE DU TEMPS
Tel: 42 73 23 08
Antique dealer who specializes in small furniture for collectors.

93/94. A. GIOE
Tel: 43 06 25 01
Decorative objects.

────────────────── **PLACE DE ZURICH** ──────────────────

59/60. JABERT
Tel: 43 06 45 55
Antique tapestries & carpets.

61/62/63. MICHEL CAFLER
Tel: 45 67 89 67 - Fax: 49 26 01 41
Art Deco furniture and art objects.
XVIII & XIX century antiques & art objects.

64. LUC JOLLIVET
Tel: 45 67 88 95
Antique furniture and lanterns.

65. J. MATEILLE
Tel: 47 83 47 08
Antique English furniture, decorative objects.

66. MAUD & RENE GARCIA
Tel: 47 83 93 03
Primitive art.

67. CATHERINE BELLAICHE
Tel: 42 73 30 05
Oriental carpets, decorative objects.

68. JACQUELINE NIMSGERN
Tel: 47 34 81 40
Antique art objects, carpets.

69. JEAN-LOUIS KARSENTY
Tel: 45 67 72 08
Antiques, decorative objects.

70. **PHILIPPE MICHEL**
   Tel: 45 67 89 67 - Fax: 49 26 01 41
   XVIII & XIX century paintings, furniture, art objects, small furniture in mahogany & marquetry.

―――――――――――――― **GRAND PLACE** ――――――――――――――

73. **L'HEURE ANCIENNE**
   Tel: 47 34 99 43
   Antiques, decorative objects.

76/76b **GALERIE MAXINE FUSTIER**
   Tel: 47 34 13 82
   XVIII & XIX century furniture & art objects.
   Specialist in Directoire and Consulat.

77. **LA CHEMINEE**
   Tel: 45 66 88 71
   Fire dogs, fireplace accessories.

89/90. **JEAN-JACQUES BESREST**
   Tel: 45 67 59 61
   XVIII, XIX century furniture and art objects.

96. **EN QUATRE-VINGT-QUINZE**
   Tel: 43 06 31 76
   XVIII & XIX century furniture, clocks.
   Carpets, tapestries & ivories.

―――――――――――― **AVENUE DE CHAMPAUBERT** ―――――――――― ―

113. **PIERRE SAVINEL**
   Tel: 45 66 09 76
   Antique and contemporary furniture adapted for stereo equipment.

158. **ANNE & PENELOPE**
   Tel: 47 34 94 54
   Furniture & art objects of China, ivories and carved stone.

―――――――――――――― **PLACE DE LUGANO** ――――――――――――――

79/80. **LE KEPI ROUGE**
   Tel: 45 67 59 83
   Historic souvenirs, lead soldiers, antique arms for collectors, historical paintings.

82. **L'HEURE DE ROBERT**
   Tel: 45 66 74 53
   Antique jewellery & jewellery repair.

83. **ANNE-MARIE DESPAS**
   Tel: 43 06 55 94
   Antique art objects. Decorative items.

84. GISELE BIZOT
Tel: 45 67 10 12
French and English antique furniture and objects of the XVIII & XIX centuries.

85. GHISLAINE CHAPLIER
Tel: 45 67 30 55
Antique collectibles & objects of curiosity.
Specialties: sewing kits, baby rattles, bouquet holders, cruets, antique jewellery.

86. GERARD SANTOLLINI
Tel: 43 06 91 94
XVIII & XIX century furniture & art objects. Art of the Atlas mountains.

87/98/99. SAADA
Tel: 45 67 59 14
Furniture & art objects of the XVIII century.

97. THIBAUD DE MONTJOYE
Tel: 44 49 06 60
Antiques, decorative objects.

100/101. GALERIE OLIVIA JACQUELINE TEBOUL
Tel: 43 06 85 30
Table arts, antique silver.

RUE ALASSEUR
---

102. GALERIE KIRIN
Tel: 45 67 39 39 - 45 67 31 21
Bertrand Henry
Asian art, especially of China & Japan.
Antique furniture, paintings, estampes.

104. INTERIEURS AND DECORS
Tel: 47 34 19 51
Antique furniture and decorative objects.

105. BESREST
Tel: 45 66 88 71
XVIII, XIX century furniture and art objects.

106. ANTIQUITIES FOUQUET
Tel: 45 40 46 89
XVIII & XIX century antique furniture.

108/109. SUR LES AILES DU TEMPS
Tel: 47 83 50 19
Antiques, decorative items.

114. GALERIE KERVAL
Tel: 47 83 67 72
Antique tapestries and art objects.

117. DANIEL
Tel: 45 66 68 44
Antique toys, Dinky toys.

118. GALERIE XANTHO
Tel: 40 56 06 18
Paintings, antique furniture and art objects.

149. MEMOIRES
Tel: 45 66 09 72
Antique furniture and decorative objects.

150. AUX TRESORS DE LA PERSE
Tel: 45 67 38 28
Persian carpets from all regions. Choice of approximately 800.

151/153. LA TOUR CAMOUFLE
Tel: 43 06 36 30
XVIII & XIX century French furniture, art objects and paintings.

152. GEORGE GOUR
Telfax: 43 06 84 61
XVII to XVIII century furniture, paintings and art objects.

154. GALERIE JULIETTE LAURENT
Tel: 47 34 27 73
XIX & XX century paintings, aquarelles & engravings.

155/156. AUX ARMES D'ANTAN
Tel: 47 83 71 42 - Fax: 47 34 40 99
Maryse Raso
Antique arms, military souvenirs.
Qualified expert.

157. YSMAILOFF
54 av. de la Motte-Piquet ■ Tel: 45 67 81 77
Persian & Caucasian carpets.

120. ENTRE TEMPS
Tel: 45 67 68 07
XVIII & XIX century antiques, art objects.

121. LES ATELIERS SAINT-GERVAIS
Tel: 45 67 29 39
Restoration of old master paintings.

122. **CARIATIDES ANTIQUES**
Tel: 45 66 05 75
XVIII & XIX century English furniture.

123. **FABIAN DE MONTJOYE**
Tel: 45 67 79 36
Antiques, old jewellery & primitive African art.

124. **PIERRE VIGUIE**
Tel: 40 56 38 37
Antiques, decorative items.

125. **GILLES BODARD**
Tel: 43 06 44 18
Antique jewellery.

126. **GALERIE MERCURE**
Contemporary marine articles and recuperation.
Second hand.

128/132. **MONIQUE DE CHAMARD**
Tel: 47 34 47 38
Paintings.

130. **JEAN-PIERRE PALEAU**
Tel: 45 66 02 33
XVIII & XIX century French furniture & art objects.
Specialty: French regional furniture.

132. **MONIQUE DE CHAMARD**
Objects.

133/134/135. **LE 7e JOUR**
Tel: 45 66 09 06
XVIII & XIX century antiques.

139. **J-P EHGNER**
Tel: 45 66 08 49
XVIII & XIX century furniture in fruit woods.

140. **L'ACROSTICHE**
Tel: 40 56 30 62
Antique furniture in fruit woods and decorative objects.

141. **GALERIE MERCURE**
Tel: 43 06 88 96
Paintings, sculpture and art objects.

142. **HEDJAZI SEYED**
Tel: 44 49 04 63
Tapestries, antique textiles & antique carpets.

143. **MONIQUE DESPRAIRIES**
Tel: 43 06 36 81
Small antique furniture, mirrors & chairs of the XIX century.

116. PHILIPPE MINARET
Tel: 45 66 02 59
Small furniture and art objects from XVIII & XIX centuries.

115. LES SPLENDEURS D'ORIENT
Tel: 45 66 08 96
Carpets from all parts of the world.

136. YVES PLASSARD
Tel: 45 66 05 55
Mirrors and furniture of the XIX century.

137. SHOP SIXTEEN
Tel: 44 49 06 38
1930 furniture, dressing tables, bars. XIX century liqueur cabinets.
American cookie jars 1930-1960, Walt Disney & others. Old glass.

──────────── **AVENUE DU GENERAL BARATIER** ────────────

144. ANTIQUITES HERBERT
Tel: 47 34 83 61
English & French furniture, XVIII & XIX centuries.

145/146. JEAN-CHRISTIAN DAVEAU
Tel: 47 83 69 31
Art Deco furniture, paintings & sculpture.

148. GALERIE MERCURE
Tel: 43 06 88 96
Paintings, sculpture, & art objects.

──────────── **SOUS-SOL COUR ANGLAIS** ────────────
(Entry on Grand Place)

1/2. HANRI KUSZELEWIC
Tel: 45 66 91 24
XVIII & XIX century French furniture, commodes, coat stands, vitrines, chairs and art objects.

3/16/18. BRITISH IMPORT ANTIQUITIES
Tel: 45 67 87 61
XIX century English furniture.

5. LUCETTE VINCENT
Tel: 43 06 48 84
Necklaces and bracelets in semi-precious stones.

6. CELINE NGUYEN
Tel: 45 67 39 55
Porcelain and miniatures of the XVIII & early XIX centuries.

6. PASCAL FESTOR
Tel: 47 83 60 59
Jeweller, antique & modern, repair & transformation.

9. LA DENTELLIERE
Tel: 47 34 46 96
Antique textiles.

11. ROIG LAMBERT
Tel: 43 06 44 63
Antique lamps, shades.

12. JACQUES COGNET
Tel: 42 73 34 43
Antiques, decoration.

13. JEAN LEVY LECLERE
Tel: 47 83 64 11
Antiques, art objects, curiosities.

16/18 BRITISH IMPORT
English furniture and objects.

21. LA LUCIOLE
Tel: 40 56 91 19
Lighting.

22. 7 FOIS 7
Tel: 43 06 83 96
XIX century paintings, art objects, & decoration.

The Flea Market
Le Marché aux Puces

The Marché aux Puces is easily reached by Metro to the Porte de Clignancourt, by taxi or by private car directly to the rue des Rosiers. There is ample parking space available in the Marché Malassis, on the roof of the Marché Serpette, the garages on the rue Marie-Curie, rue Docteur-Bauer and rue Eugène-Bertoux.

All the main markets, Biron, Vernaison, Malassis, Dauphine, Serpette and Paul-Bert, are entered from the rue des Rosiers, which acts as the main street.

There are plenty of restaurants and cafés to rest your tired feet and have a meal. Unless you have a particular dealer in mind and a specific purchase, plan to spend at least half a day browsing. A full day is even better. And do not forget: bargaining is the order of the day and the good negotiator is always patient. Don't be hasty and be sure to ask for a certificate of guarantee if you are being sold an antique or an old painting.

The hours are not fixed. Some merchants are open from Friday to Monday, but the hours are mainly Saturday and Sunday from 9:30 to 18:30 and Mondays by appointment. It is best to call to avoid disappointment.

In consideration of the sheer size of the Flea market and the limitations on time, the editors have made certain selections which the professional should find interesting.

There is of course much more to explore if time is unlimited.

99 rue des Rosiers

This is a small, compact market which contains a few good dealers. It is certainly worth a visit and is adjacent to the Marché Vernaison.

BOUTIQUE C
XVIII and early XIX century small furniture, chairs and armchairs in mahogany and walnut. XVIII and XIX century paintings and porcelain.

FRANCK ANTIQUITES - Boutique H
Tel: 40 11 82 60 - Fax: 42 39 14 97
XIX century Japanese and Chinese furniture, curiosities and decorative objects.

FRANCK ANTIQUITES - Boutique I
Tel: 40 11 82 60
English furniture and decorative items. XIX century English silver, paintings and boxes.

BOUTIQUE G
Tel: 40 11 82 60
Oriental carpets, kilims and tapestries.

MILAD ANTIQUITES - Stand F
Tel: 40 11 52 83
Antiques and architectural elements from India.

POT, Michel - GOLD HORN - Boutique J
Tel: 40 10 09 84
XVI to XX century books, drawings, engravings and paintings, some furniture.

VAURY, Gisèle - Boutique A
Tel: 40 10 09 93
Excellent collection of canes and their stands.
Art glass and showcase collectibles.

85 rue des Rosiers and 118 av. Michelet

The Marché Biron is one of the most convenient markets in the Puces. Allée 1 is almost exclusively dedicated to the classic furniture styles, art objects, Art Nouveau and some good silver and glassware dealers. Allée 2 is particularly devoted to XVIII and XIX century country furniture from Brittany and Normandy.

ALLÉE 1

ABECASSIS, Paul - Stand 125
Tel: 40 12 82 38
XIX century furniture and portraits.

AKER, Albert - Stand 16

AMBRE - Stand 68
Tel: 40 12 17 01 - Fax: 40 26 61 06
XVIII century furniture, paintings, objects, decorative elements. XVIII century Italian furniture.

ANDRE, Jeanine - Stand 35

ANDRE, Marcel - Stand 110, 110 bis

ANTICA - Stand 23
XVIII and XIX century furniture, lighting and objects.

ARMAND, Bernard - Stand 164

ARNOUX Christian - Stand 85
Tel: 40 11 04 21 - Fax: 40 10 13 08
1860 to 1960 lamps, vases, decorative objects, small furniture. Specialist in Art Nouveau, Art Deco.

ARTCOS - Stand 80 and 81
Tel: 40 10 00 85
XX century furniture.

ART TRANSIT - Stand 63
Tel: 40 12 24 97
Shippers.

LES AUTHENTIQUES - Stand 130
Tel: 40 12 12 50
Antique jewellery.

AVNER ANTIQUITES - Stand 47
Tel: 40 11 19 23
XIX century furniture, marquetry and decorative objects.

BAKERDJIAN, Eric - Stand 18
Tel: 40 11 20 89/48 78 93 39
Antique tapestries and Oriental carpets. Restoration and cleaning.

BARBANEL, Claude - Stand 88
Tel: 40 12 33 35
XIX century furniture and objects. XVIII and XIX century glass.

BAROCO - Stand 117

BENOIT - Stand 70
Tel: 40 11 58 45
Art Nouveau lamps and vases in pate de verre, Gallé, Daum, Rousseau, Muller, Schneider. Art Deco glass objects.

BENSON, Raphael - Stand 37

BERGER-CHICUREL, Bella - GARANCE - Stand 108

BERMAN FRERES - Stand 9
Lighting.

BERRO, Pascal - Stand 72
Tel: 40 12 14 18 - Fax: 48 78 43 82
Art Nouveau, Art Deco 1900-1930. Glass objects by Daum, Gallé, Walter, Rousseau, Muller. Bronzes, ceramics, furniture.

BIRON - Stand 75 ter
Tel: 40 12 40 46 - Fax: 40 10 13 08
XIX and XX century paintings by confirmed artists. Post-Impressionist and modern. Sculpture, Art Deco.

BITOUN, Jacques - Stand 8
Tel: 40 11 96 54
Antique porcelain. XVIII and XIX century Meissen and other German XVIII century porcelain.

BOLAND, Elisabeth - Stand 98
Tel: 40 11 38 22
Art Nouveau and Art Deco. Lalique glass and perfume bottles.

BREGHEON, Jackie - Stand 61
Tel: 40 11 58 15 - Fax: 40 12 04 62
XVIII century provincial French furniture.

BROC'ART - Stand 113
Tel: 40 12 31 10
Art of Japan and China. Objects in ceramic, porcelain and lacquer. Chinese and Japanese furniture. Animal bronzes and Japanese paintings.

BROPHY, Peter - Stand 135 bis
Diverse and interesting furniture, objects. Great garden benches.

BROUN, Robert - Stand 12

BROUN, Roseline - Stand 39

BRUDASZ, Joe - Stand 86 bis
Tel: 40 12 87 04/48 54 43 43 - Fax: 40 10 13 08
Art Deco and Art Nouveau: sculpture, lighting, wrought iron, pate de verre, Lalique. Lithographs.

CAHIER, Raymond - Stand 106

CAMET, Huguette - Stand 124

CARPENTIER, Henri - Stand 33
XIX century furniture.

CARPENTIER, Sylvie - Stand 127
Tel: 40 12 51 15
French silver. Bronzes, marble, Napoléon III furniture.

CHARLIAT, Jeanine - Stand 35

CHICHE, Samuel - Stand 122

CHRIS/ANDRE - Stand 110 and 110 bis

CLAUDE - Stand 15
Tel: 40 12 01 38
XIX century furniture, marquetry, art objects, chandeliers, opaline, porcelain mounted on bronze.

CLERC, Philippe - Stand 121 bis
Tel: 40 11 59 69
Neo-Classical (1780-1830) mahogany furniture, art objects, drawings and engravings.

COHEN, Clara - Stand 11

COTTAGE 46 - Stand 46
Tel: (16) 40 12 02 49 - Fax: (16) 40 10 13 08
Napoléon III furniture and objects.

COUET Alain (See AMBRE) - Stand 68

DANIEL - Stand 55

DAVID'S ANTIQUITES - Stand 21
Tel: 40 12 40 04 - Fax: 40 10 13 08
XIX century furniture and decorative objects.

DAYAN - Stand 58

DELOR SIMONET - Stand 104

DELPLACE, Patrick - Stand 60

DESNOUES, Jacques - Stand 4
Tel: 40 10 26 70
XIX century furniture and objects. XVIII century reproduction marquetry, bronze objects. Porcelain mounted on bronze.

RODOLPHE - Stand 59

DOUCHIN, Jacques - Stand 134
Tel: 40 11 35 89
Antique English mahogany furniture.

DUCHEMIN, Therese - Stand 24

DUINAT, Marie - Stand 129

DUPRE, Maurice - Stand 91

EDOUARD, Jacqueline - Stand 29
Tel: 40 10 23 00
Rare watches, silver, exceptional art objects.

ELISABETH - Stand 66
Tel: 40 11 12 00 - Fax: 47 47 02 82
Art Nouveau and Art Deco glass and furniture. Glass by Gallé, Daum,
Schneider, Sabino, Murano, Lalique, with certificates. Miniatures, boxes in
gold and silver. Russian objects and collectibles.

EMBERGER, Henri - Stand 25
Tel: 40 10 99 26 - Fax: 40 10 13 08
Toys, games and decorative objects.

EVELYNE ANTIQUITES - Stand 13
Tel: 40 10 09 99 - Fax: 44 53 08 58
Napoléon III art objects, furniture, porcelain.

FRIOUR, Michelle - PHILOMENE - Stand 19

GAIGNON, Claude - Stand 7
Mixture of furniture and objects.

GALERIE R.B. - Stand 39
Tel: 40 12 96 75/41 18 90 37 - Fax: 40 10 13 08
Art Nouveau, Art Deco furniture and glass. Paintings and objects 1950-1960.

GARRY - Stand 10
Tel: 40 10 09 87
Russian art: icons, jewellery, silver, objects.

GERMOND, Maryvonne - Stand 165

GITTON, Thierry - Stand 101
Tel: 40 11 52 46 - Fax: 45 74 19 70
Charles X and Napoléon III opalines and furniture. Italian water colors.

GOLDENBERG, Leon - Stand 84

GOULIGNAC, Pascal - Stand 114

GOZES, Ghislaine - NOSTALGIE DU PASSE - Stand 126

GRANDIDIER, Gerard - Stand 42

HEIMROTH, Alain - Stand 51
Tel: 40 11 02 37/45 20 76 73
XVIII, XIX and XX century furniture and objects.

HOFFMANN, Roland - Stand 75
Tel: 40 12 87 29
Furniture, art objects, wood panelling (boiseries).

HUBERT, Claude
Tel: 48 74 25 08/40 12 44 27
Fabrication of chairs. Restoration of antique furniture.

HUREL, Claude - NEW ART - Stand 27

IRAM - MINET, Annie - Stand 62 bis

ISABELLE - Stand 112
Tel: 40 10 12 90
XIX century furniture and unique objects.

JAM - Stand 1
Tel: 40 10 84 09
Posters and paintings.

JACKIE - Stand 61
Tel: 40 12 36 66 - Fax: 40 12 04 62
French antiques, provincial furniture in fruit woods. Chandeliers in crystal and iron, wood panelling (boiseries) and large book cases.

JEAN-CLAUDE - Stand 64
Tel: 40 12 36 66 - Fax: 40 12 04 62
Provincial furniture in fruit woods, lighting and decorative objects.

KALFON, Guy - Stand 31

KAPE, Simone - L'ESCAPADE - Stand 90

KNUTH Studio 26 - Stand 26
Tel: 42 12 24 57 - Fax: 40 10 13 08
XVIII and XIX century furniture and objects.

KOLSKY, Gisele - Stand 53
Specialty: tables.

KRIVONOS, Michel - Stand 41
Table arts.

LALUQUE, Claude - Stand 92
Tel: 40 12 85 51 - Fax: 40 10 13 08
Art Nouveau glass, Gallé, Daum, bronzes and objects.
Qualified expert.

LAMBREQUIN ANTIQUITES
Tel: 40 12 07 71/(16) 86 96 51 24
Antique furniture, paintings, drawings and decorative objects.

LARGEAULT, Nicole - Stand 107
Tel: 40 12 83 54
Art Nouveau and Art Deco.

LAROUSSE-TROMBETTA - Stand 69

LASSERIE, Edith - Stand 136

LEDELEY, Patrice - Stand 67

LEGRAND, Eliane - Stand 86

LEPOT, Françoise - Stand 65

LEVANNIER, Alice et Luc - Stand 50

LE MAIRE, Jean-Michel - Stand 109

LE MANOIR - Stand 116

LEMOINE, Maurice - Stand 74
Tel: 40 11 37 94
Art Nouveau, Art Deco: glass, furniture, engravings, sculpture.

LEPAGE, Phillippe - AU PETIT MAYET - Stand 103

LOEFFLER, Charles (see BROC' ART) - Stand 113

LUCCA ANTIQUITES - Stand 139
Tel: 64 93 10 30
XVIII and XIX century furniture, glass and crystal.

M.J.M. - J. BESSON - Stand 89

MAGNE, Simone - Stand 93
Tel: 40 12 55 48
Antique arms and military objects.

MANIERES, J.F. - Stand 133

MARC, Marcel - Stand 54
Tel: 40 10 24 80
Antiques, lighting, repair of chandeliers.

MARX, Jean-Claude - Stand 64
Tel: 40 12 36 66/40 11 58 15 - Fax: 40 12 04 62
Furniture and decorative accessories, chandeliers and large book cases.

MARZET, Claude-Annie - Stand 97
Tel: 40 11 95 49
Art Nouveau glass: Rousseau, Walter, Decorchemont. Gallé and Daum.
Ceramics.

MASLIAH, Guy - Stand 111
Tel: 40 12 61 56/47 47 48 37
XVIII and XIX century antiques from Japan and China: furniture, bronzes,
ceramics. Some French antiques.

MEKIESS, Claude - Stand 36

MEKIESS, David - Stand 20

NACHTIGAL, Olivier - Stand 87
Tel: 40 11 28 91
Art Nouveau and Art Deco.

NATLYNE - Stand 49
Tel: 40 11 04 64 - Fax: 40 10 13 08
Regional French XVIII and XIX century natural wood furniture and decorative objects.

NEFF, Roger - Stand 120

NEW ART, Claude Hurel - Stand 27

NOSTALGIE DU PASSE - Stand 126
Tel: 40 10 83 57
Collectibles.

ODIN, Elisabeth - Stand 66

OLIVE, Didier - Stand 115
Art Nouveau.

PERQUIS - LA GRANDE ROUE - Stand 82
Tel: 40 11 55 53 - Fax: 48 85 31 36
XVIII, XIX, XX century: furniture, objects, paintings.

PHILIPPE - Stand 32
Tel: 40 11 75 75/40 10 03 90 - Fax: 40 12 33 90
XVIII and XIX century fireplaces, furniture and objects.
Architectural elements, marble, boiseries (wood panelling), grills, railings, gates, doors. Bronze and copper for the interior, custom made.

PHILIPPE, Michel - Stand 119

PHILOMENE - Stand 19

PISTINER, Gisele - Stand 73

PORTEFAIX, Huguette - Stand 121
Tel: 40 10 13 40
Art Nouveau and Art Deco.

LA PROVIDENCE - Stand 84

RAFFY, G. - Stand 83
Tel: 47 70 36 51
Old books, maps, engravings.

RENAUD, Geoffroy - Stand 102

RENAUD, Yves - Stand 99

RIDEL, Rosette - Stand 45

ROBERT, Yvette
ANTIQUITES - Stand 48
Tel: 40 11 26 72 - Fax: 40 10 13 08
XIX century lighting, lamps, porcelain, tole, bronze, bronze sconces, mirrors.

SABATIER Nadine - Stand 135
XVIII and XIX century furniture, bronzes and decorative objects.

SAINT-PIERRE, Catherine - Stand 123
Tel: 40 10 29 80 - Fax: 40 10 13 08
XIX century furniture and objects of curiosity.
XVII to XIX century antique French and other fabrics. Antique trimmings.

SAMY ANTIQUITES - Stands 122 and 52
Tel: 40 11 56 78 - Fax: 44 53 08 58
Napoléon III furniture, crystal, chandeliers and art objects, luterie, clocks, sculpture.

SASSON, David - Stand 21

SAY, Alexia - Stand 100
Tel: 40 12 11 07
Art Nouveau (Daum, Gallé, Walter), furniture of Ecole de Nancy, bronzes.

SCHAFFLER, Paul - Stand 75 bis

SCHWETZ, Charles - Stands 5 and 15
Tel: 40 11 98 94
Meissen porcelain, paintings, pastels. European and Oriental porcelain, small furniture and table arts.

SIMON - Stand 44

SOYET, Bernard - Stand 118
Tel: 40 12 76 41/42 58 64 92 - Fax: 40 10 13 08
Furniture in fruit woods and paintings.

STERG, Didier - Stand 131
Tel: 40 11 99 20/42 81 35 52 - Fax: 40 10 13 08
XIX century furniture and art objects.

STERG, Albert - Stand 22
Tel: 40 12 93 27
XIX century furniture, paintings, art objects, grand pianos, decorative filing cabinets.

SZLOS Daniel et Fils - Stand 55

SZLOS, Norbert - Stand 40

TEBOUL, Alain - Stand 38

TEISSIER, Renaud - Stand 114
Tel: 40 12 31 83
Art objects, collectors' post cards and antique arms.

TOUPENET, Raymond - Stand 6
Tel: 40 12 71 77/40 31 73 93
1900 to 1930 furniture and objects, glass by Gallé and Daum, sculpture. Everything to do with the Ecole de Nancy.

TOURNIGAND, Valerie - Stand 94-95
Tel: 40 12 20 17
Lighting and furniture.

TOURNIGAND, Yvette - Stand 34
Tel: 40 11 05 55
Lighting.

TRADITION - Stand 56
Tel: 40 12 66 91

XVIII century furniture and XIX century paintings.
Qualified expert in furniture.

TROJANOWSKI, Louis - Stand 43

TROJANOWSKI, Samuel - Stand 52

TURYSK, Michel - Stand 28

TZAFA, Avner - Stand 47

VALERIE - Stand 94-95

VERRACHIA, Christiane - Stand 110 bis

LES VERRES DE NOS GRANDS-MERES - Stands 2 and 3
Tel: 40 12 72 19 - Fax: 40 12 65 13

Glass and crystal. Assortment of antique and contemporary glasses, odd
lots and complete sets, decanters.

AU VIEUX MOULIN - Stand 12
Tel: 40 11 11 82

XIX century French and English furniture, objects, chandeliers, pier glasses, office furniture.

VYNCKE, Andree - Stand 14
Tel: 40 12 92 75

Art Nouveau, Art Deco.

WAJEMAN, Robert - Stand 132
Tel: 40 11 18 63/42 54 12 84

XIX century furniture in mahogany and walnut. XVIII and XIX century faience,
copper and brass.

ZOI, Philippe (See PHILIPPE)

ZYSSET, Morel - Stand 19
Tel: 40 10 11 50 - Fax: 40 10 13 08

Art Nouveau glass: Gallé, Daum, Icart. Sculpture in bronze and marble of
the XIX century. Books, paintings and engravings.

ALLÉE 2

Allée 2 has great collections of French country
furniture. There are some fine examples of armoires
from Normandy and Brittany and interesting furniture
from old shops, offices, bakeries, pharmacies,
architects' desks. There are also a couple of dealers in
fine classic Louis XV and Louis XVI furniture as well
as good collectibles.

ABDELLATIF, Mona - PRESENCE DES SIECLES - Stand 188

ANGELOU, Dominique - Stand 141
Tel: 40 12 66 29
XVII and XVIII century furniture and decorative objects.

ANTICA - Stand 140
ATHIAS, Monique
Tel: 40 12 93 85
Posters.

ANTIQUITES 205 - Stand 205

BESSON, Jacqueline - Stand 197

BICHON, Simone - Stand 183

BLANC, Gerard - Stand 160
Tel: 40 12 43 75
Old store furniture and curiosities.

BOURIQUET, Jacques - Stand 199
Tel: 40 10 23 56
XVIII and XIX century furniture in natural wood and paintings.

BOUTELOUP, Huguette - Stand 169
Tel: 40 12 24 08
XVIII and XIX century furniture in fruit woods. Art objects.

BOUTET, Gerard - Stand 160 bis
Tel: 40 10 82 50
XVII, XVIII and XIX century furniture.

BOYER, Brigitte - Stand 176
Tel: 40 12 26 49
Furniture and objects.

BRIS, Maurice - Stand 186

BUOB, Monique - Stand 204

CABILI, Albert - Stand 144

CAZENAVE, Christine - Stand 153
Tel: 40 12 80 32/46 47 68 67
XVIII and XIX century French furniture.

LA CERISAIE - Stands 151 and 152
BARREAU, Jamy
Tel: 40 12 02 56
XVIII century furniture in fruit woods, paintings and decorative objects of the XVIII and XIX centuries.

CLAVERIE, Elisabeth - Stand 179
Tel: 42 59 51 57
Oriental Art: furniture, art objects and sculpture.

CUER, Christian - Stand 155

DANIELE B. - Stand 146
Tel: 40 12 83 59
XVIII and XIX century furniture and decorative objects.

DAUTAIS Catherine - Stand 168
Good quality.

DELAGE - Stand 194 bis
Tel: 40 11 26 09
XVIII and XIX century furniture.

DESCHAMPS, Philippe - Stand 144
Tel: 40 11 68 93 - Fax: 42 52 78 87
XVIII century furniture.

DESPRAIRIES, Monique - Stand 143
Tel: 40 11 59 69/45 32 51 83
XVIII and XIX century furniture in fruit woods.

DE RIDDER, Thierry - Stand 201
Tel: 40 11 28 38
French rustic furniture of the XVIII and XIX centuries.

DJIAN, Yves - Stand 184
Tel: 40 11 24 42 - Fax: 42 72 96 97
XIX century furniture, chairs and paintings.

DOREL - Stand 174
Tel: 40 12 57 70
Antique musical instruments, lecterns, music stands. French furniture.

DUMONS, Jean-Louis - Stand 178

ENTRE-TEMPS - Stand 168
Tel: 40 10 25 94
XIX century furniture and decorative objects.

ETENDART, Sylvia - Stand 190

FERRAND, J.L. et B. - Stand 147 and 148
Tel: 40 10 25 88 - Fax: 40 02 95 34
XVIII century French regional furniture in natural and painted wood.

AU FIL DES TEMPS - Stand 161
Tel: 40 11 78 77 - Fax: 40 10 13 08
XVIII to early XIX (1833) century furniture.
Certificates of expertise furnished. Will undertake restoration by confirmed artisans if necessary.
Qualified expert.

GOLDENBERG, Leon - Stand 195

L'HERMITAGE
M. Chaumont - Stand 189
Tel: 40 10 93 75
XVII, XVIII and XIX century furniture.

KLASSER, Andre - Stand 181
Tel: (16) 40 11 25 45
Scientific and optical objects, old cameras and antique arms. Film memorabilia.

KUSZELEWIC, Henri - Stand 177
XIX century furniture.

LACHAUX, Phillippe - Stand 156 and 157

LAMREQUIN ANTIQUITES - Stand 183 bis
Tel: 40 12 07 71
Antique furniture, pantings, drawings and decorative objects.

LANOUX, Lylian - Stand 191 and 192

LASSERIE, Edith - Stand 137

LAURANT, Gisele - Stand 159
Tel: 40 11 25 99
XVIII and XIX century furniture and paintings.

LE LAVANDIN - Stand 172
GOAEC, Jeanne
Tel: 40 10 83 89
XVII, XVIII and XIX century furniture.

LUCCA, Lucien - Stand 139

MACHEFERT, Guy - Stand 200

MARTINEAU-CHERIGUENE, Helene - Stand 171
Tel: 40 11 59 69
Old office and shop furniture, book cases, work tables, Filing cabinets.

MOSES, Raymonde - Stand 149

MUSSON Michel - Stand 196

ORSO ANTIQUITES - Stand 185
Tel: 40 11 66 40
Charles X and Louis-Philippe furniture in mahogany and clear woods. Chairs and tables. Napoleon III gilded mirrors.

PALERO, Henri - Stand 158

PIPERAUD, Pascale - Stand 154

PREFERENCES - Stand 202
Tel: 40 11 63 67
Antiques, brocante, furniture, objects, paintings and jewellery.

LA PROVIDENCE - Stand 195

RENAUDIE, Claude - Stand 180
Tel: 40 11 59 69 - Fax: 40 10 13 08
Antique furniture from offices and shops and decorative objects.

RETI, Thomas - Stand 193 and 194

REVON, Dominique - Stand 203

RICHARD, Colette - Stand 182
Tel: 40 12 11 99 - Fax: 40 10 13 08
XVIII and XIX century French antiques and pop art objects in wood.

SICARI, Mireille - Stand 145
Table arts.

SWOBODA, Marcel - Stand 167

TABLES DU PASSE - Stand 142
Tel: 40 10 00 57 - Fax: 94 81 13 67
XIX century table arts: faience and porcelain.
Complete table services of glasses and china in perfect condition.

THIEBAUT, Bertrand - Stand 173
Tel: 40 12 48 85 - Fax: 40 10 13 08
Antique scientific instruments, marine objects, curiosities.

TREY, Anatol - Stand 166
Tel: 40 10 01 57
Russian art objects.

TREY, Boris - Stand 163
Tel: 40 10 01 57
XIX century painted regional furniture.

WAJEMAN, Robert - Stand 138
Tel: 40 11 18 63/42 54 12 84
XIX century furniture in mahogany and walnut. XVIII and XIX century faience,
bronze and copper.

WILMES, Maria - Stand 150

140 rue des Rosiers

A sprawling new building, all under glass: it houses 300 dealers, from whom the editors have selected a few with antiques, art and decorative objects of interest.

This market also displays an overwhelming amount of second rate merchandise.

A.B.J. CHEMINEES - Stand 105 and 4 rue Lécuyer
Tel: 40 11 44 78 - Fax: 40 12 87 44
Excellent selection of antique fireplaces, antique wood panelling, parquet, oak beams and all material for restoration.

ADENIS, Lionel - Stand 135
Tel: 40 11 67 10/46 42 16 26 - Fax: 47 36 25 67
African Art: masks, statuary, old fetiches, necklaces, chairs, fabrics, musical instruments, arms and archaeological objects.

AMADORY - Stand 74
Collectibles.

ANSALDI - Stand 243
Antique fabrics and linens.

ART COL ANTIQUITES - Allée Sud Stand 77
Tel: 40 12 88 79
XIX century furniture. Showcase collectibles.

ARTHUR TOYS - Allée Sud Stand 97
Antique toys, curiosities.

A TRAVERS LA VOILETTE - Allée Sud Stand 95
Tel: 47 71 25 18
Collectibles: perfume bottles, powder boxes, presentation cases, old advertising.

B&B - Stand 109
XVII and XVIII century furniture.

BARBERA - Stand 57
XVII, XVIII and XIX century furniture.

BARBIER, Theodore - Stand 236
Tel: 40 10 26 39
Decorative objects, old drawings and engravings, lighting.

BENJAMIN, Paul - Stand 185
Tel: 40 11 90 08
Paintings of all periods.

BENMAOR, David - Stand 55
Old linen and fabrics.

BESSARD, Claude - Stand 187
Tel: 40 12 86 88
Collectibles, contemporary art.

BESSIS - Stand 176
Paintings of all periods and frames.

LE BILLET DOUX - Stand 104
Tel: 40 11 31 93
XIX century furniture. Specialist in Napoléon III objects, liqueur cases. Boulle furniture.

BODART - Stands 224-225
Oriental art.

BODINIER - Stand 62
Paintings of various periods.

BOULET-DECAUX - Stand 249
XVII, XVIII, XIX century furniture.

BOURDETTE - Stand 152
XVII and XVIII century furniture.

BOUTARD - Stand 126
Oriental art objects.

BOUTELOUP - Stand 239
Paintings of various periods.

CABORNE-RONDEL, Yvonne - Stands 122-123
Tel: 40 11 59 70
Objects of curiosity and decoration, garden furniture and painted furniture.

CAMET - Stands 32-33
Art Nouveau and Art Deco.

CASTAGNE - Stand 41
Art Deco and objects of the 1950s and 1960s.

CHARMOY, Xavier - Stand 96
Books, documents, paintings.

CHEVALLIER-BULLES - Stand 172
Silver and antique jewellery.

CIEL, MA PUCE! - Allée Sainte-Sophie Stand 177
Tel: 40 11 26 76
Art Deco and Art Nouveau. Paintings, bronzes, lighting, perfume bottles, ceramics and glass.

CONSTANTIN, Jean-Michel - Stand 69
Decorative objects.

CORREAS - Stand 232
Perfume bottles.

COUDERC - Stands 34-44
XIX century furniture.

COVILLE, Jean-Pierre - Allée Sainte-Sophie Stand 47
Tel: 40 12 87 96
XIX century furniture and collectibles.

DAHROMANI - Stand 24
Carpets and tapestries.

DAOUD - Stand 84
Paintings of various periods and antique jewellery.

DARJOU-BARREAU - Stand 1
Tel: 40 12 88 75
XVII, XVIII and XIX century furniture and paintings.

DARNAULT, Veronique - Stands 17-18
Tel: 40 12 70 15
XVII, XVIII and XIX century furniture, paintings and antique jewellery.

DECANTICA - Allée des Rosiers Stand 244
Contemporary paintings, gouaches, water colors, drawings, small furniture and collectibles.

LE DRAGON MAGIQUE - Allée Sainte-Sophie Stand 67
Tel: 40.12.72.41
XIX century Chinese furniture and objects. Boxes, curiosities of the Far East.

DUBOIS DE MAROLLE - Stand 36
XVII and XVIII century furniture.

FERNANDES - Stand 194
Decorative objects and collectibles.

FERNANDEZ - Stand 29
Art Deco.

FERRY-CLEMENT - Stand 171
Tel: 40 11 54 46
Art Deco objects, watches and bracelets. Masonic objects, objects of curiosity and old paintings.

FEUGERE - Stand 91
Porecelain and faience.

FRANCK ANTIQUITES - Allée Voltaire Stand 103
Tel: 40 12 72 43
Korean and Japanese furniture. Objects of the Far East.

GALLAND, Alain - Stand 87
Tel: 40 12 88 98
Decorative objects, furniture and paintings of all periods.

GOLDMANN - Stand 92
Old articles of travel.

GONZATTO - Stand 110
Faience and porcelain.

GUERRICHE - MG GALERIE - Stand 183
Crystal and glassware. Furniture and paintings of all periods.

GUIGNARD - Stand 154
XIX century furniture and paintings.

GUILLAUME - Stand 153
XIX century furniture. XVII and XVIII century paintings.

HENRY DE TOURVILLE, Stephane - Allée Sainte-Sophie Stand 20
XVII, XVIII and XIX century furniture.

IMPRESSION 21 - Stand 214
Paintings of all periods.

J.B.R. - Stand 215
Books, comic books, documents.

JOIRKIN Pascal - Stand 1
Architectural elements, fireplaces and accessories.

JUAREZ - Stand 13
XVII and XVIII century furniture.

KHOSRAVI - Stand 78
Carpets and tapestries.

KLEIJMAN - Stand 156
Paintings of different periods. Some old linens.

KLEIN, Michel - Stand 151
Tel: 40 12 28 03
Furniture of the Haute Epoque, XVII and XVIII centuries.
Paintings of the XVII and XVIII centuries.

LAMBERT, Philippe - Stand 241
Tel: 42 12 69 95
Old drawings, paintings, engravings and books.

LAZAROVICI, Bernard - Stand 28
Tel: 40 10 00 45
Old engravings, estampes, original lithographs of the period 1863 to 1934,
principally of the caricaturist SEM.

LEDA DECORS - Stands 60-61
Tel: 40 12 74 88 - Fax: 34 87 06 53
XVIII and XIX century furniture, tapestries and chairs.
Gilded mirrors, decorative objects, tole, lighting.

LEDAY - Stand 149
Architectural elements, decorative objects.

LEDUC - Stand 65
Paintings.

LELLOUCHE, Guy - Stands 93-94
Tel: 40 12 87 08 - Fax: 42 81 43 48
XIX and XX century paintings and Oriental art objects.

LOPEZ - Stand 209
Crystal and glassware.

LYS DE FLORENCE - Stands 136-137
Art Deco

MARTIN, Michel - Stand 184
Marine objects.

MARX - Stand 106
Lighting
Stands 107-108
Architectural elements and decorative objects.

MASSON, Fabrice - Stands 120-121
Tel: 40 11 56 08
XVII and XVIII century furniture and decorative objects.

MELONCELLI - Stand 189
Collectibles.

MILAN - Stands 250-251-252-253
Rustic furniture.

MOREL - Stands 99-111-133
Crystal and glassware.

NARDOUX - Stand 141
Furniture of various periods. Collectibles.

NIKNAM - Stand 178
Oriental art objects.

OHANA - Allée Sainte-Sophie Stand 50
Tel: 40 12 88 56
Antique musical instruments: harpsichords, XVIII to XX century Italian violins.
Paintings.

OLIVIER - Stand 98
Antique jewellery.

ORSO ANTIQUITES - Stand 35
Tel: 40 11 80 44
Furniture: Restoration, Charles X (commodes, desks, bookshelves, tables, in mahogany and clear woods), Louis-Philippe (chairs and tables), Napoléon III gilded mirrors.

LE PATIO ANTIQUE - Stands 53-54-55
Tel: 40 12 77 19
XVII and XVIII century furniture. Decorative objects.

PEARCE, Catherine - Stand 268
Table arts.

PEARON, Michel - Allée Sud Stand 81
Tel: 40 10 99 10
Collectibles and furniture of diverse periods.

PELLIER - Stand 160
Rustic furniture.

PETITOT - Stand 206
Contemporary art.

PICAULT, Dominique - Stands 276-277
Tel: 40 12 84 01
Paintings.

PIERRON - Stand 205
XVII and XVIII century paintings.

PINTA-FAYELLE - Stand 200
Paintings.

RASPAIL, Richard - Allée 1 Stands 68-79
Decorative objects and furniture of different periods.

REDIER, Helene - Allée Sainte-Sophie Stand 85
Tel: 40 11 17 72
French and Russian silver and antique jewellery.

REDONDO - Stand 181
Paintings of various periods.

REMY - Stand 201
Art Deco. Paintings.

RENVOISE LE GAL - Stand 169
Collectibles. Furniture of all periods.

RIBES - Stand 9
XVII and XVIII century furniture.

RICCI, Jean - Stand 16
Tel: 40 12 32 10
Old watches.

SARFATI, Marie-Paule - Stand 39
Tel: 40 11 28 07
Furniture and paintings of diverse periods.

SAUQUET - Stand 80
XVII to XIX century furniture.

SECCHI - Stand 125
Art Deco.

SEFFER-BOUCHEZ - Stands 179-180
Diverse furniture, old fabrics and linen.

SELVES, Marcel - Stand 269
Table arts.

SOLARZ - Stand 265
Collectibles.

SOLEIL NOIR - Allée Dauphine Stands 58-59
Tel: 40 12 74 09
Chinese and Egyptian archaeology.
Han, Tang, Ming. XVIII and XIX century Chinese and Japanese furniture, Indian and Thai sculpture from the XI to the XVI century.

SONIGO - Stands 284-285
Fireplaces and accessories. Some furniture of various periods.

SOPEXIM - Stand 266
Carpets and tapestries.

SOURICE, Benilde - Stand 42
Tel: 40 12 88 00
Showcase collectibles, antique jewellery.

SOUYRIS - Stands 6-7-8
Paintings.

TANZINI, Luigi - Stands 207-212
Sculpture and collectibles.

THIEBLEMONT - Stand 233
Old watches.

VAYSSE - Stands 223-229
Art Deco.

VERRECHIA - Stand 193
Decorative objects and collectibles.

ZEM - GALERIE MUZE - Stand 202
Tel: 40 11 18 03
Art Deco and decorative objects.

142 rue des Rosiers and rue Jean-Fabre

A handsome modern building with its own parking facility in the basement. Fully equipped with escalators, coffee bars and excellent lighting, the market displays a broad mix of the good, the bad and the ridiculous. A few of the merchants, with well defined specialties deserve a visit.

ALBERTINI, Anouk - Stand 38
Tel: 40 11 72 67
Modern paintings and photographs.

ALPHA ANTIQUITES - Stand 73
Tel: 40 11 99 33
Antiques, decorative objects, gilded bronze and crystal.

ANTIQUITE 56 - Stand 56
Tel: 40 11 88 98 - Fax: 45 98 01 40
XVII and XVIII century furniture, paintings and decorative objects.

LE BRICK A BARC - Stand 95
Tel: 40 11 32 31
Marine and science antiquities and curiosities.

CABORNE-RONDEL Yvonne - Stand 72
Tel: 40 10 17 78
Garden furniture, painted furniture and decorative objects.

COLLECTIONS - Stands 77-78
Tel: 40 11 47 67
XIX and XX century bronze sculptures. Decorative objects and ceramics.

L'ESCALIER DE CRISTAL - Stand 44
Tel: 40 11 37 34
Napoléon III furniture, porcelain de Saxe, fans.

GALERIE 33 - Stand 33
Tel: 40 11 21 25/46 36 74 03
Specialist in silver and ceramics from 1870s.

GOCINE - Stand 13
Tel: 40 11 16 75
Movie, photo and music items for the collector.

L'HOMME DE PLUME - Stand 211-12-13
Tel: 40 11 49 33 - Fax: 43 44 63 12
XIX century furniture and objects with a special focus on the desk.

INTERIEURS - Stand 174
Tel: 40 11 72 18
XIXth century curiosities and furniture.

LEFAUCHEUX - Stand 76
Tel: 40 11 13 19
Products for maintenance and restoration of furniture, objects, marble, flooring. Advice, demonstrations and sale by correspondence.

LELLOUCHE, Guy - Stands 84-85
Tel: 40 11 48 93 - Fax: 42 81 43 48
XIX and XX century paintings and Oriental art.

LIBRAIRIE BOULOUIZ - Stand 168
Tel: 40 11 85 58/40 35 66 17
Old books with beautiful bindings, old documents, old maps, modern books of the great illustrators, books on art and decoration, signed bindings.

LUCIE H. - Stand 28
Tel: 40 11 79 15
XIX and XX century curiosities, paintings, drawings, ceramics, glass and furniture.

LORGERE, Herve - Stand 225-226
Tel: 40 11 06 66
Antique furniture and decorative objects from the XVIII century to the 1940s.

MAEVOR - Stands 218-219
Tel: 40 11 13 09
XIX century furniture and decorative objects, specializing in Biedermeier and French.

MAKASSAR FRANCE - Stands 120-121
Tel: 40 11 13 56
Art Deco furniture, paintings, bronzes, lighting and decorative objects.

OPUS 93 - Stand 93
Tel: 40 10 90 96
Paintings from various periods. XX century furniture, objects, clocks and curiosities.

RONDEURS DES JOURS - Stand 176
Tel: 40 11 48 98
Ceramics from Provence and curiosities.

SMOKER ANTIQUITES - Stand 132-133
Tel: 40 12 24 40/47 70 73 62
Antiques and collectibles related to smoking.
Boxes in marquetry, writing stands and canes.

URANIUM - Stands 187-188
Tel: 40 11 29 82
Clocks, jewellery, silver and paintings.

ZAMBAKEJIAN, Zohrab - Stand 3
Tel: 40 11 29 82 - Telfax: 34 28 77 01
XVIII and XIX century furniture and art objects, especially Boulle and Napoléon III. Paintings, bronzes, clocks and fireplaces.

ZERLINE - Stand 209-210, 98-99
Tel: 40 10 92 51
XIX century furniture, decorative items and faience.

104 rue des Rosiers and 18 rue Paul-Bert

The Marché Paul Bert is one of the largest and most typical of the Paris Flea Market. With over 200 shops covering every imaginable specialty, it has become a favorite shopping mall for professionals from all over the world. The dealers of the Paul Bert are good negotiators, but the quality of their wares certainly deserves hard bargaining from both buyers and sellers. Most of the market is outdoors so summertime browsing becomes a real pleasure.

ALLÉE 1

ANGEL- Stand 33

AUX TEMPS PASSEE - TOVI - Stand 12

BABY BOOM PLASTIC - Stand 104
Tel: 48 07 27 21
70's furniture, specialty in colored plastic.

BACHELIER ANTIQUITES - Stand 17
Tel: 40 11 89 98 - Fax: 40 11 72 08
Kitchen objects, wine objects, potteries from the southwest, Provence, Alsace, Savoie, wicker-work and baskets. Old shop furniture and rustic furniture.

BARGHEON, Yvette - COLLECTIONS ANTIQUITES SHOPPING - Stand 22
Tel: 40 12 55 10/47 85 01 00
Antique furniture, decorative objects. Antique toys and dolls.

BERGFELD, Simon & Madeleine - Stand 59

BERNARD, J.-Claude - Stand 61

BERNARD, Franco - Stand 55

BERTRAND, Ester - Stand 14
Furniture and objects from 1830 to 1900.
Garden furniture and baker's furniture.

BOUCQ - Stand 6

BRANDOSSER - Stand 27

CANAL - Stand 120

CARPENTIER - Stand 11, 19
Tel: 45 22 53 16 - Fax: 45 22 53 16
Decorative objects and lighting.

CHAMAK, Didier - Stand 45

CHOUVET, Gerard - Stand 9
Tel: 40 11 23 09
Far Eastern art.

CLOS, Jacques - Stand 41

COHEN BOULAKIA, Armand - Stand 16
Tel: 40 12 19 32
Furniture, paintings and decorative objects from all periods.

COHEN Daniel - Stand 69

COUDOVEL - Stand 126

LES CROCOS - Stand 37
Tel: 40 09 01 35
1940's to 1970's paintings, objects, furniture and sculpture.

DAGOMMER, Chantal - Stand 71

DE FONTENEY, Antoine - Stand 144

FARMAN - Stand 73

FHALS, Francis - Stand 51

GONZALEZ IBANEZ - Stand 75

HERSCHTRITT, Laurent - Stand 2
Tel: 40 11 50 06/42 77 53 87
XIX and XX century cameras and photo equipment.
Qualified expert.

HOFFMAN, Rachel - Stand 55, 57, 128

IMBERT, Jean-Pierre - PATALANO, Evelyne - Stand 29
Tel: 40 12 39 73 - Fax: 44 81 81 47
Old furniture for shops, decorative architectural and garden objects. Wood panelling (boiseries) and architectural elements.

JOUEN, Daniel - Stand 65

JUKE BOX CAFE, Jean-Claude Trauchessec - Stand 21
Tel: 40 11 40 00 - Fax: 40 11 03 36
1940's, 50's, 60's American furniture, collectors items: Juke boxes, neon signs, pin ball machines, guitars, soda parlor bars, stools and booths, 45 rpm records, pick-ups.

LACOUR, Bernadette - Stand 63
Tel: 40 10 05 30
Collectibles.

LESCHEVIN - Stand 136

LEVY, James - Stand 100

LUBICKI, E. - Stand 13
Tel: 40 12 65 40/42 08 46 73 - Fax: 48 03 42 16
XIX century furniture, chandeliers, diverse decorative objects.

JAUDEL, Marie - Stand 116
Objects of curiosity.

MARTIN, David Georges - Stand 122
Tel: 40 11 27 83
Specialty: XIX century paintings and drawings.
Old furniture and decorative objects.

MOLINARI, Michel - AU CLAPIER RUSTIQUE
Tel: 40 11 94 67 - Stand 67
Rustic furniture.

OBRY, Jean - Stand 108

PASSE SIMPLE - Stand 118

PEYRE, Jean-Gabriel - Stand 130
Tel: 40 10 92 00 - Fax: 42 61 14 99
XVII and XVIII century French faience and XVIII French porcelain.

PFENNIGER, Marie-Claude - Stand 15
Tel: 40 12 36 90
Decorative objects and curiosities.

PHILIPPE, Jeanine - Stand 25
Leather armchairs from the 1940's and 1950's. 1930's lighting and copies
of the 1930's.

PIRON, Gabriel - Stand 124 bis

PLANTARD - Stand 35

PRAVER PETIT - Stand 47

RAPIN, Philippe - Stand 112

RUIZE, Dominique - Stand 134
Tel: 40 10 90 84
Art objects and furnishings of the 1930's.

O.B.A. - BERTHON, Olivier - Stand 24
Tel: 40 12 72 41 - Fax: 45 35 16 51
Decorative objects, pop art, furniture, lighting.
Architectural elements in stone and marble.
Restoration of stone fireplaces and sculpture.

THEVENEAU, Philippe - Stand 25

VALLADE, Christian - Stand 43

VARENE, Susan - Stand 20

VOSFER ANTIQUITES - Stand 124

ALLÉE 2

ALPER, Henri - Stand 137

BAZIN, Patrick - Stand 123 bis
Tel: 40 12 60 36
Furniture and decorative objects.

BELAYCH, Christian - Stand 129
Tel: 45 00 44 96 - Fax: 45 00 70 27
Paintings of the XVI to XIX centuries. XVIII and XIX century furniture.

BERNARD, Jane - Stand 32
Antiques, decorative objects, gilded and sculptured wood, lighting, furniture.

BEBEYRIE - Stand 123

BOUCHER - Stand 40

CAMPANAX, Jean - Stand 26

CARPENTIER, Guy - Stand 34
Tel: 40 12 64 67
Antiques, brocante, chandeliers, billiard table lamps, bakers' shelves.

CHEZ DANY - Stand 105
Tel: 40 11 13 60
XVIII century chandeliers, furniture and art objects. Napoléon III lighting.

COHEN, Armand Boulakia - Stand 16
Tel: 40 12 19 32
Antique furniture and decorative objects.

CORMERAIS - Stand 129

GOLDBERG - Stand 115

HASSAN - Stand 111

HERSCHTRITT, Laurent - Stand 2
XIX and XX century cameras and photographic equipment.

H.P. ANTIQUITES - Stand 131
Tel: 40 11 94 09/45 35 44 54 - Fax: 45 35 44 54
Antiques, decorative objects and old drawings.

H.P. ANTIQUITES - MARIAGE, Philippe - Stand 133
Tel: 40 11 91 42
Decorative objects and curiosities.

INCLAN, Gisele Renaud - Stand 141, 143
Tel: 40 11 37 59
Furniture and decorative objects.

JABOUILLE - Stand 38

JALLES, Yves - Stand 132 bis

JALLOT, PERLE - Stand 32
Antique textiles. XVIII and XIX century embroideries, silks, needlepoint, tapestries. Antique Asian embroideries.

LELIEF - Stand 119

LETELLIER, Jean - Stand 36
Tel: 40 12 04 45/40 12 71 01
Pianos from 1880 to 1940. Objects, furniture and paintings.

MAUMY, Nicole - Stand 99
Tel: 40 11 15 17
Objects of curiosity, silver and glass.

"LE MERCURE" - SABRIE-DROUART-LAURENT - Stand 127
Tel: 40 10 92 62
Paintings and objects of the XVIII and XIX centuries and contemporary.

MEMIN, Gilles - Stand 44
Tel: 40 12 26 17
Antiques and decorative objects.

MESSAGER, Michel - Stand 46

NETTER, Mariane - Stand 103

EURL O.C.A.C. - Mathon, Gerard - Stand 135
Tel: 40 11 72 03
XIX century glass "cloches maraîchères". Harnesses, carriages, other objects related to the horse, the hunt and engravings.

L'OCCAS DE L'ONCLE TOM - Stand 113
Tel: 40 12 78 38/47 81 85 71
XVIII and XIX century porcelain.

PFENNIGER, Florence - Stand 42
Furniture and objects of the XVIII and XIX centuries.
Porcelain of Bayeux.

PIERRET, Robert - Stand 121
Tel: 40 11 29 74
Decorative objects and frames.

THIERY, Didier - Stand 117

ALLÉE 3

ANDRE et JEAN JACQUES - Stand 147
Decorative objects.

AUVERNOISE - BUSSON, Yvonne
Tel: (16) 60 80 34 45/40 11 67 91 - Stand **58 ter** - Decorative garden accessories - Stand **60** - Painted furniture - Stand **161** - Mirrors - Stand **163** - Wrought iron - Stand **165** - Doors

BAGHERA, Robin - Stand 151
XX century objects.

BESSON, Roger - Stand 167
Tel: 42 48 02 91
XVIII, XIX and XX century decorative objects.

BOLGE, François - Stand 149
XX century decorative objects.

BOUCHETARD, Marc - Stand 169
Tel: 40 11 59 44
Wrought iron fire dogs, pop art pottery, furniture and chairs in pine.

BOUCHETARD, Catherine
Tel: 40 11 59 44 - Stand **280** - Fireplace accessories - Stand **282** - Chairs,
lighting, pop art and diverse objects.

CHABOLLE et GUERRE - Stand 48
1930's objects.

DERREY, Catherine - Stand 157
Tel: 40 11 17 58/40 10 93 28
Furniture and architectural elements of the XVIII and XIX centuries.

DELFLAT, Eric - Stand 153
Objects of curiosity.

DETAVE, Jean-Claude - Stand 56

HAVAS, Christophe - Stand 52
XVIII century objects.

GALERIE DEMONS et MERVEILLES - JEUILLARD, Michel - Stand 145
Tel: 40 12 25 55 - Fax: 54 42 12 01
XVI and XVII century European and Far Eastern archaeological and art
objects.

LERVIN, Henri - Stand 155
General brocante.

MAURISE - Stand 58
General brocante.

MARTIN, Charles - Stand 58 bis
Diverse decorative objects.

ROMAIN, Jean-Claude - Stand 54
Antique baggage and trunks.

SIMONET, Serge - Stand 155 bis
Paintings and furniture in marquetry.

VALENTIN-SMITH, Michel - Stand 159
Decorative objects.

ALLÉE 4

ANDREONI, Adrienne
"PAPILLON" - Stand 172
Tel: 40 11 17 22
Antique dolls, dolls houses, dolls clothes, old teddy bears and other stuffed
animals. Old cinema photographs, some autographed.

AZNAVOUR, Evelyne - Stand 203

BUREL, Thierry - Stand 160

BUSSON - Stand 176
Decorative objects.

CARLOTTO, Marc - Stand 209
Tel: 40 11 92 63/42 59 37 15
Antique paintings, objects, art objects and furniture.

CHABOLLE, Françoise - Stand 160 bis

CHRISTINE et ALAIN - Stand 199

CLEMENT - Stand 156

EVRARD, Michele - Stand 158
Furniture and decorative objects.

FRIGERI - Stand 146

GUENIFFET, Patrick - Stand 180
Tel: 42 62 99 80 - Fax: 43 63 26 72
Japanese antiques: arms, armour, prints, lacquered objects, bronzes, ivory, books.

HELLSTROM, Eric - Stand 215
Paintings.

HOUWINK, F. - Stand 213

KLEJMAN-JINTI - Stand 211

LALBALTRY, Hélène - Stand 164
Decorative objects.

LASNE, Christian - Stand 217
Marine objects.

LECLERCQ, Elisabeth - Stand 223
Tel: 40 10 23 03
Brocante, antiques and decorative objects of the 1940's.
Art Deco.

LENGLARE, Laurence - Stand 174
Tel: 40 11 91 47
Napoléon III furniture and objects.

LERICHE, Vicky - Stand 182
Tel: 45 04 38 87
1930's objects, ceramics.

LORGERE, Hervé - Stand 150
Tel: 40 11 06 66
XVIII and XIX century furniture, pier glasses, arm chairs, chandeliers, decorative objects.

MARTANO, Robert - Stand 166 - 168
Tel: 40 12 53 58
Decorative objects, faience and porcelain.

MEMOIRE - EPOCA - Stand 225
Tel: 40 12 67 20 - Fax: 45 44 85 82
Brocante, decorative objects, paintings.

MERLIN, Jean-Michel - Stand 154
XIX century furniture.

MEYER, Jean-Claude - Stand 162

MILLANT, Catherine - Stand 219, 221
Tel: 40 11 87 83
Objects of curiosity.

NAUDIN - Stand 205

PARISOT, Jean-Luc - Stand 178
Tel: 40 12 41 59
Military arms and memorabilia.

PEDEZERT, Maryse - Stand 148
Tel: 40 11 85 05
Decorative objects and furniture of all periods.

PHILIPPE, Charles - Stand 201

REYNAL, Christophe - Stand 227
Tel: 40 12 90 77 - Fax: 45 51 44 61
Antique frames from the XVII, XVIII, XIX centuries. Restoration and framing.
Old engravings and drawings.

ROUSSAT, Marie-Louise - Stand 211 bis

SCHWEIZER, Lisette et Henri - Stand 170
1930's objects.

SPIGELSHEIM, Lucie - Stand 152

THIRIOT, Alain - Stand 207

METCHKOUB, Loulon - Stand 229

ALLÉE 5

ARDALAN - Stand 192
Decorative objects.

AURINEL - Stand 229
Decorative objects.

BAINVEL - Stand 216
Old drawings.

BOUCHETARD, Marc - Stand 220
Tel: 40 11 35 55
Pottery.

BOUCHETARD, Marc - Stand 222
Tel: 40 11 35 55
Wrought iron fireplace accessories, garden furniture.

CAZENTRE - Stand 233
Decorative objects.

CERVANTES - Stand 251
1940 to 1950 objects.

CHAIZE, Eric - Stand 259
Tel: 40 10 08 04
XVIII and XIX century pier glasses. XVIII and XIX century furniture from Bordeaux. Mirrors in gilded wood.

DEVLAY, Ivan - Stand 235
Tel: 40 12 70 87
Objects of curiosity.

GALERIE DREVET - Stand 214
Tel: 40 11 91 14 - Fax: 42 54 74 69
Crystal chandeliers from the XIX century. Furniture and objects.

FLY - Stand 210
Decorative objects of the 1940's to 1950's.

GRISOT - Stand 218
Travel souvenirs.

GUEENON - Stand 202
Decorative objects.

JACQUELIN, M.N. - Stand 198
Tel: 40 12 88 31
Objects, curiosities and collectibles.

JEAN-PIERRE - Stand 194
Paintings.

LEVY-ALBAN, Sylvain - Stand 212, 253
Tel: 40 10 10 61
Antiques and decorative objects of the XVII and XVIII centuries. Specialty: tole and gilded and painted wood.

LE VIGOUREUX - Stand 257

DE MAS LATRIE, Jean - Stand 249, 208
Tel: 40 10 29 21
Furniture and antique objects from the XVIII century to the early XX century. Gilded sculptured wood, crystal chandeliers, wall sconces, candelabra.

MASSEN - Stand 196
Decorative objects.

NHO - Stand 255
Decorative objects.

PERRUCHOT - Stand 206
Diverse furniture.

PROSPER - Stand 231
Decorative objects.

REYNAUD, Martine - Stand 247
Tel: 40 12 28 40
Furniture and French pop-art objects, wrought iron and curiosities.

STOUPINA - Stand 245

URZANDI, Varus - Stand 204 bis
Old shop furniture.

ALLÉE 6

AGACE, Annette - Stand 232
Tel: 45 48 15 71/(16) 44 51 61 45/Fax: (16) 44 51 61 54
Antique luggage from 1850's to 1950's: Louis Vuitton, Hermes, Goyard.

APELSTEIN - Stand 79

ARMENJON, Agnes - Stand 224

CHAMAK, Raymond - Stand 93
Tel: 40 12 67 82
Chairs, armchairs, desks and objects in bronze. Paintings, drawings.

DELCLUZE, Guy - Stand 228, 230

DEMETER - Stand 89
Tel: 49 45 00 30/47 47 48 01- Fax: 45 56 02 84/46 40 07 99
Furniture and art objects from the end of the XVIII century to 1940. Neo-Classical furniture. XIX century paintings.

DEMOLLIENS - Stand 226

PIERRES D'ECOUEN - MARC MAISON - Stand 83
Tel: 34 19 81 03/40 10 12 15
Antique elements for interior and exterior architecture: objects in cast iron, wrought iron railings and gates, stone floors and fireplaces.

FOURTIN, Patrick - Stand 81
Tel: 40 10 17 87 - Fax: 42 81 40 66
1940's furniture and decorative objects, sculpture and lighting.

GOLLAIN - Stand 85

J.P. GROS - Stand 95

LARUE, Stephane - Stand 232 bis
XIX century furniture.

LOUOT, Axel - ARMES ANCIENNES - Stand 77
Tel: 40 10 99 89
Antique arms, military items.

NEBOUT - PIANOS - Stand 97
Tel: 40 10 94 15
Pianos.

PERRIER, Jean Luc - DECO BISTRO - Stand 87
Tel: 40 10 92 73 - Fax: (16) 85 40 76 17
Old bars and counters from bistros and cafes. Complete bistro decors.

THUILLIER, Marc - Stand 234

ALLÉE 7

BRAVARD - ILOUS - Stand 409
Tel: 40 10 23 74
Art Deco.

LE BRAQUEMART - Stand 286
Antique arms and military memorabilia.

D'ANTAN - Stand 420
Classic styles.

GAUTHIER, Alain - Stand 408, 418
Art Deco.

G.B.C. Antiquités - Stand 288
Art Deco.

HEDLEYS HUMPERS - Stand 414
Shippers.

ILOUIS - Stand 411
Art Deco.

LINES - Stand 284
Classic styles.

LOUIS BLEU - Stand 410
Decorative objects.

MARTIN, Catherine - Stand 417
Art Deco.

MATTERN, Charles - Stand 404
Tel: 43 66 45 14
Decorative objects.

THEMES - Stand 402, 416
Tel: 40 11 33 01 - Fax: 40 53 02 96
Art Deco furniture 1930 to 1940.

VILLA BORGHESE - Stand 401, 403, 405, 415, 423
Classic styles.

WALLIS - Stand 406
Modern paintings.

110 rue des Rosiers

The Marché Serpette is not only one of the most fascinating markets in the Puces, but it is the most accessible.

Located inside, just below the rooftop parking lot, it is a marvellous place to explore any time and especially in bad weather. The range of antiques, art and collectibles is as wide as you will find anywhere, from the XVII century through Art Nouveau and Art Deco to the contemporary.

ALLÉE 1

PYTEL - Stand 1
Tel: 40 10 16 10
XVIII and XIX century furniture, paintings and showcase objects. Specialist in art of the hunt.

VALDO - Stand 2

CANTO - Stand 3

CHINN - Stand 4
Tel: 40 10 03 40

RAUD - Stand 5
Tel: 40 11 04 76
Statuary of the Haute Epoque.

CABOTSE, Michel - Stand 6
Tel: 40 11 29 16/(16) 47 47 16 72 - Fax:(16) 47 20 72 20
Early XX century paintings, old and recent drawings and watercolors. XX century furniture.

SANCHEZ - Stand 7
Tel: 40 11 54 14 (Ext. 59)
Old paintings, portraits, art objects. Old furniture, chairs and lighting.

MAURY ET DERIJINSKY - Stands 8-9
Tel: 40 10 17 88
Antique arms and military orders.

COUGOULE ET DEVERGNE - Stand 10

BENNAZAR, Pierre - Stands 11-14-15
Tel: 40 10 29 36
Paintings and gilded bronzes.

AKER, Albert et Colette - Stand 12
Tel: 42 64 63 72
Decorative objects, furniture, bronzes, lighting and marble.

BON, Michel - Stand 13
Tel: 40 11 85 80/43 29 87 15
XVIII, XIX and XX century furniture, objects and paintings.
Certificates of expertise upon request.

LE SAVOIR FER - Stand 16
Tel: 40 12 13 58/60 12 09 45 - Fax: 60 12 45 70
Copies of XVIII century table bases and chairs in wrought iron. XVII and XVIII century decorative wrought iron objects.
Contemporary line of cafe tables, chairs, armchairs and consoles.

FONTAINE - Stand 17
Tel: 40 10 22 24
Antiques and decorative objects.

LACAZE - Stand 18
Tel: 40 10 22 24
Antiques and decorative objects.

GUIGNARD ANTIQUITES - Stand 19-20, 29
Tel: 40 11 17 85
Certified antique furniture, art objects and paintings of the XVIII and XIX centuries.

KLEJMAN - Stand 21
Tel: 54 47 32 13
Primitive Art of Africa, Oceania and the Americas.

GLB CREATION - Stand 22
Tel: 40 12 91 60
Furniture and art objects.

DESPAS - Stand 23
Tel: 40 11 83 83
XVIII century furniture and decorative objects.

TIXIER - Stand 24
Tel: 40 11 83 83
Antiques and decorative objects.

BENCHETRIT - Stand 25
Tel: 43 39 19 54
Furniture and art objects.

GOSSELIN, Jean-François - Stand 26-26 bis
Tel: 40 10 13 50
XVIII and XIX century furniture, paintings and decorative objects.

GAMMES - Stands 27-30
Tel: 40 11 63 60
XVIII and XIX century objects and furniture.

LARDE, Monique - Stand 28
Tel: 40 10 02 21
Antique lace and household linens. Period clothing.

PREVOST - Stand 29 bis
Tel: 40 11 54 14
Marine and science antiques.

TIMSIT - Stand 30 bis
Tel: 40 10 18 94
Paintings and jewellery.

MAHE - Stand 31
Tel: 40 12 81 22
XVIII and XIX century furniture and objects.

LEDAY - Stand 32
Tel: 40 10 26 51
XVIII and XIX century furniture.

TESI, Pierre - Stand 33
Tel: 40 11 11 83
Modern paintings.

MOITY - Stand 34
Tel: 40 10 12 93
Engravings, gilded wood and paintings.

SUSSET, Olivier - Stand 35
Tel: 40 12 45 05
XIX and XX century paintings.

AUGEARD, Francine - Stands 36-36 bis
Tel: 40 10 00 94
XVIII and XIX century decorative objects.

VALENTIN-SMITH - Stand 37
Tel: 40 11 54 14

FORTIN, Clémence - Stands 38
Tel: 40 12 87 40
XVIII and XIX century painted and gilded furniture.

SAINT-OUEN ANTIQUITES - Stand 39
Tel: 40 12 75 62
Jewellery and paintings.

GABORIAUD, Marc et Gisèle - Stand 40
Tel: 40 11 26 92/47 90 19 09 - Fax: 47 90 18 86
Silver, decorative objects and furniture of the XIX century.

FORTIN, Lucien - Stand 41
Tel: 40 10 02 43

BENICHOU, Didier - Stand 42
Tel: 40 12 46 05
Carpets and antique furniture.

SERRE ET GATTOLIN - Stand 1
Tel: 40 11 72 88
Lighting.

RAUZADA, Alain - Stand 2
Tel: 40 12 54 62
XIX century furniture and decorative objects.

GUY-CLAUDE ANTIQUITES - Stand 3
Tel: 40 12 70 60
Art Nouveau and Art Deco lighting. Objects and glass of the 1900s. Decorative objects from Louis XV to Napoléon III.

REGNIER, Jean-Claude - Stand 4
Tel: 40 11 56 06
Decorative objects.

PEDROL, Alba - Stand 5
Tel: 40 12 05 63
Decorative objects, jewellery and hats.

CASSAN, Georges-Guillaume - Stand 6
Tel: 40 10 12 15/42 62 21 98
XVII to XX century sculpture, decorative elements. Furniture of the 1940s. Some paintings and curious chairs.

VARENNE, Catherine et Alexandre - Stand 7
Tel: 40 10 06 56
XX century paintings.

LANTZ, Isabelle - Stand 8
Tel: 40 11 54 14 (Ext. 55)
Diverse objects and curiosities.

VUAILLAT, Renaud - Stand 9
Tel: 40 11 06 08
Decorative objects.

MAKASSAR - Stands 10-11-12
Tel: 40 12 44 76
Art Deco furniture, paintings, bronzes, lighting and decorative objects.

JOSCAUD - Stand 13
Tel: 40 11 53 97
Paintings. Qualified expert.

GALERIE DOMINIQUE WEITZ - Stand 14
Tel: 40 11 84 12/43 78 15 29 - Fax: 43 78 95 04
Drawings, water colours and figurative paintings from the early XIX century to 1940. Photographic art from the end of the XIX century and between the years 1930 and 1970.

FEUZ - Stand 15
Tel: 40 11 08 51

LEBEL - Stand 16
Tel: 40 12 05 89
XVIII century furniture and objects. Paintings.

RENOULT, Françoise - Stand 17
Tel: 40 11 30 65
Objects of charm and curiosity.

ALLÉE 3

BABLEE - Stand 1
Tel: 40 10 02 43/40 12 87 40

LAFON - Stand 1 bis
Tel: 40 11 54 14 (Ext. 44)
Art Nouveau and Art Deco 1900-1950.

COSTEY, Jean-Paul - Stands 2-3-4
Tel: 40 12 26 38/42 71 72 04 - Fax: 42 71 72 05
Art Deco cocktail bars and furniture in precious and exotic blond woods,
restored by French artisans in the Costey ateliers.

MARAUT - Stand 5
Tel: 40 12 90 44
Bathrooms 1900.

GAUD ET PIRMAN - Stand 6
Tel: 40 11 54 14 (Ext. 50)
Furniture and art objects.

FOREST, Olwen - Stand 7
Tel: 40 11 96 38
Costume and designer jewellery from the 1920s to 1960s. Hollywood jew-
ellery worn by the stars. Art Deco crystal, plated silver, bathing beauties.

PREUX - Stand 8
Paintings.

CHEREST, LEVIEUX ET BRIAU - Stand 9
Tel: 40 12 63 64
XVIII and XIX century furniture and objects of curiosity.

GALLAND - Stand 10
Tel: 40 10 85 63
Paintings and art objects.

FOREST, Jacques - Stand 11
Tel: 40 11 96 38
Art Deco: paintings of bathing beauties, statuettes, ceramics, small furni-
ture and curiosities.

KIRILUK ET BONNET - Stand 12
Tel: 40 11 54 14
Cocktail bars and lighting.

BERTHON - Stand 13
Tel: 40 12 10 58
Old cigarette lighters and fountain pens.

GREGORIAN - Stand 14
Tel: 40 12 45 88
Regional furniture of the XVII and XVIII centuries.

LE MONDE DU VOYAGE - Stand 15
Tel: 40 12 64 03

LEJEUNE - Stand 16
Tel: 40 11 54 14
Natural wood furniture and decorative objects.

TOUSSAINT - Stand 17

QUITARD, Pierrette et Pierre - Stand 18
Tel: 40 10 00 24/34 87 61 88 - Fax: 34 87 63 22
XVII and XVIII century furniture and objects. Decorative wood panelling for libraries. Fireplaces in stone and wood. Tile and flagstone.

BRETONNIERE, Philippe - Stand 19
Tel: 40 12 31 75/ 42 65 13 63 - Fax: 42 66 28 96
XIX and XX century paintings, watercolors, drawings and sculpture. Qualified expert.

LA BOUTIQUE MAUVE - REMY - Stand 20
Tel: 40 11 00 75

MOREL, Pierre-Louis - Stand 21
Tel: 43 01 82 32
XIX century paintings of the Ecole de Paris and antique furniture.

ROCANTIC - Stand 22
Tel: 40 12 42 48
XVIII and XIX century decorative objects.

GANTELMI D'ILLE, Ghislaine - Stand 23
XIX century paintings.

HEIDENGER, Mino - Stand 24
Tel: 40 11 54 14
Decorative objects.

ALLÉE 4

BISTROTS D'AUTREFOIS - Stands 1-2
Tel: 40 12 90 06 - Fax: 42 79 97 51
1900-1930 bars and bar accessories, bistro and cafe furniture, completely restored. An excellent selection.

ROSENTHAL, Philippe - Stand 3
Tel: 40 11 54 14
Leather easy chairs and club chairs.

LEMAIRE, Anne-Marie - Stand 5
Tel: 40 12 36 56
Impressionist, Post-Impressionist, Post-Cubist and modern paintings.

TAMPESTA, Marly - Stand 6
Tel: 40 10 13 93
Objects from the XV century to the 1960s.

HARROS - Stand 7
Tel: 40 12 55 25
XIX and XX century decorative objects.

LES BILLARDS DE L'ANTIQUAIRE - Stands 8-9
Tel: 40 12 85 68

HALTUF, Radovan - Stand 10
Tel: 40 12 28 08
Art Deco lighting.

ROSENTHAL, Marie-Eve - Stands 11-13
Tel: 40 12 04 85/39 69 45 77 - Fax: 39 69 46 21
The best collection of XVIII century gilded wood mirrors, XIX century gold leafed fireplace mirrors. XVIII and XIX century pier glasses. Art Nouveau mirrors 1925. Most of the mirrors have their original gold leafing.

COLLIGNON, Jacques - Stand 12
Tel: 40 12 04 85 - Fax: 39 69 46 21
Paintings from the XIX century to the 1930s.

PERLOFF, Georges - Stand 14
Tel: 45 39 81 97
Medals, antique collectibles and objects of curiosity.

CRIEF-LOPEZ - Stand 15
Tel: 40 10 80 32
XVIII century furniture and faience.

MOUTON - Stand 16
Tel: 40 10 26 40
Art Deco decorative objects.

LENGLET - Stand 17
Tel: 40 10 23 25
European faience and porcelain of the XVII and XVIII centuries.

JO ET JO ANTIC - Stand 18
Tel: 40 10 01 50
XVIII and XIX century furniture, objects and paintings.

WROBEL, Georges - Stand 19
Tel: 40 11 54 14

SARFATI - Stand 20
Tel: 40 10 26 88
Decorative objects.

OUTEIRO - Stand 21
Tel: 40 12 21 07
Decorative objects.

BROULARD - Stand 22
Tel: 40 10 09 88
Antique decorative objects.

MORCOS - Stand 23
Tel: 40 10 08 79
Art objects and furniture.

COUGOULE ET BARROUX - Stand 24
Tel: 40 12 46 65 - Fax: 40 12 10 62
High quality antiques. XIX century natural wood, painted and gilded furniture.
Large warehouse.

GRUNENWALD, Christian - Stand 25
Tel: 40 10 12 44
Furniture and objects of the Haute Epoch. French and European faience.

ALLÉE 5

ARTISANAT PERSAN - Stand 1 Cour
Tel: 40 11 84 26/07 61 32 55 - Fax: 43 87 53 32
XVIII and XIX century Aubusson carpets, tapestries and tapestries for chairs.
Old Persian and Caucasian carpets and kilims. Cleaning and restoration.

D'YTHURBIDE, Olivier - FAUQUENOT, Benoît - Stand 2 Cour
Tel: 40 12 82 91/07 41 88 09
XVIII and XIX century paintings, furniture, art objects and silver.

GARMILLA MACON ET BON-MARIT - Stand 3
Diverse furniture and decorative objects.

PINEAU, Lucien - Stand 4
Tel: 40 11 45 75
Orientalist paintings from the French School, American, Italian and Belgian
Schools. Oriental furniture with mother of pearl inlays from Syria and Tunisia.
Art glass from the School of Nancy, Gallé, Daum, Lalique.

GALERIE ATALANTE - Stand 5
Tel: 40 11 81 99
XIX century paintings.

GARANJOUD ET BALESTIE - Stand 6
Tel: 40 11 26 69
XIX century furniture and decorative objects.

BEJANIN - Stand 7
Tel: 40 11 54 14 (Ext. 51)
XVIII and XIX century furniture.

COSTET, Hélène - Stand 9
Tel: 40 10 05 87
Furniture of the XVIII and XIX centuries, lamps, paintings, Napoléon III liqueur cases and showcase collectibles.

PEDERSEN - Stand 10
Tel: 40 12 98 87
Objects of curiosity.

SEGAS, Miguel et Gilbert - Stand 11
Tel: 40 12 28 11
Saddles.

GALLIBERT, Nicole - Stand 12
Tel: 49 45 06 07
XIX century furniture.

VIDAL, Micheline - Stands 13-15
Tel: 40 10 93 70
Art Nouveau, Art Deco.

BENNAZAR, Paul - Stand 14
Tel: 40 10 93 61
XIX to early XX century paintings from the French School and other European Schools.

GERONIMI - Stand 16
Tel: 40 11 81 06 - Fax: 45 00 15 11
XVIII and XIX century antiques.

PLAISANCE-BEAUCOURT - Stand 17
Tel: 42 82 10 90
Venetian glass and lighting. XX century furniture.

MASSERIE - Stand 18
Tel: 40 12 20 19

ALNOT, Colette - Stand 19
Tel: 40 11 54 14 (Ext. 49)/42 21 37 93 - Fax: 40 41 93 83
XIX century animal paintings and objects of curiosity.
XX century Italian glass.

CARIATIDES - Stand 20
Tel: 40 10 15 40
Decorative stained glass from the XVII century to 1930.
Speciality: Art Nouveau and Art Deco stained glass. Sculpture in marble, terra cotta and biscuit.

AFLALO, Pili - Stand 21
Tel: 40 11 27 48
XVIII to early XX century etchings, paintings, drawings, watercolors, engravings and decorative frames.

DUCHATEAU ET BRUNEAU - Stand 22
Tel: 40 11 97 15
XVIII and XIX century furniture and decorative objects.

ROY, Joël - Stand 23
Tel: 40 12 56 98
Paintings.

BAILLET - Stand 24
Tel: 40 12 77 43
Furniture in natural woods.

GANZL, Jacques - Stand 25
Tel: 40 10 91 17
Paintings, estampes, oriental art. Tsubes, lacquer, netsukes, okimones, arms, armour, bronzes from Japan, China and Tibet.

LEFEVRE - Stand 26
Tel: 40 12 40 78
Regional furniture.

HUSSARD - Stand 27
Tel: 40 11 42 55
XVIII century and Napoléon III decorative objects.

ALLÉE 6

DUBREUIL - Stand 1
Tel: 40 11 44 59

LOMBARD, Eric - Stand 2
Tel: 40 11 73 43
Decorative art objects from 1880-1940.

CHONIGBAUM ET FILS - Stand 3
Tel: 40 11 54 14 (Ext. 67)
Furniture and objects of curiosity.

ANTIQUES LINES - Stand 4
Tel: 40 11 54 14

LA BOUTIQUE - Stand 5
Tel: 40 12 26 21 - Fax: 40 10 99 16

JANKOWSKI - Stand 6
Tel: 40 11 99 16
Bathroom lighting, furniture, bronzes, mirrors and showcases for shops.

MEDIA NOCHE-MEZZANOTTE - Stand 7
Tel: 40 12 29 69
Glass art: Lalique, Verlys, Etzing. Table services.

RAVELINGHEIN - Stands 8-10
Tel: 40 12 40 89
Art Deco.

CHOLLET, Xavier - Stand 11
Tel: 40 12 22 14
XIX century furniture, lighting, curiosities and decorative objects.

GALERIE JAGER - Stand 12
Tel: 49 45 07 05
XX century paintings, sculpture and objects of curiosity.

CARETTO - Stand 13
Modern paintings and contemporary art.

ART DECO ANTIQUITES - Stand 14
Tel: 40 12 02 87
Art Deco furniture and objects.

DUPONT - Stand 15
Tel: 40 10 82 52
Furniture and objects of all periods.

PAQUEBOT - Stands 16-17
Tel: 40 12 34 28
Furniture and decorative objects of 1900 to 1940.

MARECHAL, Laurent et CHASTEL, Aline - Stand 18
Tel: 40 11 54 14 (Ext. 43)
Furniture of the 1930's and 1940's.

ORLIK, Richard - Stand 19
Tel: 40 11 54 14
Old paintings.

ROUSSEAUX - Stands 20-21
Tel: 40 11 54 14 (Ext. 66)
Rustic regional furniture.

ESTUPINA - Stand 22
Tel: 40 11 54 14
Specialists in antique luggage.

HARTER ET SINCEUX - Stand 23 Cour
Tel: 40 11 20 35
Decorative objects.

NOEL, Christian - Stand 24 Cour

ART CONCEPT - Stand 25 Cour
Tel: 40 11 12 26 - Fax: 40 11 83 85
Paintings, furniture, sculpture, lighting (1900-1950). Objects of curiosity and collectibles.

MORGE - Stand 13 Cour
Tel: 40 12 36 00
Armchairs.

FUTUR ANTERIEUR - Stands 14-15 Cour
Tel: 40 11 43 05
Art Deco furniture.

7 rue Jules-Vallès ■ Tel: 40 11 54 41

A covered gallery with over 100 shops dealing in everything from old books to feathered masks, prints, glassware and curiosities. Lots of objects of curiosity.

———————— MARCHÉ DES ROSIERS ————————

This market is in a small, self-contained, building which houses a concentration of dealers in Art Nouveau and Art Deco. It is just off the rue des Rosiers at 3 rue Paul-Bert.

ART NOUVEAU ART DECO
PAUL GENER - Stand 14
Tel: 40 12 43 62
Art Nouveau and Art Deco glass. Some furniture.

MICHEL GIRAUD GALERIE - Stand 7
Tel: 40 11 21 15 - Fax: 46 41 00 65
Specialist in Art Nouveau and Art Deco, 1900 to 1930.
What they don't have, they'll find for you. They are experts in 1900s cameo glass.

BERNARD LIAGRE - Stand 6
Tel: 40 10 18 91/(16) 85 56 39 89 - Fax: (16) 85 78 77 55
Art Nouveau and Art Deco glass, ceramics, bronzes, lighting and furniture.

CHRISTIAN SERRES - Stand 8
Tel: 40 12 97 65 - Fax: (16) 85 92 06 78
Art Nouveau and Art Deco glass and lighting.

———————— MARCHÉ L'USINE ————————

18 rue des Bons-Enfants ■ Tel: 40 12 42 14 (Guardian)

A remarkable collection of architectural elements for interior and exterior. 10,000 square feet on two levels.

A favourite for professionals. The best time to go is early Thursday or Friday.

99 rue des Rosiers and 136 av. Michelet

From the 300 merchants in the Vernaison, the editors have carefully selected those they consider the best and most reliable. There are many others who deal in some antiques, art, second hand furniture and decorative objects of interest to those who have the time to meander through the stalls until something catches their eye. But we have tried to keep our focus on those merchants who might have something of value for the decorator, the architect or the discriminating individual.

ANTIQUITES DE LA TABLE - Allée 6 Stand 115
Tel: 42 05 07 86
Table arts.

ANTIQUINDUS - Allée 1 Stand 3
Tel: 49 45 07 32
Art and antiques of the Far East and the Islamic world, including old carpets, paintings, lithographs. Some old French faience and porcelain.

L'ARLEQUIN - Allée 7 Stands 128-128 bis
Tel: 40 11 16 38
Household linens, antique lace, decorative objects.
Old fashion accessories.

ATMOSPHERE - Allée 1 Stand 23
Mirrors.

AUBERT, Bernard - Allée 9 Stands 203-204
Antique furniture, objects and jewellery.

BALBON, Denise - Allée 8 Stand 185
Tel: 40 12 75 35 - Fax: 40 12 75 35
Specialist in XVII to XX century glass and liqueur cases.
Qualified expert.

BARRERE - Allée 8 Stand 183
Tel: 40 12 77 16 - Fax: 46 55 35 97
Old crystal, Baccarat, Saint-Louis. Gold leafed frames, bronzes.

BLANC, Jean-Paul - Allée 9 Stand 209
Tel: 40 12 57 27
Old toys, advertising signs and posters of 1900 to 1970.

BOURDONNAIS, Maite - Allée 5 Stand 90
Old post cards.

BOUVIER - Allée 10 Stand 260
Tel: 40 12 46 52
All styles of furniture.

CAMILLE - Allée 9 Stand 215
Tel: 40 12 66 47
Excellent collection of armoires and rustic furniture.

CASTILLO, Francisco - Allée 9 Stand 224
Icons and art objects.

👑 **CATAN** - Allée 9 Stand 227
Tel: 40 10 19 41
Remarkable extra large tables made of a combination of old wood elements and new. XVIII century rustic natural wood furniture, bridal armoires, tables, commodes, buffets.

CHAUVET, Jean-Paul - Allée 1 Stand 34 and Allée 4 Stand 82
Tel: 40 11 93 78/40 11 64 95
Good selection of XIX century French silver, solid and plated. Crystal objects mounted on silver bases.

CROLET, Erick et Tracey - Allée 9 Stand 205
Tel: (16) 44 78 54 85
Old furniture and objects. Restoration.

DAHAN, Françoise - Allée 1 Stand 4
Tel: 40 11 26 95
XVIII and XIX century fans, silver, showcase collectibles.

👑 **DE LATTRE, Marie-Ange et Dominique** - Allée 1 Stand 47
Tel: 40 12 68 89
XIX and XX century posters and books. One of the best poster collections in Paris.

DEROUET, Jean-Paul - Allée 10 Stands 255-257
Tel: 49 59 12 41
Large choice of rustic furniture of the XVIII and XIX centuries. Specialist in marvellous tables.

DERREY, Catherine - Allée 8 Stand 176
Tel: 40 11 17 58
XVIII and XIX century architectural elements, wood panelling (boiseries), furniture and store furniture. Statues and large decorative objects.

DIGIART - Allée 1 and 3 Stand 14 (corner)
Tel: 40 11 61 34/40 12 68 95 - Fax: 40 12 12 60
Specialist in marble, fireplaces, consoles, tables. Lighting: chandeliers, lanterns, sconces. XVIII century pendulum clocks. XIX century paintings, sculptured wood consoles, fireplace accessories, mirrors, porcelain from China and Japan. Silver. Custom work in marble and bronze.

DUPERRIER, Claude - Allée 7 Stand 141 bis
Tel: 40 10 01 18
Marvellous old luggage.

FARD, Torbati - Allée 8 Stand 196
Tel: 40 12 76 80/46 63 34 62
Antique rustic furniture and objects.

FARHAD, Imankhan - Allée 9 Stand 219
Tel: 40 10 23 68/48 27 71 27
Specialist in rustic furniture.

FRANCINE DENTELLES - Allée 7 Stands 121-123, 140 bis
Tel: 40 10 93 96/40 12 05 58
Wonderful collection of old linen, lace, fabrics, objects and 1900s fashion.

FRANÇOISE - Allée 1 Stand 4 and Allée 4 Stand 74 bis
Tel: 40 11 26 95
XIX century silver, objects.

FUSIER, Lucien et Bernard - Allée 10 Stands 239-240-242-244
XVIII and XIX century furniture and decorative objects.

FUTUR ANTERIEUR - Allée 10 Stand 246
Tel: 44 85 97 59 - Fax: 44 85 39 15
Egyptian antiques: bas-reliefs, masks of sarcophogae, divinities in bronze and wood, vases in alabaster, amulets, ceramic statuettes (oushebtis).

GALLAND, Alain - Allée 1 Stand 31
Tel: 40 12 88 97/39 83 50 90
Beautiful and high quality regional furniture and objects.

GIOVANNONI, Janine - Allée 7 Stand 141
Antique linens and fabric.

GIOVANNONI, Nicholas - Allée 3 Stand 146
Table arts.

GISELLE - Allée 1 Stand 19
Rustic tables and book cases.

GOLDMANN, N. - Allée 10 Stand 250 and Allée 6 Stand 17
Porcelain and vases.

HAULLE, J.- C. - Allée 8 Stand 181
Tel: 40 10 81 16
Antique books.

HORDE, Olga - Allée 6 Stand 111
Tel: 69 09 51 60
Antiques and second hand.

"INSOLITE"
Iliane Pelta-Robert - Allée 6 Stand 106
Tel: 40 11 19 63
Antiques, second hand decorative objects.

INVITATIONS - Allée 7 Stand 146
Tel: 40 10 17 91
Specialty: antique table arts, Limoges porcelain, crystal of Baccarat, Saint-Louis, Daum. Silver of Christofle and Ercuis.

IRMA - Allée 9 Stand 203
Tel: 40 10 08 57
Old household linens, old lace and decorative objects.
Collectors buttons and some glassware.

JAMES, Michel - Allée 10 Stands 49-49 bis, 50-51
Tel: 40 12 88 36 - Fax: 40 12 95 23
XVIII and XIX century furniture.

KAGAN - Allée 2 Stand 83
Silver and objects for the table.

LHOMOND, Yves - Allée 1 Stand 11
Tel: 45 23 13 80/45 23 13 84
XIX century furniture and decorative objects. Specialist in antique "cartons" of Aubusson tapestries.

LISS, Lily - Allée 9 Stand 211
Tel: 40 11 71 90
Art Deco furniture, chandeliers, chairs, mirrors and decorative objects.

MATLIS, Bernard - Allée 9 Stand 226
Tel: 40 11 99 94
Old toys and games.

MAUREL, Isabelle et Paul - Allée 1 Stand 41 and Allée 7 Stand 154 bis
Tel: 40 11 11 59/42 36 73 40 - Fax: 42 36 50 07
Old books of the 1900s, old children's books, Art nouveau and Art deco posters 1900 to 1950. Advertising engravings of Paris.

MOREL, Violette - Allée 8 Stand 186
Tel: 40 10 89 01
Old English books and second hand objects.

MORIN, Michel R. - Allée 6 Stand 112
Tel 40 11 19 10
French pop art and antiques.

MURIELLE - Allée 9 Stand 225
Tel: 40 10 99 27
Antique dolls, teddy bears and Barbie dolls.

MOUTON, André - Allée 9 Stand 221
Unusual objects.

NOVELLA
Leduc, Sylvie - Allée 1 Stand 8
Tel: 40 10 15 90
Antique arms, old musical instruments, XIX century bronzes and paintings.

OPALESCENCES - Allée 9 Stand 224 bis
Tel: 40 10 15 14
Art Nouveau, Art Deco glass. XVIII and XIX century lighting.

ORIGINES DE L'HOMME-FAVRE, M. - Allée 8 Stand 160
Tel: 40 12 42 65
Minerals, archaeological artifacts.

PEPIN, Luc - Allée 9 Stand 199
Tel: 40 11 93 97
Collectible toys, autos, trains, planes, boats, automated toys, figurines.

PIERREL, Alain - Allée 9 Stands 231-235-237
Tel: 47 70 57 82 - Fax: 40 10 28 13
XVII, XVIII and XIX century furniture in natural woods.

PIERRELOT - Allée 1 Stand 26 and Allée 2 Stand 61
Furniture and decorative objects.

REMINA ANTIQUITES - Allée 10 Stand 262
General antiques and second hand items.

REMON, Nicolas - Allée 7 Stand 148 bis
Tel: 40 10 29 32
Old books, especially illustrated books and engravings.

RICHARD, François-Gilbert - Allée 3 Stand 107
Tel: 40 11 29 13/64 59 97 76
Specialist in scientific antiques and curiosities.

LES TROUVAILLES DE THEA ET JEAN-MARC - Allée 9 Stand 233
Tel: 40 11 87 60
Old toys and doll furniture, paintings and collectibles.

VERNAISON TAPIS - Allée 1 Stand 21
Tapestries, old and reproductions. Oriental carpets.

VERRIER, Michel - Allée 6/3 Stand 105 bis
Tel: 43 24 04 77
An unusual mixed bag of furniture and objects.

VIALFONT, - Allée 9 Stand 217
Generalist in all sorts of things. Old cameras, radios, toys and some lighting.

VINAIS, G. - Allée 1 Stand 17
Tel: 40 11 39 57/47 45 08 79
XIX century furniture and objects. Specialist in the period of Napoléon III.
Allée 7 Stand 24
Bronzes and pendulum clocks.

ZOI, R. ET FILS - Allée 1 Stand 14
Tel: 40 10 13 76
XVIII and XIX century antiques, porcelain, pendulum clocks, paintings, sculptures, fireplaces, lighting.

--------------------------------- **RUE ANSELME** ---------------------------------

YANE ET LE BATON MAGIQUE
73 rue Anselme ■ Tel: 40 11 55 48 by appointment
Contemporary works of art: paintings, drawings, sculpture.

An outdoor market which offers some good merchants:

LA DECORATION ANGLAISE

36 rue Jules-Vallès ■ Tel: 40 11 54 44

Lamps in pate de verre, "black men" statues, English objects of curiosity, English style furniture in pine, carved wooden animals, signs and advertising posters.

GALERIE CHRISTINE

16 rue Jules-Vallès ■ Tel: 40 12 22 79/48 93 69 19

XVIII and XIX century furniture, engravings, paintings, bronzes, chandeliers, mirrors, art objects, dolls.

MARC MAISON

15 rue Jules-Vallès ■ Tel: 40 12 52 28/40 12 48 95 - Fax: 40 12 26 47

Stock of a large selection of architectural elements, exterior and interior. Fountains, grills and gates in wrought iron, flooring, fireplaces and elements for the garden. They are also located in the Louvre des Antiquaires (Allée Boulle, Stand 19) and in the Marché Paul-Bert (Allée 6, stand 83).

LA REMISE

19 rue du Plaisir ■ Tel: 40 11 42 81

Regional furniture.

This street is the Flea Market as it used to be. Lots of second hand and a couple of very good dealers who should not be overlooked.

A.B.J. CHEMINEES

4 rue Lécuyer ■ Tel: 40 11 44 78 - Fax: 40 12 87 44

Antique fireplaces: stone, marble, wood. Parquet, wood panelling (boiseries), statues in wood, marble, cast-iron.
Open all week.

LIBRAIRIE DE L'AVENUE - H. Veyrier

31 rue Lécuyer ■ Tel: 40 11 95 85/46 33 20 18

Rare books. This second hand book store has an excellent collection. Antique engravings.

J.L.V. ANTIQUITES

18 ter rue Lécuyer ■ Tel: 40 12 30 84 - Fax: 40 11 59 17

XVII, XVIII and XIX century paintings, furniture and decorative objects.

MARCHE LECUYER

8 rue Lécuyer ■ Tel: 40 11 46 51

Ten stands who sell to the trade. Rustic and period furniture. Stained glass, engraved glass, gilded wood, old and contemporary paintings, decorative objects.

New merchandise arrives on Thursday and Friday mornings.

RUE PAUL-BERT

Lots of real Flea Market merchandise. This street runs off the rue des Rosiers and leads to the Marché Paul-Bert. There are several interesting merchants who rate a visit.

ART INTER

1 rue Paul-Bert ■ Tel: 40 11 11 80

Decorative objects of the XIX century to Art Nouveau. Lamp bases, chandeliers, objects in crystal and earthenware.

SEMA
ROGER ADJINSOFF ET FILS

13 rue Paul-Bert ■ Tel: 40 11 25 69

Architectural elements, fireplaces in stone, wood and marble, wood panelling, wrought iron gates and grills, parquet, fountains, garden statues. Also at 55 rue des Rosiers.

RUE DES POISSONNIERS

ALDO FRERES
ZOI, DINO

39 rue des Poissonniers ■ Tel: 40 12 66 55

Antique architectural elements: fireplaces in marble and stone, wrought iron grills and gates, wood panelling, doors, decorative elements for interior and exterior.

RUE DES ROSIERS

This is the main street of the Marché aux Puces.

There are several high quality dealers in antiques, mirrors and collectibles. Here is our choice.

ANTIQUITES 107

107 rue des Rosiers ■ Tel: 42 62 77 08/40 10 23 15 - Fax: 42 64 81 99

Lighting and decorative objects

AU TEMPS JADIS

127 rue des Rosiers ■ Tel: 40 12 85 99

Paintings, bronzes, miniatures, old drawings, art objects and curiosities.

AUCLERT, Christian

73 rue des Rosiers ■ Tel: 40 11 09 22/40 12 60 52

Antique four-poster beds, chairs, marquetry furniture. Restoration.

MAISON BEYS

118 rue des Rosiers ■ Tel: 40 12 69 99/40 12 79 90 - Fax: 40 12 42 71

Large and interesting collection of XVII to XIX century furniture, fireplaces in marble and wood, clocks of the XVIII and XIX centuries, XVIII and XIX century paintings, faience, arms, glass and decorative objects.

ETS CAMUS

88 rue des Rosiers and 5 rue Eugène-Lumeau ■ Tel: 40 10 88 59/43 44 14 02 - Fax: 40 11 82 17

Antique fireplaces in marble and wood, sculptures for the garden, statues, fountains. Architectural elements.

COHEN, Eliane

99 rue des Rosiers (Corner of the Marché Vernaison) ■ Tel: 40 11 05 73

XIX century to 1900-1930 bronzes, lighting and small furniture.

DECO LIGHT ART DECO

107 rue des Rosiers ■ Tel: 42 62 77 08/40 10 23 15 - Fax: 42 64 81 99

Art Deco lighting, furniture, armchairs, cocktail bars, dining room suites.

DUGAY

92 rue des Rosiers ■ Tel: 40 11 87 30 - Fax: 40 12 26 32

Supplies for restoration and maintenance of furniture and all art objects. One of the largest and best stocks in Paris.

LA GALERIE DES GLACES

138 rue des Rosiers ■ Tel: 40 11 17 52

Good collection of antique mirrors.

HUBERT, Claude-Bernard

78 rue des Rosiers ■ Tel: 40 12 44 27/48 74 25 08

Custom chairs. Restoration and upholstery in fabric or leather. Restoration of antique furniture.

KROUGLY, E.

41 rue des Rosiers ■ Tel: 40 11 35 78

Decorative hardware for furniture in bronze and iron.
Old locks, "sabots", casters, and lots more.

IVANOVIC

152 bis rue des Rosiers ■ Tel: 40 50 04 75

Old clocks and small furniture.

PRUDOU

2 rue des Rosiers and 18 rue Pavée ■ Tel: 42 74 10 34

XVIII and XIX century porcelain and faience, fabrics, showcase collectibles, European ivories, silver and plated silver. XIX century art glass, paintings, drawings and engravings.

GALERIE EMMANUEL ZELKO

89 rue des Rosiers ■ Tel: 40 12 24 58/40 11 21 01 - Fax: 34 67 03 45

Amazing collection of XIX century furniture, mirrors, lighting, clocks and decorative objects. Great fireplace accessories. Suppliers to many of the palaces of the Orient.

─────────────── **OTHER POINTS OF INTEREST** ───────────────

BERNARD STEINITZ

Atelier of restoration ■ 6 rue Marie-Curie ■ Tel: 47 42 31 94 - Fax: 49 24 91 16 ■ Mon-Fri 9:00-19:00/Sat 11:00-18:00

XVIII century furniture and art objects.

SALLE DES VENTES DES PUCES

45 rue des Rosiers ■ 14-16 rue Jules-Ferry ■ Tel: 40 10 01 21/40 12 35 35 ■ Fri-Mon 9:00-19:00

Warehouse sales of everything, including furniture and decorative objects.

Le Village Saint-Paul

This market is located in the Marais (the Fourth Arrondissement), one of the oldest and certainly one of the most historically interesting quarters of Paris. It is situated on the rue Saint-Paul with access by car from the Quai des Célestins through to the rue de Rivoli. This charming market houses a collection of mixed quality. We recommend it for the gifted amateur eager to find the small treasure and the occasional bargain.

ANTIQUITES ERIC DUBOIS
9 rue Saint-Paul ■ Tel: 42 74 05 29 ■ Open every day 11:00-19:30
Antiques, second hand, pottery, African art.

ANTIQUITES JAPONAISE
17 rue Saint-Paul ■ Telfax: 42 77 98 02 ■ Thurs-Mon 12:00-19:00
Japanese antiques.

ANTIQUITES L'OTTOCENTO
5 bis rue Saint-Paul ■ Tel: 42 71 81 90 ■ Thurs-Mon 11:00-19:00
Restoration of antique furniture, sale of furniture and miscellaneous objects.

L'ASTREE D'OR
5 rue Saint-Paul ■ Tel: 40 29 94 30 ■ Every day 11:00-19:00
Art Nouveau, Art Deco furniture, mirrors and decorative objects. Paintings, engravings, pastels, lighting, bronzes.

BRASIL EXPO
2 rue de l'Hôtel Saint-Paul ■ Tel: 42 74 08 64 - Fax: 42 74 34 33 ■ Tues-Sat 10:30-13:30/15:00-19:00
Brazilian artisanal products. Precious and semi-precious stones.

DUMAS, Marion
27 rue Saint-Paul (courtyard) ■ Tel: 42 71 21 45 ■ Thurs-Mon 11:00-19:00 and by appointment
XIX century small furniture, XVIII and XIX century fabrics, old glass and china, decorative objects (tôle, opalines).

ELI'S ANTIQUES
14 rue des Jardins Saint-Paul ■ Tel: 42 71 07 71 ■ Thurs-Sun 14:00-18:30
Antique furniture, jewellery, paintings, kilims (old and new).

FORLANI, Jacqueline
7-9 rue Saint-Paul ■ Tel: 40 29 01 97 ■ Every day in the afternoons
Old mirrors, lamps, frames, decorative objects.

FUCHSIA

2 rue Saint-Paul ■ Tel: 48 04 75 61 ■ Every day 12:00-19:00

Antique lace, styles of 1900 to 1930. Old bed linens, table linens, table arts, antique fans, old fabrics and braids, dolls accessories.

LE JARDIN SAINT-PAUL

24 quai des Célestins ■ Tel: 42 78 08 89 - Fax: 42 78 40 98 ■ Mon-Sat 9;30-18:30

Garden furniture in wrought iron and cast-iron in the styles of Napoléon III and 1900. Florentine lighting, wall lanterns, cast-iron street lamps. Marble and bronze statues.

Le Village Saint-Honoré

Visit this tiny little Impasse at 91 rue Saint-Honoré in the First Arrondissement. You might find a lovely piece of silver or an article of furniture that works perfectly. There are about a dozen dealers. Here are three we like:

ANTIQUITES TRIPTYQUE

Tel: 42 33 23 74 ■ Tues 14:00-19:30/Wed-Sat 12:00-19:30 ■ Gabrielle Gourvellec and Richard Bialas speak English

Silver of the XVIII and XIX centuries and of the 1930s.
1930s glass. Objects of curiosity.

LA CREDENCE

Tel: 40 26 05 44 ■ Mon-Sat 11:00-19:30 ■ Denis and Christine Chalem speak English

Furniture, paintings and objects of curiosity of the XVIII and XIX centuries.

LADYBIRD

Tel: 40 13 98 54 - Fax: 46 13 77 88 ■ Mon-Sat 12:00-19:00 ■ Brigitte Hinderze speaks English

XVIII and XIX century French and English furniture. Lamps and lampshades.

THE PALANCAR COMPANY LTD

PALANCAR
**the Maxi-media Company presents
its multi-media publications for 1995-1996**

1995: The TOUT PARIS SOURCE GUIDE TO
THE ART OF FRENCH DECORATION
Watch for the exciting new CDROM

1996: The television series, "THE COMPAGNONS"
"The Great Artisans of Europe"

1996: The TOUT PARIS GUIDE TO FRENCH
PRET-A-PORTER
Also on CDROM

1996: The TOUT PARIS GUIDES FOR THE
BUSINESSMAN
With CDROM

1996: SHODATA

*The exciting new database for the television
professional. Every film or tape ever produced
anywhere in the world. Full details on contents,
casts, producers, writers, directors, sales, prices, etc.*

Database, catalogues and CDROM

**THE PALANCAR COMPANY LTD.
The Courtyard, 12 Hill Street,
St. Helier, Jersey, C.I.**

Alphabetical Index

410 - ALPHABETICAL INDEX